SOCIAL CAPITAL AND WELFARE REFORM

SOCIAL CAPITAL AND
WELFARE REFORM

Organizations, Congregations, and Communities

JO ANNE SCHNEIDER

COLUMBIA UNIVERSITY PRESS

NEW YORK

Columbia University Press
Publishers Since 1893
New York   Chichester, West Sussex

Library of Congress Cataloging-in-Publication Data
Schneider, Jo Anne, 1959–

    Social capital and welfare reform : organizations, congregations, and communities /
Jo Anne Schneider.

        p.   cm.

    Includes bibliographical references and index.

    ISBN 0–231–12650–6 (cloth: alk. paper) — ISBN 0–231–12651–4 (pbk.)

    1. Public welfare—United States. 2. Social capital (Sociology)—United States. I. Title.

    HV95.S353 2006

    361.2′5′0973—dc22

                                                                                2005048411

Columbia University Press books are printed on permanent and durable acid-free paper.
Printed in the United States of America

c 10 9 8 7 6 5 4 3 2 1
p 10 9 8 7 6 5 4 3 2 1

CONTENTS

ACKNOWLEDGMENTS

This book has been a journey of more than 10 years with many people and institutions providing support along the way. There are many more than I can name here. First and foremost, I wish to thank the families and organizations that shared their experience with me and the other researchers involved in the various projects. Several organizations and community members deserve special thanks: Ed Schwartz and the staff at the Institute for the Study of Civic Values, Colleen O'Connell, Kristen Rantanan, Reverend Olen Arrington Jr., Olatoye Baiyewu, Guida Brown, Tony Garcia, Dan Melyon, Marcus White, Jim Bartos, and Wendy Humphreys.

State government officials in both Pennsylvania and Wisconsin graciously provided data and facilitated research for the project. I particularly thank Edward Zogby, David Florey, Don Jose Stovall, Dennis Putze, Adeline Robinson, Jim Kennedy, Ed Kamin, Jeffrey Sachse, J. Jean Rogers, and Eliza Lebkicher.

Many students from several colleges worked with me in conducting this research. Most were involved in internships, service learning classes, independent studies, and graduate thesis and dissertation work while attending Bryn Mawr, Haverford, Hope College, the University of Pennsylvania, the Community College of Pennsylvania, the University of Wisconsin–Parkside, and University of Wisconsin–Milwaukee, among others. I am grateful for their assistance. Colleagues from the University of Wisconsin–Parkside and the University of Wisconsin–Milwaukee were also integral parts of the Neighborhood Settlement House research team, and Maria Lydia Spinelli, an independent researcher, worked on the Kenosha Social Capital Study. Several students and colleagues deserve particular recognition. In Philadelphia, they include Robin Ebright, Melissa Smiley, Mathew Wickens, Julie Simon, and Sophia Javid. The Kenosha research project team included Theresa Embury, Maria Lydia Spinelli, Carol Jones, Calvin Lucas, Tania Rodriquez, Karen Szalapski, Elda Torres, Traci Rabelhoffer, Marin Rocha Jr., Latisha Riser, and Meghan Mumford. Milwaukee research was conducted by James Harris, Michael Barndt, Florence Kyomugisha, Amanda Beaver, Katie Cahoon, Theresa Embury, Mildred Spann, and Anne Statham. Regina Miller, Melanie Grant, Lane Blaquiere, and Jason Brady assisted in organizing data for analysis.

Photographs from Milwaukee and Kenosha were provided by Tom Fritz Studio. Joseph Labolito supplied photographs of Philadelphia. Initial design for tables and figures was done by Robert Cronan, Lucidity Design.

Funding for the research came from the Philadelphia Private Industry Council, the Petit foundation, the Aspen Institute Non-profit Sector Research Fund, and the Palmer Foundation. The Annie E. Casey Foundation was instrumental in providing support for development of the manuscript and publication assistance for tables, photos and other costs for the book. I particularly want to thank Doretha Carter, Audrey Jordan and Ralph Smith at the Casey Foundation for their ongoing support. A companion policy report to the book, *The Role of Social Capital in Building Healthy Communities,* is available through the Casey foundation. Analysis of the relationship of social geography and social capital, originally included in this manuscript, is also available as a Casey foundation report: *Social Capital and Social Geography.*

A number of colleagues and friends provided helpful comments on earlier drafts of the book. I am especially thankful to Marcella Ridlen Ray, Arthur McKee, Michael Foley, Richard Wood, and Bob Wineburg. Alison Anderson and Ellen Coughlin provided editorial assistance. I am also grateful to John Michel for his guidance in developing this project.

Finally, I thank Virginia Hodgkinson and the staff at the Center for the Study of Voluntary Organizations and Service at Georgetown Public Policy Institute, Georgetown University, and Dean Hoge, Michael Foley, and the staff at the Life Cycle Institute, Catholic University, for providing the supportive institutional environments needed to develop this book.

SOCIAL CAPITAL AND WELFARE REFORM

CHAPTER 1

Introduction

Jaysa[1] moves from welfare to work, taking a day-care job at the nonprofit that hosted her community-service job placement. Jaysa had become part of the close network of program participants and staff at the agency, establishing trusting friendships through shared culture. She uses the resources of the social service agency to supplement her wages and provide social supports for herself and her children. Connections allow Jaysa to fulfill the goals of welfare reform, yet she earns poverty-level wages. Although her abilities fit well with this social service agency, she has not yet developed the skills or connections to find a better-paying job.

An interfaith coalition develops a model program that teams church members with low-income families to help them negotiate between the worlds of work, family, and government aid. Despite important successes, the program runs into several problems. Limited funding through short-term grants makes it difficult to keep staff with appropriate skills. More important, some churches find that the families they intend to help have problems beyond the skills of volunteers. Even with a well-designed program and connections to organizations that can successfully implement programs, this initiative runs into structural problems that cause it to be discontinued after one year.

The 1996 U.S. welfare reform legislation depends on the ability of states and localities to move large numbers of people on public assistance from welfare to permanent work paying family-supporting wages. The Personal Responsibility, Work Opportunity Reconciliation Act of 1996 ended the entitlement to cash and medical assistance for low-income people with children that had existed in the United States since the 1930s (Handler and Hasenfeld 1991; Katz 1989). Federal Aid for Families with Dependent Children (AFDC) was replaced by a block-grant system that gives states enormous flexibility in designing their programs, provided that they prove that an increasing percentage of their welfare caseload are engaged in "work-related activities." Recipients are permanently barred from getting any public assistance after receiving aid for a cumulative five years over a lifetime.[2] Like Jaysa, many welfare recipients have found jobs under the new system. However, again like Jaysa, a large number do not earn enough to fulfill their basic needs without either government or private supports.

Understanding the dynamic among government, nonprofit, and for profit service providers, families receiving service, and employers becomes important in designing successful programs. Welfare recipients will not magically find family-supporting employment. The legislation envisions a host of programs designed to help people locate jobs; gain adequate basic and job-specific skills; and provide day care, transportation, and social supports. In the U.S. system of "third party government" (Salamon 1987:110), most of these services will be provided through subcontracts to nonprofits, for-profits, and faith-based organizations. For example, the interfaith model program provided a supplement to government-contracted welfare-to-work programs. This program, and the agency that served Jaysa, both played instrumental roles in implementing welfare reform. However, like the interfaith program, these programs have had mixed results and faced challenges due to reduced funding, unexpected participant needs, and a number of other issues.

Using data from a series of projects in Pennsylvania and Wisconsin, this book addresses two questions regarding U.S. welfare policy in the 1990s:

1. Why do some families in a community succeed in meeting their education, work, and lifestyle goals while others fail?
2. What is the role of community institutions in this process?

APPROACHES TO SOCIAL WELFARE POLICY

Both implementing the enormous changes engendered by the 1996 reforms and working toward future welfare reform legislation requires understanding why social programs succeed and fail. Most public policy and management theory is based on the assumption that provider organizations and government are making a product as a factory does. In the case of welfare reform, the raw materials are welfare recipients. Government sets the design specifications for the production process by creating legislation and regulations for specific programs. Government then contracts with providers to build the product: welfare recipients who will permanently move into the paid labor force. If the contracting agencies follow the design specifications correctly, they should produce this desired outcome.

But people are not widgets. The "raw material" consists of people with free will and a variety of strengths and weaknesses. Welfare recipients are extremely diverse. Each type of family needs appropriate aid in order to succeed. Nor do

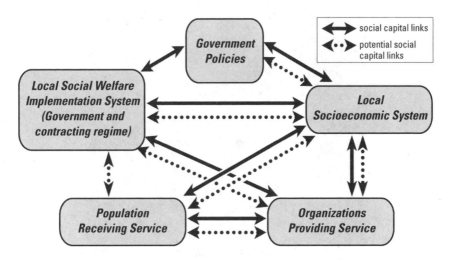

Figure 1.1. Five factors influencing implementation of welfare reform.

the contracting agencies function like factories with well-oiled machines. They are community institutions staffed by people with their own unique sets of strengths and weaknesses. These organizations are as varied as the people they serve. They respond to a variety of constituencies, including government, in creating their programs and carrying out their work.

Multiple models offer appropriate alternatives to different populations. Welfare-reform policies continue to fail, in part, because they do not recognize the diversity within both the population served and the organizations providing service. Policy based on factory models also ignores the impact of larger socioeconomic factors and government regulations themselves on both recipients and providers. Understanding the implementation of social welfare policy involves looking at the dynamic among these multiple factors. Welfare-reform policy will succeed only when it recognizes that the diversity of programs is the real strength of contracting with the for-profit and nonprofit sector. Government also needs to realize that individual institutions are capable of effectively serving a portion of the public assistance population only because they arise out of one sector of the local community.

The appropriate role of government in this scenario is to facilitate the relationship among organizations with different strengths by creating policies that encourage agencies to foster bridges among different populations seeking services and various kinds of employers and other institutions that can fulfill their needs. To effectively function in this facilitator role, government must develop an understanding of local-level complexity. Complexity is not chaos but variation within a set of key factors (figure 1.1):

1. The government policies that shape programs
2. The nature of the organizations providing service
3. The nature of the local implementation system
4. The socioeconomic system of the locality
5. The nature of the population receiving service

By looking at the relationship among these critical components, policy makers and community leaders together can discern the patterns within the local community and develop appropriate programs to best meet the general goals of welfare reform. Understanding relationships among these various components in a complex system involves examining the interactions among the various institutions and individuals that participate in that system.

Social capital serves as the intervening element among these five components. Social capital refers to *the social relationships and patterns of reciprocal, enforceable trust that enable people and institutions to gain access to such re-sources as social services, jobs, and government contracts.* It includes two ingre-dients: 1) trust-based relationships with people or organizations with access to resources and 2) knowledge of cultural capital cues that indicate that an indi-vidual is a member of a group and should be given access to those relation-ships. The same definition applies to both organizations and individuals. So-cial capital enables organizations to gain government contracts, place their program participants in jobs, and find people to serve.

People and institutions engage in two types of social capital networks: closed and bridging. *Closed social capital* refers to networks that include people or institutions that are similar to each other and participate in exclusive shar-ing relationships. It involves strong ties within subcommunities, for example, a neighborhood or ethnic group. Everyone belongs to at least one closed social capital network. It may be family, people who graduated from a certain school, or simply local community networks. People in these closed networks are fa-miliar with one another, practice the same culture, and trust one another. *Bridging social capital* involves long-term trusting relationships but crosses boundaries of class, race, ethnicity, religion, or type of institution. As Portes (1998) points out, social capital can be either positive or negative. In the welfare-to-work system, social capital can both help and hinder attempts to negotiate the local social, political, and economic system in order to aid low-income people attempting to move into stable, family-supporting employment.

DATA AND METHODS

I use examples from Wisconsin and Pennsylvania to demonstrate similarities and differences across localities. I draw on several separate studies to weave to-gether a complex, dynamic portrait of the role of various factors that influence social capital and welfare reform. An outline of the projects that serve as the basis for this book is provided in box 1.1. Discussion of methods and data is available in appendix A. The research combines eight projects conducted in Philadelphia from 1992 to 1997 and four projects in Wisconsin conducted from 1997 to 2000. Additional data on welfare policy were collected for Pennsylvania in 2001 to update earlier research.

The projects involved three cities: Philadelphia in Pennsylvania, and Mil-waukee and Kenosha in Wisconsin. Philadelphia and Milwaukee are both the largest cities in their respective states and the major locations for concentrated poverty. As in many large U.S. cities, both Philadelphia and Milwaukee have become increasingly diverse over time. According to the 2000 U.S. census, Philadelphia racial breakdown is 45 percent white, 43 percent African Ameri-

Box 1.1 Research Projects

Pennsylvania Projects

Social Networks, Career and Training Paths for Participants in Education and Training Programs for the Disadvantaged (Social Network Study): Statistical study of 338 people enrolled in nine training programs or community college in Philadelphia conducted in late 1995 through 1996. Study participants came from a stratified sample of people in training programs that served the range of low-income individuals in the Philadelphia area.

Life Experience of Welfare Recipients: Life-history interviews of 20 individuals and participant observation of more than 100 public assistance recipients in education and training programs in Philadelphia. These data were supplemented with data from case files from the Alternative Work Experience Program from 1992 through 1997.

Community Women's Education Project (CWEP): Anonymous Survey Analysis: statistical study of all participants (373 women) enrolled in the CWEP workstart program over five years. CWEP is an innovative adult basic education and career-preparation program for women. At the time of the study, 69 percent of the study population was on welfare and 76 percent had been on welfare at some point in their lives.

The Alternative Work Experience Program Evaluation: Evaluation of a model service learning workfare program for two-parent families on welfare, based on program statistics for 154 individuals and ethnographic observations of that program from 1993 through 1995.

Economic, Racial, and Educational Census Mapping Project: Analyzes census maps of Philadelphia and the Philadelphia region (SMSA) on race, Hispanic origin, income, poverty, education levels, rates of employment and unemployment, types of employment, housing, welfare use, and travel to work.

Survey of Training Providers in Philadelphia: Survey of 29 training programs in Philadelphia conducted 1992–1999.

The Education and Training System in Philadelphia: Ethnographic study of organizations and government agencies involved in training in Philadelphia examining Philadelphia PIC, Commonwealth and federal documents on training and welfare reform, as well as my notes on working with training programs. Research was conducted between 1992 and 1997.

The Rapid Attachment Study: Analysis of an administrative database for a short-term job-readiness and job-placement program in Philadelphia. The database includes demographic information; government program utilization; information on substance abuse and criminal history; work and training history; interviewer assessments of presentation, attitude, dress, and interviewing techniques; TABE math and reading scores; and job-placement information for 718 people who participated in this program from February 1996 to February 1997.

Wisconsin Projects

Kenosha Conversation Project: Community needs assessment on welfare reform in Kenosha. Research consisted of focus groups with stakeholders involved in welfare reform (program participants; Kenosha County Job Center (KCJC) and Department of Human Services administrators, program managers, and line staff; social service agency staff; employers; government officials; church representatives; and concerned advocacy organizations, combined with interviews with key people involved in welfare reform and participant observation in KCJC and one advocacy organization. Research conducted in 1997–1998.

Neighborhood Settlement House Evaluation Study: Evaluation of the effects of changing welfare and child-welfare policy on a Milwaukee community-based organization, its neighborhood, and its participants. Multimethod team study: 1) ethnography of the organization and its partner agencies, 2) depth-interview study of community families (forty-eight families), 3) community resource analysis through statistical mapping of the neighborhood, windshield survey of community organizations, and interviews with selected organizations and churches, and 4) analysis of agency administrative databases and correlation of those data with available demographic resources on the community. Research conducted in 1998–1999.

Kenosha Social Capital Study: Study of the Latino and African American subcommunities of Kenosha focusing on the dynamic between Latino and African American community-based organizations and churches, community residents, employers, and the citywide community organization and church context. This multimethod team study consisted of four components: 1) ethnography in key organizations and churches serving these communities, 2) life-history interviews with twenty-six families (fifteen Latino, eleven African American) regarding social resources, work, education, and involvement in organizations and churches, 3) interviews with key actors in Kenosha and the African American and Latino communities, and 4) survey of employment practices of Kenosha employers. Research conducted in 1998–1999.

Milwaukee Interfaith Welfare Project: Research with Milwaukee Interfaith in 1997–2002:1) one and one-half years of participant observation of the agency and its advocacy programs, 2) analysis of written material from the agency on these efforts, and 3) interviews with key staff in addition to participant observation notes.

can, 4 percent Asian, and 8 percent Latino; Milwaukee is 50 percent white, 37 percent African American, 3 percent Asian, and 12 percent Latino. Both are rust-belt cities hit hard by deindustrialization and the recession of the early 1990s. Local economies have rebounded, but much employment has shifted to surrounding suburbs, and city-centered employment provides more service-sector and high-technology-based employment than in the past.

Kenosha is a small city located on the border between Illinois and Wisconsin with a population of 90,352 (2000 census). Kenosha also was a rust-belt city dominated by one employer until the mid-1980s. Unlike Philadelphia and Milwaukee, Kenosha quickly shifted to a mixed economy and had a thriving job market in the late 1990s. Like many smaller U.S. communities, Kenosha is predominantly white. According to the U.S. census, population figures are 84 percent white, 8 percent African American, 1 percent Asian, and 10 percent Latino. Kenosha was also one of the models for one-stop-shop, employment-focused welfare reform envisioned in the 1996 welfare-reform legislation.

This book departs from most studies of poverty and related issues by looking at communities as a whole, instead of focusing exclusively on the populations that use government programs or the agencies that offer welfare-related services. Discussion of families ranges from persistently poor families to those who have moved into the professional middle class. Although most of the book focuses on organizations that serve the poor, these agencies are placed within the wider context of all organizations providing certain services in a locality. Research in faith communities includes institutions serving people from several race and class backgrounds.

The research used ethnography, the methodology of anthropology. Ethnography looks at a problem like poverty holistically, exploring the dynamics within a system that affect the implementation and outcomes of social welfare policy. Research of this type relies on multiple methods: 1) participant observation—the regular observation and recording of events in a setting over time, 2) qualitative interviews, 3) analysis of secondary source materials such as government documents, agency reports, and media, 4) analysis of government data sets like the U.S. Census, Department of Labor statistics, and welfare-department statistics, and 5) survey research on particular populations.

Qualitative research and analysis of secondary source material were combined with statistical studies to develop a comprehensive picture of the social welfare policy process and the role of social capital in welfare reform. Ethnography provided two kinds of data: 1) micro-level data on changing behavior patterns and ideology of program participants, agencies, and government through participant observation and life-history interviews of a smaller population and 2) macro-level data on government policy implementation, local labor-market conditions, and segregation. The ethnographic data explained patterns found through quantitative analysis on larger samples (macroanalysis). I further linked micro to macro by situating patterns of experience in sample populations within two contexts: 1) demographic data on segregation, gender, and poverty available through public-use data sets such as the U.S. Census and Department of Labor and Department of Public Welfare (DPW) statistics and 2) local and national academic and policy literature on these topics.

My strategy of approaching social welfare policy from a community-wide perspective comes from three observations. First, as other researchers have noted (Stack 1974, 1996; Newman 1999), many impoverished people are part of family systems that include people with a full range of economic and education backgrounds. This is particularly common since the downsizing of government starting in the 1980s and deindustrialization that accelerated after 1970. Tracking the interplay among family members with different resources provides a much fuller and more nuanced understanding of poverty than concentrating only on welfare-dependent or low-income households. Second, comparing the experience of families who end up in different economic circumstances despite similar beginnings shows how various factors such as skill, work experience, education, and social capital influence long-term outcomes. Finally, through research on local institutions and communities, these projects found much interaction among people from different economic backgrounds in churches and local organizations. These interactions involved not only formal helping activities but also informal support and friendship. Understanding this circle of care is important in appreciating individual life paths.

The same pattern held true for nonprofit organizations and faith communities. Organizations with a particular purpose were linked to one another through associations and other mechanisms regardless of the segment of the populations they served. Faith communities were linked to nonprofits and government in many ways. Understanding the role and capacity of faith communities as socializing entities, sources of social capital, and providers of social welfare services involved placing these institutions within a wider community context.

DEFINING SOCIAL CAPITAL

Social capital evolved as an extension of economists' understanding of human capital: education and skills people have to offer in the labor market. Social capital, most generally, refers to social relationships based on trust that have value or can be used productively. Although the wording of the major definitions of social capital is similar, various scholars conceptualize social capital differently. Robert Putnam and his followers see social capital as a generalized civic good whereas other social scientists define social capital as a structural variable influencing access to social resources (Foley and Edwards 1999).

Putnam defines social capital as: "the features of social organizations such as networks, norms and social trust that facilitate the coordination and cooperation for mutual benefit" (1995:67). Social capital is fostered by face-to-face interaction in voluntary organizations such as bowling leagues. He suggests that societies with strong social capital based on civic culture thrive (Putnam

1993), while countries such as the United States that lack this social capital ethos are at risk (Putnam 2000).[3] Putnam sees weak social capital as influencing all spheres of U.S. society: "Just as a screwdriver (physical capital) or a college education (human capital) can increase productivity (both individual and collective), so too social contacts affect the productivity of organizations and groups" (Putnam 2000:29).

This definition of social capital objectifies the concept into participation in activities that foster a sense of shared community. Social capital becomes a commodity like the skills set of "human capital" that can be acquired through networking or community involvement. Following the attention in policy circles given to Robert Putnam's (1995) work, the term was transformed into a metaphor for civic participation.[4]

Numerous scholars have protested Putnam's assertions regarding the civic health of the United States (Rich 1999; Portes 1998; Ammerman 1997). People in the United States participate in many forms of joint activity. More important, the homogeneous communities envisioned as the recent past in this country never existed (Lynd and Lynd 1929). Putnam's definition of social capital ignores the conflictual and unequal aspects of a society divided by class and race (Portes 1998; Foley and Edwards 1997). The body politic cannot draw on social capital to develop a cohesive society precisely because social capital involves defining boundaries among small groups against others outside of their social networks. Various subgroups within this society are very effective at mobilizing social capital in support of their own needs (Portney and Berry 1997; Wood 2002). In most cases, social capital functions as a mechanism to exclude outsiders lacking connections from jobs and other social resources (Waldinger 1995; Stepick et al. 1997). Although Putnam's (2000:350–361) work recognizes that "bonding" social capital exacerbates race, class, and gender divisions, his solution is to call for increased civic participation (2000:402–414), particularly creating bridging social capital through participation in diverse forums (Putnam and Feldstein 2003). As discussed in later chapters, contact among people from disparate groups does not automatically lead to trust-based relationships.

In contrast, structural definitions of social capital highlight the existence of closed small groups within a larger society. In the sociological tradition, two distinct definitions of social capital exist based on the writings of Coleman (1988) and Bourdieu (1986; Bourdieu and Wacquant 1992). Both definitions recognize that social capital is a process that facilitates access to economic capital and enables individuals to acquire and use human capital.[5]

Coleman (Coleman 1988:s98) seeks to draw together the work of sociologists and economists, defining social capital "by its function": "a variety of different entities . . . that facilitate certain actions of actors—whether persons or corporate actors—within the structure. Like other forms of capital, social capital is productive, making possible the achievement of certain ends that in its absence would not be possible . . . Unlike other forms of capital, social capital inheres in the structure of relations between actors and among actors." Coleman portrays social capital as instrumental relations that come from face-to-face interactions. Applications of Coleman's model also focus on face-to-face relationships (for example, Teachman et al. 1997).

Bourdieu is far less instrumental—based in the poststructuralist social science milieu of Levi-Strauss, Marx, and Weber, he attempts to comprehend the totality of capitalist societies. Bourdieu (1984, 1986) examines the complex conjunction of factors that reproduce existing social inequalities. For him, social capital is one of "three fundamental species" of capital—economic, cultural, and social—and a process variable linked to cultural and economic capital: "Social capital is the sum of the resources, actual or virtual, that accrue to an individual or a group by virtue of possessing a durable network of more or less institutionalized relationships of mutual acquaintance and recognition" (Bourdieu and Wacquant 1992:119). In Bourdieu's formulation, each class faction reproduces its way of life and position by maintaining closed networks of people who share the same cultural habits and economic resources. Newcomers are kept out because they do not possess the constellation of social relations, even though they may acquire the wealth and cultural traits of a given status.

The definition used by Portes (1998; Portes and Sensennbrenner 1993:1325) draws on both Bourdieu and Coleman, stressing that social capital depends on "enforceable trust." Social capital is redefined as: "those expectations for action within a collectivity that affect the economic goals and goal seeking behavior of its members, even if these expectations are not oriented toward the economic sphere" (Portes and Sensenbrenner 1993:1323).

The definition used in this book draws on both Portes (1998; Portes and Landolt 1986) and Bourdieu (1986, 1984). I identify two interrelated types of social capital: closed and bridging. Both are equally important for individuals and organizations. Bridging social capital tries to create trusting relationships between closed social capital networks. Bridges are built through intentional and slow processes.

CLOSED AND BRIDGING SOCIAL CAPITAL

My use of *bridging* and *closed social capital* differs from the use of *bonding* and *bridging social capital* by Putnam (2000:22–23) and followers in two ways. First, although I agree with Putnam that bonding social capital involves strong ties in insular groups, I do not see bonding and bridging social capital as mutually exclusive. To the contrary, strong closed social capital networks sometimes serve as safe space in which to develop bridging skills.

Second, I agree with Putnam (2000:22–23) that bridging networks are "better for linkages to external assets and for information diffusion," but I do not see bridging social capital as consisting of weak ties across groups, a perception underlying many discussions on bridging social capital but not those by Putnam himself. In fact, Putnam recognizes that bridging social capital takes time to develop (Putnam and Feldstein 2003:9). I differ from Putnam because I do not see face-to-face ties as essential for developing bridging social capital. Instead, institutional networks can serve the same function, developing bridges that extend to individuals who may not know one another but trust the common bonds created through organizational connections.

Participants in effective bridging networks develop long-term, trust-based relationships similar to those in closed networks. However, participants in bridging networks may not share the same cultural or economic capital. To successfully bridge differences among closed social capital networks, they need to either develop tolerance for varying views or share culture based on other criteria. Common ground could come from shared attributes, for example, professional experience or generalized shared religious values. Bridging culture can also be a new creation of the group. For example, the civil rights movement developed new ways of working together and approaches to social inequality.

Social capital can serve as either barrier or bridge in complex society. Classic anthropological studies of the poor illustrate instrumental strategies of resource sharing through social capital that allow people to survive despite social exclusion (Stack 1974; Susser 1982). More recently, Stack (1996) showed how African Americans who developed social capital and knowledge of government-agency cultural patterns through employment in the northern United States use this new bridging social capital, combined with long-established networks in the South, to provide government-funded resources to poor African American families in their southern home communities. To succeed, welfare reform must bridge exclusionary boundaries as in Stack's (1996) case study. Understanding the processes involved in creating bridges necessitates returning to structural definitions of social capital.

Both Putnam and Coleman ignore the power issues central to social capital. In contrast, Bourdieu sees social capital as a mechanism to maintain existing power structures. As Wacquant (1998) shows, unequal power relations are fundamental to continued poverty. Applying social capital involves first understanding the power relations inherent in the concept. Successfully altering individual career paths and changing social welfare policy involves paying attention to the power structures inherent in existing social and cultural capital. Understanding the process of power is essential to modifying current conditions. Creating bridges and breaking down boundaries ultimately results in formation of new social and cultural capital.

TRUST

The structural definition of social capital used here depends on context-specific trust. Members of a social capital network know that others will share resources because of trust-based relationships holding together the entire network. Resource sharing involves delayed reciprocity based on long-term relationships (Mauss 1954). For example, Chyrstal may provide groceries to her friend Jaysa. The favor would be returned several months later by Jaysa's lending Chyrstal her car. Because Chrystal and Jaysa belong to the same social capital network, they know that favors will eventually be balanced out. As in Stack's (1974) research, network members who betray the trust-based expectations of reciprocity among group members will be eliminated from the network. Thus, long-term trust becomes essential to maintaining social capital.

Members of the network do not necessarily have relationships with all other members, but a common bond through a shared network fosters trust. For example, a reference from a college adviser to a trusted colleague at another institution leads a program to offer a scholarship to a student despite the fact that the colleague has never met the student.

This definition does not require a closed network of known individuals. Like the "imagined communities" of ethnic nationalism, social capital relies on reference to known networks through cultural symbols (Anderson 1983). Individuals gain access to resources through reference to a recognized individual or organization and displaying appropriate cultural behaviors, not simply through face-to-face interaction. Representing a trusted entity such as an interfaith coalition or graduating from a respected school can provide social capital similar to a reference from a known individual or services provided by one person to another.

Context-specific trust differs from the generalized trust inherent in Putnam and Fukiyama's definitions of social capital. Putnam anticipates that engagement in common activities will lead people to trust in society as a whole. His studies of Italy (Putnam 1993) highlight generalized trust in successful communities. He harkens back to the patriotism of the Word War II era in the United States—when citizens trusted in the United States as a good society. Fukiyama describes social capital as "the component of human capital that allows members of a given society to trust one another and cooperate in the formation of new groups." Again, trust is a generalized value among society members.

To the contrary, the context-specific trust of social capital comes from understanding that not everyone in society can be trusted. The college professor trusts his colleague over others because he knows that teachers often write good recommendations for students regardless of their long-term potential. Chrystal borrows Jaysa's car because she knows it is reliable whereas the bus or taxi might not show up on time. Jaysa asks Chrystal for groceries because she knows that Chrystal will not gossip to others about her running out of food. Social capital is necessary precisely because of a lack of generalized trust.

SOCIAL CAPITAL AND COMMUNITY

Social capital is also linked to the concept of community. Although numerous definitions of community exist (Bell and Newby 1972:21–54), most scholars and practitioners assume that community means a "cohesive, integrated social system" (Merry 1981:15), such as a social capital network. However, instead of socially cohesive bounded units, scholars often found a multitude of social worlds (Lynd and Lynd 1929) or "a series of distinct non-overlapping social networks occupying the same geographical space" (Merry 1981:15). Hunter (1974:4–8) describes two dimensions of community as ecological (geographic) and normative (social interaction, social structure, and symbolic/cultural elements of community). He argues for a multidimensional understanding of community that measures spatial, sociostructural, and symbolic elements of community. In modern society, local community becomes more formalized through organizations; participation in "community" becomes voluntary.

Community is multiplex and voluntary. In contrast, localities—for example, a city or neighborhood—are complex, not necessarily cohesive geographic and social spaces where individuals move through contexts structured by macro-social factors (economy, race, class, gender) and micro-level settings (organizational structures, social networks) in an ever-changing process.

I define "community" as the conjunction of instances when individuals develop the common recognition of shared interest, culture, and potential for trust envisioned as the basis for social capital and mutual action. My understanding of community combines the anthropological concept of subculture with the voluntary and variable theory of symbolic ethnicity. Descriptions of symbolic and emergent ethnicity (Gans 1982; Waters 1990; Yancey et al. 1976) show that people move in and out of subcultures at will. For example, an individual may participate in an ethnic club or attend a cultural event because of his or her connection to that ethnic community but participate in other communities based on work, neighborhood, or political affiliation. Individuals may participate actively in a community at one point in their life but change communities as they age. People may also participate in many communities simultaneously.

Although social capital networks are often associated with communities, social capital is not the same as community. Communities are larger entities that include people who may have no connection to one another. Closed social capital networks develop within communities, whereas bridging social capital networks cross community boundaries. For example, the low-income African

American community includes many closed social capital networks based on geography, kinship and friendship networks, church affiliations, and participation in social service organizations. People within a community are likely to share similar cultural capital that enables expanding closed social capital networks more easily than attempting to develop bridges across dissimilar communities.

LINKS BETWEEN SOCIAL AND CULTURAL CAPITAL

Recent ethnographic work in communities of color (Stack 1996; Newman 1999; Fernandez Kelly 1995) shows that social capital functions hand in hand with cultural capital to help or hinder low-income people seeking financially stable lives. Using social capital involves both access to the social resources of a small group that facilitate their ability to carry out their work and knowing the cultural habits, mores, and behaviors that indicate membership in the group. Bourdieu (1986) defines cultural capital as one of the three primary forms of capital, along with economic and social capital. The social capital networks that an individual or institution engage in depend on the cultural milieu of that society. Culture becomes cultural capital when specific elements of a culture are used to identify someone as a member of a group. Cultural capital is a commodification of a particular culture or subculture that individuals or organizations can use through social capital to access resources of that group. These cultural capital cues can be subtle social patterns or clear symbols, such as speaking a particular dialect or reference to specific political beliefs.

A number of scholars recognize the links between social and cultural capital, but some substitute cultural capital for social capital or subsume cultural capital under social capital. Coleman (1988) includes mores and norms of the group as part of social capital. Fukuyama (1995:90) uses social capital to refer to the culture of particular societies, stating that social capital depends on "a prior sense of moral community, that is, an unwritten set of ethical rules or norms that serve as the basis for social trust." The same mixing of social and cultural capital occurs in the literature on welfare reform and charitable choice. For example, Sherman (1997:130) confuses social capital with a combination of human and cultural capital when she states that social capital refers to "training I received from my parents, peers, schools, and church that has equipped me with some valuable life skills."

Following Bourdieu (1986) and Fernandez Kelly (1995:222), I see social and cultural capital as intertwined and linked, but not merged, phenomena. Whereas Fernandez Kelly sees cultural capital as a by-product of social capital, I view the two concepts as separate, but reproducing each other. Connections can be shared with outsiders and social cues can be learned. However, for an individual to gain entry into an existing social network, the members of that closed community must both offer connections and teach the culture of that group.

Links to Economic Capital

As Wacquant (1998) notes, social capital is also inextricably linked to economic capital. People in power use both individual networks and formal institutions to exacerbate race/class inequality. Social science research documents prevailing economic, social, and governmental structures that keep poor people of color and women out of good jobs and power structures that determine the distribution of goods and services in this country (Edin and Lein 1997; Stack 1974, 1996; Susser 1982; Piven and Cloward 1977; Katz 1989; Gordon 1994, 1990; Massey and Denton 1993; Gordon et al. 1982; Skocpol 1995). Success or failure of welfare reform will depend on altering existing patterns of social, cultural and economic capital to allow excluded populations access to wider social resources.

Social and Cultural Capital and Individual Career Histories

The remainder of this chapter uses ethnographic case material to clarify the various parts of the definition of social capital used throughout this book. Social capital involves three related elements working together: 1) network connections, 2) reciprocal, enforceable trust, and 3) practice of network-appropriate cultural cues. The constellation of these factors are acknowledged by everyone participating in the network, particularly when social capital crosses the unequal boundary of employer/employee, service provider/program participant, or policy makers/community advocates. The kinds of individuals and institutions that use social and cultural capital in welfare-reform-related efforts are outlined in table 1.1. Although the same three ingredients go into social capital in each case, the actual resources needed, expected outcomes, potential causes of failure, and ways to enhance social and cultural capital differ in each situation. I explore these relationships across these various categories of individuals and different types of formal organizations and coalitions. Because successful welfare reform involves individual, organization, and coalition networks, it is important to explore the role of social and cultural capital in each context. I begin through examples with individuals.

TABLE 1.1 SOCIAL/CULTURAL AND CAPITAL INGREDIENTS

Individuals	Possible Existing Social Network Resources	Required Cultural Capital	Sources of Enforceable Trust	Potential Results	Social Capital-Related Reasons for Failure to Meet Goals	Mechanisms to Enhance Successful Completion of Goals
Individual job seekers	• Individual: friends; family; people known through educational institutions, community, social service organizations, and voluntary association activities • Employer: previous employers or employers connected to people in individual networks	• Individual: working knowledge of appropriate language, dress, and behavior patterns for network • Employer: working knowledge of appropriate language, dress, and behavior patterns for workplace	• Individual: reputation of individual, family member, or other referring social network resource; previous experience with individual • Employer: résumé, application, or job letter; reports from references; reputation of references	• Stable employment • Successful career path	• Lack of appropriate networks to find work • Lack of resources to provide supports such as child care, transportation, health care, and emotional/mentoring support • Lack of appropriate cultural capital	• Development of mentoring relationships and networks • Development of cultural capital

(continued)

TABLE 1.1 (continued)

Organizations	Possible Existing Social Network Resources	Required Cultural Capital	Sources of Enforceable Trust	Potential Results	Social Capital-Related Reasons for Failure to Meet Goals	Mechanisms to Enhance Successful Completion of Goals
Formal social service organizations	• To find program participants: former program participants, government/ social service agency referrals, connections to schools, community-based organizations, and other appropriate locations to advertise programs • To gain contracts: government/ funding agencies: other social service organizations (both formal association and informal networks), political connections, key staff individual social networks	• Program participants: knowledge of participant cultural patterns • Employer, government, and other agencies: knowledge of appropriate cultural patterns	• Reputation of the agency for successful service through actual experience, word of mouth, and sometimes program outcome statistics	• Successful program outcomes, continued contracts	• Lack of appropriate social networks or cultural capital to reach various constituencies, contracting/ funding organizations, and/or employers • Failure to translate social or cultural capital for some program participants or employers due to lack of enforceable trust	• Hiring staff with appropriate social/ cultural capital to reach various constituencies; developing programs that consciously develop social and cultural capital among participant/ employee • Partnering with other agencies with different social/cultural resources to bridge participant/ employee gaps • Participating in government, agency, and political coalitions related to the service

Community-based organizations and churches	Established ties to other institutions and employers; social networks of organization leaders and organization participants	Knowledge of appropriate cultural capital cues for both people receiving service and potential social and institutional resources like employers, government or social service agencies; Knowledge of appropriate cultural capital cues to help people receiving service learn to bridge between home/community culture and agency/employer culture	Reputation of the organization; ability to foster a sense of community/individual trust among organization participants; Ability to use accepted discourse and cultural symbols to communicate effectively with agencies, government officials, and employers	Linkages between individual job seekers and appropriate agencies/employers; Instrumental, emotional, and mentoring support to facilitate job placement, retention, and advancement	Lack of appropriate networks; Failure to use appropriate cultural cues to gain access to resources and support job seekers; Too closely established patron–client relationship with funders/policy makers	Developing understanding of relevant context factors (family circumstances, agency mission, relevant legislation), cultural cues and discourse for organization participants, agencies, and employers; Enhancing networks through ties to other organizations/agencies and expanded board/participant outreach

(continued)

TABLE 1.1 (*continued*)

Advocacy Coalitions	Possible Existing Social Network Resources	Required Cultural Capital	Sources of Enforceable Trust	Potential Results	Social Capital-Related Reasons for Failure to Meet Goals	Mechanisms to Enhance Successful Completion of Goals
Provider coalitions	• Ties to similar organizations, government/funding organizations, politicians, employers, and sources for program participants such as the school system or community-based organizations • Individual institution social networks	• Knowledge of coalition cultural cues, appropriate cultural cues, and discourse for government, politicians, and employers	• Individual agency reputation • Coalition reputation; ability to use appropriate discourse when talking to government, other coalitions, employers, and program participants	• Ability to establish and change policy and program standards; ability to successfully carry out goals of program or participating agency	• Limited knowledge of policy agendas or appropriate cultural cues • Lack of social capital connections to government, other related organizations, or participants • Too closely established patron-client relationship with funders/policy makers	• Developing understanding of relevant context factors (family circumstances, relevant legislation) • Developing effective use of cultural cues and discourse for participants, policy makers, government agencies, and employers

| Advocacy coalitions | • Ties to target population for advocacy efforts (for example, welfare recipients); member organization and individual member networks
• Connections to agencies and/or government | • Knowledge of appropriate cultural cues and discourse for the general community, policy makers, agencies, and target population | • Reputation of coalition participants or member organizations; coalition reputation
• Ability to use appropriate discourse for a given forum; social network ties of coalition participants | • Ability to change policy and program direction and implementation strategies | • Failure to use appropriate discourse; reputation of advocates or target population; failure to understand policy or implementing agency constraints and rules
• Failure to establish consensus within the advocacy coalition | • Develop thorough knowledge of policy and programs; establish networks with appropriate agency, government, or political actors
• Develop appropriate cultural cues and discourse |

INDIVIDUAL SOCIAL NETWORKS

The first ingredient of social capital that successfully brings welfare recipients into stable employment involves the availability of networks with connections to needed resources. Chapter 7 describes the five types of families studied: those with limited or no work experience; low-skilled workers; displaced workers/ stable working class; rising educated middle class; and migrants and refugees. Differences among these five types of families often hinged on available social capital, as illustrated by the case examples. In one example, John was a white man in his mid-40s with no high-school diploma but an established career working in factories. He had migrated to the United States as a child from Germany, entering elementary school without speaking English. He was quickly tracked into special education and as a result never received formal education. "I was in special ed and can't read," he told us. Despite these deficits in human capital, John never had trouble finding work. His family and friends found him jobs whenever he was in need. Although he had turned to welfare for support after running through his unemployment, he cheerfully told me, "I'll find a job." Three months later, a family friend helped him find work driving a truck.

John's experience was typical of that of most of the displaced workers. People relied on known employers, finding work through established social networks. Employers, in turn, trusted the skills and work habits of these workers. Jobs lasted until companies went out of business or left town. However, social capital does not simply mean having friends and family to rely on for advice and employment referrals. Both low-skilled workers and displaced workers had plenty of friends and family to provide employment information. In many cases, however, the jobs found by low-skilled workers through social networks did not offer the stability and good wages of jobs displaced workers found though their networks. The difference stemmed from the fact that low-skilled workers, primarily people of color and women, had connections only to low-paying jobs.

Chrystal's story illustrates how low-skilled workers' networks led them to unstable, low-paid employment. Chrystal started working at age 10, doing odd jobs at the laundromat where her family washed their clothes. She graduated to temporary jobs cleaning suburban hotels found through "a girlfriend's cousin. She had some cousins who worked there. And they knew some openings, so that's how I got that." When cleaning jobs ended, she found work at the neighborhood store where she shopped. All these jobs paid less than $6 an hour and did not offer health insurance. Frustrated with low-level employment, she found through a newspaper a short-term nursing-assistant training program that trained her and placed her in a home health position—still part-time, paying low wages. When we met her, she was enrolled in the welfare-to-work program through a community college. She had also decided to attend this school through social capital referrals: "I had a sister-in-law who attended Community. And the talk she gave me about Community made it sound pretty appealing."

Social Capital and Reciprocal Trust   If social capital simply meant networks, fostering connections to work would be easy. However, social capital equally involves reciprocal trust. Anna's experience illustrates the way that lack of this element of social capital belies available human capital. Anna was an African American low-skilled worker who had completed an associate's degree while working as a secretary. Her skills, attitude, and work habits were good. Before returning to college, Anna had worked on and off in sales positions. Even though she was placed in an internship where her skills were valued, that employer did not hire her because of funding problems. Anna, disappointed by that experience, told another program participant how the agency had "promised a job" but did not come through. She started ignoring her internship program's phone calls about job leads, instead "looking for work through friends and the newspaper." After more than a year of job hunting, she returned to a sales position in a department store. She remained in that job for several years.

Social capital involves trusting the network that provides job leads and support as much as it does the prospective employer's recognizing an employee's skills. Trust resides in the network as a whole, but it is activated or broken through individual actions. Trust relations with new networks, such as a social service agency, are often fragile. For example, Anna's agency had a reputation among both employers and welfare-to-work program participants for finding good jobs. However, welfare-related agencies generally have a justifiably poor reputation in the African American community (Wacquant 1998; Kingfisher 1996). Anna decided not to use social capital offered by her sponsoring social service agency after they lost credibility when the internship agency did not hire her. The link with the new network was broken because they lacked enforceable trust in her eyes. She returned to tried-and-true social capital within her community, which kept her as a low-skill worker regardless of her training.

The Role of Cultural Cues   Accessing networks and enforceable trust depend on common cultural capital associated with the network. This particularly becomes an issue for newcomers attempting to break into stable labor markets. Christine had graduated from a highly regarded clerical program with exemplary skills. Although no one in her primary social networks of family and friends could help her find secretarial work, she was confident that she could find a job. However, employer after employer turned her down. After several unsuccessful interviews, her training program checked with some of the potential employers. The interviewers initially camouflaged their concerns with such statements as "she wouldn't fit in." Eventually they told us that the problem was that she dressed in clothing too tight and too brightly colored for conservative Philadelphia workplaces, wore a great deal of gold jewelry, and spoke black English.[6] Employers did not believe her credentials because she did not follow the cultural cues used by employees they found acceptable.

Sandy's story shows how using appropriate cultural capital makes the difference in ability to bridge into mainstream employment. Sandy was an African American woman who came from a neighborhood similar to Christine's and had graduated from a Philadelphia technical high school known for quality clerical training. Through school and her community, she had learned the expected attire for "mainstream" workplaces, the ability to switch between black and white English, and required work habits. Because she stopped working when her children were born, she did not learn word-processing skills needed for office jobs. Despite these skills deficits, she was quickly hired by an agency where she had served as an intern. Management at her agency commented that they were sure she could learn computers because she fit in and did such a good job with other clerical tasks. Social capital came through the welfare-to-work program connections. However, Sandy's cultural capital superseded human capital in the hiring decision. Sandy would not have been hired if she had lacked both human and cultural capital.

Socialization, Class, Race, and Social Capital   Primary social networks serve as the most reliable source of social capital that leads to stable employment because they often provide direct access to cultural and economic capital. African American and Latino families in the stable working class and rising middle class lacked historical ties to industry but possessed social skills expected by employers. Working-class families acknowledged the need to learn to switch accents, dress, and other cultural habits that allowed these individuals to succeed in a white workplace. The ways in which social and cultural capital are developed are discussed throughout this book. Chapter 7 outlines life histories for different worker types. Chapter 8 compares the experience of different worker types with education and work. Chapters 9 and 10 look carefully at the role of social service organizations and faith communities in developing social and cultural capital. The next section explores the role of organizations in providing social and cultural capital.

The Role of Formal Social Service Agencies and Training Providers

The welfare-to-work programs in both Wisconsin and Pennsylvania call for agencies to find jobs for welfare recipients. As outlined in table 1.1, the same elements function in similar ways when an agency serves as the locus for social capital that moves people across the boundaries of local communities. Exploring the role of agencies in social capital also reveals two additional elements of the concept: 1) patterns within the new employment context and 2) the importance of community-based institutions in helping individuals move into different social arenas.

Martha's case illustrates the role of agencies in successfully marshaling social and cultural capital to reinstate stable employment. An African American woman from a working-class background, Martha received clerical training from a well-respected technical high school. The school helped her land her first job. Later, she returned to community college to obtain training as a legal secretary. The next job came from a community referral, but the reputation of the training programs proved particularly important in finding employment. She eventually left that position to care for a sick child, also intending to complete a four-year degree in social work.

Required to participate in mandatory community service as part of welfare reform, she was placed at a social service agency as a secretary. Recognizing her skills, the agency quickly offered her a full-time secretarial job that paid less than her last private-sector employer had. We spent many hours talking about whether she should take the position. She told me that she didn't want "to take a job paying $7 an hour" when her previous jobs had paid more. She particularly feared that she would have no time or way to pay for college: "It's my turn for school; I don't want to lose that." On the advice of the welfare-to-work program, she told the employer her concerns and they agreed to help pay for her social work education. She took the secretarial position, and less than a year later they hired her for a social service position.

Martha's experience illustrates several key elements of social and cultural capital development linked to organizations. First, school-based social capital proved critical in finding her first job. The reputation of the school and its connections to employers provided resources not available through her family. However, cultural capital came from a combination of her upbringing and lessons learned in school. Formal education alone did not provide the ingredients necessary to access social capital.

Similar mechanisms helped place Martha in the social service position later in her career. The social service agency contracted to provide internships had an established relationship with the social service agency that hired her. This organization had the knowledge and social capital trust with that agency to suggest an appropriate placement for Martha. The agency also drew on the cultural capital that Martha had obtained through home, school, and work in evaluating her for employment and promotion. This mix of connections and cultural cues led to her success. Many agencies were much more successful placing people from working- and middle-class backgrounds than they were with graduates lacking those cultural skills.

Placement entailed an agency's attempts to match participants to organizations in the agency's social networks. Organizations rely on established social networks to fulfill their contracted placement goals. Analysis of the employers who hired people from the Rapid Attachment Study program supports this theory. Training Solutions, an organization in Philadelphia, provided a list of the placements for all employers who hired people from this program for two years. This comprised 384 jobs with 200 employers. Two patterns were evident. First, over half of the placements were individual jobs throughout the city, most likely jobs found through personal networks. Second, blocks of between three and twenty jobs were placed with several employers. Most of these positions were with health care providers, a few were clerical, and some were blue-collar jobs with companies like UPS.[7]

These major employers shared several characteristics. None was a major firm in the city such as a large hospital, hotel, or university. Nor was Training Solutions able to make many successful contacts with the suburban firms that have most of the employment opportunities in the area. The agency reported limited success in making connections outside of the city.

The majority of the block employers were midsized firms that had previous ties to the agency: nonprofit agencies, and government offices that work with Training Solutions. The list of employers included several of these. Training Solutions relied on its own social capital to fulfill its contract. Ethnographic research with other organizations in the city showed similar patterns. Organizations could place their program participants with the employers with which they had already established patterns of trust, supplying their own good name as credit to the job readiness of their program participants. They were unable to develop similar trust with organizations outside those established networks.

Chapters 9 and 10 explore the interplay between agency social capital and family use of these organizations. These chapters demonstrate that social capital through agencies involves two kinds of trust. First, participants must trust the agency in order to successfully use their services. As chapters 8 and 10 show, families of the five worker types respond differently to various agencies. Second, agencies must develop trust-based relationships with funders and other organizations in order to carry out their work. The dynamic between organization and individual social capital influences outcomes.

THE ROLE OF INSTITUTIONS NOT CONNECTED TO WELFARE REFORM: SOCIAL CAPITAL AND COMMUNITY

As outlined in the third category in table 1.1, social capital resources were provided to low-income people by several kinds of institutions, including formal social service agencies and community organizations. Faith communities often provide similar kinds of social support. Mary's case illustrates this trend. Mary had moved to Kenosha from Chicago to be near her mother, who had relocated to Wisconsin several years earlier. Mary was a single parent with six children, no high-school diploma, and limited work experience. Her mother provided transportation and child-care support, but the most important connection involved bringing Mary into her church. The congregation offered a community, as well as guidance on choosing a career path. Noticing that Mary enjoyed caring for children, the pastor suggested that she volunteer in the church day-care program to try out this job. Mary focused on child care when contacted by the welfare agency to find work. Her choice came partly from loyalty to the pastor; she expected a part-time job in the church day-care center. When I asked her why she wanted to work for the church when other employers could pay better, she told me that she knew "the church and the people" and felt more comfortable in this known environment. The congregation continued to provide social, emotional, and instrumental support as she continued through the government-sponsored program.

Community-based organizations and faith communities often play an important role as bridging institutions. As in Mary's case, the church provided a safe, recognized environment to practice the cultural cues and work habits expected by other employers. Since the congregation members knew Mary, they had a wider context that enabled them to understand when she was not able to fulfill every expectation. Reciprocal trust worked both ways. At the same time, the church provided bridging mechanisms through advocacy to the welfare-reform organization. Congregation members also helped Mary develop cultural capital, teaching her the language and strategies to best navigate the government programs and other social networks she needed to learn to move toward stable employment. The church served as a trusted bridge between the recipient of government services and the wider community, providing both social and cultural capital.

CLOSED AND BRIDGING SOCIAL CAPITAL

These various examples illustrate the importance of both closed and bridging social capital. As with Mary and John, closed social capital networks become the resource families use to fulfill their needs. John found work through his closed networks of family and friends. Mary developed a number of supports through closed networks. She is most comfortable functioning in the closed social capital community of the church. In cases like Christine's, the needs and expectations of those closed social capital networks supersede opportunities to branch out into other worlds. Every family we met in this study relied on closed social capital communities for base resources and the beliefs they used to interact with others from different networks.

This research consistently shows that closed networks form the basis for bridging relationships. Sandy and Martha relied on a combination of home, church, and school to develop the social and cultural capital that they needed to succeed in mainstream workplaces. Home and congregation networks taught that they should learn how to become bicultural in order to make it in a largely white world. Members of Mary's church are working to help her develop the same skills.

Bridging social capital develops over time as people form networks across closed social capital groups. Sandy and Martha developed strong, long-term ties to people outside their home communities. In these cases, bridging social capital came through school and work. In other cases, discussed later in the book, church pastors, nonprofit programs, and school personnel deliberately help families make connections to people from other groups. In all cases, bridges are built slowly and carefully.

SUMMARY: INGREDIENTS OF SOCIAL CAPITAL FOR INDIVIDUALS

Taken together, these examples of individual and institutional social support delineate the basic factors of social and cultural capital. Social capital provides networks that link people to jobs and other resources. In many cases, these contacts include face-to-face interactions among known individuals. However, this is not always the case. The reputation of training providers serves as a stand-in for personal interaction. The networks of faith communities and social service agencies can serve the same function. As a member of her congregation, Mary could contact other organizations familiar with that church and expect special attention because of the reputation of the organization. By participating in a faith community or a social service organization, people learned about additional resources and appropriate cultural capital needed to access them.

In each case, social capital involved understanding appropriate cultural cues, not merely knowing the right people. This became most clear for people attempting to cross racial or national divides. The problem was most acute for formal organizations when trying to place people who lacked expected cultural capital. In all cases, the relationship between cultural cues and social trust went both ways. Like Anna, they were unwilling to depend on network resources that they did not trust.

The disjunctures among training, agency supports, and social and cultural capital highlight the fact that social and cultural capital remain mechanisms for creating in-groups and exclusion. Mary trusted her church but not others. Employers would not hire or keep trainees like Christine who lacked appropriate cultural behaviors regardless of skills or the reputation of the agency. It is possible to bridge the exclusionary networks of social and cultural capital, but it requires an added measure of trust across networks and cultures. Support from closed social capital networks is often an important ingredient in the development of bridging social capital.

Agencies exist within their own social networks that influence their range of potential employers. Contracting relationships and accepted values also shape organizational goals and strategies. Fully understanding the role of social and cultural capital in welfare reform requires comprehending the interorganizational dynamics that provide social capital to organizations and shape their programs.

Social and Cultural Capital and Interorganizational Dynamics

The basic social capital elements work for organizations in the same way as for individuals. However, exploring the role of social and cultural capital in organizations implementing welfare reform raises two additional points. First, social and cultural capital influences not only who gets and keeps work or social services but also the very nature of the services offered. Second, the power relationships among the various actors in policy-structured social service contexts profoundly influence the process of policy implementation and change. The dynamics of social and cultural capital in the three communities of Philadelphia, Milwaukee, and Kenosha illustrate different patterns.

Research on nonprofit social welfare focuses on the dynamic between government and nonprofit contractors (Smith and Lipsky 1993; Salamon 1995). According to much of this research, these relationships tend to control and routinize the activities of nonprofits implementing government policy (DiMaggio and Powell 1988; Smith and Lipsky 1993). I explore this issue in more detail in chapters 4 and 10. DiMaggio and Powell (1988:84–85) comment that hiring networks select people within a defined sphere who conform to the same cultural traits as others in the organization. Thus, social and cultural capital combine to structure organizational behavior.

As discussed in more detail in chapter 5, other scholars posit several interorganizational contexts that support various organizational structures (Warren 1967; Milofsky 1988; Milofsky and Hunter 1995). Consistent with the social capital approach, nonprofits come out of vertically defined relationships with contractors, network relationships among similar organizations, and more localized "communities in themselves" (Milofsky and Hunter 1995). Warren (1967) assumed competition among agencies instead of the implied cooperation of social capital, describing organizations competing to bring forward specific values through participation in the differing interorganizational contexts of federative, coalitional, and social choice relationships. In the Milofsky and Hunter model, social and cultural capital can play a role in each of these relationships. The research presented here focuses on these aspects of interorganizational dynamics as agencies use social capital to implement welfare reform.

Who Provides Service?: Social Capital and Provider Interorganizational Dynamics

Welfare-reform rhetoric calls for new service-provision models and for expanding the pool of providers to include for-profit organizations and faith communities along with a wider array of nonprofits. However, as illustrated under "Formal Social Service Organizations" in table 1.1, in both Wisconsin and Pennsylvania contracts went to those with established social capital ties to government and proven track records providing welfare-related services.

Milwaukee agencies were the most deliberate in developing noncompetitive social capital relationships that structured service provision. Relying on preexisting network relationships (Milofsky and Hunter 1995), they developed the kind of provider coalition described in table 1.1. Prior to bidding on contracts, most agencies participated in regular meetings to discuss the process. Agencies had agreed on which organization would bid for a given region before submitting proposals. As W-2, Wisconsin's welfare-reform program, was implemented, agencies continued to meet on a regular basis to discuss ongoing issues (W-2 agency administrator, personal communication). These relationships framed responses to both the state and local advocates. Chapter 5 describes the systems that agencies develop in order to carry out their work. Chapter 10 discusses the role of social capital in agency response to welfare reform and design of individual programs. Chapter 13 discusses advocacy strategies used by contracting organizations and others to shape and change the policy of Temporary Aid to Needy Families (TANF).

As mentioned in table 1.1 under "Social Capital–Related Reasons for Failure to Meet Goals" for provider networks, the power relationships inherent in interorganizational dynamics among local providers and government mean that providers have limited ability to change programs. One example from Milwaukee illustrates this tendency. The Wisconsin program carefully delineated services to people once they either had found a job or were deemed to need additional preparation for employment. However, the program had no income-support provisions for people who agencies thought were "job ready" but who had not located employment. Both community activists and some W-2 agencies protested this policy. One Milwaukee W-2 agency announced that it would not classify anyone as "job ready." State officials ignored these protests but changed their minds after an organized legislative and community protest campaign orchestrated by both advocates and the religious community. Although providers were unable to change policy, outside agencies succeeded in changing government strategy. Examining the interorganizational dynamics of community dissent clarifies concepts of social and cultural capital and highlights strategies to use them to move people out of poverty.

SOCIAL AND CULTURAL CAPITAL AND SHAPING WELFARE REFORM THROUGH COALITION ACTIVITIES

Putnam's (2000) model of social capital seeks a society in which everyone participates in civic activities and debate. Social capital is structured through face-to-face interactions in voluntary associations and other organized civic venues. If this model held true, Kenosha, with its limited but actively supported social service arena, would illustrate a wealth of social capital whereas the larger cities would illustrate a decline in social capital. Chapter 5 describes the dynamics in each city that facilitate or hinder service provision.

In each community, the population most needing welfare services has increasingly become poor people of color, a pattern that follows a national trend (De Parle 1998). This means that the population least likely to access existing social and cultural capital resources remains outside mainstream employment networks. Building bridges to these communities and modifying programs to address their special needs become increasingly important (Wilson 2000). Social and cultural capital takes on a different dimension in this context. Rather than refer to activities that connect individuals in need to jobs or services, the same community resources are used to influence how individuals access government funds and the character of program supports. Shaping government-funded programs establishes how various community residents have access to the social goods of that community. For example, people who are provided no means of support while they look for work are limited in the kinds of social or human capital resources they have time to access before finding employment. Using social and cultural capital in advocacy efforts may make a long-term difference in the ability of welfare-reform initiatives to cross class and race barriers to connect low-income people to family-sustaining resources. Coalitions in the larger cities have proved most effective in this role.

As summarized in the last category in table 1.1, "Advocacy Coalitions," two aspects influence the ability of communities to effectively mobilize social capital to modify policy: 1) trust patterns among participants in the debate and 2) the language of discussion that signifies cultural cues inherent in cultural capital. In both cases, religious-based social and cultural capital had the most success in changing policy.

Cultural Capital and Recognized Authority   The importance of the "enforce-able trust" (Portes and Sensenbrenner 1993:1325) in shaping policy debates is perhaps best illustrated by the failure of Kenosha coalitions to address success-fully community concerns about welfare reform. The city's social service and advocacy community participated regularly in coalition meetings hosted by the W-2 agency regarding the progress of welfare reform. Representatives of government and social service agencies frequently voiced concerns over some aspects of W-2 implementation. Yet the W-2 agency continued to discount suggestions for change as the comments of a few malingerers.

This failure comes from the inability of the social service providers and ad-vocates to draw on established cultural capital authority resources to back up their concerns. When I first called the major interfaith coalition, the organizer told me that they would welcome an informational talk on W-2: "We want people to educate us, not expect us to do something."

This comment arose from associating me with a welfare-rights advocate who had been my initial contact with this coalition. Agnes was respected as a community volunteer but ignored as one of the outsiders who violate commu-nity norms by calling attention to race/class inequities. The faith communities have led efforts to support the local health clinic as well as other community initiatives. However, coalition members remain split on expectations for wel-fare reform. Some support the ideology behind W-2; others see it as a punitive program. As a result, concerned pastors participated in activities to support the poor through the existing social service activities for the homeless and in-dividual congregation initiatives, but no orchestrated coalition activities had raised community consciousness regarding any aspect of W-2. Because the voices of authority that represent cultural capital within the community do not participate in the debate, advocates for change can be identified as repre-senting primarily their own interests or as having a limited view.

Dynamics Between Social and Cultural Capital in Organization Contexts   An-other Kenosha example illustrates the ways in which social and cultural capital are both connected and independent. Pastor Carter is a newcomer to Kenosha who has recently moved from outsider to insider status in the social capital networks that run this city. A highly educated former Illinois school-district administrator serving as the minister of a large African American church in Kenosha, he maintains the cultural habits of many African American clergy, including impeccable suits, a practice of pointing out racial disparity, and use of titles with everyone he meets. These practices exacerbated established Kenoshan's view of him as an outsider because the city's culture emphasizes egalitarian ethos through refusing to acknowledge racial or educational differ-ences, calling everyone by his or her first name, and always dressing casually.

His move from outsider to insider involved both conscious efforts to develop social capital and modifying cultural capital practices to better fit into this small city. He developed social capital by consistently working in citywide organizations and engaging his previously isolated congregation in a range of interfaith and interracial activities. He slightly modified his cultural style for Wisconsin by downplaying his educational and employment background and foregrounding concern for the Kenosha population as a whole. For example, he never mentioned his credentials in public meetings. Although when among African Americans he expressed concern about how children of color were treated in school, in citywide forums he would talk about working "for all the children" of Kenosha. By modifying cultural capital enough to fit in, he now has the reputation as a bridge builder in a racially divided community. If he had entirely maintained his previous cultural style, he would still be known as a mistrusted African American minister who "hollers at" officials in public meetings.

Cultural Symbols and Community Social Capital. As with Pastor Carter's way of phrasing concerns, the language of debate also makes a difference in the ability of community representatives to foster policy modification. Language often represents the cultural symbols inherent in cultural capital. A town meeting in Philadelphia shows how the same message delivered using different cues can lead to very different results. The town meeting, held early in the welfare-reform process, was labeled as a forum for sharing information and expressing community concerns. The audience included most of the social service providers in the city, representatives from all the advocacy groups, and several organized groups of program participants. The city's welfare-reform administrators sat behind tables on the stage, offering information and responding to comments.

A representative from Women Warriors, a radical welfare-reform group, spoke first. She angrily described being homeless and without skills, demanding that the government give her benefits and a good job. She complained about several aspects of the implementation of the program. The government facilitator's response was terse and clearly reflected annoyance.

Shortly thereafter, a representative from the archdiocese made a presentation from an advocacy coalition. This coalition was nonsectarian, but the nun's speech relied on religious language and deliberately sought common ground with the government position. The substantive points of this message were largely the same as those of the Women Warriors representative. The government administrator responded with a series of questions and a promise for consideration. After further negotiation, some modifications were made to the welfare-reform program.

This story shows how social and cultural capital go beyond simply drawing on trusted actors to achieve a measurable end. As in Milwaukee, the respect and trust resident in the religious community enabled social capital to facilitate change. The language used in presenting messages to government made a significant difference. The cultural capital cues that imply that social actors belong to the same community are encoded in the religious community activist's words. These individuals are able to present messages that alter the resources available to low-income people because they invoke accepted cultural capital conventions, creating the expectations of enforceable trust inherent in social capital networks. It is this sense of civic commitment through shared values that Putnam (1995, 2000) mourns as missing in life in the United States. These examples show that social capital is not missing but depends on culturally coded relationships.

SUMMARY OF SOCIAL CAPITAL FOR ORGANIZATIONS

This discussion of social capital for organizations shows that it has many similarities to social capital for individuals. Organizations use their social capital networks to find funding, establish policies, win contracts, and attract program participants. Organization social capital relies on reciprocal trust developed over time: agency reputation enables them to place trainees in jobs and continue relationships with government. Cultural capital also plays a role in social capital for organizations. As the examples with the interfaith and welfare-rights coalitions show, the cultural symbols of language and shared belief are a powerful component that enables organizations to use their social capital effectively.

Although individuals associated with organizations bring social capital to their roles in those institutions, organization social capital means much more than the sum of the networks available to individuals connected to those institutions. Chapters 10, 11, and 12 explore the dynamics between institutions and individuals in welfare reform.

Much of this book examines the interplay between organizations and families in the context of local policy and socioeconomic systems. Interorganizational dynamics and larger community interactions also play a role in social capital and welfare reform. I rely on definitions of social capital outlined here to discuss the various issues detailed throughout the book. In some cases, I look in more depth at what social capital means while illustrating how organizations and individuals develop and use social capital to meet their goals. However, the book looks less at definitions than at practical applications of theory outlined here. Theory arises from the interplay between on-the-ground data and theoretical assumptions. Future policy and programs stem from careful understanding of research within the framework of theory. I follow these goals of combining theory and practice throughout the book.

Plan of the Book

The first half of the book describes the five factors that create a local social welfare system and discusses the role of social capital in each factor. Chapter 2 outlines the state and federal government policies, and chapter 3 demonstrates how policies shape programs in Philadelphia, Kenosha, and Milwaukee. Chapter 4 discusses the nature of the organizations providing service, and chapter 5 describes the nature of the local implementation system. Local labor markets are briefly described in Chapter 6. Chapter 7 details the five worker types outlined earlier in this chapter. Chapter 8 analyzes differences among typical families.

The second half of the book looks at the interplay of these five factors in various contexts. Chapter 9 looks at the way individuals use social service agencies. Chapter 10 examines the role of social capital in responses to welfare reform by social service agencies. Chapter 11 asks the same questions of faith communities. Chapter 12 looks at the interaction between congregations, nonprofits, and government in the context of a larger community. Chapter 13 focuses on advocacy and social change. The concluding chapter brings together all these elements to make concrete policy and programmatic suggestions for welfare reform using social capital as an aspect in program design and implementation.

A Note on Group Labels

Social scientists use several terms to describe groups of people who supposedly share similar attributes. Such terms as *race, nationality,* and *ethnicity* have political meanings that continue to generate debate as well as ongoing social science discussion. In my own work, I have found that *race* is generally used to refer to group identity supposedly based on biological ancestry but that implies power relationships among people identified as African American, white, Latino, Asian or Native American. *Ethnicity* also refers to putative ancestry, but based on country of origin. In the United States, *ethnicity* is often used to refer to soft aspects of identity such as culture and values rather than power relationships. Both race and ethnicity are social constructions in the United States, they have little to do with actual biology, nationality, or traits of any given group. Group labels for racial and ethnic groups continue to change and serve as the basis for ideological differences. In this book, I generally use *African American, Latino,* and *Asian* to refer to people of African descent, Spanish-speaking populations, and people whose ancestors came from Asia, respectively. However, the terms *black* and *Hispanic* also appear in case examples when I am quoting individuals or other sources that use those terms.

Nationality has a specific meaning in this book. I use it exclusively to refer to the country of origin of immigrants to the United States. When talking about people of a specific nationality, I identify their country of origin.

When discussing community-based organizations or demographic factors, I use *race/ethnicity/nationality* together as one term except when I address one aspect of identity exclusively.

DEFINITIONS OF CULTURE USED IN THE BOOK

Anthropologists define *culture* as the whole way of life of a people, including their economy, political system, social structure, beliefs and values. In anthropology, a subculture is a society within a society that practices different patterns but is dependent on the socioeconomic system and political structure of the larger society. As with the Amish or inner-city African American or Latino subcultures, sometimes the values and practices of the subculture are in deliberate opposition to those of the dominant culture. However, class factions within a society are also subcultures—the elites in each city also have their own unique patterns.

Subcultures can be related to larger subcultural systems; for example, several competing subcultural patterns exist within African American communities that cross class and race (Anderson 1990, 2000). These patterns all developed as a response to past and current racism in the dominant society but reflect different strategies to address these challenges. For instance, one subculture emphasizes professional demeanor, ability to speak standard (white) English, and excellence in school and the workplace whereas another, equally prevalent subculture develops cultural styles deliberately different from their perception of the white majority, considering such behaviors as succeeding in school as "acting white" (Fordham and Ogbu 1986). The cultural content of a subculture responds to a combination of group history, current patterns in the dominant culture, and patterns specific to that subculture. The content and style of any subculture changes over time, and boundaries among subcultural systems may shift as society changes.

Popular definitions of culture, and those used in other social sciences as well as by scholars of organizational dynamics, tend to use *culture* to refer to beliefs, values, and unique patterns of a particular group or organization. I primarily use the anthropological definition throughout this book, but when referring to culture in organizations I speak primarily of unique patterns engendered by the cultural system to which a particular agency belongs.

PART I

FACTORS INFLUENCING IMPLEMENTATION
OF WELFARE REFORM

Social capital plays a role in the way that individuals, families, and organizations access resources to achieve their goals. It means *the social relationships and patterns of reciprocal, enforceable trust that enable people and institutions to gain access to such resources as social services, jobs, and government contracts.* Social capital involves two related elements working together: 1) network connections based on reciprocal, enforceable trust and 2) practice of network-appropriate cultural cues.

Social capital implies that society is organized into networks of individuals and institutions that work together to formulate public policy, develop social welfare programs, and meet community or family needs. Connections among people or institutions necessarily involve the exclusion of those who do not share policy views, come from a different backgrounds, or simply compete for the same resources. However, developing and implementing welfare policy also necessitates crossing small-group boundaries. Two kinds of social capital work simultaneously in local systems. *Closed social capital* refers to networks that include people or institutions that are similar to one another and participate in exclusive sharing relationships. *Bridging social capital* involves long-term trusting relationships but crosses boundaries of class, race, ethnicity, religion, and type of institution.

Social capital becomes the conduit among the various elements that impact on implementation of social welfare policy. Both exclusionary and bridging social capital also functions within each factor, helping or hindering people and institutions seeking to meet their goals. This section describes the following five elements essential to implementation of social welfare policy at the local level and the role of social capital in each factor:

1. The government policies that shape programs
2. The nature of the organizations providing service
3. The nature of the local implementation system
4. The socioeconomic system of the locality
5. The nature of the population receiving service

Chapter 2 outlines the state and federal government policies that shape programs in Philadelphia, Kenosha, and Milwaukee described in chapter 3. The TANF programs created through 1996 welfare-reform legislation gave states block-grant funding to implement their own programs. States develop diverse strategies, but all must create programs that place an increasing number of welfare recipients into work-related activities. Both Pennsylvania and Wisconsin rely on "work first" strategies for welfare reform. Both states used pilot programs as the basis for their TANF programs. Although most of the Pennsylvania research took place before welfare reform, case material includes pilot programs that led to current initiatives.

Pennsylvania relies on a rapid attachment model. *Rapid attachment* refers to short-term job-search and job-placement activities that stress quick placement into paid employment. Participation in a rapid attachment program is the first step in the Commonwealth of Pennsylvania's TANF plan. Prior to implementation of this strategy, AFDC recipients applied for employment and training programs on a voluntary basis. Research reported here includes data on people participating in both voluntary and mandated employment-development strategies.

Wisconsin's welfare-reform initiative (W-2) is one of the most radical reform efforts in the United States. W-2 completely eliminates cash assistance, replacing it with a work-based system that provides supports to low income working people and cash grants to eligible unemployed people only if they participate in work-related activities (Wiseman 1996). Because only W-2 participants engaged in work-related activities receive benefits through this program, people who are unable or unwilling to participate in W-2 must rely on local community resources.

Chapter 4 looks carefully at the types of organizations providing services to families in these three cities. Case examples show the different structures and resources available to organizations oriented to help people with particular problems or those from a specific neighborhood or race/nationality/ethnicity group. To explain the role of social capital for each group, I identify the constituencies that influence organization behavior and describe how social capital between agencies influences their resources.

Chapter 5 explores the nature of the local implementation system. Both state programs rely heavily on the private and nonprofit sectors to provide services. Competitive requests for proposals that fit each state's program were let out for bid in 1996. The provision of services through nonprofit, for-profit, and quasi-governmental institutions means that individuals served in each locality may experience different resources and varying program processes. However, in each city, organizations are part of three interlocking systems. Each system functions through social capital and contracting relationships among participating organizations.

Chapter 6 examines the labor markets that impact on the ability of organizations to find jobs for their participants and influence individual career histories. Milwaukee and Philadelphia proved surprisingly similar as socioeconomic contexts for welfare reform. As the largest city in each state, these two localities housed the greatest concentration of welfare recipients in the state and had the most trouble moving people out of their caseloads. At the end of 2000, nearly half of Pennsylvania's welfare recipients lived in Philadelphia, a significant increase from previous years (Pennsylvania Department of Public Welfare, personal communication). By March 1998, nearly 86 percent of Wisconsin's remaining welfare cases lived in Milwaukee, up from 66 percent six months before (Dresang 1998:B1). Both Milwaukee and Philadelphia are extremely segregated cities (Goode and Schneider 1994; Massey and Denton 1993:221). Most employers have left for the suburbs, and transportation available to low-income, inner-city workers is extremely limited.

Kenosha offers an important contrast to the large cities. By March 1998, the caseload had been reduced from over 1,000 to 338. Kenosha had a booming economy but limited public transportation. It also had a small, well-known circle of social service agencies to provide supports for low-income people. By mid-1998, their W-2 populations included mostly hard-to-serve cases, increasingly people of color.

Chapter 7 looks carefully at the ways individuals navigate the economic system in these cities. People in all three cities could be categorized into five worker types based on their career trajectories over time. Using case examples, I explore the differences between each family type and the way they use social capital. Chapter 8 takes this examination of individual experience further by comparing worker-type experience with education and child care. In order to provide a more detailed understanding of the ways that families use social capital, this chapter also looks at the role of closed and bridging social capital for each family type.

Key to Case Examples

The book uses numerous case examples. The appendixes provide a quick reference and short guide to these organizations and families. Appendix B lists all the organizations and churches profiled in the book, and appendix C provides basic information about the key individuals and families.

CHAPTER 2

The Federal and State Policy Context for Welfare Reform

U.S. social welfare policy shapes the support system for families in several ways. First, government programs provide basic income and payment systems to cover food, child care, transportation, housing, and health care for some families. Second, government funding supports education, training, programs for children and youth, and an array of other forms of social support provided through government agencies and private organizations. Third, social welfare policies govern the types of programs offered to families and what they must do to qualify. This chapter addresses two questions:

1. What social supports are available through government?
2. What rules govern access to these social supports?

DEVELOPMENT OF U.S. SOCIAL WELFARE POLICY

Social welfare provision in the United States consists of a complex mix of programs with wide variation among states and localities. Programs are housed in different government agencies, each with its own rules and structure. People needing service, agencies offering it, and interest groups alike find the U.S. system fragmented and confusing. Although public assistance, unemployment, and education and training initiatives now have uniform federal guidelines, benefit levels and program details are established by each state. Nongovernmental entities provide services under government contract. This system grew out of historic development of social welfare in the United States, which emphasized local control and private provision of public assistance.

PRECURSORS TO THE FEDERAL SOCIAL WELFARE PROGRAMS

Until passage of the Social Security Act of 1935, basic needs and social services for people without other means of support were provided at the local level, primarily through private institutions. Originally based on the English Poor Laws, each town or county provided assistance to the indigent through a locally devised system that involved a patchwork of local government support and private charity through churches, fraternal associations, and other private agencies. By the mid-nineteenth century, these systems were generally regarded as inefficient, chaotic, and corrupt. In response to growing concerns, state oversight of local welfare services began slowly after 1860. Massachusetts instituted the first Board of State Charities in 1863; sixteen states had similar entities by the turn of the century (Trattner 1994:87; Skocpol 1992).[1]

As the industrial revolution expanded the U.S. population through immigration, concentrated population in cities, and changed the nature of work to factory production, social welfare needs altered dramatically. Civil War casualties and social dislocation created an extensive population of widows, orphans, and disabled veterans, leading to founding of the first federal pension system to support this population. Post–Civil War reformers expressed concerns regarding increasing poverty, child labor, juvenile delinquency, poor housing and sanitation, and a host of related social ills. Two movements led primarily by elite women, the Charitable Organization Society (COS) and the settlement-house movement, began the slow evolution from local social welfare provision to Federal government public assistance.[2] Leaders in the settlement-house movement were instrumental in spearheading state and federal legislation in support of women and children through the Children's Bureau, mothers' pensions, and related initiatives. By the early twentieth century, the COS and settlement-house leaders had joined forces to work for social welfare legislation at the state and federal level (Trattner 1994:163–192, 214–233).

These initiatives in the late nineteenth and early twentieth centuries shared several characteristics that are echoed in social welfare reform of the 1990s. First, legislative initiatives stemmed from fast-moving changes in the economy combined with a new consensus on appropriate behaviors for low-income families. Second, government policy was initiated by the private sector. Finally, legislation started with the states, providing models for federal legislation.

U.S. public assistance policy provides an example of this trend. AFDC came out of state initiatives for mothers' and widows' pensions enacted between 1911 and 1934 to help widowed or abandoned mothers stay home to raise their children, to prevent juvenile delinquency and decrease foster-care placements, and to curb child labor.[3] The legislation reflected changes in the economy that prompted an increasing number of working-class women with children to go to work. Mothers' pensions also sought to expand the middle-class pattern of women staying at home to care for children.[4]

Whereas leadership for these initiatives came from elite, politically active women involved in the settlement-house and COS movements, grass-roots support came from women's organizations at the local level. As a result, every state but Georgia and South Carolina had passed legislation for mothers' pensions by 1934 (Trattner 1994:214–232; Skocpol 1992:424–479). However, the benefit levels and the specifics of each state program varied widely. These variations would later be incorporated into federal law. At the same time, union movements sought better working conditions, wages, and benefits through employers. As a result, current social supports for unemployment, workers' compensation, health insurance, and the elderly focus on employer-funded benefits (Skocpol 1992:205–310).

THE SOCIAL SECURITY ACT AND LATER INITIATIVES

The economic crisis of the Great Depression in the 1930s spurred the creation of federal-level social supports for U.S. citizens. The 1935 Social Security Act created income support systems for unemployed workers, children in low-income families, the disabled, and the elderly. The systems for both unemployed and low-income families incorporated preexisting unemployment insurance and mothers' pension programs, and both developed as state–federal partnerships, with the federal government providing general guidelines and states establishing program details. Funding for both programs came from a combined state and federal match.

Unemployment Insurance   Changes in the economy led to erosion of the unemployment insurance system from the 1970s onward. When initially designed in the 1930s, the system presumed that most wage earners would be full-time factory workers who would return to previous positions after a temporary recession. Unemployed people are usually eligible for benefits for up to six months—or more during an economic downturn—but to qualify they must have worked a state-determined number of hours and reached minimum earnings criteria. Part-time workers and low-wage service-sector employees seldom qualified for unemployment insurance. In recessions prior to 1970, approximately 50 percent of unemployed workers qualified for benefits (General Accounting Office 1993:3). Women and people of color were least likely to receive unemployment insurance.[5]

As the employer mix shifted from manufacturing to service-sector employment in recent decades, and states lowered unemployment insurance taxes on businesses, the unemployment insurance trust funds proved too small to cover needed benefits during multiple recessions. States turned to federal government loans to cover unemployment costs. The federal government responded by passing legislation in 1983 that required states to raise business taxes and reduce benefits. These changes in benefit structures, combined with escalating numbers of workers in jobs that traditionally were not covered by unemployment insurance, have led to a steady decrease in the percentage of workers qualifying for unemployment benefits. Although 97 percent of workers were covered by unemployment insurance in 1993, in the 1990 recession only 39 per-

cent of the unemployed received benefits (General Accounting Office 1993:2). Only 31 percent of unemployed women and 28 percent of people of color received benefits in 1990 (General Accounting Office 1993:45). However, during the 1990 recession, overall unemployment insurance recipiency rates in Pennsylvania (47 percent) and Wisconsin (44 percent) were higher than the national average. Still, fewer families qualify for unemployment insurance today than previously. As discussed in chapter 6, stable-working-class people who remained unemployed for longer than six months were forced to take low-wage jobs or turn to welfare. Changes in the economy make this trend more likely: only 15 percent of workers were expected to return to their previous positions after the 1990 recession, compared to 44 percent in previous recessions (General Accounting Office 1993:2).

Public Assistance   Mothers' pensions became Aid to Dependent Children (ADC) in 1935 as part of the Social Security Act. However, benefits for children of deceased workers were moved to the Supplemental Security Income (SSI) system under Social Security.[6] This meant that the "worthy widows" envisioned for the mothers' pension program received help under another part of the Social Security system. The remaining ADC population consisted primarily of the children of unmarried women.

Support for mothers was added to ADC in 1950, and the program name was changed to Aid to Families with Dependent Children in 1962. Some states also created General Assistance programs for adults without children; these were administered under the aegis of AFDC. Following concerns about tendencies of AFDC to divide two-parent families, the program provided the option to support two-parent households that met income and work eligibility requirements in 1961. The two-parent family option, known as Aid to Families with Dependent Children–Unemployed Parents Initiative, was made mandatory in 1988.

Income eligibility criteria for AFDC meant that few low-income working families qualified for assistance. Struggling working people increasingly resented public assistance recipients. Racist portraits of welfare recipients as lazy "welfare queens" by conservative politicians during the 1980s further eroded support for public assistance.

Public assistance in the United States has always included a strong moral component, with different types of aid provided to the "deserving" and "undeserving" poor (Katz 1989). However, the definition of undeserving poor has changed over time. Unemployed workers, veterans, and the elderly were deemed "deserving." From the late nineteenth century through the 1960s, "worthy" women caring for their children at home were also considered deserving poor. Most African Americans were left out of Social Security until 1950, based on exclusion of agricultural and domestic workers. Local administration of AFDC that allowed county social workers to determine which single-parent households were deserving of aid also contributed to the small numbers of African Americans receiving AFDC (Quadagno 1994). AFDC rooted out the "unworthy" through intrusive social work practices, for example, by making inspections for men living in the house.

The twin movements for civil rights and welfare rights in the 1960s helped many eligible families receive public assistance (Handler 1995:28; Trattner 1994:324–317; Piven and Cloward 1977). Between 1960 and 1970, the welfare rolls doubled, to approximately twelve million people (Trattner 1994:314). This expansion in public assistance resulted from several factors. First, mechanization of agriculture in the 1940s and 1950s, combined with African American migration to the North in search of better-paying jobs, led many African Americans to northern cities. Similar situations brought Latinos from other countries to the urban United States. However, these newcomers moved to industrialized areas as factories moved south and overseas in search of cheaper, nonunion labor. Along with the newcomers, many of those in the existing industrial working class found themselves turning to welfare as family-supporting jobs disappeared.

At the same time, legal action by welfare-rights groups and other advocates for the poor increased the number of applications for public assistance. Welfare-rights initiatives did away with moralistic methods of determining benefits, replacing them with federal eligibility criteria based on income. As a result, the focus of AFDC administration changed to determining income eligibility and rooting out fraud.

In 1964, a separate federal food-stamp program was added by the Department of Agriculture. Health insurance for the poor, Medicaid, was enacted as an amendment to the Social Security Act in 1965 (Trattner 1994:324–327). Although these programs were administered separately and have different eligibility criteria, until passage of TANF, eligibility for these three programs was generally determined as a package. Housing assistance was available through yet another series of programs administered through the Department of Housing and Urban Development, and assistance for the homeless was often provided through private organizations that sometimes received partial government support.

Because AFDC benefits were not indexed for inflation, benefits steadily eroded, leading to an average drop of 51 percent in the real dollar value between 1970 and 1996 (Stoesz 2000:24). Although more people received AFDC, the program kept recipients well below the poverty level. For example, in 1996, combined cash assistance and food-stamp benefits amounted to 67 percent of the federal poverty level in Pennsylvania and 73 percent of the federal poverty level in Wisconsin (Stoesz 2000:25–26). As a result, AFDC lost credibility as an antipoverty program.

The primary reason for AFDC as support for women to care for children at home also disappeared as more women entered the labor force and two-parent families found that it often took two incomes to support a family. As a result, welfare now provided a benefit no longer available to working-class women. Many working- and middle-class women no longer thought of staying at home to watch children as a primary or preferred goal. As nonworking welfare mothers became deviants from the social norm for mothers, the image of welfare recipients quickly changed to one of lazy women who spent their days watching television. Instead, working mothers were regarded as appropriate role models for their children, building self-esteem through self-support and modeling responsible behavior.

Workforce development and income-support programs remained separate until 1967.[7] The Family Support Act (FSA) of 1988, commonly known as the Jobs Opportunities and Basic Skills (JOBS) training program tied receipt of cash assistance to workforce development for the first time. JOBS mandated that a portion of the public assistance population participate in activities to encourage economic self-sufficiency (Hagen and Lurie 1992).

Workforce Development   The U.S. government developed large-scale employment programs in only two time periods: the Works Project Administration and related programs during the Depression of the 1930s and Comprehensive Employment and Training Act (CETA) work programs in the 1960s and 1970s (Rose 1995).[8] CETA provided entree into new career paths for a number of populations, particularly women, but gained the reputation of being riddled with fraud and administrative abuses (Rose 1995; Spar 1983). Moreover, the program did not have the intended effect of moving large numbers of people out of poverty, raising concerns about cost-effectiveness and program outcomes (Spar 1983:9). The Job Training Partnership Act (JTPA) replaced the CETA program in 1982. JTPA provided funding for training programs for adults and youth. Like other government employment and training initiatives, JTPA has been criticized as continuing gender-based segregation through the nature of available training opportunities (Harlan and Steinberg 1989). Additional funding for training was available for displaced workers through legislation designed to lessen the impact of large plant closures.

Summary

The differing political evolution of benefits for veterans, workers, and non-working parents created a system with wide disparity in benefits based on gender and race. Populations perceived as earning benefits, such as unemployed workers and veterans, were treated more generously (Skocpol 1992, 1995). Male workers receive much better benefits than poor women with children (Gordon 1994).

By the mid-1980s, the social assistance system provided a relatively stable income to the elderly that was indexed to inflation, reducing the percentage of older people below the poverty level. However, the unemployment and AFDC systems increasingly provided lower benefits to fewer people. As Theda Skocpol (1995:301) observed, means testing of government assistance meant that most people "in the middle" received no government supports. Lack of support for working families contributed to the call for welfare reform in the 1980s and 1990s.

Evolution of the social assistance system also involved further fragmentation across the states as all benefit programs are combined state/federal initiatives. Since benefit levels are determined by each state, levels of assistance vary widely across the country.

Social Welfare Programs in the 1990s

As in the early twentieth century, economic changes and shifting expectations of family behavior led to calls for public assistance reform. Starting on a large scale with the FSA, welfare reform was aimed at making AFDC recipients more like the rest of the population through wage work.

Like the mothers' pensions initiative that led to AFDC, pilot programs for welfare reform were initiated at the state level. The federal government promoted state waiver programs that provided models for the 1996 legislation. At the same time, some states tried to increase benefits for the working poor by changing eligibility criteria for child-care assistance and medical assistance. As in the early twentieth century, private-sector grass-roots lobbying also played a key role in welfare reform. In 1996, calls for devolution to the private sector and initiatives to increase the role of faith-based providers came from local, state, and federal lobbying efforts.

The decade of the 1990s saw several shifts in the goals and provision measures for income assistance and workforce-development programs. In general, programs for cash assistance and housing changed from providing basic supports to moving families off the public assistance rolls. Workforce-development goals were changed several times in an effort to link education and training more closely to employment and create more consumer choice.

Structures for providing assistance shifted at the same time. Public assistance and workforce-development programs were consolidated. Medicaid was also originally slated to be included in the new system but was removed from the 1996 reform package by Congress.

Although the federal government still provided general guidelines for administration of public assistance and workforce development, policy changes in the second half of the 1990s ceded design control for social welfare programs to the states. Given already existing diversity of state public assistance programs, and preexisting waiver programs in many states, this shift from federal to state control over program design simply expanded already existing trends. However, devolution of welfare programming to the states meant that few national standards for safety-net provision remained in place.

Public assistance reforms also increased the potential role of for-profit, nonprofit, and faith-based organizations in providing service. Government has always contracted with nonprofit organizations to provide services, but the reforms of the mid 1990s changed existing patterns in three ways. First, the legislation allowed for-profit organizations to provide social welfare benefits directly for the first time. Proponents of for-profit contracting felt that market competition would improve services, whereas opponents feared quality would be lost in the quest for profits (Frumpkin and Clark 1999).

Second, TANF allowed nongovernmental agencies to administer cash assistance, a significant change in the policy that had been in place since the turn of the twentieth century. As with for-profit social welfare provision, expanded contracting was meant to discourage poor service through market competition. Opponents raised concerns that increased contracting would lead to fragmentation and inconsistent provision of services.

Third, Charitable Choice provisions encouraged government to contract with faith-based institutions to provide service. While religion-related institutions have provided social welfare services through government contracts since the beginning of the U.S. welfare state (Cnaan et al. 2000), the new legislation softened provisions under previous law that strictly disallowed any reference to religious affiliation or comingling of funds related to religious purposes for institutions offering government-contracted services.

CASH ASSISTANCE SYSTEMS

The basic benefit structure for AFDC remained in effect until passage of the 1996 welfare reform act, commonly known as TANF. The FSA was a supplement to AFDC that required nonexempt recipients to participate in education, training, and employability activities in order to receive benefits.[9] Adult participants could lose benefits through sanctions if they refused to participate without good cause. Most program activities involved job-search or educational activities, with an emphasis on educational programs. Two-parent families on public assistance were required to participate in 16 hours of community service per week.

Although the FSA mandates reflected conservative approaches to welfare reform, the program structure reflected liberal strategies to promote self-sufficiency. Each participant was supposed to be evaluated by a trained case manager and develop an employment-development plan reflecting the individual's education and training needs. The legislation funded a wide range of education and training programs, including college. The FSA program also provided funds and mandates for child-care and transportation allowances to enable participation in training programs. In addition, it required states to develop child-support enforcement mechanisms, an initiative that would be expanded under TANF.

The FSA was never completely implemented owing to refocusing of welfare-reform legislation toward work-first initiatives in the Clinton administration. TANF represented a radical shift from previous public assistance policy in three ways. First, TANF replaced AFDC with a block-grant system administered by the states, giving them flexibility to design their own programs within federal guidelines. Federal legislation required all states to include a time limit for welfare, develop a child-support enforcement system, and submit plans to reduce the number of out-of-wedlock births and teen pregnancies. Under federal regulations, state plans stipulated that recipients under the age of 18 obtain a high-school diploma or GED and that teen parents live with an adult or in a supervised setting. Most legal immigrants were banned from receiving public assistance. Beyond these general requirements, states had wide latitude in designing their programs. Each submitted to the federal government a plan that outlined its proposed program. State plans were revised and renewed on a regular basis.

During the first five years of the program, states received an annual allocation based on their welfare caseloads in 1992, a year of high welfare use due to a recent recession. States could use their funds in a wide variety of ways. The 1996 legislation included employment and training activities, formation of individual development accounts (savings accounts for low-income families), case management, child care, transportation, and other forms of assistance. Some state programs, including those of Pennsylvania and Wisconsin, were based on waiver programs that had already been piloted by state governments.

Second, TANF ended the federal entitlement to public assistance that had been in effect for sixty-one years. TANF sets a five-year lifetime limit for receipt of government assistance. A state could exempt up to 20 percent of its caseload from the five-year limit.[10] In Pennsylvania and Wisconsin, the lifetime clock started after cases were transitioned from AFDC to TANF in 1997. People who remained on AFDC for five continuous years could lose their benefits by 2002. However, lifetime limits for most families would not come into effect until much later because most public assistance recipients cycle on and off the system. For example, a family that regularly used TANF for one year every other year would lose benefits after ten years. Another federal requirement of TANF legislation was that adult recipients be involved in a work-related activity after twenty-four months. States also had the option to limit lifetime benefits to two years. Neither Pennsylvania nor Wisconsin chose to adopt a two-year time limit.

States can refuse to provide aid if TANF recipients do not meet state eligibility criteria or do not fulfill obligations of work-related activity. Systems for sanctioning people who do not fulfill TANF work obligations were developed by each state. While food stamps remained a separate program with separate eligibility criteria, states could choose to include food-stamp allocations among sanctioned benefits.

Third, whereas AFDC focused primarily on providing income support, TANF is geared toward helping program participants gain economic self-sufficiency. Like FSA, TANF called for welfare workers to develop individual responsibility plans with each recipient that would outline activities required to receive assistance, thus shifting the role of front-line workers from determining income eligibility to casework.

TANF allowed states to choose from a wide array of work-related activities that could lead to long-term employment.[11] The 1996 legislation listed work-related activities as including 1) regular employment, 2) work experience—employment with wages paid, either in full or in part, by the government, 3) on-the-job training, 4) job-skills training directly related to employment, 5) six weeks of job-search and job-readiness assistance, 6) up to one year of vocational training, 7) education directly related to employment, 8) attendance at high school or a GED program, 9) community service, and 10) providing child care to an individual participating in a community service program.

TANF offered states both opportunities and challenges in developing their state plans. A state's TANF allocations could be reduced if it did not enroll a certain percentage of its caseload in work-related activities. The variety of activities allowed under the 1996 legislation could lead to improved employability for welfare recipients, but TANF did not include poverty reduction as one of its goals. States could establish their own philosophy for providing assistance to state residents. They also needed to develop ways to support families unable to fulfill TANF work-related-activity requirements because of disability, age, or other issues.

STATE PLANS

Both Wisconsin and Pennsylvania were under Republican administrations when TANF went into effect, and both states focused on work-first strategies. However, the two plans differed significantly when first developed. Over the first three years of operation, state trajectories led to further divergence in plan strategies and goals.

Wisconsin Works (W-2)   Wisconsin's TANF plan is one of the most radical in the country, completely substituting a work-based program for AFDC. The overview document on the W-2 Web site states: "Under W-2, there will be no entitlement for assistance, but there will be a place for everyone who is willing to work to their ability."[12] The design structure for Wisconsin's plan relied on the thinking of conservative scholar Lawrence Mead (1992, 1997), who believes that persistent poverty was caused by lack of a work ethic. Designers of the Wisconsin plan hold a strong faith in advancement through work. A key administrator told me:

> A phrase that is a mantra throughout the development of our proposal and the implementation is: "everyone starts somewhere." There is no such thing as a bad job, there is no such thing as a dead-end job because by definition what we are able to do as individuals on the employment ladder determines where we are to go . . . and it's the thing we have to keep reinforcing in order that it doesn't backslide.
> The rest of it was to make the [system] simple to access, simple to understand. The third piece, though we didn't voice this one in our written descriptions, was to teach consequences—good and bad. Out of that is the third biggest goal, which is building a sense of hope back into an individual, a family, a community. It's pretty hard to have any motivation if you have no hope that what you do is ever going to matter. . . . How is it that you get your approbation in life? Probably through your work . . . and yet [that was] the

piece we had—inadvertently—taken away from people. Hope comes from having something you feel good about.

The aim of welfare reform was to change the "victim mentality" of public assistance recipients. The program focused on adults instead of children because, as the administrator explained:

Children—like it or not—are done to. And who is it that does the doing? It's the parent and the government. So let's get the fix at the right level, because if we get the fix at the parent then the fallout to the child is going to be positive. . . . How do children learn? They learn through role models.

W-2 began with a pilot program in two counties under the name Work Not Welfare in 1993. According to a key plan designer, the "goals of the pilot were to have people spend a very limited time within the welfare structure and become employed as soon as possible." The program had a time limit of two years.

Prior to passage of TANF at the federal level, Wisconsin governor Tommy Thompson had attempted a series of small reforms that were generally considered ineffective. In response to Work Not Welfare, Wisconsin democrats proposed that the governor replace AFDC with a new system by 1998. This initiative came from Milwaukee politicians, who, like the governor's Republican advisors, believed that the current welfare system impaired the ability of poor families to escape poverty. They argued that welfare should be replaced by a system that made work pay, included a public service jobs program for people who could not find work on their own, offered adequate income supports for those who could not work, and provided child care and health care. This challenge to "end welfare as we know it" was added to an authorization bill for the Work Not Welfare initiative. Although most Democrats presumed that the governor would not sign the legislation, and some of his advisors counseled against it, Thompson accepted this challenge to completely reform welfare. However, using a line-item veto provision, he eliminated liberal language about the nature of the new program, leaving in a statement that AFDC must end and the governor must propose a replacement. In 1995, the governor offered W-2 as his replacement program, and it was passed by the Wisconsin legislature in March 1996.[13]

Governor Thompson created a bipartisan task force to determine the details of W-2. It included a five-year time limit, and each person requesting assistance was required to meet with a Financial and Employment Planner (FEP) who would evaluate his or her employment prospects and develop a self-sufficiency plan. As Kaplan (2000:105) notes, FEPs "have complete discretion to determine whether child care is available and full authority to decide whether a participant must find an unsubsidized job." Although employability plans are designed with the recipient, the FEP holds authority in the process. The recipient is obligated to follow the written plan, including locating work. Following the philosophy described by program designers, W-2 employability plans focus on building responsibility, which will presumably lead to self-sufficiency. The FEP serves as guide, aide, and enforcer in this process.

W-2 created a four-level employment ladder with the following steps:

1. *Unsubsidized employment*: Those who found work became eligible for food stamps, Medicaid, child-care assistance, and the earned income tax credit (EITC), depending on their income. Employed people on W-2 also received some case-management assistance.

2. *Trial jobs*: People who had trouble finding work could be placed in regular jobs subsidized by the government for a three- to six-month training period. These people were also eligible for food stamps, Medicaid, child care, EITC, and case management. This employment strategy is rarely used.

3. *Community-service jobs* (CSJs): People who were not likely to find employment quickly were placed in community-service positions that were expected to provide work experience for participants. People worked at their CSJ placement for thirty hours a week and attended training for another ten. They received a cash grant of $673 per month, which could be docked if they missed hours without good reason. Those in CSJs were eligible for food stamps, Medicaid, child care, and case management.

4. *W-2 transition*: People with major problems that kept them from performing independent, self-sustaining work were placed in this last category. These people received cash grants of $628 per month and were eligible for food stamps, Medicaid, child care, and case management. They were expected to participate in work or developmental activities for twenty-eight hours per week and education and training for twelve hours per week. The program assumed that people would eventually transition to CSJs and then unsubsidized employment.

W-2 also provided several forms of additional assistance. The goal of case management changed from determining whether someone was eligible for assistance to helping participants solve problems that stood in the way of work. Assistance was available for transportation to required programs and job interviews. The program required local agencies to provide drop-in child care for participants. Job-access loans were available to help cover the costs of such items as clothing, work-related tools, and a car to get to work.

W-2 also increased enforcement of child support. A mother who applied was required to name the father of her children so that the state could ensure that he provided cash support. People who were working received all the money that the state collected from the father; those in the cash-grant program received 41 percent of child-support payments.

Although the W-2 program carefully outlined the various kinds of assistance available to people once they were placed in the system, it was less clear about support while they looked for work. AFDC supplemented income with cash assistance for people working in low-paying or part-time work. These benefits disappeared under W-2. From 1997 to 2000, people working in part-time or low-wage jobs could receive more in food stamps, but no additional cash assistance. The W-2 program began offering prorated cash grants to people working part-time under the 1999–2000 TANF plan, through cash assistance in exchange for participation in community-service or education programs. W-2 program applicants deemed job-ready were offered workshops and other assistance to find employment, but no cash support during their search.

Under AFDC, relatives caring for family members' children received cash benefits. W-2 replaced this with Kinship Care, which provided $215 per month for each child, often less than AFDC benefits. Kinship Care also required extensive background checks for relatives caring for children, for which no funding to localities was provided. Kinship Care funds were also limited, creating waiting lists for assistance in some areas.

As a work-first program, W-2 focused on work rather than educational benefits. CSJ participants can take GED or other educational programs. Until the federal Workforce Attachment and Advancement (WAA) program started in 2000, the amount of time that people could spend in training was limited. The new program still emphasizes work but also provides funding for qualified people to attend technical or vocational training that will help them obtain a job or advance in their career path.

Wisconsin also significantly changed the administration of social welfare benefits under W-2. Separate agencies for social services and labor were combined into the Department of Workforce Development. The state program carefully outlines the types of services available to recipients, but the details of W-2 administration are determined at the local level through a request-for-proposal process. Wisconsin introduced market competition by allowing county government, nonprofits, and for-profit entities to bid on local contracts. This resulted in subtly different plans in each locality in the state. Although the Department of Workforce Development maintained administrative control of W-2 through the contracting and implementation process, state administrators felt that local authorities could best develop services in their communities.

Wisconsin's plan maintained the same structure over the first three years of TANF. State-level administrators realized the need to revise job-development curricula based on participants' needs as well as the necessity for specialized counselors for substance abuse and other issues. However, the W-2 administrators remained largely steadfast to the original goals of the program, fearing that "chipping away" at the original structure would lead to the demise of a successful reform effort.

Pennsylvania's Road to Economic Security Through Employment and Training (RESET)   Like that of Wisconsin, Pennsylvania's TANF plan focused on early employment through rapid attachment to the workforce. However, Pennsylvania's system differed from W-2 in several important ways. First, RESET retained the general benefits structure of AFDC. Second, although RESET focused on work, the program included a much stronger emphasis on training as an essential component of welfare reform. Finally, Pennsylvania's plan showed much more flexibility than W-2, shifting focus and adding components as the program evolved.

Pennsylvania's approach to welfare reform reflects a philosophy toward recipients that is very different from that of W-2. Politically and demographically the states are very similar, with one large city containing most of the public assistance population, surrounded by largely rural and conservative areas. However, Pennsylvania welfare administrators shared a concern for the needs of public assistance recipients. The reform initiatives came from two sources: 1) the Department of Public Welfare (DPW) and 2) the Republican administration of Governor Thomas Ridge. DPW had already started welfare reform under Governor Casey, a Democratic. A commonwealth policy developer recalls:

> I think one of the things I've learned—from my whole experience in welfare—you need to go get information from the people out in the field. Not just staff but clients, providers, people who deal with our clients. I may come up with the hypothesis that something's wrong and feed it to the stakeholders and see if it's wrong.

Unlike Wisconsin, Pennsylvania responded to the concerns of people using the welfare system. Ideas also came from research on other state initiatives and the Center for Law and Social Policy (CLASP), a liberal think tank based in Washington, DC. Reforms in the late 1980s and 1990s focused on changing the culture of the welfare offices and doing away with disincentives to leave the welfare rolls for work. The Pathways to Independence program focused on developing an "agreement of mutual responsibility" between the client and the caseworker. The idea was piloted in several counties, with a focus on developing a script that engaged the caseworker in talking with the program participant about a self-sufficiency plan. The program also sought to encourage work through a 50 percent earned-income disregard and related measures.

Administrators in the Republican Ridge administration were eager to develop work-first reforms in Pennsylvania. However, Ridge appointees also listened carefully to suggestions from staff members, leading to programs that combined a variety of initiatives. The centerpiece was Rapid Attachment, an 8-week job-search system required of all new applicants and nonexempt recipients. The program included both independent job search and a system of job search and job readiness provided through contracted agencies. Rapid Attachment was piloted successfully in 1995.

Key administrators described Rapid Attachment as a triage system that would help the most employable welfare recipients find work, leaving more resources to support harder cases. Administrators also stressed that they anticipated helping employed recipients move up in the workforce through education and training.

Most of Pennsylvania's TANF plan was enacted as state law under Act 35 in 1996. It included the Rapid Attachment initiative, earned-income disregards, and the mutual-responsibility agreement. The plan required minor modifications to accommodate federal time limits and hours-worked requirements.

The agreement of mutual responsibility outlines program activities to move the participant toward self-sufficiency. The plan is reviewed and modified every six months. A participant who did not follow his or her plan could be sanctioned.[14]

The Pennsylvania plan also included generous income and resource disregards to encourage families to work and move out of poverty. These included a 50 percent continuous earned-income disregard, under which only half a person's income would count toward setting benefits. Educational savings accounts, loans or grants for education, one car (regardless of value), a primary residence, and life-insurance policies also did not count in determining extent of public assistance. In its second state plan, Pennsylvania added individual development accounts (IDAs)—savings programs that include matching funds from the state—as one of its TANF initiatives. IDAs were also excluded from income for purposes of calculating TANF benefits.

Despite the work-first emphasis, the Pennsylvania plan also included an education component. In the first twenty-four months on TANF, recipients could spend up to one year in vocational education, general education, English as a Seond Language (ESL) classes, and job-skills training without performing any other activity. Educational activities could continue after one year along with work, work experience, or community service. After twenty-four months, participants had to work or be in community service but could still continue educational activities. In the second state plan, Pennsylvania emphasized the strategy of combining education with work, adding outreach and case-management initiatives to help recipients manage education and work.

In addition to incentives and supports for recipients, Pennsylvania also initiated "time out," or time off the five-year time-limit clock, for participants who had done more than what was required to achieve self-sufficiency. A welfare administrator explained:

> But what we looked at were incentives to clients. So if you're doing more than is required, like working 30 hours, [we're] giving you a time-out. Our thought process was that if you're doing 30 hours for a year, which is as long as the time-out lasts, chances are you're not going to be on welfare much longer. And it's good public relations, good policy to look at things like that. We [also] did one around domestic violence.

Like many states prior to TANF, Pennsylvania also had a General Assistance program that provided small cash grants plus medical insurance to people who did not meet the family composition criteria for AFDC. Pennsylvania began to limit the amount of time for which employable individuals could receive General Assistance in 1982. Further limits were placed on this population in 1994, and employable individuals were eliminated. With TANF, continuous General Assistance was also reinstated for people meeting income eligibility criteria but restricted to people caring for an unrelated child under the age of 13, children under the age of 21 who were full-time students, domestic-violence survivors, disabled people, and people in approved substance-abuse programs.

In an effort to assist disabled people in qualifying for SSI and other related benefits, Pennsylvania established the Disabilities Advocacy Program (DAP) in 1985. However, the disabled are not automatically exempt from TANF.

Administration of the TANF plan followed already existing systems. The county assistance offices are responsible for providing benefits, determining eligibility, and establishing individual employability plans. Uniform rules apply across the state. RESET job-search programs and other educational and support services are provided directly through contracts with the Pennsylvania Department of Public Welfare.

Although the Department of Public Welfare retained principal authority for administering TANF, the agency worked closely with the commonwealth departments of labor and education in administering various programs under the plan. One administrator commented that state agencies in Pennsylvania had some of the strongest collaborative relationships in the country. Pennsylvania designed a number of contracted programs to serve various parts of the public assistance population. Contracted programs initially focused on Rapid Attachment and related programs but by 1998 included community service, supported work, and employer-linked job-training and job-placement programs. Recipients under the age of twenty-two received intensive case management through a contract with the Department of Education. According to Department of Public Welfare data, 89 percent of the young participants in this program graduated during the 1999–2000 contract year. In more recent years, Pennsylvania added contracts for services to help employed participants retain jobs and advance in the workplace. This program also provided services to low-income workers who had lost jobs. Pennsylvania has contracted with community-based groups for many years. In 2001, the commonwealth expanded this goal through a program specifically targeted to reach socially isolated participants though agencies working with refugees, non-native speakers of English, and other populations of concern. As outlined in figure 2.1, the majority of these initiatives partnered with the local Private Industry Councils/Workforce Investment Act entities through agreements with the Department of Labor.[15]

Flexibility and change in the Pennsylvania program come from close evaluation and interaction with participants, local advocacy agencies, and county welfare offices. The Pennsylvania plan also maintains a strong relationship between work and education that started with the FSA programs. In fact, Pennsylvania continues to run its FSA program alongside other TANF initiatives.

THE WORKFORCE-DEVELOPMENT SYSTEM

Education and training for low-income people are funded and regulated through three very different government policies: 1) the general post-secondary-education system funded through Pell grants, student loans and tuition payments, 2) the adult basic education (ABE) system, and 3) the skills-training system created for disadvantaged populations.

The General Training System Funded Through Grants, Loans, and Tuition Payments   Government has played a key role in expanding access to post–secondary education for several decades. Much of the growth in training occurred in two-year, vocationally oriented programs. Grubb (1992:225) states that the percentage of the population in post–secondary education that first sought training in two-year institutions nearly doubled, growing from 23 percent to 49 percent between 1960 and 1987. Proprietary school enrollments reportedly grew during the same time period. Particularly for low-income students, these programs were funded through Pell grants and student loans in voucher systems that supposedly bring market values to government expenditures (Salamon 1995:208). Institutions benefiting from this expansion in public funds included public and nonprofit colleges as well as nonprofit and for-profit trade schools.

The expansion in funding for higher education led to a proliferation of programs to provide skills training. The expansion of trade schools also meant the

TABLE 2.1 PENNSYLVANIA TANF PROGRAMS

Child Care Services	Pennsylvania's subsidized child-care system is a single, integrated service-delivery system serving TANF and low-income working families. Child-care costs are covered in full for TANF families involved in education and training activities, while working families participate in the cost of care through a sliding copayment system based on family size and household income.	PRWORA, Act 35 (1998-2002)
Community Solutions	Provided services to welfare recipients based on their job-readiness level. The Employer-Linked Job Placement Program Local Collaboration Program targeted more job-ready clients. Services included limited education and skills-training enhancement, a 90-day intensive job-development period, and job coaching to ensure long-term retention. Both programs offered paid work experience and subsidized employment. The Innovations Demonstrations Program targeted less job-ready clients. Services included intensive job preparation, search and development, basic skills, and customized job training.	PRWORA, Act 35 (1998-2001)
Directed Job Search Program	Thirty days of intensive job-placement services for post-24-month clients who have a high-school diploma, GED, or work history and are not currently employed. Clients placed in employment receive an additional 90 days of job-retention services.	PRWORA, Act 35 (1998-2002)
ELECT	Education Leading to Employment and Career Training Program. Year-round case-management-centered program to assist pregnant or custodial parents who receive TANF benefits to stay in or return to school.	PRWORA, Act 35, Food Stamp Act (1998-2002)

(*continued*)

TABLE 2.1 *(continued)*

Rapid Attachment	Rapid Attachment to the Work force and Job Retention Program. Provided intensive job placement services to welfare clients.	PRWORA, Act 35 (1998-2001)
Single Point of Contact Program	Provides comprehensive education, skills training, job-placement and job-retention services to welfare and food stamp clients with significant barriers to employment.	PRWORA, Act 35, Food Stamp Act (1998-2002)
Supported Work Program	Job-search activities and on-site assistance to help participants in obtaining unsubsidized employment. Designed to prepare and assist recipients with a ninth grade education or less in finding and maintaining employment.	PRWORA, Act 35, Food Stamp Act (1998-2002)
Up Front Job Placement Program	Intensive job-search activities during the initial months of TANF. Up to three months of workshops and job-development and job-placement services. Clients placed in employment receive an additional 90 days of job retention services.	PRWORA, Act 35 (1998-2002)
Welfare-to-Work Program	Intensive job-search activities for TANF and hard-to-serve, long-term welfare clients who are not now working or training and education for clients who are employed. Clients placed in employment receive an additional six months of job-retention services.	Balanced Budget Act of 1977; PRWORA, Act 35 (1998-2002)
Work Activities Expansion Stand-Alone Program	Eastablished to ensure that clients who have received cash assistance for 24 months and participated in other employment and training programs, and failed to find lasting employment, are provided with 20 hours per week of work activities. Education and skills training are also provided, along with intensive job search.	PRWORA, Act 35 (1998-2002)

(continued)

TABLE 2.1 (*continued*)

Community Connections Initiative	Expansion of community-based and faith-based organizations' efforts to encourage TANF clients to make good and early choices to engage in opportunities for self-sufficiency.	PRWORA, Act 35 (2001-2002)
Job Retention, Rapid Re-Employment	Job Retention, Advancement and Rapid Re-Employment Program. Provides services to ensure that working welfare clients and parents below 235% of the Federal Poverty Income Guidelines retain employment, advance into better jobs, and are assisted in quickly finding new jobs if they lose their current jobs.	PRWORA, Act 35 (2000-2002)
Maximizing Participation Project	For TANF clients with multiple barriers or undiagnosed barriers to employment. Provides opportunities and incentives such as intensive case management, medical rehabilitation, substance-abuse treatment, mental health counseling, and education and training opportunities.	PRWORA, Act 35 (2001-2002)
Maximizing Participation Extension	Maximizing Participation Project Extension. Supplements the services provided to TANF clients during their participation in MPP. Provides the necessary employment and training services.	PRWORA, Act 35 (2001-2002)

Source: Pennsylvania Department of Public Welfare.

proliferation of programs reported as providing substandard training (Ackelsberg testimony). For a variety of reasons, many graduates from these programs did not find jobs, causing many of the program graduates to default on their student loans.

Until passage of the Higher Education Act amendments of 1992, monitoring of these programs was extremely limited.[16] As the number of defaulted student loans escalated and the legal services community mounted a sustained advocacy effort to curb abuses, both federal and state legislators moved to more closely monitor institutions receiving federal funds for education. The resulting legislation was implemented in 1994, cutting off student-loan dollars to schools with excessive default rates and requiring for the first time that these institutions evaluate whether students could complete their programs and find employment.

Adult Basic Education   Education and training programs specifically for the disadvantaged involve much closer contract monitoring than the more general educational system does. Several systems also exist for the population that fits the criteria for programs funded directly by government contracts. This population primarily includes people with limited income, dislocated workers, and refugees. Funding for adult basic education comes from the Department of Education to provide basic literacy and GED programs. TANF funds can also be used for adult basic education. Refugees receive ESL training through funds allocated under the Refugee Act of 1980. Both adult basic education and specific skills training is funded through a federal pass-through system to the states. States, in turn, subcontract most programs to nonprofits or more local government entities.

Skills Training for Disadvantaged Populations   Two major pieces of legislation funded training in the United States during most of the 1990s: the JTPA and the FSA. The JTPA required states to create service delivery areas (SDAs), each with its own Private Industry Council (PIC) to deliver training programs, provide policy guidance, and oversee local job-training programs, including subcontracted training (Spar 1983:12–13). The PICs are nonprofit entities that act as local government.

The JTPA also specified administrative expenditures and performance standards, including federal stipulations that 90 percent of program recipients be "disadvantaged." States were also required to meet standards for the number of JTPA participants who enter employment, wage rates, and cost per participant.[17]

The JOBS training program for public assistance recipients were similar to those for adult basic education and JTPA but had specified required hours. However, the length and placement goals for JOBS programs were not as strict as for JTPA.

JOBS and JTPA were only the two largest of numerous government training programs. From the early 1990s on, the Clinton administration sought to combine training into block grants that combined funding for job training, displaced workers, and vocational rehabilitation. Separate funding and program structures are outlined for three major populations: adults, dislocated workers, and youth. However, passage of the Workforce Investment Act (WIA) moved through Congress much more slowly than TANF and was signed into law in 1998. It went into effect in Wisconsin and Pennsylvania in 2000.

WIA programs are available to a wider range of people than those of JTPA, which was focused primarily on low-income or at-risk populations. Most government training programs prior to WIA funded contracts for training with providers, PICs, welfare departments, and similar entities, referring participants to available training slots. WIA puts training choices in the hands of the participants. Most training is provided through Individual Training Accounts (ITAs), which provide vouchers for training. Local areas are required to create one-stop shops where participants learn about approved training programs. And, unlike in earlier programs, government is required to develop certification and performance measures for approved training programs. The legislation requires that performance data be available for consumers to help them choose quality programs.[18]

WIA replaced the PIC structure with local Workforce Investment Boards. In many ways these local entities are similar to the PICs, except that they cannot provide training themselves. In both Milwaukee and Philadelphia, PICs were restructured into WIA boards. Kenosha was combined with neighboring Racine into one entity for WIA purposes.

Wisconsin Workforce Development System   Wisconsin has a well-developed technical college system that provided both adult basic education and technical training using funds from the various federal funding streams. This system continued to offer a wide array of training programs throughout the 1990s. For example, most adult basic education in Milwaukee was provided through the Milwaukee Area Technical College, which placed teachers at community-based agencies through subcontracts. Prior to TANF, government also contracted with local nonprofits to provide JOBS education and training programs. However, the TANF focus on job placement meant that linkages between welfare and workforce development were largely dropped after 1997. As with TANF, local WIA boards developed their own plans with separate program details. This led to as much diversity in local programs for workforce development as there had been with TANF.

Pennsylvania Workforce Development Programs   Most adult basic education in Pennsylvania was funded directly through the Department of Education. Literacy and GED programs involved loose monitoring that focused primarily on the number of clients served. In an example of social capital, contracts were granted primarily to agencies with established ties to the Department. Funding restrictions limited the ability to enhance program quality because of the inability to hire additional staff.

Pennsylvania used funding from the Family Support Act to expand the Single Point of Contact (SPOC) program under the title New Directions. Although New Directions made significant inroads in coordinating services across agencies, the program still focused on short-term training using JTPA models. The Pennsylvania SPOC program also included entered-employment rates based on JTPA.[19]

The commonwealth continued the SPOC system under TANF, using federal funds from the block grant and additional Welfare to Work funds added by Congress to help public assistance recipients find work and advance in the workplace. Many of the same contractors offer programs similar to those under JTPA and JOBS.

CHILD CARE

Parents need child care in order to take jobs or participate in TANF and workforce-development activities, and federal legislation for JOBS and TANF both included significant funding for a range of child-care services. TANF child-care funds included a child-care block-grant program passed in 1990 as part of the block grant. As with TANF, states can design their own programs for child care.[20]

Both Wisconsin and Pennsylvania provide child care to both low-income working families and TANF recipients. The Pennsylvania system, called Child Care Works, covers the full costs of child care for TANF recipients engaged in approved education, employment, and training activities. Low-income working families pay part of child-care costs through a sliding co-payment system.[21]

Wisconsin also uses a uniform child-care system for both W-2 recipients and low-income working parents. People are eligible for child care if they are working, enrolled in high school or a GED program if under the age of 20, or participating in a W-2 activity. People involved in skills training can access subsidized child care only if they have held a job for 9 months. Child-care support was available to anyone earning up to 165 percent of the federal poverty level from 1997 to 1999. In 2000, that was raised to 185 percent. In Wisconsin, single parents must also name the noncustodial parent for purposes of child-support enforcement to qualify for child care, a rule that has caused some parents not to access the system. In Wisconsin's system, there is a co-pay for child care that is based on income, number of children, and type of care.

HEALTH INSURANCE

The U.S. health-insurance system has been in crisis for a number of years. The Clinton administration attempted to enact a universal health-insurance system in 1992, but that effort was defeated by lobbying campaigns.[22] Nearly half (47.5 percent) of low-income full-time workers do not have health insurance.[23]

Health insurance is particularly an issue for low-income working people. Part-time workers often do not qualify for benefits. Many firms do not offer coverage to new employees until they have worked for a certain period of time. Further, it is increasingly common for employers to cover the costs of insurance for employees but not their family members. Smaller employers and service-sector employers are less likely to offer health insurance at all, or they require employees to cover more of the costs. For example, a fact sheet reported that inexpensive family policies in companies typically paying over $15 an hour cost the employee $84 a month, compared with $130 in firms paying half that hourly wage. Family coverage through work averages $7,035 a year and costs much more if purchased on the open market as an individual.[24] For this reason, many people eligible for insurance through the workplace choose to remain uninsured.

The federal Medicaid program covers people who are "medically needy" as well as people receiving cash assistance. However, people must "spend down" their income and assets in order to qualify. This means that recently unemployed people and most low-income working adults do not qualify for assistance. As with other government assistance programs, Medicaid's benefit systems and eligibility requirements are set at the state level, leading to much variation in the percentage of the low-income population covered by insurance. Noting the number of children not covered by insurance owing to the cost of family policies, Congress passed the State Children's Insurance Program (CHIP) in 1997. After initial low enrollments, states engaged in extensive outreach, which has increased the number of people insured through this program. States may also experiment with Medicaid waivers in order to design their own systems. The 1996 federal TANF legislation also includes a one-year extension of Medicaid coverage for families leaving public assistance.

Wisconsin combined Medicaid and CHIP into a managed-care system called Badgercare. Families are funded through either Medicaid or Badgercare depending on Medicaid eligibility criteria, but the system appears as a single entity to the consumer. There is no assets test. However, families are ineligible if the employer pays for 80 percent or more of family coverage.[25]

Pennsylvania maintains separate programs to cover Medicaid-eligible and CHIP populations. However, it offers one uniform application form for all commonwealth-sponsored health-insurance programs. Families leaving TANF earning up to 185 percent of the federal poverty level are eligible for extension of their Medicaid for one year. The Pennsylvania CHIP is available free for children under age 19 in families earning up to 200 percent of poverty level ($28,296 for a family of three). Those earning 235 percent of poverty level ($33,252) are eligible for subsidized health care. Healthy Beginnings covers pregnant women and children based on a third set of income eligibility criteria. Finally, medically needy adults can also receive services, but the maximum annual income is only $10,200 after deductions.[26]

FOOD STAMPS

The federal food-stamp program remained unchanged during the 1990s. The system is administered by state welfare programs following uniform federal guidelines. As with TANF, legal immigrants could no longer receive aid after 1997. Some food-stamp recipients are required to participate in employment programs in order to receive benefits.

CONCLUSION

The U.S. government's social welfare system provides a limited safety net for people due to the legacy of a late and small role for government in providing for basic needs. Significant variation among states in social welfare provision represents expansion of federalist tendencies characteristic of the U.S. system throughout its history. This system is fragmented and provides supports only to the most needy citizens. Both Pennsylvania and Wisconsin attempted to broaden this system somewhat in developing their TANF and CHIP programs. Each state created a unique program that reflected the values of its political actors and local economic systems. How does each state system play out at the local level? The next chapter explores this issue.

CHAPTER 3

Local Government Systems

Both Pennsylvania and Wisconsin created systems that encouraged local variation in TANF plans through local contracting and other mechanisms. This
chapter outlines the nature of the local government programs and the results
of that policy in the first three years of TANF implementation. The chapter explores two questions:

1. How is social welfare policy implemented in each city?
2. What is the role of social capital in the local policy system?

LOCAL PROGRAM IMPLEMENTATION

The two states' systems shaped local policy implementation in different ways.
The Wisconsin system ceded program details to the local level but maintained
control through hierarchical structures and proscriptive guidance. Local-level
W-2 agencies reported a steady stream of memos clarifying aspects of W-2 implementation. The state also insisted that all W-2 contractors use CARES, the
state data system (Client Assistance for Re-employment and Economic Support). Although uniform reporting made evaluation easier at the state level,
local providers sometimes did not have access to needed data.

Most important, the state envisioned that one provider—the W-2 agency—
would be responsible for all aspects of W-2, including the organization of processing for child care, food stamps, and medical assistance. W-2 agencies could
subcontract for services. This top-down structure meant that W-2 agencies assumed most of the risk and authority for outcomes at the local level. This hierarchical structure discouraged collaborative relationships between state and
local-level agencies.

The W-2 contracts covered administrative and staffing costs. Each agency
was also allocated money to fund cash grants and other payments to program
recipients based on an estimate of the number of people who would use the
system in that area. Agencies that placed more of their participants into jobs
could keep a portion of the cash in this account as a "profit" to put toward new
programs. Because the W-2 caseload fell rapidly during the first year of imple-

mentation, agencies in both Kenosha and Milwaukee had plenty of money to spare. However, agencies, fearing that cases would increase in the future, spent little of the surplus. The state responded by cutting back on funds. Local agencies still had their profits, partly mandated as community reinvestment funds. The W-2 agencies argued that much of their activity went unrecorded in the CARES system because services to those not receiving cash assistance did not count. After 2000, the state changed its allocation formula to include these additional services.

MILWAUKEE

Milwaukee was divided into six W-2 regions based on the welfare caseloads in different parts of the city. Five agencies received contracts to serve the city. Prior to the competitive request-for-proposal process for W-2 contracts, Milwaukee County was removed from bidding as lead agency. A state administrator recalls: "Milwaukee could've bid, but Milwaukee knew they didn't have the infrastructure to get the job done in and of itself. They would've had to go out and hire the very people they were bidding against to operate."

As discussed in chapter 1, Milwaukee agencies agreed among themselves who would bid for which region prior to W-2. According to the administrator, the state generally supported these proposals:

> Four of the agencies were operating precursors to the jobs connection piece. First of all, you don't tear down all of your structure. You need to have something to build on. And what was the piece we needed to build on? All other factors being equal, the employment piece, and they were the employment piece.

These agencies had run various JOBS programs. Each agency proposed its own structure, within the guidelines of the W-2. As implemented, the systems reflected the prior experience and philosophy of each agency. For example, Community Solutions, profiled in the next chapter, had an already established program that worked with hard-to-serve clients. Their proposal included an emphasis on job-retention services. They also subcontracted services to smaller, community-based agencies, a unique innovation. Despite the work-first format, their program also included an emphasis on training. One administrator stated: "I'd say overall it's the same . . . because we know the ultimate goal is employment. We will at this point pay to get people through those trainings so they can be employed so we don't have to pay the benefits down the road."

Whereas this agency incorporated community-based organizations from the start, others attempted to subcontract after the state requested that agencies work with churches in order to fulfill charitable choice mandates. As the extent of substance-abuse problems became apparent in the W-2 population, some agencies contracted with specialists to provide these services.

Although different agencies placed more or less emphasis on education over immediate job placement, the uniform guidelines for W-2 and the nature of the population receiving service led to similar outcomes across agencies by 2000. Between 34 and 39 percent of agency caseload was in case-management-only categories—sometimes receiving food stamps, child care, and/or Medicaid. The W-2 transition category, used for people needing significant remedial education or support, included less than 20 percent for each agency but still encompassed a significant part of the caseload. The bulk of the remaining cases were in community-service jobs. Including cases of pregnant women and mothers of newborns who received cash assistance without any work obligations, this meant that over half the cases depended on the state as their primary income source after five years of activity-linked welfare reform.

KENOSHA

Kenosha's W-2 program was largely in place by 1997. In 1990, Kenosha opened a one-stop job center that became a national model. The Kenosha County Job Center has since the early 1990s successfully run a work-first program that included many elements of W-2, including the presumption that any job would lead to self-sufficiency. However, the precursor to W-2 started with five days of assessment and job-readiness seminars. Implementing W-2 thus entailed few initial changes in the program design.

As detailed elsewhere (Schneider 2001), the Kenosha one-stop center offered fourteen agencies under one roof, including in-house programs for education, job placement, human services, senior services, and child care. Owing to budget cuts in 2000, fewer support programs were offered in house at the job center, and some services were offered less frequently. The adult-education program offered through the job center was replaced by in-house technical college classes. Parenting classes were also eliminated; people needing this service were referred to programs offered by local nonprofits.

Kenosha's program does not distinguish between W-2-eligible people and other county residents needing employment services. W-2-eligible people use the same job resource room as others seeking work in the county. Job development and assessment workshops include both W-2 recipients and other community residents. All job placement and related programs in the center are available to any county resident equally. This strategy is meant to combat the stigma attached to receiving welfare.

The Kenosha W-2 contract also kept a preexisting case-management system unique in Wisconsin. Case management and employment services are

provided by a team. Rather than one FEP who is responsible for decision making and referral for a W-2 case, the Kenosha program includes a team of economic support specialists, case managers, job-placement specialists, and
employment-support specialists. Two of the team members are employees of a
nonprofit partner, bringing an ethos to interactions that is very different from
that of the government eligibility-determination specialists. The initial employability plan is developed through a team discussion. Any additional needed
services involve staff throughout the job center.

The Kenosha partnership model also included additional case management
for particularly at-risk families through the Emergency Services Network, a
group of safety-net and child-welfare agencies offering support services. These
agencies kept close watch on targeted families through home visits and other
means. In addition, Wisconsin allows counties to run a General Assistance program. Kenosha uses General Assistance funds to support emergency services.

The Kenosha system downplays education and training. The city's PIC had
a small office at the job center but was not a major player in welfare reform.
The links between employment and training became even more attenuated
once Kenosha was combined with Racine under WIA. One administrator said:

> I think Racine has spent $600 out of that money in the last year and a half.
> That's it. It requires almost a 50% match. But there's creative ways to use it
> for the TANF population and we've got to figure out ways to do that to off-
> set [some of the budget cuts due to reduced TANF funds] and do some new
> things.

Philadelphia

In contrast to Wisconsin, Pennsylvania maintained control over the design of social welfare policy. The county welfare offices worked closely with state government to develop and modify program details. Contracts for TANF and JOBS services were either direct relationships between providers and the state or subcontracts with the PIC. In Philadelphia, the state contracted with the school district, the local housing authority, agencies of city government, nonprofits, for-profits, and churches.

The contracting system led to a two-track system for welfare services. Within the county welfare offices, two workers were assigned to handle each welfare case: the income eligibility worker and the employment and training caseworker. Initially, these workers often did not communicate well with each other. One welfare administrator commented, "I never realized how people sitting next to each other never shared information." However, with emphasis placed on changing the casework environment, this situation has slowly changed over time.

Contractors also maintained their own case-management system, sometimes acting as advocates for their program participants with welfare caseworkers. The county community-service office acted as liaison with the contracting agencies and other parts of the local community. This office acted as educators about TANF and facilitators between the county and the contractors. Workforce development also relied on contracting, but contractors were oriented more toward the PIC and the state rather than toward the county welfare office.

State and federal regulations limited contractors' freedom to design their programs (Smith and Lipsky 1993). Program components were strictly specified.[1] The issue that caused the most concern to subcontractors was performance-based contracts. All PIC contracts held back approximately 30 percent of the total contract amount, paying only for participants who found jobs or transferred to an appropriate program. Performance-based contracts gave more favorable payment terms to for-profit contractors.[2] Agencies that contracted directly with the state faced similar dilemmas. Both county government and local agencies responded to state policy through informal conversations and formal meetings with the state to discuss policy. Many of the innovations in welfare reform in Pennsylvania came out of conversations with providers and clients, indicating a role for social capital.

Social Capital and Public Policy

The development of welfare policy in both states reflects the influence of social capital on policy strategies. Wisconsin policy developed through the connections among the governor, his key welfare program administrator, and conservative scholars. Pennsylvania used information from peers in other states to develop their own strategy. Each state sought input from a variety of constituencies in developing policy. However, connections to policy makers do not necessarily equate with social capital, which involves established trust between parties participating in the policy process. This is most evident when examining unequal power relations, as among the state, local policy implementers, and advocates for those receiving or providing service.

These types of social capital relationships were largely absent between state-level policy makers and the local level in Wisconsin. The state developed limited relationships with local administrators, instead maintaining control over the policy process. The state was quick to help agencies that came to the Department of Workforce Development for assistance in implementing W-2. For example, one administrator praised an agency for seeking support: "They didn't start out with the knowledge they needed but their hearts were in the right place and they listened, they were good learners, fast learners."

In response, Milwaukee W-2 agencies developed strong social capital networks among themselves. Regular forums afforded opportunities to discuss various aspects of W-2. These social capital networks influenced program implementation more than policy.

Pennsylvania's relationship to advocates and nongovernmental service providers was initially similar to that of Wisconsin. Early in the Ridge administration, advocates accused the government of not providing enough community forums for policy input. Social capital ties between communities and state policy makers were limited. However, Pennsylvania started to reach out to these constituencies early in the TANF development process. In addition to seeking research advice on policy development, various constituents were invited to participate in advisory panels. One administrator recalls:

> The income maintenance advisory group has been around for years so we get recommendations. [One coalition] came to us, they were established, and we suggested because they have a good cross-section of groups that deal with the department [that they join the advisory group]. . . . When we make any changes in TANF we give it to our income maintenance advisory group first . . . and have them get back to us with comments and concerns they may have.

The advisory committee includes representatives from welfare-rights and community legal services from throughout the state. The strength of these social capital relationships has grown over time; the commonwealth plans to include some of these advisors as proposal reviewers in the latest round of contracts.

Pennsylvania developed even stronger relationships with county assistance offices. Philadelphia has a major role in these forums. One Pennsylvania commonwealth administrator commented:

> What we do is, we draft policies and share them with our counties to get some feedback. We have management meetings where we have all the "EDs" around and we tell them what's coming up the pike. Let us know what you feel. They're all involved but [the Philadelphia administrator] is really more involved because he's really concerned [about] the impacts on him. He comes to the monthly TANF implementation meetings.

Different social capital relationships with local welfare offices and organizations play a role in the evolution of TANF policy over time. Wisconsin policy through 2000 changed little, showing limited influence from local-level implementers. Pennsylvania, on the other hand, continually added components to its program as it assessed the impact of TANF at the local level. Sharing ideas with trusted advisers from throughout the state clearly influenced policy direction. These relationships influence not only policy development but what outcomes are considered important. I next briefly describe results of welfare reform.

Overview of Results of Welfare Reform

Between 1994 and 1999, welfare caseload declined across the country, with a 51 percent drop in public assistance receipt (Liebschutz 2000:13). Wisconsin led the nation in caseload decline; between 1995 and 2000, the number of families receiving cash assistance fell by 91 percent. However, a larger number of families receive some kind of case management or other support from the state. Pennsylvania also saw large decreases: 47 percent between 1995 and 2000.

The large cities have had the greatest difficulty moving cases off the welfare roles. However, sizable caseload decreases in Milwaukee (86 percent) and Philadelphia (41 percent) reveal significant changes in these localities too. Milwaukee and Philadelphia account for an increasing percentage of the caseload for each of their states. Milwaukee had 51 percent of the state AFDC cases in 1995; by 2000 they represented 78 percent of state cash caseloads. The change in Philadelphia has been less dramatic: in 1995 Philadelphia represented 39 percent of the state welfare caseload, compared with 49 percent in 2000.

Kenosha began to dramatically reduce its cash assistance caseloads in the mid-1990s, prior to W-2. By 1998, it had a low of 140 families receiving cash assistance, with another 190 receiving supportive case management. However, even in 1998, many Kenosha families were still so poor that they qualified for Medicaid and food stamps. A total of 4,010 families received some form of government assistance that year. Those numbers continued to rise as the economy slowed. In 2000, 1,247 families received TANF in Kenosha, with nearly 43 percent in case-management-only categories. However, 4,901 families received Medicaid, food stamps, or a combination of the two—several hundred families more than were on public assistance in 1990, prior to reforms.

Caseload reductions do not tell the entire story, however. In Wisconsin, child-only cases have been moved to Kinship Care; Pennsylvania still includes these families in their TANF caseloads. Wisconsin also completely eliminated partial grants in 1997, whereas Pennsylvania continues to provide income support to low-income working families through earned-income disregards. One study reported that the percentage of families living in extreme poverty increased in Wisconsin (Zedlewski 2002:69), a change that was probably influenced by the loss of government assistance.

AFDC/TANF is only one form of cash assistance available to families. Table 3.1 shows caseload changes in three major income-support programs: SSI, TANF, and General Assistance for Pennsylvania.Caseloads declined for TANF and General Assistance but rose for SSI. In part, this change reflected efforts to move disabled AFDC recipients onto SSI. By 2000, SSI accounted for nearly 70 percent of cash assistance from the commonwealth.

Use of food stamps and Medicaid also declined with TANF implementation. For example, food-stamp enrollments in Milwaukee declined by 30 percent from 1995 to 2000 (Fendt et al. 2001:3). Analysis of food-stamp enrollments in Pennsylvania showed similar declines. The decreases are due partly to increased income, but many eligible families do not get benefits because of TANF diversion policies and the administrative hassles of getting assistance (Zedlewski and Gruber 2001). Administrators of the federal food-stamp program raised concerns about these declines, leading to more emphasis on food-stamp enrollment in 2000.

Many families lost Medicaid coverage when they left public assistance. However, implementation of CHIP and Badgercare has begun to increase the number of people using public insurance. Both Wisconsin and Pennsylvania saw declines in Medicaid enrollment after TANF implementation. In Pennsylvania, the Medicaid caseload declined 5 percent between 1997 and 1999. After initial declines, Wisconsin began adding cases in 1998. Total Medicaid enrollment is now up .6 percent from 1997 (Ellis et al. 2000:6). Most of the additional cases came from expanded CHIP and Badgercare enrollment rather than increased use of Medicaid. States and localities have implemented creative measures to raise the number of families receiving supplemental benefits. For example, Kenosha has sent staff with laptop computers to low-income employers to enroll families. In Pennsylvania people can enroll online for food stamps and medical assistance.

Families turned to churches and nonprofits for assistance when obtaining government aid became more difficult. One Milwaukee report indicated that

TABLE 3.1 PENNSYLVANIA AND PHILADELPHIA CASELOAD CHANGES

	1994–1995	1995–1996	1996–1997	1997–1998	1998–1999	1999–2000	2000–2001
Pennsylvania							
Total state cases	1,141,448	1,149,995	1,082,496	1,057,506	1,070,816	1,095,576	1,090,755
SSI	255,537	267,213	274,355	273,973	280,823	285,983	290,607
% of total cases	22.39%	23.24%	25.34%	25.91%	26.23%	26.10%	26.64%
TANF	207,999	193,901	172,218	141,096	117,241	98,512	89,939
% of total cases	18.22%	16.86%	15.91%	13.34%	10.95%	8.99%	8.25%
GA	118,409	83,395	68,613	59,603	52,498	46,601	42,855
% of total cases	10.37%	7.25%	6.34%	5.64%	4.90%	4.25%	3.93%
Medicaid only	559503	605486	567310	582834	620254	664480	667354
% of total	49.02%	52.65%	52.41%	55.11%	57.92%	60.65%	61.18%

(continued)

TABLE 3.1 (*continued*)

Philadelphia

Total city cases	300,565	301,979	275,303	261,538	259,099	264,091	270,119
SSI	72,753	76,377	78,580	78,052	80,408	83,258	85,229
% of city cases	24.21%	25.29%	28.54%	29.84%	31.03%	31.53%	31.55%
% of state cases	6.37%	6.64%	7.26%	7.38%	7.51%	7.60%	7.81%
TANF	82,122	78,893	73,586	65,542	57,219	48,689	44,096
% of city cases	27.32%	26.13%	26.73%	25.06%	22.08%	18.44%	16.32%
% of state cases	7.19%	6.86%	6.80%	6.20%	5.34%	4.44%	4.04%
GA	47,775	36,951	32,685	29,532	27,060	24,441	22,390
% of city cases	15.90%	12.24%	11.87%	11.29%	10.44%	9.25%	8.29%
% of state cases	4.19%	3.21%	3.02%	2.79%	2.53%	2.23%	2.05%
Medicaid only	97,915	109758	90452	88412	94412	107703	118404
% of city	32.58%	36.35%	32.86%	33.80%	36.44%	40.78%	43.83%
% of state	8.58%	9.54%	8.36	8.82%	9.83%		10.86%

Source: Pennsylvania Department of Public Welfare.

food assistance rose 58 percent between 1998 and 2000. Although evictions increased only 13 percent between 1997 and 2000, emergency calls for shelter rose 88 percent. Local hospitals reported an 89 percent increase in uncompensated health care between 1995 and 1999 (Fend et al. 2001). Reports from Kenosha and Philadelphia indicate similar trends.

These findings show that welfare reform in these two states has achieved caseload-reduction goals. However, families leaving welfare still need supports for basic needs. The increase in the use of nonprofit and church service providers demonstrates a partnership between government and civil society to support families. Contracting relationships also indicate a similar partnership in service provision.

CONCLUSION

Contemporary scholars contrast state with civil society, seeing civil society as the voluntary associations that support society. The state represents enforcement of law, potentially by institutions unsympathetic to low-income citizens (Edwards et al. 2001:2–6). Devolution of social welfare provision from government to local nonprofits has been interpreted in two ways. In one formulation, devolution returns social welfare provision to the more supportive forces of civil society. Federal guidelines for welfare and other social services establish a general framework for assistance—the regulations of the state—whereas civil society marshals the wider community to provide aid. Other interpretations see devolution as abandoning the poor to the vagaries of the market without a state-enforced safety net.

Oppositional concepts of state and civil society make limited sense when analyzing the creation of social welfare policy. This brief outline of policy development shows interaction between state and civil society to formulate state-governed assistance. Policies evolve out of local-level concerns about social needs, incorporating the strategies and ideologies of the time. As Gramsci (1971:263) observes, the state consists of political society plus civil society, with law enforcing structures of those currently in power. The state is also the center for contesting strategies, as groups negotiate power. Law reflects the fluid interactions among citizens engaged in developing policy. Social capital influences who has access to policy making and how they interact with key actors. Understanding social policy development as a confluence of civil society actors involved in state policy explains the variation in social welfare policy among states and localities described here.

This dynamic between state and civil society becomes more important when analyzing the contracted system for providing social welfare services in each city. The next chapter describes this system.

CHAPTER 4
Social Service Organizations

As outlined in the last chapter, government implements welfare policy through a partnership between government and private organizations based on contracts for services. The effects of this mixture of government, nonprofit, and for-profit service provision on agencies and program participants are discussed in chapters 9 and 10. This chapter focuses on the second factor that influences implementation of social welfare policy: the nature of the organizations providing service. I also explore the role of social capital in developing and maintaining these institutions. I address the following questions:

- What kinds of organizations provide social welfare services in Milwaukee, Philadelphia, and Kenosha through government contracts?
- Does nonprofit status, for-profit status, or relationship to a particular racial/ethnic/national or faith-based community influence organizational form and service provision tactics?
- How does the size of an organization affect service provision?
- Do the focus and constituencies of an organization differ among citywide institutions, community-based organizations, and faith-based institutions?
- What role does social and cultural capital play in organization development and activities?

DEFINING CONCEPTS

The social welfare system encompasses a plethora of organization types and theories to understand how these various institutions interact. Terms like *nonprofit, for-profit,* and *government* engender complex and often conflicting assumptions about the meaning and style of each organizational form among scholars and practitioners. Policy makers often base social welfare policy on assumptions about nonprofits and government. To clarify the background of the terms related to organizations used in this book, I briefly discuss the theory of organizations used here. I also relate these concepts to social capital.

GOVERNMENT, BUREAUCRACY, AND CONTRACTING REGIMES

Many assumptions about government social welfare provision rely on concepts of bureaucracy developed by Max Weber (1948). Bureaucracies provide services based on universal criteria. For example, means-tested government assistance programs such as food stamps and Medicaid theoretically provide services to anyone who meets income eligibility requirements, regardless of race, age, gender, or any other characteristic. Bureaucracy also refers to a type of organization structure. In a bureaucracy, decisions flow from the head of the organization down through the ranks to the front-line employees. Employees are rational cogs in this system, carrying out orders from above.

Bureaucracy has both good and bad connotations. On the positive side, bureaucracies theoretically provide service to everyone in a uniform manner, doing away with the prejudices and idiosyncrasies of local closed social capital networks. Government bureaucracies supposedly have more resources than local organizations because they draw on the tax base.

However, in practice, government bureaucracies seldom live up to the theory. Michael Lipsky (1980) notes that the street-level bureaucrats who implement government policy use their own discretion in doing their jobs. Scholars of government social welfare services describe underfunded organizations in which overworked employees behave in an impersonal and rude manner as they attempt to cope with ever-increasing paperwork requirements to determine eligibility for government programs (Lipsky 1980; Kingfisher 1994; Morgan 2001). In the public mind, government bureaucracy has become synonymous with uncaring and slow service. The move toward devolution described in the last chapter partly involved attempts to shift toward a friendly, customer-service-oriented culture by contracting to nonprofit and for-profit institutions that supposedly embodied these positive characteristics.

Some scholars of nonprofit organizations assume that government contracts incorporate nongovernmental institutions into government bureaucratic agendas through the contracting process (Smith and Lipsky 1993). Research on institutional isomorphism (DiMaggio and Powell 1988) shows that organizations tend to become more like each other as they respond to the same government regulations, share funding sources, and borrow service-provision strategies from one another. The examples here reveal a tension within agencies between such structural factors as contracting and funding sources that encourage organizations to become alike and efforts to maintain an organization's unique mission. Government contracts do require some changes in institutions that use government funds. However, as demonstrated by the multitude of organizational responses to government contracting described here and in chapter 10, participation in partnerships with government does not necessarily lead to development of bureaucratic forms in nonprofits or routinization of program forms among organizations.

NONPROFIT AND FOR-PROFIT ORGANIZATIONS

As discussed in the last chapter, policy makers continue to debate whether nonprofit or for-profit organizations provide "better" service. These debates rest on a series of assumptions regarding the goals of these two types of organizations. In welfare policy debates, some scholars raise concerns that organizations focused on the profit motive will sacrifice quality service for the bottom line (Frumkin and Andre-Clark 1999). On the other hand, some policy makers presume that for-profit institutions will offer higher quality and more efficient service given their focus on market competition. Nonprofits, on the other hand, are portrayed either as caring, personalized service providers or as wasteful, inept institutions.

The descriptions of organizations throughout this book take a different view of the role of for-profit and nonprofit status. For-profit and nonprofit organizations are creations of the U.S. federal tax code. For-profits can access a wider range of funding sources, make a profit, and declare bankruptcy if the organization fails. Nonprofits are exempt from federal taxes, but government regulations require mission-based service provision that profits no individual as well as board responsibility for organization activities. I agree with Smith and Lipsky (1993:33–34) that social service organizations may take either nonprofit or for-profit form, for a variety of reasons. Nonprofit or for-profit status may have nothing to do with the motives or service-provision tactics of an organization.

For example, one well-established nonprofit organization in Milwaukee developed a for-profit subsidiary to implement their W-2 contract because they feared that the other programs of the parent organization would suffer if the W-2 agency failed to meet performance-based contract goals. Potentially, W-2 organizations could run a deficit that parent nonprofits would be expected to absorb. In this worst-case scenario, a for-profit organization could simply declare bankruptcy or go out of business. The nonprofit created the for-profit subsidiary to allow an easier way out should the agency have trouble running its W-2 program within budget. Creating a for-profit subsidiary also distanced the parent nonprofit's other programs from any bad press related to TANF. Despite its for-profit status, this organization maintained the service ethos of its parent nonprofit in implementing its W-2 program.

Many of the for-profit institutions profiled here share an ethos of service identical to that of their nonprofit counterparts. Focus on mission and quality service provision rather than profit distinguished them from other for-profit

social service providers offering shoddy service or putting placement goals before participant needs. For this reason, throughout the book I use the term *social service organization* to refer to nonprofit and for-profit organizations
together.

That said, there are some important differences between nonprofit and for-
profit institutions. Regardless of their motives, for-profits receive special status
from government in developing their contracts. Primarily, contracts presume
that the organization is able to make a profit in exchange for quality service. In
Philadelphia, for-profits also seem to have a wider range of program participants than most nonprofits do.

Nonprofits, on the other hand, exist to provide a service to a specified population based on a board-defined mission statement. The chief goal of the organization is to implement that mission through programs for its constituent
community. The board is obligated to see that the organization fulfills mission goals. Nonprofits are challenged to retain focus on their primary mission
in an environment in which funders (government, foundations, and others)
may have different goals. Scholars of nonprofits refer to organizations that
move away from their primary mission in order to meet the needs of government as experiencing "mission drift." In this chapter, I touch on the impact
on agency mission of funding sources and board composition as the first
step in addressing issues of government bureaucratic authority and mission
drift.

FAITH-BASED AND FAITH-RELATED ORGANIZATIONS

Public policy has increasingly focused on the role of religious-based institutions as service providers. Much of this debate sounds like the for-profit/nonprofit or government/nongovernmental institution conflict using different names. As with nonprofits in earlier debates, religious-based institutions presumably embody the best and worst of social welfare service provision. Proponents of faith-based service assume that religious-based institutions provide caring, connected, and less expensive programs. Opponents invoke the separation of church and state and raise concerns about potential discrimination based on religious belief.

Most of this argument ignores the fact that religious-affiliated institutions have been the primary provider of social welfare services throughout most of U.S. history (Cnaan et al. 2000; Hall 1990, 1996). Today such institutions dominate nonprofit provision for some social problems.[1] Faith in Action, one of the major employment and training organizations in Philadelphia profiled below, has religious roots and maintains a significant presence from its faith community on its board and among its top management staff. However, people and institutions interacting with this organization would find no reference to religion in their service provision. As Smith and Sosin (2001) point out, the term *faith-based organization* has been used to refer to anything from the mission activities of church congregation to organizations such as Faith in Action that are similar to their nonsectarian counterparts. I use *faith-related organization* (Smith and Sosin 2001) to refer to these organizations, which have religious roots but behave like other nonprofits—a significant amount of social capital may come from the religious community, but agency culture reflects a combination of religious-based culture and that of the wider social service community. For this reason, when describing types of organizations later in this chapter, I treat nonprofits and faith-related organizations as one category.

However, not all religiously tied institutions provide only nonsectarian services. Some organizations deliberately use their faith in the development and execution of their programming. Throughout the book, I call these *faith-based organizations.* As described below, the mission focus and social and cultural capital resources of these institutions may differ from those of their less sectarian cousins. The Salvation Army, which is a church with a service mission, may be the most well-known faith-based organization. This book concentrates on smaller institutions.

I also distinguish between the mission activities of churches and the programs of formally incorporated faith-based organizations. As discussed in chapter 11, church activities most consistently embody religiously inspired community creation, with social service activities a by-product of this primary mission. Religious-based service is one expression of faith. Although churches, faith-based organizations, and faith-related organizations are often linked through common networks of social and cultural capital, they represent a continuum ranging from direct expression of faith through mission activities to institutions that use faith-community social capital as a background for professional nonprofit service. Individual organizations can fall anywhere on the continuum, but church-congregation activities generally provide the closest links between faith and action.

CITYWIDE AND COMMUNITY-BASED ORGANIZATIONS

Some scholars of nonprofits describe them as serving "the community," presuming that institutions created by people with a common concern and serving a particular population represent a single community.[2] However, the history of social service contains numerous examples of the establishment of nonprofit social welfare organizations by elites to provide services or socialize populations very different from themselves (Trattner 1994:77–107). In many cases, these organizations represented people from one closed social capital network using their resources to provide a service to people from different groups (Schneider 1999b). Elite social service often maintained or reinforced boundaries between groups in a community rather than creating bridges connecting groups.

Other social service organizations rely on professionals from diverse class and racial/ethnic/national backgrounds to provide services to people with a particular need. Hospitals, training programs, and other social service organizations may have staff members who share background characteristics with program participants or who have sought similar services elsewhere. However, the boards of these organizations are more likely to draw from citywide elites and professionals associated with the service the agency provides. For example, the board of the Women's Literacy Project, which provides educational development and training for women from throughout Philadelphia, consists primarily of established middle-class women active in social welfare and education in the city, a very different group from the participants of their program. Throughout the book, I use the term *citywide organizations* to refer to organizations that provide a service to anyone with a particular need living anywhere in the locality and belonging to any racial, national, ethnic, or religious group.

Community-based organizations, in contrast, focus on either one neighborhood or people from a group with specific characteristics such as African Americans, Jews, or gays/lesbians. These institutions are more likely to focus exclusively on the needs of people in closed social capital networks. They are also more likely to have people from that community as active participants on their boards. For example, Latinos United has a board that consists of a mix of Latinos from the closed social capital network that founded the organization, Latinos who are newcomers to Kenosha, and citywide elites.

Examination of nongovernmental organizations providing social welfare services in Philadelphia, Milwaukee, and Kenosha relies on interpretations of organizational theory based on findings from organizations in these three cities. Regardless of its form or focus, each organization responds to several stakeholder groups: its program participants, its board and funders, and other organizations that provide similar or complementary services. These three groups may represent one closed social capital network or span diverse sets of social capital resources. Stakeholders may come from similar or different communities.

To clarify the role of social capital for organizations, I next provide examples of different organization types used throughout the book. These examples clarify the concepts used throughout the book as well as show the ways in which an organization's type, size, and interactions with different stakeholder groups influence its history and present strategies.

TYPES OF ORGANIZATIONS

The organizations providing social welfare services in Milwaukee, Kenosha, and Philadelphia fall into three general categories: citywide social service organizations, community-based nonprofit organizations, and faith-based organizations. Each type of organization has a different relationship to its key stakeholders of board, funders, and participants. The mission focus of each category also differs. Organization patterns vary by size within each general category; large organizations with more than two hundred staff members and multimillion-dollar budgets have different concerns than small or midsized organizations. Within the category of social service organizations, nonprofits and for-profits exhibit some divergence in their relationship to funders and program participants. Faith-based organizations can either focus on a particular community or serve the entire city. Comparison of organization types illustrates the diversity of institutions providing social welfare services in each locality and showcases institutional responses to welfare policy.

Although I use particular organizations to represent one organization type, it is important to note that many organizations cross categories. For example, Community Solutions is a citywide nonprofit social service organization that was developed to serve a particular racial/ethnic community. Despite its political orientation toward that ethnic community, it serves anyone who meets government-determined program criteria.

CITYWIDE SOCIAL SERVICE ORGANIZATIONS

All three localities include both for-profit and nonprofit citywide social service organizations. The two large cities have both large and small/midsized organizations whereas Kenosha's social welfare institutions are all small to midsized. The general patterns among organizations in all three categories today vary little. Citywide organizations were developed by citywide or community-wide elites in all three localities. However, Kenosha, having originated as a union town with limited need for safety-net services, developed citywide institutions much later than those of the two larger cities.[3] Social service organizations in Philadelphia and Milwaukee tended to be developed by professionals, religious or business elites, or elite women. In contrast, Kenosha's citywide nonprofits also included significant support from unions, churches, and other civic institutions that are less involved in citywide organization development in the larger cities.

Small/Midsized Nonprofit/Faith-Rated Organizations   Citizens United is a small Philadelphia-based nonprofit providing education, research, advocacy, and direct service to people in neighborhoods throughout the city. The organization was started in the 1970s by a small group of elite activists and educators. Its focus has changed several times during its existence, but the institution generally maintains a pattern of working with neighborhood-based organizations on current concerns. During the study period, the organization focused on civic involvement and self-sufficiency. Welfare-related activities included an adult basic education program, a welfare-to-work program, and several research and advocacy projects associated with welfare reform.

It had a paid staff of six and many volunteers. However, most of its programs were partnered with neighborhood organizations that also contributed staff and volunteers to programs initiated by Citizens United. Its participant base consisted primarily of low-income city residents. Its key constituencies were the neighborhood organizations, other citywide social welfare institutions providing similar services, and government.

During the study period, the organization had a budget that ranged between $200,000 and $300,000. Although funding came from a combination of private foundation grants and government contracts, most of the staff was hired through government contracts that contributed three-quarters of the budget. Delayed government payments or loss of a key contract caused extreme cash-flow problems for this organization.

Despite its reliance on government funds, Citizens United remained committed to its core mission when applying for them. For example, the organization agreed to run a welfare-to-work program only if they could use its own model of working with low-income communities and their institutions to offer services. The government-funded adult basic education program partnered with neighborhood-based organizations to offer literacy services throughout the city. All the programs maintained the core philosophy of the institution and its mission-based attributes of working with community organizations to provide services to neighbors in need.

Sunrise is a citywide homeless shelter in Kenosha. The organization was started by elite church women to help displaced families during massive layoffs when the community was deindustrialized in the 1980s. These women gathered the support of the union and most of the city's civic and religious institutions to start a soup kitchen. Over the years, the organization has grown to include a homeless shelter that offers a food pantry and several related programs. Sunrise is a unique community effort. It has a small staff of fewer than twenty people, but it has between eight hundred and one thousand volunteers who help operate the programs. Until the mid-1990s, it was virtually a 100 percent volunteer effort. The organization still follows its original model, with a different religious or community group taking responsibility for the soup kitchen one night a week. Most single people are housed in the basements of churches whose (white) members are core contributors to the organization.

The organization's funding also reflects this mixed support base. The budget ranges between $800,000 and $900,000, not counting in-kind contributions. The administrators feel that Sunrise is underfunded and understaffed, and that too much paperwork is required. The executive director noted that "If you look at community-based support for the agency, financially, we are right at about 50 percent of our operational budget [coming] through direct contributions" from individuals, community organizations, and local businesses. The other 50 percent comes from a variety of grants, government, and other sources. In addition, the shelter's resources are supplemented with in-kind contributions of commodities, clothing, and other materials. Like the monetary contributions, this support comes from a combination of the government (in this case, the commodities program) and community donations. For example, many community organizations and businesses have contributions bin for Sunrise or sponsor food drives.

The shelter's board consists of representatives from core contributing churches and civic organizations as well as local elites. Most of the volunteers come from the same constituency as the board, but the African American churches and a wide array of such civic groups as the unions and Boy Scouts also participate in the volunteer efforts. In contrast, those served by the organization consist mostly of low-income people. An increasing number of program participants, particularly in the family shelter, are African American.

Although the rules for the various government housing and commodities programs affect Sunrise's accounting and paperwork activities, for the most part the organization sets its own agenda. The wide social capital base in the community helps the shelter's administrators develop the trust they need to accomplish their own mission-based agenda in the community. Government supports Sunrise with little interference. For example, a key government official observed that annual funding for this organization, although officially provided under a fee-for-service contract, actually "functioned as a grant" to support an important community institution.

Empowerment Education is a small but rapidly growing organization in Milwaukee that provides adult basic education/GED, child care, and specific skills training. The organization also hosts a W-2 site under contract to Community Solutions, profiled below, and offers community-service jobs for W-2 program participants assigned to the site.

The organization was started as an alternative school for troubled teenagers in the mid 1970s by a faculty member at a local university and a small group of elite educators and activists. It gradually expanded its participant base to include people needing adult basic education/GED, from a variety of backgrounds but with an emphasis on low-income populations. Until recently, the organization had a budget of $40,000 and six staff members, half of whom were volunteers or paid sporadically. They ran their education program out of several sites in churches and the offices of faith-based organizations and citywide nonprofits. Some of these sponsoring organizations contributed to teachers' salaries.

In the late 1980s, they contracted with Community Solutions to provide their core program under one of the larger organization's government contracts. This relationship led to additional contracts, and a shift in the size and scope of the organization. Asked to host the W-2 program by Community Solutions, they bought a building and expanded to include day care in the late 1990s. They now have a budget of several hundred thousand dollars and a staff of seventeen. Most of the new employees are day-care workers hired from the W-2 program.

Although Empowerment Education was established by citywide elites, the agency has always maintained a partnership with its diverse participant base. One of the agency's key staff members—a former program participant—explained:

> We're very client-based, very client friendly. We run our organization more like a family. We try and make sure that everyone has an equal part. Our program director and director of children's' services, they all sit on our board. We used to be worker managed, where everyone who worked for us sat on the board, and that worked for many years until we had so many employees we would have an enormous board.

As noted, Empowerment Education maintains a clear focus on its participants and has always collaborated with city elite with similar philosophies.

They began collaborating with other organizations in the community only after developing the relationship with Community Solutions. Key staff members described their relationship with other organizations providing similar services as "very aloof," adding that they had been asked whether Community Solutions was "really going to hook up with those crazy old hippies." Through the support of the larger partner agency, they now participate in a number of citywide networks.

Involvement in W-2 has shifted the focus of the organization's client base, but it has not changed its ethos or mission. As described in chapter 10, Empowerment Education insists that the W-2 staff comply with agency standards instead of the other way around. However, it is equally clear that maintenance and growth of the agency depend on continuation of government contracts that fund the building and staff.

Small to midsized citywide organizations share several characteristics. First, each was started by citywide elites to address a particular social problem. Elite philosophy and connections influence the direction of the organization. Organizations in both of the large cities drew from liberal elites focused on helping less advantaged citizens in their locality. In Kenosha, Sunrise reflected elites' concern with maintaining quality of life in a working-class community during hard times. Although each organization has expanded its activities over time, all remain committed to their original mission and philosophy for providing service. The service-delivery model used by each agency to provide government service reflects this unique mission. Citizens United works with its constituent neighborhoods, Empowerment Education develops partnerships with program participants, and Sunrise involves its community-wide volunteer base in supplying food and shelter for the hungry and homeless. Their government contracts and affiliations with larger organizations stem from an appreciation of their core missions and strategies.

Each organization has a small staff and relies on strong volunteer and social capital networks to survive. In all three cases, active volunteers and people from affiliate organizations far outnumber staff. These institutions serve as bridging forces among people and institutions throughout the city who share the agency's concerns. They also rely on the social capital they have developed with their partners in order to carry out their work.

All these organizations are vulnerable to the vagaries of funding cycles and government payment structures. While each has the technical expertise to manage government contracts, they lack multiple sources of funding for operations that larger organizations rely on to support core operations. These small institutions also lack the economies of scale that larger organizations rely on to provide service. I now compare these smaller organizations to large institutions to show the similarities and differences among citywide organizations.

Large Citywide Nonprofit/Faith-Related Organizations   Larger citywide organizations are less vulnerable to funding cycles—they have a greater presence in social service provision in their localities, and their strong social capital connections to government means they can depend on continuing contracts. They regularly work with the smaller organizations, either through subcontracts or in coalition activities.

Faith in Action is a $33-million, multisite faith related organization in Philadelphia. Its mission is to "enhance the employability and self-sufficiency of the people it serves." This is a highly professional organization with a complete planning and administrative staff, multiple funding sources, and a nearly hundred-year history. They participate in most of the employment- and training-related government-funded programs in the city, including several TANF, adult basic education, and JPTA/FSA/WTW contracts. They function within citywide networks of social service providers but also have well-developed ties to employers throughout the region.

Their program participants, who come from a wide range of city residents in need, tend to vary according to the nature of a particular program. For example, Faith in Action's Transitionally Needy program consisted exclusively of welfare recipients. Half the program participants were female and 70 percent were either African American (60 percent) or Latino (10 percent). Most had more than two years of work experience.

In contrast, Substance Abuse Support, another Faith in Action program, served only people with a recent history of substance abuse. That population consisted of 46 percent whites, 30 percent African Americans, 19 percent Latinos, 3 percent Asians, and 1 percent Native Americans. Seventy-two percent of the program participants were women, and 90 percent had less than two years of work experience history.

Individual program administrators pay close attention to their funding sources and contracting requirements but are insulated from the day-to-day crisis atmosphere of the smaller organizations. Also, they can refer clients to a placement unit or other training programs in house, allowing them to focus more closely on program mission and outcomes.

Community Solutions is a large, multiservice organization in Milwaukee. It started in the late 1960s as a franchise of a national organization with a mission to provide employment and training primarily to people of one racial group. Over the years, it has been involved in most government employment and training initiatives. Its current budget is between $25 million and $30 million, and it has numerous staff at several locations. It is currently a W-2 agency in addition to holding other contracts.

The organization receives general mission guidelines and some technical support from its parent organization. However, local affiliates have significant autonomy. Community Solutions has developed strong relationships with government and other organizations providing similar services in Milwaukee. Despite its focus on one low-income community of color, the organization also works with the people and organizations associated with its target community. In many ways, the organization has become a patron and leader of smaller community-based institutions with similar goals. This includes subcontracting with smaller organizations that serve their target populations in order to provide more community-based support.

Our research on the agency indicated some stresses as Community Solutions modified its programs to meet the mandates of its W-2 contract. However, the organization did not seem controlled by government. Rather, it used its multiple resources to cushion the new expectations in the same way that Faith in Action did. This organization also became an active participant in advocacy efforts to change some aspects of W-2 at the state level. In terms of program focus, they maintained a fair amount of autonomy within the guidelines of their W-2 contract. This same philosophy prevailed in their relationship with their two subcontractors, which also shaped W-2 to fit their agency ethos with Community Solutions's blessing.

These larger institutions have multifaceted programs and centralized planning, financial, and human resources staff. They thus represent an economy of scale different from that of smaller institutions. As with the job-development unit at Faith in Action, they were able to create specialized departments that offered activities needed for many programs. This flexibility extended to administrative capacity—whereas smaller organizations used staff to perform both administrative and program activities, these large organizations were able to devote more staff exclusively to administrative tasks. This administrative capacity resulted from several advantages of large size. First, these organizations were better equipped to develop funding sources for general operations—for example, the United Way, United Jewish Appeal, corporations, and individual donors. In addition, these larger agencies were able to pool the amounts that their government contractors allowed for administration more effectively than small organizations that had only one or two government contracts.

Being large does not necessarily mean that an organization's staff is more professional, however. In fact, we saw a great range in professional behavior and employee credentials across all organizations. However, large size does lend an aura of legitimacy sometimes lacking in smaller citywide and community-based institutions.

These larger organizations relied much more heavily on paid staff than the smaller institutions. Although each had ties to community-based institutions, the large organizations served as the dominant partner in each of these relationships. These organizations recognized that sometimes the tradeoff for economies of scale is difficulty serving some participants. For example, the Social Network Study found that these large institutions faced challenges placing immigrants and some people of color in jobs (Schneider 1999a). The organizations dealt with the potential weakness of large institutions—that is, that they are less likely to offer specialized service—in several ways. Community Solutions used community-based partners to customize service delivery. Faith in Action primarily developed in-house programs tailored for particular populations, like the two programs profiled above. However, it also developed partnerships with community-based institutions to enhance their service provision. The executive director described such partnerships as a "win–win" solution in which the small organization benefited from the larger institution's capacity while the large institution gained grass-roots connections that its centralized programs might lack.

The strong relationships that large citywide institutions had with government, other service providers, and some grass-roots organizations indicate that they rely on social capital through both vertical and horizontal relationships to maintain and expand the organization. Social capital was also tied to cultural capital. As with the smaller citywide organizations, these large institutions had clear missions that governed their activities and their choice of partners. They were more likely to partner with organizations that shared their values and general service provision goals.

For-Profit Organizations   The for-profit organizations in this study ranged in size, focus, and operation. In some cases, for-profit entities were founded by citywide elites as a more flexible way to provide services. These institutions resembled citywide nonprofits of similar size in most ways. Others were founded to provide a particular service for a profit.

Bakers is a for-profit proprietary school in Philadelphia that offers several curricula. It functions within the network of vocational schools and maintains strong ties to its trade association and with employers that hire their graduates. It has a staff of twenty-five, most of whom are teachers but also a designated administrative staff and job developer. Ninety-five percent of its income comes from tuition and fees and five percent from government. Although most tuition payments include government-sponsored grants and loans, there is little fiscal oversight and the school receives the bulk of its funds up front as tuition payments.

The client base is 70 percent white, and all have at least a high-school education. Unlike smaller Philadelphia employment and training agencies that get referrals through the PIC, the Department of Public Welfare, or word of mouth, the media and other referrals account for most of Bakers's intake. Administrators claim that 95 percent of their participants are placed in training-related jobs. They are concerned with providing quality training in order to maintain their reputation with employers, funders, and potential participants.

Government proponents of for-profit service provision often envision organizations like Bakers because they feel that the close ties to employers and competition for students will lead to higher-quality service. However, the quality of trade schools varies enormously. Research on trade schools in Philadelphia revealed that many programs provided substandard training and failed to place their program participants into jobs.[4] However, other for-profit schools had reputations as a key stepping stone for people interested in careers in clerical work, as professional chefs, or in other skilled occupations. In addition, use of the for-profit form by citywide social service elites and larger non-profits as mechanisms for service provision allows few generalizations about for-profit organizations.

Although for-profits rely on marketing data to attract their client base, their major focus is not on program participants as a constituent group. Instead, social capital links are cultivated with funders, employers, and similar institutions throughout the city and state. This research found that quality trade schools served as social capital links between their trainees and the employers in agency networks. These reciprocal relationships depended on established trust among the trade school, its participants, and employers that the training program would produce people who would succeed in jobs in these companies.

Trade schools that were less successful in placing their graduates often had ties to other trade schools and government but fewer links to employers. These lower-quality schools used the reputations of successful schools to draw participants seeking stable work who lacked social and cultural ties to the longer-established institutions.[5] However, with limited ties to employers, program graduates found it difficult to find work after completing their training.

Relationships of for profit institutions with government were mediated through the trade school association's lobbying organization, which developed strong connections with politicians and regulators. In fact, Philadelphia advocates complained that the regulating body consisted largely of trade-school officials. This created a closed social capital system that limited unbiased oversight of these organizations and led to regulations favorable to for-profit institutions.

For-profits share with other citywide social service organizations an orientation toward people with a particular need rather than one community. This problem focus is the major factor that distinguishes these institutions from community-based organizations. I next profile these types of institutions.

COMMUNITY-BASED ORGANIZATIONS

Although a community-based organization serves a designated community, its board and staff do not necessarily come from that constituent base. In some cases, citywide elites with ties to a particular community form an organization that concentrates on that community and its needs. In most present-day community-based organizations, some members of the board and staff come from the community, and community members tend to have some input into the organization's activities. Other organizations are formed by local community people to serve themselves and others in the same closed social capital network.

As with citywide institutions, comparing community-based organizations in Philadelphia, Milwaukee, and Kenosha reveals many similarities across all three localities. The organizations take similar forms and have common strengths and weaknesses. In contrast, the citywide institutions' access to bridging social capital into citywide elite closed social capital networks varies enormously depending on the nature of the staff, board, and history of the organization. As with the citywide institutions, again, comparisons across the three localities revealed nearly identical institutions in the two large cities. The only difference was that Philadelphia's institutions were older, with a slightly different history that reflected national shifts in social service provision over time. As was the case with the citywide institutions, Kenosha lacked the larger type of community-based organization, a difference attributable to a combination of community size and the more recent development of nonprofit social welfare agencies in this small city.

Settlement Houses: Midsized Community-Based Institutions   The settlement-house model consists of multiservice institutions founded by community elites for a particular neighborhood. The settlement-house movement started in the late nineteenth century as a way to alleviate poverty in urban neighborhoods. Unlike many elite social welfare institutions of the time, the settlement house had staff who lived in the neighborhood and concentrated their efforts on working with local community residents to meet their needs (Trattner 1999:163–191). Today, most settlement houses have changed to resemble either neighborhood-based community organizations or citywide social service organizations, but the agency mission remains focused on working with neighborhood residents to meet their self-defined needs. Settlement houses in both Milwaukee and Philadelphia involved bridging social capital because elites from other groups—particularly the religious community—initiated these agencies. However, today boards and staff include people defined as being "from the community." Settlements are often bridging institutions that work with citywide organizations that provide similar services. The same pattern holds in both large cities.

Milwaukee's Neighborhood Settlement House started in 1958 along with the development of the Uptown Housing Development. The Housing Authority wanted a community center for the housing project, and, based on advice from the pastor who directed a well-known Milwaukee settlement house, the center was chartered as a settlement house for the entire community. The center started operations in 1960, using a small part of the building for Uptown's management. Through the 1960s and most of the 1970s, Neighborhood Settlement House focused on youth programs and day care, with some activities for seniors. Program budgets were modest. For example, the 1967 budget was $59,751, and 94 percent of funds came from United Community Services, the precursor of the United Way. Program participants were mostly white and working class.

The organization continued on a small scale through the mid-1970s. In 1976 a new executive director brought sustained energy and creative vision that rapidly transformed the organization into a burgeoning multiservices organization. The 1982 budget was seven times the 1967 budget. In 1997, the organization had $2,341,504 in income from multiple sources and hosted a W-2 agency, a health clinic, an alternative middle school, safety services, a family resource center, adult basic education and computer courses, youth summer and after-school programs, day care, community organizing, senior programs, a food pantry, and nutrition programs. Despite increasing budgets, the core staff remained small and the administrative staff consisted of four people. At the time of this study, the organization was planning its fourth addition to the building and beginning initiatives for a charter school and several youth safety and enrichment programs off site. The 1997 annual report listed 30 collaborative partners (funders and program providers) in addition to the United Way.[6] Fifteen of the thirty partners represented organizations that either conducted programs in Neighborhood Settlement House facilities or worked with Neighborhood Settlement House to develop activities.

As the organization has grown, the racial composition and nature of its programs have changed. Beginning in the late 1970s, more African Americans started using its services. According to several employees, program participants slowly transitioned to almost completely African American by the late 1980s. According to one former employee who watched this change, the transition started with the youth programs and day care, and gradually spread to the other programs. At present, only the seniors program serves whites, and this program includes very few African Americans. The organization also now serves many people from outside their defined service-delivery area; agency statistics showed that over 50 percent of program participants live outside the target neighborhood. Many of these participants come from older African American sections of the city.

Beginning in the 1980s, the focus of Neighborhood Settlement House began to change from general community activities to programs for the most disadvantaged citizens. The youth and day-care programs remain open to anyone who comes in, on a first-come, first-served basis. The same is true of the GED and computer courses. However, some other programs primarily serve various disadvantaged populations based on funder-defined categories. More agency programs are directed toward the "disadvantaged" and "at-risk," including the food pantry, the W-2 agency, safety services and the alternative school. As these categorical programs have expanded, some general programs (for example, aerobics) have been discontinued, and the seniors program was moved out of the building into a park service facility about a mile away.

These changes reflect a combination of entrepreneurial vision, the organization's perception of the needs of its community, and a keen understanding that nonprofit development must involve links to government. Like many nonprofits (Smith and Lipsky 1993), Neighborhood Settlement House now gets over 70 percent of its funds from government, and these government sources sometimes restrict funding to specific at-risk populations or those who meet various low-income criteria. This has led to change in programs and contributed to the inclusion of people from outside the service-delivery area. United Way funds cover the traditional activities such as youth development that are no longer popular in funding circles. Neighborhood Settlement House also has an active board and creative management staff that succeed in finding private funds and foundation grants to cover the range of activities.

However, the shift in programs does not simply represent mission drift as agencies respond to funders' expectations (Smith and Lipsky 1993). The administrators of Neighborhood Settlement House are determined to maintain their mission. They are contemplating discontinuing the alternative school and replacing it with a charter school because the alternative-school population comes primarily from outside the service-delivery area.

Neighborhood Settlement House responds to several constituencies. First, they focus on the closed social capital networks of their program participants. Although Uptown's residents are the agency's core concern, the agency also serves a combination of Milwaukee African Americans and residents of all colors from the geographically defined neighborhood. The agency's community also includes a large group of home-based day-care providers under the organization umbrella and the local business association. The organization also has limited ties with neighborhood churches.

Second, the organization develops strong social capital links with its collaborative partners, primarily a local university, its W-2 partner Community Solutions, the Milwaukee Technical College, and a variety of local and citywide youth-serving organizations. The agency pays equal attention to the government agencies and private citywide foundations that provide their funding. Neighborhood Settlement House also participates in networks of similar organizations throughout the city. Participation in these citywide social service networks has raised the visibility of the organization, but it is not known as a strong collaborative partner among local social service agencies.

The settlement houses had strong connections to citywide institutions and government similar to those of large citywide social service organizations.

However, unlike their citywide counterparts, these organizations focused on a particular geographical community. They also had multiple programs aimed at fulfilling different needs within their target community. Neighborhood Settlement House currently functions as a comprehensive social service entity providing services to people of all ages.

Like the large, citywide nonprofits, these organizations shared administrative functions across programs. Each had dedicated staff who addressed financial matters, fund-raising, and related issues. However, unlike their citywide counterparts, these community-based organizations tended to have fewer staff members to work in these areas, and their administrative structures tended to represent a small portion of their budgets. Administrators were pulled in many directions as they tried to maintain social capital ties with key stakeholders and perform other needed administrative functions. As a result, program staff in settlement-house organizations were more likely than their counterparts in the larger citywide institutions to participate in grant-writing and administrative record-keeping.

The settlement houses maintained ties with two very different types of stakeholders. As organizations participating in citywide social welfare service provision, they maintained relationships with government, funders, and similar organizations throughout the city. However, partnerships with other large community-based organizations or smaller citywide institutions were centered on providing the same service to people in different parts of the city rather than the patron–client relationships characteristic of partnerships between large citywide social service organizations and their partners. However, social capital relationships with citywide institutions did allow these community-based institutions to serve as local partners with large citywide institutions. Neighborhood Settlement House partnered with several citywide quasi-governmental organizations, such as the Housing Authority and social service agencies.

These organizations also developed strong social capital relationships among the communities they served. People from these communities used the organization's services, joined the staff, and served on the board. While attending to the expectations of their funders and larger partners, these organizations always concentrated first on the communities they were chartered to serve. This emphasis on working with the community defined these larger institutions as community-based organizations despite their offering programs also provided by citywide institutions. The community focus makes these organizations similar to smaller community-based agencies.

Small Community-Based Organizations   Smaller organizations in this study were race/ethnicity/nationality-based, neighborhood-based, or a combination of the two. In Kenosha, smaller race/ethnicity/nationality-based organizations served the entire city, and sometimes neighboring localities as well, because of

the small population base of people of color and the fact that no one neighborhood was dominated by African Americans or Latinos. In contrast, both
Milwaukee and Philadelphia were racially segregated cities. Race/ethnicity/
nationality-based organizations could either exclusively serve residents of one
geographical section of a race/ethnicity/nationality-based community or serve
everyone from the particular group. In all three localities, people active in the
organization were self-selected from one of several closed social capital networks within the race/ethnicity/nationality group. Staff and board members
may come from another faction in the community, but they also tended to
represent closed social capital networks. Sometimes board members also included citywide elites in order to foster bridging social capital to help obtain
funding or government contracts.

Latinos United started as a community center and direct service organization for Latinos in southeastern Wisconsin in 1969. The original organization
was founded by a local priest serving the Mexican migrant community and
some established residents of Mexican American descent. A branch office was
soon founded in Kenosha. In the mid 1970s, an area Latina with strong social
capital ties in the Mexican migrant and Mexican American community became the assistant director of the Kenosha branch. Although officially under
the auspices of its parent organization, the Kenosha office rapidly developed
its own range of programs. It also developed strong ties with other African
American and Latino community-based organizations as well as bridging ties
to Kenosha government and citywide elite.

The board consisted almost entirely of established Mexican Americans
from a particular closed social capital network in the area until the organization had a financial crisis in the early 1990s. Latinos United was forced to close
the Racine office; the Kenosha branch was able to continue only through a
bailout by citywide leaders. The bailout package included the requirements
that the organization work closely with the United Way to reestablish its funding base and broaden its board to include Latinos from outside the controlling
closed social capital network as well as some city elites. During the research
project, the organization's board consisted of representatives of all three constituencies, although leading roles were still held by people tied to the original
closed social capital network.

Over time, the participant base and programs also changed. Since the 1970s,
agency focus has shifted toward programs for needier populations, including a
food and clothing pantry, gang prevention, ESL education, energy assistance,
and translation services. The organization also hosts Kenosha County government workers providing Medicaid outreach to the Latino population. To better serve the wider Latino community, the organization also offers tax assistance and hosts events for community members.

The organization still concentrates on its core mission to serve the Latino community, but the Latino population served by the program's ESL and support programs consists largely of newcomer Mexican immigrants, a closed social capital network very different from that of the stakeholders who form the core of the staff and Latino board. In addition, the organization relies on government funds for a significant portion of its budget. The government grants included such citywide services as energy assistance and gang prevention that bring in people from other racial and ethnic groups. The executive director estimated that one-third of the program participants are now Latino, one-third white, and one-third African American.

The agency's budget ranged between $250,000 and $300,000 during the study period. Money was always tight, and the organization was always understaffed. Funding came from several government contracts, local foundations, the United Way, and community donations. For additional income, the board ran a bingo game for white seniors once a month. The staff was supplemented by community volunteers, senior volunteers through a program sponsored by another community-based organization, and community-service parolees supplied through a government program.

The agency focused on several constituencies, the primary one being various parts of the Latino community. It also developed strong social capital ties with local government and citywide business elite, as well as with citywide organizations providing services used by its program participants, including the local hospital, doctors, citywide organizations like Sunrise that serve similar populations, and the other organizations serving communities of color in Kenosha.

Second Chance is a program for African Americans based in one of the poorest neighborhoods of Philadelphia. This organization was founded by the neighborhood's African American community. Its administrators claim a staff of twenty-two, but most are part-time workers or volunteers. Ninety-five percent of the staff and all participants are African Americans. Eighty-five percent of its funding comes from government and the remainder from small foundation grants. Second Chance provides a combination of GED and skills training, working in partnership with a larger training organization as well as offering their own programs. It does a particularly good job of creating a community among its participants, many of whom return to serve the agency and local community as volunteers. The administrators constantly disagree with the Department of Public Welfare about client activities, wish they could be involved more in education as opposed to mandated skills training, and describe government paperwork as a "bureaucratic nightmare" that gets in the way of running programs.

Second Chance focuses primarily on the closed social capital networks of its program participants, board, and staff. It also has developed relationships with government and other funders, but these relationships are not as strong as for the other organizations profiled above. It has network ties to other African American organizations but is not very visible in the social service community providing similar programs.

Small community-based organizations are most likely to rely on closed social capital networks for board, staff, and participants. Although the staff, board, and participants did not always overlap, these organizations were most likely to have people from the same closed social capital networks in all three roles. As a result, agency mission and service-provision strategies were often tied to the culture and needs of the participating community. Small community-based organizations thus often had more success reaching local communities than citywide institutions did. Through multiple ties within the community, these institutions were most likely to share social and cultural capital trust with the populations that were hardest to serve.

In all three cities, small community-based organizations were also most likely to lack the technical expertise or capacity to manage the organization well and successfully compete for government contracts. The limited staff in these organizations performed both administrative and program tasks, and the same people were responsible for developing and maintaining social capital ties with government agencies, funders, and other social service agencies needed to sustain the organization. With the workers pulled in many directions, some tasks necessarily fell by the wayside. Although many agencies had highly qualified staff, the low salaries these organizations could afford made it difficult to keep junior staff members who did not have a firm commitment to the organization. This was particularly true of administrative staff.

Small community-based organizations supplemented their limited staff with working boards and volunteers. The expertise and labor contributed by these volunteers allowed many small community-based nonprofits to provide quality service despite small budgets and limited staff. Participation by boards and volunteers in these organizations represented much larger contributions of time than in any other type of organization. Volunteers were also more likely to carry out such key functions as staffing programs, performing administrative tasks, and writing grant applications.

Government agencies increasingly reached out to these organizations because they often have access to the most isolated public assistance recipients. As one Pennsylvania Department of Public Welfare administrator acknowledged, government sometimes encourages these organizations to partner with larger nonprofits to relieve limited financial, grant-writing, and program-management systems. As with citywide organizations, size makes a difference in the activities and organizational structures of community-based nonprofits.

However, regardless of size, community-based institutions are most likely to arouse concerns about serving one piece of a community. This happened most often with community-based nonprofits that drew board, staff, and participants from the same closed social capital networks. The same concerns have been raised about faith-based institutions.

FAITH-BASED ORGANIZATIONS

Like citywide and community-based organizations, faith-based institutions took a variety of forms and have different strengths and weaknesses. Truly faith-based organizations in all three localities tended to be small to midsized. Salvation Army chapters were sometimes larger in the major cities, but most locality- and faith-based organizations had staffs of fewer than fifty people. Most of the faith-based organizations in this project had staffs of fewer that thirty and budgets under $500,000.

In all three localities, faith-based organizations looked to the wider religious community and sometimes citywide or race/ethnicity/nationality social capital networks for resources, participants, and funding. Because the faith-based organizations providing social welfare services in each locality are similar in size, the three examples presented here illustrate different organizational forms for this type of institution.

Share the Wealth is the latest mission project of Pastor Rice, a well-known clergyman serving low-income African American community residents in Kenosha. Pastor Rice also ran a prison ministry and provided community-service jobs for parolees through church programs. He started Share the Wealth in the late 1990s as a nonprofit mission activity associated with his church that provided basic necessities at little or no cost to families hit hard by welfare reform. The program was staffed by church-members volunteers or community-service parolees, primarily serving people in the closed social capital network of low-income African Americans.

Pastor Rice was consistently turned down for funding by citywide government and private sources. The lack of success was due not to lack of information—he identified a number of funding opportunities—but to inability to present proposals in expected format. He also failed to obtain support from other African American churches and the African American middle class. One citywide professional active in the community who had been asked to help Pastor Rice said, "I am an unwilling participant because I feel that the organization needs to be totally restructured." Deficiency of basic organization did not inspire community-wide confidence. Other Kenosha African Americans suggested that the kind of cultural capital practiced by Pastor Rice and his constituents clashed with the patterns of the more economically stable parts of the African American community.

Share the Wealth's social capital supports come exclusively through Pastor Rice's ties in one closed social capital network in the Kenosha African American community, and the same people are served by the organization. Pastor Rice has connections to the rest of the Kenosha African American and citywide social service and government elites but lacks the trusting relationships with these stakeholders to develop bridging social capital with other organizations.

The Faith Community Welfare Support Project was a model welfare initiative of an interfaith organization in Milwaukee. The parent organization is an umbrella institution for parts of Milwaukee's religious community. It also represents a bridging social capital force with ties among Milwaukee elites, left and liberal advocates, politicians, and the social service community. Funding comes from the member religious bodies, as well as some small foundation grants. The entire organization had a paid staff of five or six people during the study period. Before starting Faith Community Welfare Support, the parent organization had initiated another social service activity that had spun off into a separate organization. They also ran a direct service project focused on intergroup dynamics.

The project operated for approximately a year and a half with funding from a local Milwaukee foundation. It linked church-based mentors with poor families to provide friendly support and advocacy and to broaden opportunities. The program, intended to supplement government-funded welfare programs, was aimed primarily at providing social supports when dealing with government, employers, and the formal social service community. Only one paid staff person was assigned full time to the project, and the agency's assistant director provided additional administrative support.

The program drew on the social capital resources of its parent organization throughout its existence. This included several constituencies. Church volunteers and referrals of program participants came from the network of churches and faith-based social service agencies that were the organization's primary constituent base. The interfaith organization also had strong ties among the advocacy and progressive social service community in Milwaukee. Staff from these organizations formed the core team that developed the program and its materials, provided training and support to church volunteers, and oversaw the project's operation.

Ethnic Mission is a Catholic church–based mission project in Kenosha designed to provide social service supports and outreach to a marginalized part of the community. It was developed by a priest serving that community and is funded by all the Catholic churches in the Kenosha diocese. It has a staff of one part-time person. A church committee acts as the board; the committee consists exclusively of members of this racial/ethnic community, and it also runs religious education programs and fills other religious governance roles associated with that community. Discussions regarding the agency reflect an equal balance of the social service needs of its constituent community and spiritual supports.

Ethnic Mission focused exclusively on its closed social capital community. Advisory committee members, staff, and participants all come from this ethnic/racial constituency. It works primarily with the other social service organizations chartered to serve the same community. Although priests oversee its fiscal operations and participate on the committee, during the study period community members were the driving force behind the organization. The white Catholic church provided background supports, including fundraising and administrative support, in a social capital relationship that represented one closed social capital network serving another.

Faith-based organizations are difficult to characterize because of the wide range of organizational forms and connections to religious bodies. All share a conscious connection between faith and action and do not try to hide the religious background of the institution. However, despite the faith basis not all social service activities entailed aspects of religious practice. To the contrary, most of the activities carried out by these institutions were similar to those of other types of social service organizations. The difference arose from the close connection between the religious body and the organization; social welfare activities expressed acts of faith more clearly than in other institutions.

The existence of these faith-based institutions did not mean that government necessarily sought them out for contracts. Share the Wealth was unsuccessful in its bid for government or private foundation assistance. Ethnic Mission chose not to seek government funding, instead expecting that the community-based organization serving the same community would partner with government. Although the interfaith organization that developed the Faith Community Welfare Support Project had the connections and capacity to seek government funding, its leaders decided that they did not want to be part of the government-funded social service system.

Faith-related organizations were more likely to seek government aid and receive contracts. For example, Sunrise has the faith-based contract for social welfare services in Kenosha. In all three cities, ability to participate in the formal service provision system depended on measures of organizational effectiveness, ability to write proposals, and extent of social capital.

Development of Social Capital by Organizations

Taken together, these examples provide general comparisons across types of nonprofits. All these organizations were founded by members of closed social capital networks to meet a defined need. Although boards for community-based organizations are more likely to include people served by the institution, all organizations include on their boards either elites from the same general community or citywide elites. Many also include people from different closed social capital networks as key staff members. Most social welfare institutions founded before the 1970s have shifted their focus toward serving more categorically needy populations as they have become involved in more government contracts. All organizations with significant government funding, regardless of when they began, want to serve a wider participant base with fewer government strings attached. As described briefly here, and in more detail in chapter 10, each organization tries hard to mold government mandates to fit their mission rather than allow mission to drift in order to garner more funding.

Size matters regardless of the orientation of the organization. Larger institutions have more sources of funding and more options for responding to government mandates while still maintaining their overall mission. Smaller organizations are more likely to experience layoffs or closure when funding gets tight. On the other hand, many of the smaller organizations rely on volunteers who can supplement paid staff when times are difficult.

Larger organizations had more capacity to administer government programs, but they sometimes lacked close connections with the communities they served. Because community-based organizations tend to focus more closely on the expectations and styles of the communities they serve, they may have more diverse, targeted program strategies than larger institutions. The citywide nonprofits customize their programs through partnering with community-based organizations and developing programs in house focused on one population.

Organizations find resources and determine the particular direction within agency mission through the activities of their board and staff. Both funding and direction depend on social capital that facilitates carrying out objectives. Cultural capital also plays a role, as cultural clashes can lead to problems with funding; Pastor Rice's experience illustrates this problem. Shifts in an agency's culture can also lead to new directions for the organization or a change in the core constituent group of program participants. Neighborhood Settlement House shows this trend. Social capital resources are developed through two major sources: board relationships and agency-to-agency relationships through staff. Board members provided access to social capital through their networks, serving as a primary source of resources.

Empowerment Education's evolution from an isolated alternative school using other institutions' space to an established agency providing social welfare programming in partnership with a W-2 agency illustrates agency-to-agency social capital development. The executive director of Community Solutions noticed Empowerment Education's work and encouraged a partnership with them to provide services through one of the larger organization's programs. Community Solutions helped Empowerment Education expand the organization and stabilize its physical plant and funding base by providing social capital links to material resources. These in turn led to additional resources. A key staff person recalls:

> [The executive director of Community Solutions] has been a wealth of knowledge for us. We have relied on him for support. When we told him we wanted to buy a building he said "Well, OK." He gave us a list of 10 people. He said go and talk to all the people on this list and they'll give you a pretty good idea of what direction you should go. People didn't even know why we were visiting them. We would just call them and say [the executive director] said we ought to meet with you. It was really odd.
>
> [A progressive banker] got us a loan. She's done a lot of community things for agencies like ours. She said, "I knew you guys would pay the loan back. I knew you would be successful. . . . It was just getting somebody else to believe us." It was amazing. People were amazed we bought the building.
>
> So then we moved into the building and we had no furniture. We had phones sitting on the floor. We needed a copier so we called [a copier company] and said why don't you come over and show us what you [have]. . . . So happens that the salesman from [the copier company], his boss was here from Chicago and this guy came in and he's just like, I mean he's just Mister Chicago. He said, "You girls ain't got no furniture." Well, hello! He said, "You know what, you guys gotta have some furniture." . . . We said, "You're right, we do but we'll get some." It turned out he had an entire warehouse full of furniture. He said, "You go down there, take a truck and take whatever you want."

This example shows how a larger, more established organization uses the social capital trust of its networks to help a smaller partner. The banker and other people contacted by this agency provided extraordinary resources-based on references from the larger organization. The executive director facilitated network building for the smaller institution by subtly suggesting that they talk to people who had access to other resources. More instrumental requests for help might not have had such positive responses. The relationships proved the key to garnering resources.

The story about obtaining the furniture is a more ambiguous example of the role of social capital because the agency was just beginning to establish contact with the copier company when they were offered furniture. This example illustrates two dynamics of social capital creation. First, once this organization had obtained some resources, others were more likely to help. The copier company executive responded to the big, empty building of an institution just starting out more readily than he might have to a small storefront agency. Second, offering furniture to Empowerment Education cemented trust between the copier company and the agency, potentially creating a long-term business relationship. This highlights the fact that social capital involves two-way relationships, which are more likely to continue for a long time.

POLICY AND PROGRAMMATIC IMPLICATIONS

Comparing the different types of organizations providing social welfare services in these three communities highlights several strategies for policy makers and agency administrators:

- Partnerships between large organizations and smaller institutions can balance the equally important issues of agency capacity and the necessity to develop strong social and cultural capital connections to communities served by the organization.
- Successful agencies develop social capital links with government, funders, and other organizations that help them to maintain organization goals.

SUMMARY

The types of agencies are similar across all three localities, regardless of state ethos or size of the city. The culture of a particular locality or community shapes organizational style in each place, but general forms remain the same.[7] All three cities include both citywide and community-based nonprofits. Citywide institutions generally focus on one problem, whereas community-based institutions concentrate on a single community. That said, citywide institutions sometimes develop programs targeted toward a particular community, and, like Latinos United, community-based organizations may engage in services that draw participants from outside their target community. The difference between these two types of organizations is in their mission focus, not their funding sources or the range of participants they serve. Mission focus influences service provision strategies, marketing, and fund-raising techniques, which will in turn have an impact on the social and cultural capital cultivated by each organization to enable it to fulfill its goals. A strong mission focus on a particular problem or community mitigates against tendencies for institutional isomorphism despite the fact that organizations of all sizes need to develop strong social capital ties with government and other agencies to survive in the current system.

All organizations providing social welfare services in these three communities rely on a combination of agency-to-agency social capital and board social capital to carry out their missions. As discussed in the previous chapter, state government uses these local institutions to implement welfare reform. Relationships such as that between Community Solutions and Empowerment Education are just one element of a larger system of networked nonprofit, for-profit, and government institutions that provide social welfare services in Philadelphia, Milwaukee, and Kenosha. I next describe these larger systems responsible for social welfare in the three cities.

CHAPTER 5

Social Service Systems

The various organizations that provide social welfare services are linked through contracting relationships with government and association with each other. Even organizations that have no government funding respond to regulations that shape the services they provide. Although most of the debate on welfare reform focuses on government programs or nongovernmental institutions contracted to provide government services, in fact, social support systems in local communities include many institutions beyond those officially providing welfare-related services. In all three cities studied, institutional social supports included four inter-dependent systems: 1) the official welfare reform system, 2) a network of social service organizations providing ancillary services such as housing, child care, and substance-abuse programs, 3) community-based systems, and 4) faith communities. Together, these systems encompass the third factor that contributes to implementation of welfare policy: the nature of the local implementation system. The role of faith communities in social supports is discussed in chapter 11. This chapter describes and analyzes the three systems that involve formal organizations and local voluntary associations.

Many nonprofit organizations participate in several of these interrelated systems. For example, Neighborhood Settlement House is a community-based organization that participates in the formal welfare system as a subcontractor to one of Milwaukee's W-2 agencies. The organization also offers a wide range of related services that families on public assistance need, such as a health clinic and youth programs. These programs involve the settlement house in Milwaukee's ancillary services system. Finally, it sponsors a network of home day-care providers in its neighborhood and partners with the local business association, all links that involve the organization in the community-based system of its neighborhood.

Faith communities are also connected to these three systems. For example, Sunrise in Kenosha was founded by several churches and voluntary associations. These churches remain major social capital resources on the organization's board, provide direct service through volunteers, offer in-kind supports through donations, and provide shelter in affiliated churches.

This chapter addresses the following questions:

- How is social welfare service provision organized in these cities?
- How do organizations that provide TANF programs relate to organizations that provide ancillary services needed by TANF recipients to accept and maintain employment?
- How do organizations that offer ancillary services relate to one another?
- How are the citywide institutions that offer welfare reform connected to community-based organizations?

INTERORGANIZATIONAL DYNAMICS AND COMMUNITY

Understanding dynamics among organizations and their constituent communities depends on conceptualizing that relationship. Powell (1990) describes three types of economic organization: markets, hierarchy, and networks. Each system has different sets of rules and dynamics among organizations. Government contracting largely reflects social capital links among known actors rather than relying on impartial market forces. Powell's (1990:303) hierarchical model involves expanding the boundaries of an organization to incorporate various parts of the production process. Although created to describe manufacturing enterprises, this form contributes to an understanding of the structures of some social welfare organizations. For example, Empowerment Education was originally developed as an alternative school and GED program. However, realizing that much of the participant population would be involved in W-2, its administrators agreed to become a subcontractor for one of the W-2 agencies. To provide the full range of services needed by their participants within their mission framework, they also developed a day-care program, expanding its operations to include a venue for community-service jobs and employment for its W-2 participants as in Powell's hierarchical model. The hierarchical model harkens back to a bureaucratic form; however, it need not have the rationalized, top-down decision structure expected of bureaucracy. For example, although the executive directors of Empowerment Education set the tone for the organization and oversee decision making for all programs under its roof, it functions as a nonhierarchical organization based on a significant amount of input from staff.

Powell's hierarchical model is similar to the unitary system defined by Warren (1967) for social service provision. Kenosha's welfare-to-work program would fit Warren's (1967) "federative" and "unitary" models, in which one organization maintains hierarchical control over partners, thus limiting competition and dissent. The W-2 program was implemented through a public/private partnership that includes a combination of for-profit, nonprofit, and government organizations. The contracted program also included several additional for-profit and nonprofit organizations providing support services. In a unitary management structure, these organizations functioned as one organization through hierarchical management frameworks drawing on much participation from staff at all levels.

The larger array of services in Kenosha needed to support low-income people are provided by a small pool of nonprofit organizations. Regardless of whether the ancillary agencies have formal contracts with the W-2 agency, they respond to it as federative partners. In federative structures, most decisions come from the top, but the units have authority over unit activities. In some cases, nonprofits cannot provide services to certain clients unless they have registered with the W-2 agency. For example, low-income people were refused energy assistance and housing vouchers if they had not first registered with the W-2 agency, even though families were not required to be on welfare to receive these services. Nonprofit agencies maintained autonomy, yet most decisions regarding welfare reform were made by the W-2 agency.

Network organizations (Powell 1990:303) rely on the kinds of "reciprocal, preferential, and mutually supportive actions" characteristic of social capital. Warren's federative structure, which involves a council of agencies that sometimes act as a unit, provides one example of a network organization. The federation acts as a single entity, but decision making rests with the member agencies. For example, Citizens United sponsored a coalition of training providers and other advocates to work on welfare issues. The coalition sponsored several research studies as well as advocacy activities. Although most of the participating organizations helped develop these initiatives, they chose independently whether they wanted to be involved in any specific activity. The coalition did not control agency decisions regarding coalition-sponsored efforts.

Milofsky and Hunter (1995) add another dimension to the literature on organizational dynamics for nonprofits. They describe four types of communities that foster the development of nonprofits with very different kinds of organizational structures, missions, internal dynamics, and interactions with the larger community. The social service organizations discussed in this chapter fall into three of the four groups in this typology. *Communities in themselves* are "groups with an intense, internal social life; sharp boundaries between themselves and outsiders; and a strong commitment to a particular way of doing things" (Milofsky and Hunter 1995:2). Nonprofits in this category include organizations like Second Chance that are founded in impoverished communities of color to help members of those communities develop skills and find work.

The majority of the institutions discussed here belong to *network organizations,* collectivities of people who are paid to do a certain kind of work and who interact with one another on a regular basis (Milofsky and Hunter, 1995:3). Most institutions in the three localities participate in some form of coalition activity. For example, all the youth-serving organizations in Kenosha

with gang-prevention contracts participate in a coalition that focuses on their common concerns. As illustrated below, these network organizations profoundly influence the activities of nonprofits.

All these nonprofits are also involved in *vertically linked associations,* in which local institutions interact with various levels of government, quasi-governmental organizations, or national nonprofits. These include the PIC and the state and federal agencies that fund these organizations and issue regulations that govern activities. Understanding social welfare provision through government/nonprofit contracts entails comprehending how individual organizations respond to the pressures from the institutions above them in these vertical links and tracing how these organizations use their social network connections to militate for change.

Most organizations operate within a combination of network organizations and vertically linked associations. Community-based organizations also, necessarily, orient toward communities in themselves. All types of organizations often include people from various communities. Board and staff members of these institutions may come from a variety of closed social capital networks, and an organization's board and staff may include people from several different types of closed networks.

Although the network relationships described by Milofsky and Hunter provide the opportunity to develop social capital through ongoing network relationships, belonging to networks does not necessarily constitute social capital. The kinds of ongoing relationships based in enforceable trust that engender social capital develop through selecting partners from among organizations known through these vertical or network ties. Gulati and Gargiulo (1999) note that organizations rely on previous partners to decide whom to partner with in the future, relying on already established trust-based relationships.

For example, Neighborhood Settlement House decided to develop a partnership with the social work department at a local university because it had already established a successful program with the nursing school at the same institution. The social work department, in turn, chose Neighborhood Settlement House as the site for this new model program based on good reports from the nursing program faculty member who had spearheaded the original collaboration and served on the Neighborhood Settlement House board. These organizations chose to continue these collaborations because of ongoing positive experiences. As Powell (1996:63) reminds us, "Trust is neither chosen nor embedded, but is instead learned and reinforced, hence a product of ongoing interaction and discussion." Social capital relationships facilitate trust; conversely, they can be destroyed by betrayal of trust, through negative interactions.

An agency's behavior also reflects the cultural capital norms of the agencies with which it collaborates. Organizations are more likely to choose partners that share their values and practices (Einbinder et al. 2000; Powell 1990). For example, Community Solutions chose to subcontract with Neighborhood Settlement House and Empowerment Education because they exhibited a commitment to the community that the larger organization was chartered to serve. The staff of Community Solutions knew both agencies from a coalition of ABE/GED programs that it hosted. The citywide organization selected these two organizations from the larger network because of this shared orientation. Cultural capital affinity served as one factor influencing the development of social capital ties.

However, despite the concern for one particular community shared by all three organizations that led to the common collaboration with Community Solutions, the two subcontractors were very different institutions relying on disparate organizational culture and service-provision philosophies. They participated in the same coalitions and held vertical relationships with Community Solutions but otherwise had no interaction with each other. "They don't collaborate," a staff member of Empowerment Education told me, referring to Neighborhood Settlement House. Other organizations with political or service-delivery strategies different from those of Neighborhood Settlement House made the same observation. In fact, however, Neighborhood Settlement House was known for collaborations with other organizations among the funding community. Several key partners praised the organization's model of providing programs in their community through partnerships with citywide institutions. However, these collaborations were very different from the kinds of mutual activities that Empowerment Education and similar organizations envisioned. Lacking shared cultural capital, organizations that could have easily developed social capital ties chose to remain unaffiliated members of common vertical and network associations.

Summary

These various institutional types and interorganizational dynamics influenced the nature of the social welfare systems and organizational practices in the three localities. Organizational theory describes two types of interorganizational dynamics that affect relationships among organizations participating in social welfare delivery systems: unequal power relationships and comparatively equal network associations. Power dynamics between government and social service organizations or prime contractors and their subcontracting organizations influence social capital relationships as well as the nature of service provision in a particular city.

Although vertical relationships with government may start when an unknown agency successfully bids for a contract, most vertical relationships arise from preexisting connections. The elements of trust that develop through ongoing social capital connections allow these organizations to maintain contracting relationships despite differences in philosophy, service-delivery strategies, or communities served. Despite differences in power dynamics and authority between dominant and subordinate partners, these organizations maintain reciprocal relationships in which each benefits from the other. The three service-delivery systems described below respond to the power dynamics at play in a particular city.

Organizations simultaneously participate in network associations. Partnerships based on network associations rely much more strongly on trust-based social capital than on vertical contracting relationships. Organizations choose to work together based on similar goals, values, and established trust-based relationships. The official welfare-reform systems and ancillary services systems maintain communication among service providers through a series of network organizations. Community-based organizations are linked to one another through common involvement in the same communities in themselves. As described in chapter 12, staff participate in a variety of groups that cross between systems through their work and personal interests. These informal connections sometimes lead to collaborations among organizations in the three different systems.

Service-Delivery Systems

I next outline the social welfare systems developed in Kenosha, Milwaukee, and Philadelphia to serve local families (figure 5.1). The three systems function

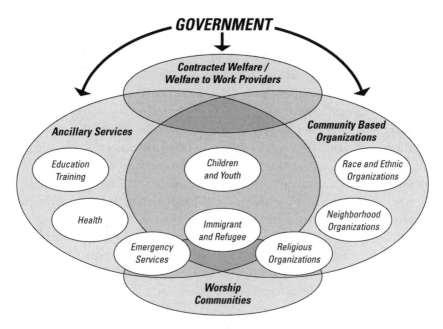

Figure 5.1. Interaction among the four systems.

independently of one another but simultaneously depend on services provided in each system to successfully carry out their work. Social capital links based on vertical and network organizations foster relationships that enable holistic service provision in these three localities. As discussed in more detail in chapters 9 and 10, organizations that are not able to develop connections with organizations providing complementary services either among themselves or for their program participants prove far less successful in helping families meet their needs.

The *official welfare-reform system* refers to government and agencies that provide TANF services through government contracts or with significant government oversight. The *ancillary services system* includes a wide array of programs that people need on a regular basis but in which the role of government varies. These include housing development and subsidized housing, education and training, health care, child care, recreational and enrichment programs for children and youth, adjustment services for immigrants and refugees (for example, ESL classes, employment assistance, and housing assistance), and emergency services. Emergency services generally refers to short-term assistance with such needs as food, clothing, household goods, furniture, temporary shelter, disaster relief, material goods for impoverished families, and special holiday packages of food or gifts for the needy.

The ancillary services system consists of several separate systems focused on a particular need such as housing, health care, and emergency services. Often agencies focused on one need have limited connections to organizations providing another kind of service. This silo style of service provision, which pervades throughout the United States, developed out of the history of service development for each need, the nature of funding systems, and long-established connections among agencies providing similar services.

Although the ancillary services system and the government-dominated system may provide some similar services, ancillary services organizations have more freedom to set program direction. For example, training providers functioning outside the welfare-to-work system have much more control over program design than those contracted to meet TANF goals. Many ancillary services organizations do receive government funds, but, as with the student grants and loans that fund Bakers, government has less control over outcomes and process.

The *community-based system* exists alongside the ancillary services and government-dominated systems. This system includes organizations chartered to serve a particular geographical area such as a neighborhood or people from a specific race/ethnicity/nationality or religion. Types of organizations include ethnic clubs, arts organizations oriented toward a particular group or neighborhood, and community-based political associations, as well as social service organizations, housing organizations, schools, and health facilities for that community.

Often, the services offered by the community-based system echo those in the ancillary services system. For example, both the community-based and ancillary services systems in Kenosha include emergency services: whereas Sunrise serves anyone in the community needing assistance, Latinos United provides food and clothing to the Latino population. In some cases, marginalized communities create separate, parallel institutions to maintain culturally appropriate services or because they think their members will not receive adequate services in citywide institutions.

Faith communities make up the fourth system, which consists primarily of houses of worship and other religious institutions such as an archdiocese or denominational conference. This system also includes institutions founded to assist people from that religion in spiritual development or their relationship to the wider society, including educational institutions and religious-based lobbying organizations.

These four systems interlock in significant ways. For example, faith communities overlap with the emergency-services organizations founded by religious communities or relying on congregational volunteers to provide service. For example, Sunrise was founded by women involved in an elite church and depends heavily on faith-community volunteers to carry out its work. As an emergency-services organization that also provides transitional housing and other social services, it belongs to ancillary services system networks for emergency services, housing, and youth services. It also has strong ties to government, particularly to obtain TANF, Medicaid, food stamps, and child-care services for its program participants.

OFFICIAL WELFARE-REFORM SYSTEMS

The different contracting strategies in Pennsylvania and Wisconsin influenced vertical relationships between each state and the agencies contracted to offer TANF services. State service-delivery strategies also influenced relationships among organizations involved in welfare reform in each locality. In Wisconsin, contracting is handled geographically, with one institution serving as the primary agent for the state in a particular locality.

Kenosha   In Kenosha, a local government agency is officially the prime contractor, but in fact the Kenosha County Job Center that implemented welfare reform was a coalition of for-profit, nonprofit, and government agencies working together from 1990 through 1999. In 2000, the Kenosha program returned to government control with significant participation from nonprofit and for-profit contractors previously involved in the coalition umbrella agency. At its peak, this coalition included nineteen agencies colocated at the Kenosha County Job Center site. Kenosha was a prime model for the one-stop shop envisioned in the TANF and WIA legislation. In many cases, these organizations worked directly together to provide services in a unitary system.

Other organizations, located both inside and outside the Kenosha County Job Center building, had contracts to provide specific services that related to the employment, training, and social support needs of Kenosha residents, functioning in vertical relationships with the job center's management. These contracts included funding for housing assistance, energy assistance, support for survivors of domestic violence, education and training, and child care. Still others simply rented space at the job center. The management structure and some services were provided by a for-profit organization. This model combined a unitary governance structure for core organizations providing services directly related to the W-2 contract with a federative model for organizations providing more peripheral services. Social capital was cemented by formal contracts and maintained through ongoing working relationships.

This model created an extremely effective program that quickly responded to the needs of individual participants through established connections among providers. For example, at Sunrise, the homeless shelter, a resident who was also enrolled in W-2 had an infant who needed specialized health care not available through her Medicaid HMO provider. Social service staff at the shelter quickly called a W-2 agency supervisor, who negotiated a specialist referral to a Milwaukee hospital. Like the nonprofit homeless-shelter caseworker working with the W-2 agency supervisor, the W-2 agency drew on community social capital to provide support through these ancillary agencies, which in turn enhanced its program's effectiveness. The W-2 agency also established networks with employers.

Kenosha focuses on local control, preferring locally established organizations to institutions with roots outside the community.[1] Most Kenosha residents practice closed social capital and expect their institutions to follow suit. Many of the organizations in the Kenosha County Job Center were locally based and had long-established ties to the Kenosha business and social service communities. Although several of the major partners in the job center's coalition were institutions established in other localities, most had developed strong roots in Kenosha through activities in the community or had hired key employees from the community. That said, the most active participants in this innovative model were outsiders brought in by government officials with more cosmopolitan roots during an administration that stressed private–public partnerships. Even though these newcomers were able to develop bridging social capital among some parts of the Kenosha elite, these ties did not last long when the county government changed back to an administration that favored government administration of local services. In less than a year, government control over these programs was reestablished and people with stronger links to Kenosha's closed social capital networks were put in control of these institutions. Contracts with outsider organizations were not renewed.

Milwaukee   The Milwaukee system maintains the geographical focus established by the state, but the city is divided into six regions with five nongovernmental agencies as prime contractors. These agencies included one nationally based for-profit organization, three locally based nonprofits, and one for-profit subsidiary of a locally based nonprofit organization. These organizations function in a federative relationship with government. All the nonprofits that served as prime contractors were local affiliates of national nonprofit institutions.[2] As described in chapter 1, they worked together in attempts to influence W-2 implementation in the city.

The national for-profit organization, JOBS INC, quickly attempted to establish local ties by hiring its key employees from among its local competitors. For a short time, this created a spate of employee raiding as other organizations followed suit when hiring new staff for these larger programs. JOBS INC was blamed for this situation, causing friction with Milwaukee's social service community. Relying on employees with established social capital, JOBS INC proceeded to develop networks to other social service providers and the advocacy community. Although it does not enjoy the same close relationship with other citywide social service agencies that many of the more established Milwaukee providers have, JOBS INC has moved beyond the bad press created by its hiring practices and begun to develop local social capital.

Milwaukee County received the contract to provide child care, food stamps, and determination of medical assistance eligibility. County government assigned employees to work at the prime contractors' regionally based facilities, and these lead agencies negotiated with county government regarding staffing, worker behavior, and other issues. While county workers were located at each of the W-2 agency sites, most of them looked to their county supervisors for authority. This created a management problem for the W-2 agencies, which were ultimately responsible for service provision in their offices regardless of who provided service. State administrators acknowledged that the county and the W-2 agencies never resolved their differences. The Milwaukee Private Industry Council also had a technical service contract to support and evaluate the prime contractors and other organizations that subcontracted with them.

W-2 agencies related to ancillary service agencies that provided child care, training, housing, food, substance-abuse programs, and other services work through a combination of formal subcontracts and informal relationships. For example, Community Solutions relied partly on its subcontracts with Neighborhood Settlement House and Empowerment Education to provide child care, GED, and computer training for its participants. Community Solutions staff also referred their program participants to other providers for these ancillary services.

Philadelphia   In Philadelphia, the commonwealth program splits authority for implementing its TANF plan between the county government agency and social service organizations contracted to provide specific RESET-related services. Both local government and social service agency providers functioned in separate vertical relationships with the commonwealth's Department of Public Welfare. For county government, this relationship resembled a unitary structure whereas contracted social service agencies maintained more of a federative structure. However, county government has input into commonwealth decisions because local representatives participate in Department of Public Welfare–sponsored conversations among local offices of the department about W-2 implementation, developing strong ties between county and commonwealth government officials. As trust developed between conservative, government-appointed Department of Public Welfare administrators and the department's local civil servants, the administrators began to listen more closely to advice from career civil servants in the local offices. As one government employee commented: "In fact, I tease some of our current leaders, 'I told you the civil service gets you all when you get over here. We convert you all because you're all sounding more progressive than I ever thought they'd be.'"

Philadelphia County government is responsible for creating individual TANF plans and providing cash assistance, Medicaid, food stamps, child-care vouchers, and the various other forms of in-kind and cash assistance that government had provided under AFDC. County government also assigns program participants to contracted nongovernmental organizations that provide the work-related services mandated by the RESET program.

Job readiness, placement, work experience, retention, and related services in the RESET program are supplied by a mix of nonprofit, quasi-governmental, and for-profit providers. Since the priorities of the Pennsylvania program have shifted over time to address unexpected developments, the numbers of state government initiatives and contractors have gradually increased. In 1996, the commonwealth funded twelve contracts to ten nongovernmental organizations to provide welfare services through five programs. The majority of these agencies ran UPFRONT programs, the precursor to RESET. In 2001, the Commonwealth funded fifty-seven contracts to thirty-four agencies to provide services under 10 separate program initiatives. Newer contracts were given to more community-based institutions, faith-based agencies, and churches focused on outreach, job-retention, and advancement services.[3]

As in Milwaukee, the Philadelphia nongovernmental welfare system followed national trends by experimenting with contracts with nationally recognized for-profit providers. Two national chains received contracts—the first agency was funded from 1997 though 2000, and the second received its first contract in 2001.

In addition, FUTURE, a smaller national for-profit organization, contributed to development of the Pennsylvania TANF plan through communications with the state administrator. The agency had garnered a good reputation with the Department of Public Welfare by providing quality service in one state region. Established ties with the department facilitated its first contract in Philadelphia. This organization has continually had contracts in Philadelphia since the beginning of the UPFRONT initiative. FUTURE sought to establish local connections by subcontracting with local institutions; although it brought in key employees from its main office, it quickly subcontracted with Citizens United to carry out its program with hard-to-reach populations. It has also established ties with local government.

As in Milwaukee, state government preferred to give contracts to agencies with preexisting social capital connections. Most of the organizations that received contracts had long-established relationships with the Department of Public Welfare or were well-known subcontractors, through the Philadelphia PIC, for providing employment and training services. These organizations included a mix of local nonprofits and for-profits of various sizes. Again as in Milwaukee, social capital held as the same organizations continued to received contracts.

As the number of contracts proliferated, the commonwealth reached out to several types of service providers. The majority of these institutions also had well-established relationships with the state to provide contracts under other Department of Public Welfare initiatives. For example, seeking to better reach communities of immigrants and native-born people of color to improve retention and advancement, the commonwealth gave contracts to several organizations that had previously provided government-funded services for refugee resettlement or services to nonspeakers of English. To better reach public housing residents, the commonwealth also contracted with the local Public Housing Authority, another governmental agency with a long-standing relationship with the Department of Public Welfare. Finally, a few newcomers also received contracts. The majority of the new agencies were faith-based initiatives associated with churches.[4]

Common Strategies   These three systems show ongoing social capital relationships between government and social service agencies at both the state and local levels. Although social capital between county government and social service agencies existed in all three localities, this relationship was not always smooth. In Philadelphia and Kenosha, county government actively worked with social service agencies by seeking them out as partners, sponsoring coalition activities to discuss TANF-related issues, and maintaining staff dedicated to relationships with local organizations. The Milwaukee county agency put less effort into fostering trust with social service agencies; as a result, service-provision relationships between the county and the W-2 agencies were strained.

Even though social service agencies in Kenosha and Philadelphia had more positive interactions with county government, local agencies often disagreed with the county about policy and sometimes complained about county services. As discussed in chapter 13, nonprofits contracted to provide social welfare services regularly participated in advocacy coalitions that sought to change TANF policy at both the state and local levels. Agencies were prepared to "bite the hand that fed them," precisely because they knew that established social capital would mean that they could still work with government even though they fought some policies. Agencies' administrators understood their role to be simultaneously protecting the rights of the people they served and participating in a government-funded system to provide services.

Because social capital is based on reciprocal obligations and long-established trust, agencies that foster relationships with established contracting regimes take care to maintain relationships among partners. Although state agencies had the power to enforce state guidelines and withhold funding or future contracts, this authority was used cautiously because both the state and local entities wanted to maintain generally successful contracting relationships. As a result, both governmental and nongovernmental providers on the local level responded to the state agency as federative partners even when the local TANF provider was an arm of government. State administrators in Wisconsin were less casual with a partnership approach, attempting to maintain unitary control through regulations and audits. Even so, Wisconsin's Department of Workforce Development expected local-level diversity and did not break off contracts with agencies that did not follow its dictates. The county welfare offices in both Kenosha and Milwaukee negotiated with the state to tailor their programs to fit local-level philosophies. Even though Wisconsin state government distrusted Milwaukee County's ability to successfully implement W-2 so much that it did not allow the county welfare office to apply for a W-2 contract, they maintained the relationship by giving the county contracts for W-2-related support services.

The same relationships held true for the nonprofit and for-profit organizations that provided services in all three localities. Notice that the majority of the social service agencies that received contracts had long-established ties to state government. The for-profit organizations that received contracts on an ongoing basis had social capital ties to state government through participation in policy development at the state level. The national for-profit organizations in Philadelphia that did not have long-established ties with government did not continue as a service provider after one contract. When asked why this agency did not receive a second contract, a state administrator explained that it "either did not bid or lost; it is possible for the big guys to lose and they do."

The agencies that successfully maintained contracting relationships with government also developed social capital at the local level that helped them do their work. The established agencies had already developed strong relationships among themselves through network organizations. They also had relationships with organizations providing ancillary services throughout the city. The successful newcomers to TANF provision quickly developed local-level partnerships in order to achieve their goals.

In all three localities, the organizations with state contracts to provide welfare services also link to other organizations to successfully fulfill their contracts. The nature of these relationships varies. In some cases, the prime contractor integrates the subcontracting organization into its service-provision structure in a unitary system. For example, FUTURE contracted with Citizens United to provide community service placements and to utilize Citizens United's established rapport with several hard-to-reach populations. Although part of this contract involved using Citizens United's already-established neighborhood-based programs to provide service, FUTURE also trained the subcontractor's front-line welfare-to-work employees to offer its regular programs. Much of the subcontract funding covered the use of Citizens United's staff to supplement employees hired by the parent organization.

As with Neighborhood Settlement House, in some cases, these relationships are formal subcontracts to provide related services using a federative model. Neighborhood Settlement House offered space to Community Solutions, its W-2 prime contractor. It also ran a program on site that provided community-service job placements in other agency programs to Community Solutions participants.

Some Community Solutions participants were also assigned to Neighborhood Settlement House's ABE/GED program to fulfill part of their employment-development plan. In addition, Community Solutions expected that this subcontract relationship would facilitate referrals to ancillary services that Neighborhood Settlement House offered, including day care, youth programs, child welfare, the food pantry, and the health clinic. In this way, the formal connections led to more informal social capital resources through ancillary services provided by the agency. Similar patterns were evident in Kenosha, where many of the organizations colocated at the Kenosha County Job Center provided services through the official welfare-reform system and others offered ancillary services through referrals from the agencies that were part of the W-2 contract. In all three localities, these formal relationships relied on ongoing referrals to the second system supporting families, that is, agencies offering ancillary services.

ANCILLARY SERVICES SYSTEM

The official welfare-reform system in each city is relatively easily described, but the network of social service organizations providing ancillary services is far more diffuse. This section briefly outlines the types of services necessary to support needy families and the connections among organizations that provide those services.

Families have diverse needs, and they may go to many types of organizations to fill them. A short list includes such basic necessities as food, shelter, clothing, and medical care; child care and programs for youth; nursing homes and elder-care programs; adult education and advancement programs through colleges and other post-secondary-education programs; assistance with mental health and substance abuse through programs or private counseling; and social/recreational enrichment through social clubs, hobbies, and other activities. A wide range of institutions offer these kinds of services. Many are provided both through citywide social service organizations and community-based institutions, particularly programs for children and social/recreational organizations.

Each city had a network of providers for key services that were known to official welfare agencies and to one another. I include in this system agencies that provide food, clothing, shelter, job training, substance-abuse programs, health and mental health care, elder care, and child care and youth programs. These services fall into four categories: 1) emergency services, 2) health care, including mental health and substance-abuse services, 3) advancement programs through education and training, and 4) family caregiving organizations (elder care, child care, and youth programs). In most cases, organizations that provided a particular service were connected in network relationships. For example, all the food pantries in Kenosha participated in ongoing meetings, developed formal agreements about the number of times families were allowed assistance, and kept track of which families each agency had served that month to prevent families from using up too much of what was viewed as a limited food supply. Likewise, training providers in Philadelphia participated in a series of ongoing coalitions sponsored by the PIC, other provider institutions, and professional associations. In Milwaukee, all the ABE/GED programs met in a coalition established by Community Solutions. Smaller child-care and youth programs were least likely to participate in coalition activities.

Network relationships drew together organizations primarily by the type of service rather than the overall mission of the agency. Multiservice organizations such as Neighborhood Settlement House often participated in several service-based networks. In this case, key staff members for that program represented the agency in a particular network. For example, Faith in Action provides employment and training services at several facilities throughout Philadelphia. One of its programs is a proprietary training school, and key staff members for this program are active members in the statewide trade-school association. Other employees participate in coalitions for refugee resettlement, welfare-to-work, adult basic education, and other services. Faith-related organizations also participated in coalitions associated with that faith, including activities sponsored by faith-based funding or administrative bodies such as Jewish Federation.

These network relationships fostered closed social capital among organizations that led to a variety of formal and informal relationships. The nature of the relationships within these different provider networks varied enormously. On the one hand, networks may lead to such formal collaborations as in submitting joint contracts to a government or nonprofit funders. For example, Neighborhood Settlement House went in on a joint contract with two other agencies to provide government-funded child-welfare services established by the state for the region covered by this particular contract. Coalitions developed advocacy and best-practices models together. Sometimes organizations learned of complementary programs and used this information to better serve their clients.

When an organization's participants regularly needed services that it did not offer, it might develop bridging social capital networks of organizations that did provide those services. For example, Quaker Residence, a housing program in Philadelphia that served both low-income people and the elderly, developed social capital links with social service organizations offering food, employment assistance, budgeting, energy assistance, substance-abuse programs, elder care, child care, and a range of other services as well as with the government agencies that provided services to its program participants.

In most cases, these social capital links developed more informally than the coalition activities among organizations with similar programs. Agencies developed social capital resources through word of mouth among agencies, formal connections to other organizations through previously developed affiliations, and interlocking board appointments, and by using formal directories created by either umbrella institutions such as the United Way or service-specific coalitions. For example, Quaker Residence was originally an offshoot of Quaker House. The executive directors of the two organizations belonged to each other's boards, and staff made referrals to the other organization as appropriate. Both Quaker House and Quaker Residence participated in programs offered through Citizens United. These formal relationships stemmed from previous links among key staff developed through prior employment relationships and participation in the same Friends' Meeting. Key staff of these three organizations often saw one another in network activities associated with a particular service offered at the organization, political activities, or other social arenas throughout the city. As program staff at one organization learned about the wider activities of the other, they were able to provide information and trust-based referrals to other staff in their employing institution. Staff at each organization also used these same bridging social capital links when looking for referrals to organizations that provided services needed by the organization or its participants. Since each of these three organizations participated in a variety of similar networks based on earlier closed social capital connections, the bridging social capital of each institutions could potentially expand exponentially.

Summary   Ancillary services systems often relied on government funding and were organized into networks based on the regulations and contracting issues governing each type of service. This silo approach to serving families meant that organizations developed social capital relationships with organizations providing similar services more easily than with those offering the range of programs families needed to meet their goals. Organizations with holistic service-provision philosophies developed social capital relationships with providers offering services regularly needed by their program participants in an idiosyncratic fashion. TANF contractors developed relationships with organizations in the ancillary services networks in the same way.

Program participants served by organizations that did not provide information and referral for needed services found themselves negotiating the same fragmented system. Sometimes government or private agency referral systems helped families find sources for assistance. More often, families relied on information provided through social capital links in their local communities.

Agencies in the ancillary services system included both citywide and community-based organizations. However, community-based organizations did not always participate in citywide networks. In addition, community-based systems were more likely to be linked to one another regardless of the kind of service provided because of common cultural and social capital networks within each community.

COMMUNITY-BASED SYSTEMS

Community-based organizations are developed for communities in themselves (Milofsky and Hunter 1995). They range in form from informal neighborhood clubs, church programs, and volunteer-based groups (for example, Girl Scout troops) to 501c3 agencies offering specific services. Often, formal and informal groups had strong connections with each other. For example, neighborhood churches and nonprofits, working together, may be instrumental in founding town-watch or antidrug activities. In some cases, formal social service agencies were well aware of voluntary associations. In other instances, formal agencies did not know about, or discounted, local resources. The more effective social welfare institutions looked for this array of community-based supports as a resource for their program participants. For example, Neighborhood Settlement House actively recruited Girl and Boy Scout troops to use their facilities. These local informal organizations complemented their after-school youth programs.

Systems of community-based organizations tend to relate to other organizations focused on the same community. Unlike the formalized coalitions among organizations contracted to provide welfare services and those providing ancillary services, the nature of social capital ties among community-based organizations varied enormously. On the one extreme, one neighborhood in Philadelphia included a dense web of organizations that worked together to develop antidrug initiatives, empowerment-zone-related initiatives, and other efforts to improve their community. The closed social capital networks among coalitions worked to develop joint proposals and new organizations and to lobby government for better services in their neighborhood. Since some of these organizations had strong bridging ties through citywide network associations, they were able to use bridging social capital to bring resources like the empowerment zone to their community.

Despite this seemingly close relationship among local groups, some organizations in that neighborhood did not collaborate with others. One organization had bridging social capital ties throughout the city and closed social capital ties to an ethnic community but did not develop social capital connections with other neighborhood-based organizations. In larger initiatives, this organization was an important player because of the citywide ties, but it was not trusted by all the neighborhood-based organizations.

At the other extreme, Neighborhood Settlement House is the only social service agency located in its Milwaukee neighborhood. It has fostered federative relationships with a businessmen's association that members of its staff were instrumental in developing, and it supports a network of home-based day-care providers that are linked through a unitary system to its government-funded day-care program. The settlement house also developed federative social capital relationships with the police, the Housing Authority tenants' group and staff for the housing project that is their core constituency, and many of the public schools in its community. They also have a limited relationship with the church on the other side of the housing project through a rental agreement for one of the church's buildings.

However, Neighborhood Settlement House took deliberate action to keep other social service organizations out of its geographical area. For example, during the study period, organization staff tried to develop a government initiative that stretched its mission and resources because they were afraid that a national organization offering similar services would come into the neighborhood. Other organizations view them as competitive, and staff members at Neighborhood Settlement House sometimes disparage the commitment of other organizations to the community. For example, one key employee commented that the church had "finally discovered" the housing project when they started developing events for residents. In this case, social capital ties among community-based organizations are limited.

Relationships among Kenosha's organizations serving communities of color represent the middle alternative to these two extreme examples. This small city had three social service organizations serving the Latino community and four organizations serving the African American community. These organizations worked together through informal ties developed through long-standing relationships. They represented two separate closed social capital networks based on race/ethnicity/nationality connected through bridging social capital ties. The staffs often spoke to one another, but these organizations rarely developed joint projects.

However, they would often refer people either to agencies in their own racial/ethnic/national community or to another organization based in a community of color. For example, when one Latino organization lost an outreach worker who spoke Spanish, they started referring more of their cases to another Latino organization that provided translation services. This situation strained the resources of the second organization, causing some stress on otherwise strong social capital relationships between these two organizations.

Community-based systems are most likely to develop ties to churches associated with the same community. For example, as with Sunrise, religious bodies are often instrumental in starting organizations. In other cases, clergy serve on nonprofit-agency boards. Sometimes churches and nonprofit organizations develop projects or activities together.

Community-based systems are linked to the two citywide systems discussed above through bridging social capital ties among organizations that have links in several closed social capital systems. For example, Community Solutions is an agency created for a community in themselves that participates in both the official welfare system and the ancillary services system. It brings in organizations associated with its racial community when developing its citywide service-delivery systems.

However, agencies that have not developed social capital ties beyond their community seldom have any direct agency links outside that local community. For example, the housing-project tenants' group that is part of the Neighborhood Settlement House network may have links to local churches and agencies in race-based communities in other parts of the city, but it has no social capital ties to social service agency networks outside these two communities.

Just as community-based systems include the widest range of organizational forms, their relationship with other systems throughout the city varies widely. That said, these community systems are often important links to more formal systems because people share information in the closed social capital networks of these institutions. They are also the places to which people are most likely to turn for help first. They represent a critical component of each community's social welfare system.

COMPARISONS ACROSS STATES AND CITIES

Comparing these three localities shows that state policies have limited influence in local systems. Wisconsin's geographical focus for its contracting system leads to more hierarchical relationships among local organizations than in Philadelphia, where organizations contract independently with the state. However, the same networks of organizations connected through the official welfare system, ancillary social services system, and community-based system exist in all three localities. Relationships among organizations in each place are very similar.

Comparisons show both the similarities and the differences among organization networks are related to city size. The official welfare system and the ancillary services system work the same way in all three localities. In the two big cities, connections between the two citywide systems and the community-based systems are far more fragmented because each locality has many more communities. For example, a citywide organization may associate only with community-based institutions in the neighborhoods where it is located or with the major populations that use its services. Neighborhood- and community-based systems are unlikely to connect with one another, and race/ethnicity/nationality-based communities are internally fragmented.

Systems in the two big cities are nearly identical, but Kenosha's systems have some significant differences. For example, it has very few neighborhood-based systems. Since the total number of social service agencies is limited, community-based organizations are much more likely to participate in either the formal welfare system or the ancillary services network through contracts with government. Likewise, Kenosha elites from communities in themselves are more likely to have developed bridging social capital into citywide networks than in the larger cities.

Although class, religious, and political factions exist within race/ethnicity- and community-based systems in Kenosha, people who differ in terms of culture, class, or philosophy are more likely to belong to the same closed social capital networks and work together (albeit usually in a limited way) than in the larger city. For example, although Kenosha's African American elites are reluctant to help Pastor Rice develop Share the Wealth, they still refer program participants to his programs and help him in other ways. Likewise, Pastor Rice is more likely to turn to other organizations within the community of color than to outsiders when seeking resources for his organizations or his constituents. In this instance, social capital ties may be attenuated, but they still exist within the broader community-based networks. In Philadelphia or Milwaukee, a Pastor Rice would be far less likely to have any functional ties among institutions outside his closed social capital networks. The small size and smaller population base mean that less fragmentation is possible in a small-town model than in a large city.

POLICY AND PROGRAMMATIC IMPLICATIONS

Organizations contracted to provide TANF-related services rely on services provided by agencies in the ancillary and community-based systems to fulfill their contracts. However, the fragmented system of social services in the United States has fostered a situation that encourages organizations to develop strong ties with organizations like themselves rather than with those offering complementary services. The following policy and programmatic suggestions are aimed at remedying this problem:

- Develop communication mechanisms to encourage partnerships among agencies providing complementary services, such as where-to-turn guides, events for organizations offering a range of services, and community-based and citywide coalitions of agencies providing complementary services.

- Include funds in government contracts to help agencies providing complementary services work with TANF service providers. Funding would cover such unreimbursed costs as additional outreach materials across agencies, staff to jointly case-manage families needing services from multiple agencies, and ancillary agency programs tailored to meet the needs of families in welfare-to-work programs.
- Provide supplementary funding and additional contracts to agencies in the ancillary agency and community-based networks to cover the expense of additional services needed because of TANF. Bischoff and Reisch (2000) and Abramovitz (2001) describe new burdens imposed by welfare reform on organizations providing ancillary services and community-based institutions. Government should cover the costs of meeting the needs caused by these policy changes.
- Encourage social service delivery strategies that serve families holistically and cross among these three service provision systems.

SUMMARY

The social welfare service-delivery system consists of both horizontal and vertical systems. Vertical relationships between state government and local service-delivery systems create social capital linkages among state government, local government, and social service agencies providing an array of services. The official welfare-reform system is one example of a vertical system. Similar systems exist to provide an array of services, including training, child welfare, and health care.

As with the official welfare reform system, the social service agencies in the system also develop social capital relationships with local government. In some cases, as in Kenosha, connections with local government also involve vertical relationships through contracting. In other cases, as in Milwaukee, relationships between social service agencies and local government are on an equal level. In Philadelphia, government and social service agency relationships involve both network and vertical ties. Maintaining relationships between local government and social service agencies when government and social service agencies are on an equal footing depends on social capital trust.

The agencies involved in each vertical system develop social capital ties among agencies providing similar services. These network organizations help local agencies influence policy and develop service-delivery models appropriate at the local level. Through working together on a variety of initiatives over time, these social service agencies become part of the service-delivery system in a community.

Although only some agencies are involved in offering TANF-related services, these organizations depend on services provided by an array of other organizations. These services are provided by organizations in the ancillary services and community-based systems. Organizations in the ancillary services system develop network organizations with agencies providing similar services, whereas those in community-based systems relate to other agencies serving the same community. The community-based system is much more diverse than the other two systems, encompassing informal voluntary programs as well as formally incorporated entities.

To meet the needs of their program participants, organizations develop social capital ties among these three systems and with organizations offering different services within the same system. However, unlike the formalized coalitions of organizations providing similar services, these connections develop in a much more idiosyncratic way. The ties among organizations providing complementary services often stem from informal relationships among staffs or word-of-mouth referral among agencies through their network associations. In many ways, the networks of similar organizations function as closed social capital networks that develop bridging social capital with organizations providing different kinds of services. Social service agencies and government must also relate to employers to fulfill the welfare-reform goal of moving adult welfare recipients into jobs. The next chapter looks at the labor market in these three cities.

CHAPTER 6

Labor Markets and Individual Career Paths

Jaysa was raised in a close African American neighborhood in Milwaukee. Her father worked full time at a large, unionized factory while her mother cared for the children. Jaysa completed high school, but she had never worked before she began volunteering at the nonprofit agency that hired her as a day care worker.

Jeff is a white man in his early thirties from Philadelphia. Both of his parents completed high school and served on the Philadelphia police force. After high school, Jeff worked at a casino and in construction before spending four years in the Air Force. He received one year of technical college training while in the military. He and his wife returned to Philadelphia after he had completed his military service. He worked in a series of skilled technical jobs: reengineering, maintaining dialysis machines, and installing surveillance cameras in stores. These jobs always ended because companies lost contracts or went out of business. In 1994, Jeff ran through his unemployment compensation and applied for welfare. He sent out around 70 résumés but could not find a job.

Xavier and Maria are middle-aged Texas-Mexicans, U.S. citizens raised speaking Spanish. Their parents were migrant workers on the Texas–Mexico border. Xavier was encouraged to attend technical college in Kenosha through a nonprofit organization for migrants.[1] He attended for one year but was then recruited to work in a factory via the same organization. Since then, he has worked steadily in various factories in Kenosha. Maria obtained a secretarial certificate and completed three years of college before quitting to get married. She worked for Latino nonprofit organizations for several years before getting a job at the local electric company, where she still works.

Tracing family life histories reveals an intertwining of community labor-market history, individual stories, and social capital connections through organizations and individuals. Individual stories are important because they show the impact on family economic strategies of macro-level factors such as economic and policy changes. The parents in each of these families found work through relatives and friends. Jaysa's and Jeff's parents belong to the stable working class, employed in factories and government. Both Jaysa and Jeff were in their early thirties when interviewed. Unlike their parents, they entered a changing labor market with more service-sector jobs. Xavier and Maria are nearly a generation older. They came to Wisconsin as the Kenosha economy was expanding, finding stable work in factories and the service sector.

Family histories like these show that children have employment trajectories different from those of their parents as labor markets change. To account for the kinds of jobs available to families, this chapter examines the labor markets that shape individual opportunities and strategies for welfare-to-work programs in these three communities, the fourth factor influencing policy outcomes in a given community. The chapter addresses four questions:

1. What are the historical labor-market conditions in Philadelphia, Kenosha, and Milwaukee?
2. How do historic trends influence present-day opportunities for individuals?
3. What kinds of jobs are currently available to individuals in these three communities?
4. What skills are required for these jobs, and what pay and benefits do they offer?

History of Local Labor Markets

Philadelphia, Milwaukee, and Kenosha are northern industrial cities that have transitioned to a mixed, primarily service-sector economy. All three cities have experienced deindustrialization and economic restructuring since the 1950s. The theory of segmented labor markets posits that two separate employment sectors exist. Primary-sector firms are large, unionized workplaces that have formal hiring practices. The traditional labor force for these firms was white men, but they have become more diverse since affirmative action. These firms have clearly established human resources practices, and most jobs require specific education, skills, and work experience. Through a process of globalization, large companies have spread their production process over a number of countries. Globalization has resulted in the departure of many of these large firms to other countries to avoid providing union wages and working conditions.

The secondary sector includes all other types of employer. Businesses are smaller and more likely to fail. Hiring practices are less formal, wages often lower, and working conditions sometimes more exploitative. The majority of women and people of color are employed in this sector. Many low-income people cannot compete in the primary sector because they lack the social networks or formal credentials required to gain entry (Gordon et al. 1982).

Echoing national trends, primary-sector manufacturing plants moved from the northern center cities to the suburbs, other parts of the country, and overseas. In all three cities, the primary-sector manufacturing economy was replaced with a mix of secondary-sector manufacturing and both primary- and secondary-sector service employment (Adams et al. 1991; Summers and Luce 1988; Jargowsky 1996; Squires 1994). In Milwaukee and Philadelphia, deindustrialization led to long periods of limited employment and slow growth in new economic sectors. Deindustrialization was also coupled with suburbanization as both service-sector and manufacturing jobs moved to increasingly populated edge cities in the surrounding areas.

Deindustrialization meant that many of the large corporations of the kind that employed Jaysa's father have left the area. Smaller factories remain, but more jobs are service employment like Maria's job at the electric company or Jeff's position as a mechanic servicing machines used in hospitals and in the retail trade. Services like the day-care center that employs Jaysa are also expanding. The three cities went through major transitions at different times, with the two large cities losing their industrial base earlier than Kenosha. Whereas Milwaukee and Philadelphia suffer from competition from nearby suburbs, Kenosha has benefited from similar trends as an outer-ring suburb of Chicago. The three communities represent common patterns in similar localities throughout the United States. I first provide a brief economic history of each city.

PHILADELPHIA

Like many older industrial cities, the Philadelphia economy was in steady decline from the 1950s to the mid-1990s. Much of the job loss involved the movement of manufacturing jobs to the South and overseas. This is a national trend (Wilson 1996:25–34). Between 1988 and 1996, the city lost nearly 100,000 jobs at an average of more than 10,000 per year (*Philadelphia Inquirer*, March 1996:A1). Philadelphia was hit particularly hard by the recession in the early 1990s. Between 1989 and 1993, the proportion of Philadelphians in poverty climbed from 20 percent to 27 percent. Economic insecurity created the paucity of employment faced by people like Jeff a year later. Businesses also moved to the suburbs. In 1970 the city provided 50 percent of the regional employment; by 1986 this had fallen to 35 percent (Goode and Schneider 1994:34).

Economic restructuring also involved shifts from manufacturing to a service economy. In 1994, 75 percent of Philadelphians worked in this sector (Goode and Schneider 1994:35). Some service-sector employment, such as

large insurance agencies, provided stable opportunities. However, service-sector employment also often meant more unstable workplaces, lower wages, and fewer benefits, as it did for Jeff (Gordon et al. 1982). The loss of manufacturing jobs was offset by increases in higher-skilled service-sector jobs. *The Philadelphia Inquirer* (March 19, 1997:A1, A12) reported that, although the city's employment levels remained steady for the first time in nearly a decade, 5,000 jobs were lost in government, finance, and manufacturing; the gains were in health care and other service industries.

The Philadelphia economy began to turn around in the late 1990s. By 2000, the city had gained approximately 25,000 jobs. Most city jobs were in services and retail trade. Employment prospects in the larger region had improved even more. Between 1995 and 2000, the Pennsylvania portion of the Philadelphia metropolitan statistical area, which includes several surrounding counties, had gained nearly 159,000 jobs. Only 17 percent were in manufacturing and construction; 60 percent were in retail trade, service, and service-related occupations in finance, insurance, and real estate.[2]

Philadelphia's employment history portrays an industrial city that lost significant employment to the globalization of industry. While high technology and manufacturing developed in the suburbs, the city was slow to develop a new economic base. This meant that many stable manufacturing neighborhoods were left without their expected employment base. The service-sector economy that replaced manufacturing offers different opportunities, has a different wage structure, and requires different skills.

MILWAUKEE

Milwaukee is a much younger city, but it followed an economic track similar to Philadelphia's in the twentieth century. Milwaukee developed rapidly from the mid-nineteenth century on, first as a center for grain exports and, by 1870, as a manufacturing giant. Industrial expansion continued in the first third of the twentieth century; in 1910 the city ranked tenth in the nation in value of industrial products. Local industry encompassed a mix of breweries and heavy-machinery manufacturing (Orum 1995:73). Most of the large plants were unionized, providing well-paying, stable jobs to generations of residents.

Milwaukee has always had a strong union presence, and Orum (1995:125) claims that labor unrest led to its economic downfall. The city began to lose jobs after a series of strikes in the 1950s. Poor labor relations led to plant closures as did the national deindustrialization of the Northeast and Midwest. By 1990, the proportion of manufacturing jobs in the city had fallen to 23 percent, down from 42 percent in 1950 (Orum 1995:126). As in Philadelphia, jobs migrated to the nearby suburbs, the South, and outside the United States.

Patterns of replacing manufacturing with service employment in Milwaukee echoed the Philadelphia experience. In 2000, 19 percent of Milwaukee employment consisted of manufacturing and construction jobs. Fifty-nine percent of employment consisted of jobs in service, retail, finance, insurance, and real estate. However, job growth in Milwaukee County between 1995 and 2000 netted only 5,541 jobs; the city has yet to rebound from earlier losses.[3]

Like Philadelphia, employment prospects are better in the suburbs, and many middle-class residents have left the city to live near suburban employment. The retail base in Milwaukee is not as strong as in Philadelphia, which means there are fewer entry-level jobs for younger workers or people with limited education transitioning from a manufacturing economy.

KENOSHA

Kenosha enjoyed stable employment for a much longer period than the two larger cities did. It is best described as an auto-manufacturing town that has rebounded from the loss of its major employer in the 1980s. Kenosha County also had a significant agricultural base, drawing migrants from Texas and Mexico to harvest crops on a regular basis. Although most farming has been mechanized, rural parts of the county are still agricultural. Founded in the 1830s, Kenosha became a regional manufacturing center between 1890 and

1920 (Keehn 1976:175–176). By 1920 the manufacturing base was dominated by auto manufacturing and heavy industry (Keehn 1976:180). By 1960, American Motors was the major employer (Keehn 1976:191). The major manufacturers unionized in the 1930s, and by 1963 Kenosha had the eighteenth highest family income in the United States (Buenker 1976:30).

This established employment pattern began to change in the 1980s, when AMC/Chrysler began to shut down production in Kenosha, finally closing everything in 1988 but the plant that made engines (Dudley 1994:7–17). Kenosha's unemployment rate hit its highest mark of 17.7 percent in 1983, and it remained high throughout the 1980s (KABA 1999:22). Although several large manufacturers remain, many of the primary-sector firms moved on.

However, in response to the announced plant closings, Kenosha's business and government leaders stepped in early to ensure that Kenosha did not experience high crime and poverty levels. Chrysler offered retraining and relocation packages for unemployed autoworkers; government worked with local banks to avoid home-loan defaults; and business and government together recruited small manufacturers and service employers to Kenosha. Around the same time, the outskirts of the city began to develop as a bedroom community for northern Illinois. This led to an increase in construction employment, as well as increased retail and service-sector opportunities, including an outlet mall as well as numerous small retail and service establishments to accommodate the new population. By the mid 1990s, unemployment hovered at approximately 3.5 percent (KABA 1999:22). However, many of the well-paying, unionized jobs had been replaced by ones with smaller employers offering lower wages and benefits.[4] Fully 39.5 percent of Kenosha residents commuted outside the county for work in the 1990s (KABA 1999:26).

In 2000, Kenosha's employment picture revealed a mix between manufacturing and service. Manufacturing and construction accounted for 29 percent of local jobs. Even though more jobs were in service, retail, and the combination of finance, insurance, and real estate than in other categories, they accounted for only 45 percent of county employment. Kenosha had gained fewer than 5,000 jobs from 1995 to 2000. Unemployment remained low, but the local economy expanded slowly. By 2000, Kenosha looked forward to a new Chrysler plant, which would provide more jobs offering family-supporting wages and benefits. However, this highly mechanized plant needed workers with much higher skill levels and critical thinking abilities than those of most Kenosha line workers.

As Dudley (1994) describes, Kenosha had developed a particularly strong manufacturing working-class culture based on employment at the "Motors" and similar establishments. Social life and social capital focused on the union hall, with churches providing the other major institutionalized source of social life and social capital. As both Dudley and I observed (Schneider 2001),

Kenosha's established residents tend to be anti-intellectual and approach employment with the demeanor and economic expectations of unionized employees. As in the larger cities, these workers needed to develop new human, social, and cultural capital to compete in the new economy. The close proximity to development in outer-ring Chicago meant that residents could find jobs in neighboring Illinois; however, most of these opportunities are also in the service sector.

Northward movement from Chicago brought new residents to Kenosha. These newcomers were oriented toward Illinois, and had different cultural, educational, and economic expectations. Many were middle class, working in white-collar jobs in both Kenosha and northern Illinois. With the influx of population, the labor force in Kenosha County included a greater mix of classes and abilities than in previous generations, but local residents were still transitioning from the earlier low-skilled manufacturing labor force. As I discuss in more detail elsewhere (Schneider 2001), Kenosha's residents are also insular and suspicious of outsiders. Many are not amenable to change, and economic shifts have meant great challenges for some families.

SUMMARY

Taken together, the labor-market histories for the three cities portray communities that previously had a strong manufacturing base and have shifted to a service economy with some remaining manufacturing. The imprint of the manufacturing past is strongest in the two Wisconsin cities. For example, even in service-sector jobs, workers speak of working first shift (7 A.M.–3 P.M.), second shift (3–11 P.M.), and third shift (11 P.M.–7 A.M.). Many retail and human-services employers accommodate this history by organizing work schedules to match these expectations.

All three cities contained a significant number of families with working-class skills, cultural capital, and social capital connections who now needed to develop new social, human, and cultural capital. Although ability and opportunity to develop bridging cultural capital varied widely, a greater range of possibilities existed in Philadelphia and Milwaukee than in Kenosha. Economic history sets the stage for current labor-market conditions. I now examine in more detail the labor-market opportunities currently available to families in these three cities.

CURRENT LABOR-MARKET CONDITIONS

The current labor market in all three cities reveals much more diversity than in previous decades.[5] Table 6.1 shows the average number of employees and aver-

TABLE 6.1 EMPLOYEES AND WAGES BY INDUSTRY

Industry	1995		1997		2000	
	Avg. Employees	% Employees	Avg. Salary	Avg. Employees	% Employees	Avg. Salary	Avg. Employees	% Employees	Avg. Salary

Industry	Avg. Employees	% Employees	Avg. Salary	Avg. Employees	% Employees	Avg. Salary	Avg. Employees	% Employees	Avg. Salary
Kenosha County									
All industries	47,249	100%	$23,018	47,746	100%	$25,163	50,443	100%	$29,951
All government	6,516	14%	$27,157	6,981	15%	$28,040	7,825	16%	$30,452
Private coverage	40,732	86%	$22,350	40,765	85%	$24,669	42,618	84%	$28,682
Agriculture/forestry/fishing	414	1%	$14,443	438	1%	$14,672	500	1%	$17,470
Mining	7	0%	$0	0	0%	$0	0	0%	$0
Construction	2,152	5%	$29,907	2,134	4%	$34,352	2,182	4%	$38,131
Manufacturing	10,761	23%	$35,588	11,231	24%	$38,287	12,619	25%	$43,186
Transportation/ public utilities	1,668	4%	$25,574	1,812	4%	$27,357	1,944	4%	$33,426
Wholesale trade	2,050	4%	$26,981	2,196	5%	$32,029	2,810	6%	$36,181
Retail trade	11,803	25%	$10,706	10,165	21%	$11,775	10,414	21%	$12,936
Finance/insurance/ real estate	1,587	3%	$24,049	1,622	3%	$25,009	1,394	3%	$30,057
Services	10,184	22%	$18,603	11,157	23%	$19,251	10,741	21%	$23,011

Milwaukee County

All industries	517,840	100%	$25,923	523,553	100%	$28,550	523,381	100%	$32,067
All government	58,464	11%	$30,749	57,981	11%	$32,766	60,388	12%	$36,172
Private coverage	459,35	89%	$25,296	465,572	89%	$28,014	462,993	88%	$31,554
Agriculture/forestry/fishing	1,442	0%	$17,448	1,538	0%	$1,846	1,575	0%	$20,945
Mining	37	0%	$0	0	0%	$0	0	0%	$0
Construction	12,129	2%	$31,566	12,887	2%	$35,076	12,757	2%	$38,975
Manufacturing	99,386	19%	$34,748	62,444	12%	$38,405	88,924	17%	$43,095
Transportation/ public utilities	27,690	5%	$28,272	27,837	5%	$31,084	29,201	6%	$35,196
Wholesale trade	25,815	5%	$31,839	26,256	5%	$34,846	24,834	5%	$39,801
Retail trade	85,457	17%	$12,621	84,984	16%	$13,671	78,407	15%	$15,199
Finance/insurance/ real estate	41,687	8%	$32,742	42,573	8%	$39,225	39,432	8%	$44,249
Services	165,727	32%	$22,310	173,211	33%	$24,541	187,811	36%	$28,315
Philadelphia MSA (PA only)									
All industries	1,664,022	100%	$32,196	1,728,100	100%	$34,999	1,822,983	100%	$44,182
All government	217,323	13%	N/A	208,053	12%	N/A	195,552	11%	N/A
Private coverage	1,445,792	87%	N/A	1,519,021	88%	N/A	1,607,974	88%	N/A

(continued)

TABLE 6.1 (*continued*)

Industry	1995			1997			2000		
	Avg. Employees	% Employees	Avg. Salary	Avg. Employees	% Employees	Avg. Salary	Avg. Employees	% Employees	Avg. Salary
Philadelphia MSA (PA only)									
Agriculture/forestry/fishing	13,358	1%	$19,994	14,567	1%	$21,571	17,558	1%	$25,184
Mining	N/A	0%	N/A	N/A	0%	N/A	986	0%	$54,492
Construction	55,391	3%	$36,052	62,794	4%	$39,701	74,232	4%	$44,325
Manufacturing	248,050	15%	$41,635	247,636	14%	$46,166	239,261	13%	$53,599
Transportation/ public utilities	75,143	5%	$37,596	77,258	4%	$40,352	81,869	4%	$46,592
Wholesale trade	87,655	5%	$40,429	85,892	5%	$44,332	88,665	5%	$51,034
Retail trade	271,956	16%	$16,354	282,999	16%	$17,476	300,050	16%	$19,863
Finance/insurance/ real estate	129,615	8%	$41,940	134,311	8%	$48,035	140,305	8%	$59,118
Services	564,624	34%	$30,166	613,564	36%	$32,636	665,048	36%	$37,870

Source: Pennsylvania and Wisconsin Dept. of Labor.

age wages by industry for 1995, 1997, and 2000 in the three communities. Service-sector employment provides the largest share of jobs, but employment is spread across various types of business. Proportions are similar in the two large metropolitan areas, with Kenosha showing an even greater mix of employment types. However, wages are higher in Philadelphia than in the two Wisconsin cities.[6]

Wage levels for various industries raise greater concern because many new retail and service-sector jobs offer lower wages, fewer benefits, and only part-time hours. Notice that the two largest categories—retail trade and service—pay far below family-supporting wages. Retail wages, in particular, provide less than half the median average wage in each community. In 1995, 47 percent of the jobs in Kenosha, 45 percent in Milwaukee, and 50 percent in Philadelphia fell into this category. This means that many working families—like Jaysa, earning slightly over $6 an hour in her service-sector job—cannot make ends meet even while working. The percentage of jobs in these low-paying sectors increased over time in both large cities but in Kenosha gradually fell to 42 percent. Over half the available jobs in the Milwaukee (51 percent) and Philadelphia (52 percent) regions were in these two categories in 2000.

The growth in these two lower-paying categories also suggests greater competition for better-paying jobs in the other sectors. Individuals used two strategies to get these jobs. First, people used social capital networks to find stable jobs similar to those providing family-supporting incomes in past generations. Because unionized factory employment often pays better and requires fewer skills, many people seek access to these jobs. As in Kenosha, people primarily use social capital networks to gain entry to unionized factory employment. For example, one retired union official in Kenosha reported receiving calls every day for help getting a job in the new Chrysler plant. In all three cities, social service agencies attempt to broker similar relationships by creating links between training programs and union apprenticeships.

The second avenue toward more stable work was education. Like many people in all three cities, each of the families profiled at the beginning of this chapter sought additional skills to obtain more stable employment. This plan had worked for Xavier and Maria a generation earlier but was less successful for Jeff and Jaysa in the new economy. In both cases, education led to jobs but not stable, family-supporting careers. For example, Jaysa obtained a day-care certificate as a prerequisite for employment. She plans to take additional classes to qualify as a teacher's aide in the public schools. However, neither education program is likely to raise her significantly above the poverty level because child-care positions pay poorly.

Jeff used technical training as an avenue to jobs offering family-supporting wages—most of his jobs paid between $10 and $13 an hour. However, stable employment continued to elude him because of shifts in the Philadelphia economy to a secondary-sector, service-based economy. These experiences suggest that obtaining skills alone will not necessarily lead to stable employment in a changing economy.

Table 6.2 examines available jobs by type of employment rather than industrial sector.[7] Job types cross industrial sectors, revealing a finer-grained picture of available opportunities. As in the industrial wage structure, wages in Philadelphia for each type of job were comparatively higher than in Wisconsin.[8]

The nine categories outlined in table 6.2 rearrange U.S. Department of Labor job categories to group together positions that require similar skills and pay similar wages.[9] *Professional entry-level* includes jobs such as emergency medical technician, drafter, or paralegal that require significant technical training at an associate's- or bachelor's-degree level. These jobs can serve as either a first step toward more highly trained professional employment or an end-stage career goal. They tend to pay family-supporting wages, in 2000 averaging more than $15 an hour in Wisconsin and $17 an hour in Philadelphia. Entry-level wages in Philadelphia were over $25,000 a year, and experienced workers earned an average of $40,679.

Human services front-line workers include child-care aides, nursing assistants, and similar occupations. Like Jaysa's child-care position, these jobs usually require only a short certificate training program. These jobs are considered first steps toward the more highly educated positions in the professional category of human services and education, they are equally likely to become dead ends if workers fail to obtain additional education. For example, in her study of training and employment in Philadelphia, Reimer (1997) found that women trained as nursing assistants did not have the basic education to begin training to become LPNs, physical therapists, RNs, or other more lucrative positions. At work, these women were socially isolated from the more professional workers, and developed an adversarial relationship with them because of the workplace hierarchy. She found that nursing assistants were not likely to develop the human capital to move up in the economic hierarchy. The social relations of the workplace also suggest that nursing assistants created closed social capital relationships that did not encourage the kinds of connections to more highly educated and skilled staff that could foster movement into the other group. Patterns in most surveys and life histories in my studies support the conclusion that few people move between these two categories.

However, one example detailed in an earlier Kenosha study (Schneider 2001:13) shows that encouragement from professional staff can help nursing assistants return to school for more education and movement into the professional human services jobs. Tania started out as a nursing assistant in a large hospital, where the doctors and nurses recognized her talents and encouraged

TABLE 6.2 TYPES OF EMPLOYMENT

	Philadelphia				Milwaukee				Kenosha			
	Average Hourly Wage		Percentage Employment		Average Hourly Wage		Percentage Employment		Average Hourly Wage		Percentage Employment	
Occupational title	1997	2000	1997	2000	1997	2000	1997	2000	1997	2000	1997	2000
Professional entry-level	$15.67	$17.07	4%	3%	$13.56	$15.91	4%	3%	$12.91	$15.57	3%	2%
Human services, front-line	$9.43	$9.99	4%	4%	$9.86	$9.16	4%	4%	$7.82	$8.39	3%	4%
Human services, education, professionals	$18.87	$19.44	5%	7%	$14.99	$18.61	5%	7%	$15.17	$12.15	7%	6%
Other professional, managerial	$22.69	$27.64	17%	17%	$19.71	$25.17	17%	17%	$20.12	$24.04	15%	12%
Sales and service, unskilled	$8.27	$9.36	17%	12%	$7.51	$8.78	17%	12%	$7.51	$8.36	28%	20%
Sales and service, skilled	$17.20	$18.51	5%	4%	$15.62	$17.70	5%	4%	$15.32	$17.95	6%	7%
Clerical, entry-level	$9.95	$10.27	3%	9%	$9.00	$11.03	3%	9%	$7.84	$9.51	3%	8%
Clerical, skilled	$12.36	$14.47	14%	16%	$11.56	$15.36	14%	16%	$11.11	$12.87	14%	14%
Blue-collar, skilled	$16.00	$18.63	17%	13%	$14.85	$17.87	17%	13%	$15.15	$18.93	10%	13%
Blue-collar, unskilled	$11.36	$12.41	15%	15%	$12.84	$12.84	15%	15%	$9.48	$11.71	13%	13%

Source: Pennsylvania and Wisconsin Dept. of Labor.

her to continue her education. Through ongoing mentoring and financial support from her workplace, she became an RN and moved into a career as a bilingual nurse educator. Research in Philadelphia yielded similar stories among rising middle-class families.

The *human services and education professional* category includes jobs such as nurse, teacher, and social worker that require at least a bachelor's degree and usually graduate education. Comparing wage levels for the two occupation types shows the difference due to education level. In 1997, human services front-line workers earned an average of $7.82 in Kenosha and approximately $9.50 in the two large cities. Wages grew by only $1 over the three-year period in all three localities. Human services and education professionals, on the other hand, earned double the wages of the front-line workers.

Paraprofessional and human services positions in these first three categories are growing occupations as needs increase for child care, elder care, and similar services. These jobs are also targeted for training programs for low-skilled workers, with the promise of growth potential. However, in both Milwaukee and Kenosha, these jobs accounted for less than 15 percent of the labor force. Human services front-line workers made up only 4 percent of the labor market in both cities. Although front-line human services jobs pay better than retail, they still offer below-poverty-level wages. Clearly, preparing a large proportion of the labor force for these jobs will not solve long-term poverty.

The *other professional* category contains the widest range of jobs and wages. It includes well-paid medical professionals, writers, artists, researchers, and other professional positions that require college education and extensive experience. Salaries vary widely within categories, particularly in such positions as interior designer and artist. All these jobs require considerable education and communication skills.

Sales and service occupations are grouped into two categories: skilled and unskilled. The *sales and service: unskilled* positions include such fast-growing positions as retail clerks, restaurant personnel, guards, and in housekeeping. These jobs pay badly, but in the growing economy of the later 1990s average wages were well above minimum wage. All sales and service jobs require communications and critical thinking skills. The *sales and service: skilled* occupations, which include hairdressers, real estate sales agents, and service-sector managers, need some experience or training. These jobs paid about double the wages of the unskilled occupations, but in 2000 accounted for only 4 percent of the jobs in Milwaukee and 7 percent in Kenosha.

All the clerical positions require some skill, but the *clerical: skilled* positions require more education or experience. The *clerical: entry-level* positions include file and data-entry clerks, tellers, and other positions that can be learned through on-the-job experience combined with quality high-school education or a short training program. The more skilled positions require either greater experience or training. There is potentially a ladder from entry-level to more skilled occupations. For example, people reported starting work as entry-level file clerks and later moving into administrative assistant positions. Skilled clerical jobs paid more than $10 an hour on average. They represent growing job categories, accounting for 22 percent of the jobs in Kenosha and 25 percent of those in Milwaukee in 2000.

However, because there are fewer entry-level jobs than skilled positions, newcomers to clerical work will have fewer opportunities to develop the skills required for the more lucrative positions. Because of the competition for better-paying jobs in all three labor markets, employers are likely to look for more experienced workers or to become more choosy about the cultural and human capital skills they require for a job. The level of competition for the well-paying jobs means that someone like Christine, profiled in chapter 1, who has good human capital skills but displays the wrong cultural capital will have fewer opportunities than in an economy with less competition for employment.

Blue-collar jobs divide roughly equally between unskilled and skilled occupations. Despite the decline in manufacturing, blue-collar jobs accounted for over 25 percent of available employment in both Milwaukee and Kenosha. Both categories paid reasonable wages, with average hourly wages for unskilled position ranging from $11.71 in Kenosha to $12.84 in Milwaukee. Skilled jobs paid more, offering an average of $17.87 in Milwaukee, $18.63 in Philadelphia, and $18.93 in Kenosha. However, middle-range wages for both job categories started at less than $7 an hour. Given these disparities in wages, finding a blue-collar job did not necessarily mean earning a family-supporting income.

Blue-collar: skilled positions require an apprenticeship or significant on-the-job experience whereas *Blue-collar: unskilled* positions require very few skills and almost no training. Unskilled positions could potentially lead to skilled positions. However, pay levels and opportunities for advancement available through blue-collar jobs depended more on whether the job was in the primary or secondary sector than in the skills of the position. Low-paying factory work in small, secondary-sector factories offered fewer lucrative opportunities, less stability, and fewer benefits than did the rapidly disappearing primary-sector workplaces.

For example, Xavier spent most of his career in unionized primary-sector firms that paid over $12 an hour and offered a complete benefits package, generous vacation and sick leave, and other benefits needed to provide a stable future for his family. However, during the worst of Kenosha's economic downturn, Xavier worked in the secondary-sector meatpacking plant that hires many Mexican migrants. This job paid less than $10 an hour, did not provide benefits, and did not have the workplace security of the unionized workplace.

Summary

All three communities had begun to recover from deindustrialization and economic slowdowns in the 1990s. Toward the end of the decade, the three cities experienced a booming economy. However, the status of their wage and opportunity structures was a mixed picture, with limited opportunities for the families
that form the bulk of the public assistance population. In all three cities, low-
paid service-sector jobs expanded at a much greater rate than better-paying
positions. In addition, the higher-paying jobs often required a college education, good critical thinking skills, and appropriate cultural capital. Sassen
(1998:140–143) describes creation of this kind of dual service-sector economy as
one characteristic of globalization. At the same time, as production is spread
throughout the world, administrative functions for global enterprise are centered in large cities. The primary areas of job growth include high-technology
jobs, but a much larger low-paid service-sector workforce is required to support these industries and their workers. The trends seen in these three cities are
echoed across the United States and in global cities throughout the world. Although the stable-working-class blue-collar, government, and clerical positions
that had offered stable employment to past generations still existed, fewer slots
were available. Given this changing economy, cultural and social capital skills
became important factors in gaining and keeping employment. I next examine
the connections among human, cultural, and social capital and the labor market in these three communities.

Labor-Market Patterns and Cultural Capital

Taken together, examination of the labor markets in these three cities indicates
that available jobs can be categorized in two ways: by the nature of the jobs and
the nature of the employers. First, the job structure is bifurcated between jobs
that offer pay and benefit packages sufficient to support a family and those offering insufficient remuneration. With the exception of the rapidly shrinking
pool of skilled blue-collar or primary-sector unskilled blue-collar jobs, the
majority of the desirable jobs generally require a college education. A full 31
percent of the available positions required advanced education, usually at an
associate's- or bachelor's-degree level or above. Twenty-nine percent of the
jobs called for either technical education in a skilled blue-collar trade or clerical skills. In these jobs employees are also expected to follow the cultural capital patterns of professional workplaces, including appropriate communication
skills, the ability to think critically, willingness to work as a team, commitment
to meeting deadlines, and readiness to take responsibility for the quality of the
work product.

The other half of the labor market consists of jobs that offer near-poverty-level wages, few benefits paid for by the employer, fewer full-time positions, and flexible hours. Most service-sector jobs—sales clerk, nursing assistant, restaurant worker, and others—call for reliability, willingness to work as part of a team, and the ability to communicate well, think critically, work in a high-pressure environment, and perform quality work. Most of these jobs seldom use advanced educational skills, but many employers require a high-school diploma.

Seventy-two percent of the occupations need communication skills. In both the preferable high-paying jobs and the low-paying remainder in the service sector, the same general attributes are expected. Most of these jobs draw on bridging cultural capital to work with a wide range of customers. Sandy, the displaced worker profiled in chapter 1, demonstrates the kinds of bicultural behaviors valued in many workplaces. Sandy is an African American in her mid-thirties who lives in a segregated, mixed-class neighborhood. At her job as the administrative assistant at a center-city Philadelphia nonprofit, she dresses conservatively and speaks white English. She has learned to understand the accents of the many foreign-born people served by the agency. She maintains a Philadelphia-appropriate professional demeanor with all people served by the agency, regardless of their race or class.

At home, Sandy participates in the labor- and goods-sharing cultural patterns of her neighborhood, as is common in low-income communities (Stack 1974,1996). Like other working-class families in similar communities (Anderson 1990, 2000; Stack 1974), in the late 1990s Sandy and her husband were an economically stable family in a city neighborhood with high levels of poverty and crime. They still remained part of the social structures of their mixed-class neighborhood. In additional to following the cultural patterns appropriate for the neighborhood, Sandy also switches to a version of black English outside of work.

Although in the office Sandy is careful to play the role of Philadelphia administrative assistant, she sometimes reveals elements of her bicultural identity when appropriate. For example, she developed a friendship with several people who had been with her in a welfare-to-work program who were also at the same agency. When on breaks and during social conversations with these people, she would switch to the cultural behaviors and language patterns of her neighborhood.

Her ability to switch between cultures and understand the problems faced by other African Americans living in poverty-stricken neighborhoods is valued at her workplace. Sandy has limited patience for people she regards as underclass. However, with people she considers simply down on their luck, she uses subtle cultural cues to show that she understands their position. This may involve dropping into black English or suggesting a resource to a program participant in need. Given her understanding of the subtleties of workplace culture from previous education and work experience, Sandy would probably not reveal her working-class African American identity as readily if she were employed in a white, middle-class, professional firm.

People like Sandy in service jobs need the highest level of bicultural skills to succeed in mainstream workplaces. While low-paying blue-collar jobs have lower expectations for communication skills, employers still want reliability, quality work, and the ability to work on a team. Many blue-collar workers develop these skills. However, as noted by several scholars of inner-city employment patterns note (Wilson 1996; Moss and Tilly 2001; Holtzer 1996), employers presume that African American men, and sometimes Latinos, will be less reliable workers based on past experience and perceptions of the neighborhood. These studies show that inability to portray soft skills appropriate for the workplace often factor into employment decisions.

Blue-collar employment is highly desirable because traditionally it has paid well and did not require advanced education. However, only 28 percent of jobs qualify as blue-collar in these three labor markets. In addition, the blue-collar jobs of today are different from the rote, assembly-line jobs held by past generations. The newer jobs often require ability to work with robotic machines and team production processes. Skilled trades have always depended on critical thinking, creativity, and quality work.

Welfare-to-work program experience among men hired at Quaker Residence illustrates the role of cultural capital appropriate for the workplace for blue-collar service-sector jobs. Quaker Residence's mission included creating opportunities for people in need for a variety of reasons, and many staff members were hired out of welfare-to-work programs or low-income neighborhoods. The maintenance jobs proved particularly appropriate for low-skilled and displaced workers with limited education because willingness to do the work, reliability, and honesty were the major prerequisites. A number of people were hired by this nonprofit agency out of Citizens United's welfare-to-work program. Most did well at these jobs, and some used these jobs as a stepping stone to higher-paying jobs in the private sector.

However, several people failed to be hired by the agency out of the welfare-to-work program because of absenteeism, drinking on the job, laziness, or poor work habits. In most cases, these were individual failings, but sometimes individual behaviors combined with cultural values to limit long term opportunities. Blue-collar cultural capital skills held by many older workers often have very different patterns than the dominant service-sector employment soft-skills set. In her book on Kenosha, Katherine Dudley (1994) describes how line workers at "the Motors" and similar employers deliberately regulated the pace of their work to impair quality. These line workers disdained higher education and middle-class people, and even maintained closed boundaries against skilled blue-collar workers. These people were ill equipped in terms of both human and cultural capital to move into service-sector employment.

Other people of color from low-income, closed social capital communities experience clashes because they refuse to acquiesce to the power imbalances of low-skilled service-sector work. For example, Linda, a woman with limited work experience profiled in the next chapter, lost one job because she got into an argument with a customer:

> I got in a fight with a lady. We was cleaning up a room and this Chinese man, I thought he was already gone. It was after checkout. So I'm knock-ing—"Housekeeping, housekeeping"—then nobody answers the door, so I take the key and I'm doing my work.
>
> Soon as I'm getting ready to leave, the man comes back askin' me, "Why you just cleanin' my house? My room? It's going to take me five, ten minutes to get dressed. I ain't dressed." I say, "You look like you dressed to me." So he's saying Chinese words. I don't know what he's saying but it sounds like he called me nigger. He say he going to go tell my [supervisor]. I cussed him out and I say, "She going to believe you anyway. Who pay the money for the room?"
>
> So I told [the supervisor] I didn't cuss him. "I didn't like this job anyway . . . you know? I quit. Before you even fire me, I quit. . . ." "If you had a prob-lem you should've come down here and told me." "If I came down there and told you I had a problem you wouldn't believe me, cause I got an attitude." So she was like, "If that's the case, you can go home." I say, "If I do good on my job today and I go home then I quit." Nobody talking to me and no Chi-nese cussing me out and I don't understand what you say. I cuss you right back out. I don't care.

Linda quit because she anticipated that she would be fired for talking back to a customer. She relied on culture that had taught her that she had no rights in such a situation. The street culture of her community also put great impor-tance on being respected by the people around her (Anderson 2000). Presum-ing her supervisor would disrespect her, she quit before the supervisor could even ask for her side of the story. She was also angry about the disrespect shown her by the hotel guest.

Phillipe Bourgois's (1995b) study in New York City describe similar patterns in which inner-city, low-income people of color refused to put up with cus-tomers and employers they felt were disrespectful to them. Research from Pro-ject Match (Berg et al. 1991), an innovative welfare-to-work program in Chicago's Cabrini Green housing project, described newly hired workers who anticipated that middle-class customers were going to disrespect them and acted accordingly. In all cases, cultural patterns developed in closed social capital networks different from those of the workplace proved problematic in multicultural service-sector jobs.

SUMMARY

People who succeed in the current labor market either match the cultural patterns expected in the workplace or have developed bicultural behaviors to switch between the worlds of work and home. Given the predominance of service-sector employment requiring communication skills and other cultural patterns more typical of each city's majority, these bicultural skills are becoming increasingly important in the competition for more lucrative jobs.

TYPES OF EMPLOYERS AND SOCIAL CAPITAL

The labor market is also categorized by the type of employer. The various kinds of jobs described in the previous section can be found in both primary-sector and secondary-sector businesses. Primary-sector employers are generally required by federal law to follow statutes for affirmative action, civil rights, family and medical leave, and other government-mandated workplace protections. These companies have the most desirable jobs, in that they pay well, offer full benefit packages, and have a set mobility ladder. In past generations, these employers offered stable jobs that could last an entire career. However, with globalization, few primary-sector employers remain in each community. For example, only 3 percent of employers in one Kenosha study had more than 100 workers (KABA 1997).

Although most people think of manufacturing plants like the remaining Chrysler plant in Kenosha as typical of primary-sector firms, large insurance companies and other service-sector businesses are more prevalent examples of primary-sector firms in Philadelphia and Milwaukee today. The electric company for which Maria works in a clerical position is one example. These firms hire data-entry personnel and workers for a variety of other low-paying service-sector jobs, but they are more likely to offer full-time work and benefits.

Secondary-sector firms are smaller, have smaller capital reserves, tend to be owned by a small group of people, and are more likely to go out of business or lay off workers when times are hard. Any small business is a secondary-sector firm. The kinds of jobs profiled above are all available in secondary-sector firms. For example, a small architecture firm would fall in the secondary sector and would hire professionals—both entry-level professionals and clerical workers. Fast-food restaurants primarily hiring unskilled service workers also fall into the secondary sector, as do small factories owned by one person or a partnership. The latter firms would hire managers, technical professionals, clerical workers, and sales personnel, as well as both skilled and unskilled blue-collar workers. Employers with fewer than 50 people may not be required by federal law to comply with the Family and Medical Leave Act the Americans with Disabilities Act, and some other workforce protections.[10]

National studies highlight differences between primary- and secondary-sector workplaces (Gordon et al. 1982). They also note that hiring practices differ in the two sectors. Officially, primary-sector employers use bureaucratic hiring practices, including a formal application and interview process. However, ethnography in these organizations shows that most of the people actually hired have social capital connections through friend or family networks (Goode and Schneider 1994; Schneider 2000). Survey research also supports the observation that factories, regardless of size, rely on their employees for referrals more frequently than other types of businesses (Holtzer 1996).

Secondary-sector businesses also hire primarily through individual social networks. For example, Newman (1999) reports that Burger Barn, the fast-food franchise in New York City that she studied, chooses among many applicants based on recommendations from the employees they value. I found the same to be true in my research. For example, the meatpacking plant that hired Xavier hires mostly newcomer Latinos because it relies primarily on word-of-mouth referrals.

Like Assan, a Nigerian immigrant profiled in the next chapter, many newcomers to the United States find jobs through temporary agencies because their friends tell them that these agencies can help them find work. Holtzer (1996:25) notes that 5–10 percent of the workforce in his study of employers consisted of temporary or contracted employees. In my earlier study of Kenosha employers (Schneider 1998b), I found that many small factories used temporary agencies as a screening device to hire workers or as a way to buffer fluctuating employment needs in a changing market and avoid paying benefits. Temporary agencies supplied clerical workers, high-tech workers, and some service-sector employees in all three communities. Low-skilled native-born workers, young adults entering the labor market, and new immigrants learn from friends and family that some temporary agencies offer ways to get a job more quickly than going through regular hiring channels. Some temporary agencies are less strict about paperwork and become employment avenues for undocumented immigrants. Like Assan, who is a legal immigrant to the United States, newcomers learn from their friends and family about this strategy to quickly earn income.

In this way, individual social capital and organizational social capital combine to help people find work. The individual networks of family and friends provide the social capital connection to the temporary agencies by recommending to their friends agencies they have used in the past. The temporary agency has organizational social capital connections to employers, which it uses to help newcomers find jobs. Through its screening system and previous successful placements, the temporary agency proves itself trustworthy to the employers, cementing the social capital relationship. Most of the firms in Milwaukee and Kenosha that used temporary agencies for large portions of their workforce were secondary-sector companies.

Research with both employers and individuals shows that social capital is a key ingredient in finding employment. Individuals use their networks to locate jobs. Their friends and family serve as references to encourage employers to hire people they know. Likewise, employers use their current workforce, educational institutions, social service agencies, and/or temporary agencies as resources for finding employees. In each case, employers rely on social capital trust established with individuals or institutions to obtain their workforce.

INDIVIDUAL WORK AND TRAINING PATTERNS

Labor-market trends, employer social capital, and employee social, cultural, and human capital intertwine to influence an individual's experience in the labor market. Table 6.3 provides data on employment and welfare use from the three Philadelphia statistical studies. All three studies show that the majority of study participants had both worked and used welfare. Most study participants had worked at many jobs. Furthermore, the Community Women's Education Project (CWEP) study, which included jobs held prior to leaving high school, found that 92 percent had started work before age twenty-one. The same patterns held true in the other Philadelphia statistical studies and in interviews in

TABLE 6.3 EMPLOYMENT AND WELFARE USE

	Social Network (%)	CWEP (%)	Rapid Attachment (%)
Never worked	13	4	N/A
One or two jobs (1–4 CWEP)	42	60	55
Three or more jobs (CWEP >4)	45	35	45
Ever on welfare	95	76	92a
On welfare LT 1 year	22	35	N/A
On welfare 1–2 years	28	15	N/A
On welfare 3–5 years	22	15	N/A
On welfare >5 years	27	35	N/A

Sources: Social Network, CWEP, and Rapid Attachment studies
a Current figure.

TABLE 6.4 MOST FREQUENTLY HELD JOBS

	Social Network (%)	CWEP (%)	Rapid Attachment (%)
Cashier	36	27	15
Clerical	27	44	23
Health/nursing assistant	17	19	14
Sales	13	22	13
Factory work	10	20	15
Restaurant work/food prep	19	19	15
Security guard	10	N/A	N/A
Maintenance/blue-collar	10	N/A	10
Professional or professional entry-level	9	N/A	11
Housekeeping	N/A	N/A	15

Sources: Social Network, CWEP, and Rapid Attachment studies.

all three communities. Recall that Chrystal, profiled in chapter 1, started work at age 10 in the local Laundromat. This experience is typical—most participants worked in stores, babysat, or participated in JTPA-sponsored summer youth-employment programs as teenagers. African Americans were most likely to start work early: 39 percent of African American CWEP participants began work before age sixteen. Researchers in other cities report similar patterns for both African Americans and Latinos (Newman 1999; Stack 2001).

The public assistance population also includes people who use welfare in diverse ways. Table 6.3 shows that most families were on welfare for less than five years. Bane and Ellwood (1994) stress that the majority of welfare recipients either cycle on and off assistance or use welfare once in a lifetime. Studies in all three cities show the same patterns. Welfare is just one piece of an income strategy for families.

The nature of the labor market profoundly affects employment patterns. Table 6.4 shows the jobs held most frequently by subjects of the three Philadelphia statistical studies. Similar trends were evident in other Philadelphia studies as well as the Wisconsin research. Low-level service-sector and front-line human services jobs dominate the employment picture in these studies. The frequency of cashier, restaurant worker, and sales positions reflects both the tendency of all workers to start out in these types of jobs and their overall predominance in the local labor market. Study participants also worked in factories and blue-collar positions, mostly in secondary-sector firms. Finally, 9 percent of participants in the Social Network Study and 11 percent of those in the Rapid Attachment Study worked in either professional or professional entry-level jobs. The majority of these people were employed in social service or education, growth occupations in all three cities.

RACE AND GENDER DIFFERENCES

Both race and gender influenced employment trajectories. U.S. Department of Labor statistics reveal that unemployment rates are much higher for people of color than for whites, in all three cities. In the Philadelphia PMSA (Primary Metropolitan Statistical Area), the 1999 unemployment rate for whites was 3.3 percent, compared with 7.4 percent for African Americans and 10.2 percent for Latinos. The disparity was even greater in Milwaukee and Kenosha: Milwaukee had an unemployment rate of only 1.8 percent for whites but 8.9 percent for African Americans and 8.2 percent for Latinos. Kenosha's figures were similar: 2.4 percent for whites, 7.5 percent for African Americans, and 11.7 percent for Latinos. Unemployment rates are usually lower for women than men, but Kenosha showed the opposite pattern for women of color. In Philadelphia, unemployment rates for white women were 3.3 percent, 7.3 percent for African American women, and 10.8 percent for Latinas, about the same as for men. In Milwaukee, patterns were mixed: 1.9 percent of white women, 7.8 percent of African American women, and 9.1 percent of Latinas were out of work. In Kenosha, few white women had trouble finding work, with an unemployment rate of 1.6 percent, compared with 9.2 percent of African American women and 15 percent of Latinas.[11]

Analysis of employment patterns in the Social Network Study also showed difference by race and gender. African American women (38 percent) and Latinas (44 percent) were more likely to work as cashiers, whereas nursing assistant positions were dominated by African American women (22 percent) compared with 6 percent for white women and Latinas. Interviews showed similar patterns for nursing assistants in Milwaukee, but more whites worked in retail than people of color. Outside of retail and food service, employment fell along traditional gender lines, with women working in clerical and helping professions while men held blue-collar jobs.

Several factors account for the disparities. Racial discrimination is undoubtedly one factor. For example, both Megan, profiled as an example of a low-skilled worker, and Mark, profiled as being of the rising educated middle class, were African Americans who experienced subtle discrimination on the job. Megan was overlooked for an assistant manager position in a retail store because the manager hired one of his white friends. Mark was the only African

American in a high-technology occupation. Although he did his job well, he was consistently passed over for promotion in favor of whites who had a bachelor's degree or better connections.

Social networks make a difference, particularly in Kenosha, where most hiring is carried out through connections. African Americans and Latinos have traditionally had more difficulty in this labor market, and the trend continues (Schneider 2001). For example, one older African American had training as a barber and a welder. However, because he had no social connections to anyone working in the large factories, he was unable to get a stable-working-class, primary-sector job. However, his family had social connections to the citywide white social service elite through his wife's participation in nonprofit activity. Using these connections, he found a job as a welding instructor at the local technical college.

Race and gender alone were not statistically significant factors in any of the surveys used for this book, and interview data reveal similar patterns. Rather, race, gender, class, and social network factors all combine to influence employment trajectories.

Policy Implications

Bifurcated labor markets like those in these three cities require two simultaneous policy directions to prepare the workers needed in a competitive global economy as well as provide adequate income, benefits, and other supports needed by working families:

- To better prepare workers for service-sector or professional employment, education for both children and adults needs to stress critical thinking and bicultural behaviors. As earlier studies indicate (Schneider 1995), people learn cultural skills best through socialization into settings where those skills are used. Modeling or mentoring activities can sometimes help people learn cultural capital skills needed in a new environment.
- Because many jobs in the new economy do not offer adequate income to support a family and many service-sector employers are unable or unwilling to raise wages significantly or provide comprehensive benefits packages, government needs to strengthen supplemental programs for working families. Government now offers aid for child care, insurance assistance, and transportation assistance for a limited number of families. These programs need to be greatly expanded so that the majority of workers who need these supports to successfully work and support their families can develop the stable lifestyle enjoyed by workers in the previous generation.

Summary

Philadelphia, Milwaukee, and Kenosha all have a mixed economy with a pre-dominance of low-paying, service-sector jobs. Jobs offering family-supporting wages and benefits exist in all three cities, but the majority of these jobs in the new economy require higher education, critical thinking skills, ability to work on a team, and reliability. Also, most employment in the new economy re-quires more human capital than in past generations; a high-school diploma is usually a prerequisite, and many jobs require additional education. However, many of the skills required to succeed in the workplace today are "soft" skills developed through socialization that are appropriate for a given workplace. In addition, the teamwork expectations of many employers are facilitated by the ability to develop social capital trust in the workplace. Since most employers use social capital to find workers, developing social capital links to employers becomes an important part of finding a job.

In an ideal situation, everyone would be able to work in either a profes-sional job or a skilled blue-collar job in a primary-sector firm. However, only a minority of jobs in these communities fit this type. Regardless of the nature of the work or the employer, people need to develop appropriate cultural capital to survive in that workplace. How do people gain the human, social, and cul-tural capital skills needed to succeed in this diverse labor market? What ac-counts for different family trajectories? Examining individual experience re-veals that human, cultural, and social capital combine to lead to various family histories. The next chapter explores such experience in detail.

CHAPTER 7

Family Survival Strategies and Social Capital

Current welfare policy presumes that the population using public assistance lacks work experience and a stable work ethic (Mead 1992). To the contrary, studies of welfare recipients reveal little difference in attitudes toward work and work experience between long-term welfare families and low-income families who work (Chambre 1977, 1982, 1985; Edin and Lein 1997). Other studies show that stable-working-class families, and even some middle-class families, use public assistance in tough economic times (Zippay 1995). Public assistance serves a diverse population, and families find themselves in different niches in community labor markets before and after participating in welfare-to-work initiatives.

Welfare provides a safety net between jobs or an alternative source of unemployment benefits to people who do not qualify for unemployment insurance (Spalter-Roth et al. 1994). The Rapid Attachment Study provides one example of the limited access to unemployment insurance. Overall, 22 percent of the people in this program had applied for unemployment compensation, but only 12 percent had actually received benefits. Ability to obtain the benefits varied significantly by gender and race. Of the 30 percent of the men who had applied, 23 percent had received them; in comparison, only 20 percent of the women had even applied and only 10 percent had qualified. Forty-three percent of whites, 29 percent of African Americans, 25 percent of Latinos and 8 percent of those categorized as *Other* had applied for unemployment. The percentages of those who actually received benefits differed even more dramatically: 30 percent of whites, compared with 16 percent of African Americans, 4 percent *Other*, and no Latinos. The small percentage of people who qualified ran through their benefits and turned to welfare because they had no other resources and could not find work.

The previous chapter described a rapidly changing, bifurcated labor market. Life histories suggest that several factors combine to influence family economic strategies. Individual career histories show even more divergence. This chapter looks at the ways human, economic, cultural, and social capital combine to influence family survival strategies. The chapter profiles five worker types found in all three cities, addressing the following questions:

- What kinds of families and individuals use the public assistance system?
- How do race, gender, and human, cultural, and social capital together influence individuals' and families' career trajectories and income strategies?

WORKER TYPES

In addition to demographic characteristics such as race and gender, a combination of different kinds of human, social, and cultural capital can influence career paths. In many cases, human capital alone does not lead to finding good jobs. Developing social capital links to employers and practicing workplace-appropriate cultural capital are also important in finding and keeping jobs. Everyone has some form of social and cultural capital. However, many people in these studies did not have social or cultural capital appropriate for the careers they envisioned for themselves. Combined, the statistical and ethnographic studies reveal a consistent pattern across communities.[1]

All the research was focused on either people of color or working-class populations; very few participants came from the stable, multigenerational middle class.[2] In two-parent families the two adults are usually from the same class. However, as observed in my earlier study (Schneider 1986), in many rising families, particularly among people of color, one person has a college education and professional work experience while the other holds a stable-working-class or low-skilled job. In such cases, class position was determined by the philosophy of the family and educational/career trajectory for children. I define middle class as people who work as small-business owners or franchise managers or in middle-level managerial positions in larger companies or professional jobs and whose families have lifestyles similar to those of others in these positions. Analyzing individual experiences provides the opportunity to investigate which factors lead to mobility and how some families remain stuck in poverty. As with Jaysa and Jeff, this research also reveals some families who have moved down the class ladder between generations because of changes in the economy. Families fell into one of five types:

1. *Limited or no work experience:* This group included long-term welfare recipients with limited work histories. People either had never worked in their adult lives or had held a few jobs for less than one year. People from all racial and ethnic groups fell into this category. The majority focused on caregiving, and lacked networks to employment and faced significant barriers, for example, disability or addiction. Lack of education was not a significant factor.

2. *Low-skilled workers:* These families cycle between work and welfare, usually spending one or two years at a time working or on welfare. Low-

TABLE 7.1 Worker Type

Type of Worker	Social Network (%)	Interviews (%)	Rapid Attachment (%)
Limited work experience	22	10	17
Low-skilled	46	43	72
Stable-working-class/displaced	22	23	8
Immigrants/refugees	8	6	N/A
Rising educated middle class	2	18	3

Sources: Social Network, Rapid Attachment, Neighborhood Settlement House Evaluation, Kenosha Social Capital, and Life Experience of Welfare Recipients studies.

skilled workers make up the bulk of the families using public assistance (Bane and Ellwood 1994).

3. *Displaced workers/stable working class:* These families are the traditional working class. Men worked in factory or blue-collar jobs, women in factory, clerical, or entry-level social welfare positions. They stayed for long periods in jobs paying family-supporting wages and benefits.

4. *Rising educated middle class:* Families in this group had at least one adult member who had completed some college and worked in a professional, technical or white-collar managerial position. In many cases, these families were the first generation with college education and had limited social networks to appropriate employment and economic resources in hard times.

5. *Migrants and refugees:* These families include undocumented immigrants, legal immigrants, refugees, and Puerto Rican citizens. They do not speak English as a native language, and many arrived in the United States with a variety of resources. These people fell into two subgroups: people who were highly educated and skilled and those with few skills and limited education.

With the exception of migrants/refugees, each family was identified as one of the five types, based on work experience and income levels.[3] Table 7.1 shows the proportion of families in each worker type in two statistical studies and the interviews. Profiles of each family type illustrate differences in experience and social capital resources.

LIMITED WORK EXPERIENCE

People with little or no adult work experience generally use the public assistance program for more than five years at one time. These families are most at

risk of running quickly through their five-year lifetime limit for TANF benefits. Although many policy makers and program administrators focus on such
individuals when they talk about welfare reform, in fact they are the minority
of families using welfare in any of my studies as well as in national research on
public assistance use (Bane and Ellwood 1994). The percentage of limited-
work-experience families ranged from 10 percent in the interviews to 22 percent in the Social Network Study. Two factors distinguish this group from others: 1) a focus on caregiving and social isolation and 2) limited ties to people or
institutions outside immediate family networks.

Jaysa represents one type of limited-work-experience household. She is an
African American single mother from Milwaukee who finished high school,
then concentrated on raising her four children with some financial support
from her parents. She went on welfare in the early 1990s and moved to the
area near Neighborhood Settlement House. She enrolled her children in the
agency's programs and began volunteering there. While volunteering, someone she met at the center suggested that she take day-care training. She obtained a day-care certificate in 1997, and the agency hired her soon after that.
Today, Jaysa's life is focused on work, her children, and volunteering at the center and her church. She maintains a strong closed social capital network with
her parents and a few other relatives. In many ways, Jaysa's life is similar to that
of other women who choose to stay outside the paid labor force while their
children are young.

Linda's experience showcases multiple problems typical of some limited-work-experience households. An African American single mother from Milwaukee in her mid-twenties, she has a three-year-old son. Her parents were both on SSI owing to various health problems, and Linda is too. She was raised in a household with much violence, experiencing both beatings and rape before the age of eighteen. Her brother and the father of her child were both in jail.

Linda left school at age fifteen after her father died. She had been in special education classes, and moved through several grades without meeting basic grade requirements. It is unclear whether she has learning disabilities or was just "slow" because of distractions from her chaotic childhood household. She explained: "I stopped going to school. I wish I hadn't. I got no GED, no high-school diploma, can't get no job. I barely know how to do fractions, percentages, decimals, multiplication." She enrolled in a GED class in her mid-twenties as part of a child-welfare program and expressed satisfaction with the program: "It has been going pretty good. I'm learning how to do my fractions. Decimals and geometry and algebra, stuff like that, I'm trying to get together, 'cause I may go [to a training program] next."

Linda had tried working three times in her late teens. She cleaned offices at a car dealership, a job found through her brother that she held for only a couple of weeks. She left a job at one hotel after two or three weeks because "it was hard work; you worked all night, you couldn't get no rest." At another hotel, as described in the previous chapter, she lost her job after an altercation with a customer. She has survived on a combination of SSI and AFDC ever since.

Linda's networks include several family members and neighbors. She has joined a church through the neighbors, which provides some support. After she was reported to a child-welfare office for child neglect, she was enrolled in a mandatory intensive program in an attempt to keep her family together. That program, run under contract by Neighborhood Settlement House, connected her with parenting classes, GED training, counseling, and an array of other income-maintenance and support services.

People like Linda are likely to have the most trouble finding and keeping work. A study by the Manpower Demonstration Research Corporation (MDRC) (Riccio et al. 1995:2) found that 23 percent of the people in its large-scale survey of welfare recipients had health or situational barriers to employment. Many limited-work-experience individuals, like Linda, want to work but need significant remedial education, psychological counseling, and case-management support. Those caring for disabled family members would need appropriate child care, medical assistance, and other supports. However, as Le Roy's (2000) study of the parents of severely disabled children found, TANF case managers rarely have the training, referral networks, or expertise to provide appropriate supports to these families.

Like both Jaysa and Linda, limited-work-experience individuals prioritize caring for their children or family members above paid work. Most such families have multiple caregiving responsibilities. In the Rapid Attachment Study, limited-work-experience participants were more likely to live in households with three or more adults, reflecting family structures that may require caring for sick adults or extreme poverty forcing households to double up. For example, in addition to caring for her children, Jaysa helped with her father, who had recently had a stroke. Linda's mother needed care. In some cases, other relatives paid these individuals to care for family members. For example, Cara explained: "It wasn't a *job* job. My daddy was paying. . . . He has a younger daughter and I was watching her house, clean the house for her. He was paying my rent, my bills."

For limited-work-experience families like those of Jaysa, Linda, and Cara, welfare provided a source of income so that the head of household could serve as a caregiver. These households were likely to remain on public assistance longer than other families. In the Social Network Study, 71 percent of limited-income households had been on public assistance for three years or more. Single parents in caregiving roles were most likely to rely on long-term welfare. However, these studies also found two-parent households in which one or both adults needed significant care. Linda's parents relied on SSI and welfare because both were disabled.

The second key difference between limited-work-experience adults and other worker types is social isolation and small, closed social capital networks. Like Jaysa and Linda, most such individuals had few connections outside their families and a small group of friends. The majority reported belonging to a church but did not describe significant networks among church members or participation in church activities. Most of their relatives and friends who did work were employed in low-paid, unstable jobs in the service sector. Going to work simply did not make economic sense because the family had no way to cover caregiving. As Edin and Lein (1997:219–220) note, working in a low-wage job often costs more than relying on welfare.

Notice that both Linda and Jaysa were able to develop networks and new resources through social service agencies. In the Social Network Study, 28 percent of the limited-work-experience participants had found a job through a social service agency or the Department of Public Welfare. These patterns suggest that social isolation can be altered through participation in organized activities. However, social network connections through agencies can be fragile when they rely solely on referral from a job-placement counselor. In the Social Network and Rapid Attachment studies, most limited-work-experience people placed by the agency lost their jobs within six months. Two elements were at work here. Although weak ties provided through agency placements can create bridges between poor neighborhoods and employers (Granoveter 1973), they do not carry the same credit with employers that the trusted social capital relationships do. Lack of cultural cues, as in Christine's case, destroyed any social capital trust between training provider and employer. This made placement difficult.

That said, people like Jaysa, who developed social networks at the agency that hired her, easily transitioned between welfare and employment. As Perlmutter (1997) notes, mentoring on the job is a critical component in job retention. As my earlier studies show (Schneider 2002), consistent case management to address social, economic, and psychological challenges, combined with modeling and appropriate community work experience over long periods of time, can help limited-work-experience individuals with significant difficulties move into stable jobs with benefits, as Linda did.

Although education played a role in work experience, not having a high-school diploma or GED did not consign people to the limited-work-experience category. In the Social Network Study, high-school education was not a factor distinguishing among groups except in the rising educated middle class. The interviews showed the same pattern. However, 71 percent of Rapid Attachment Study participants in the limited-work-experience category had not completed high school. On the other hand, 6 percent of the limited-work-experience group in the Rapid Attachment Study had attended college and 13 percent had attended a post-secondary-education training program.

Some scholars note the high levels of domestic violence in the histories of long-term welfare recipients (Wittman 1998). These researchers claim that inappropriate behavior patterns learned in dysfunctional families make it difficult for long-term welfare recipients to keep jobs later in life. Current domestic violence can also prevent women from finding or keeping work. I agree that intimidation is a major barrier for women in violent households, but domestic violence alone does not place a woman in the limited-work-experience category. Nor were limited-work-experience individuals the only people who had developed interaction styles that were counterproductive in the workplace.

Stereotypes of welfare recipients most often portray limited-work-experience families as typical of those on welfare. To the contrary, all my studies showed that these families were the minority of the population using public assistance at any given time before TANF reforms. Bane and Ellwood's (1994) national study also highlighted that, while long-stayers use the most welfare benefits, they were not the majority on the welfare roles for most of AFDC's history.[4] However, because TANF programs assist welfare recipients with better work histories to find jobs, in all three communities long-term welfare recipients were beginning to dominate the welfare roles in the late 1990s.

LOW-SKILLED WORKERS

Low-skilled workers combine low-skilled, low-paying jobs with welfare as a lifetime survival strategy, cycling between work and welfare every one or two years. They most often lose their jobs as a result of business economic instability—they work in places with frequent business closures, fluctuating workforces, or seasonal work. Other reasons often cited for leaving low-wage jobs are lack of child care and a need to find a job that offers health insurance. Low-skilled workers make up the majority of families on the welfare rolls, ranging from 43 percent in the interviews to 73 percent in the Rapid Attachment Study. Bane and Ellwood (1994) estimate that approximately half of the welfare population cycles between work and welfare. Low-skilled workers came from two types of families: multigenerational low-skilled households and stable-working-class families who could not find similar work. For both types of low-skilled worker families, social networks consisted primarily of people who held similar jobs. Low-skilled workers tended to start work as teenagers and continued to find work through friends and family over time.

An example of such a worker is Megan, an African American single mother in her late twenties from Milwaukee with one school-aged son. She began work at age sixteen: "It was at this church and it was just a summer job. My auntie got me this job, just as a youth worker. I liked it, though; it was fun." Her next job, as a cashier in a local store, was found through her mother. After about a year, she quit because the family moved. She took another job at a local department store but left that when she became pregnant with her son in twelfth grade. After that, she alternated between working in retail and helping her mother.

One job lasted four and half years, but she quit when she was passed over for a promotion to an assistant manager. She told us, "I started off working third shift and then I went to second shift and then the managers started having me do other things and then I got promoted to the price administrator. And I did a good job at it . . . I did a lot, I did a lot." She then worked at several gas stations and eventually found a job at a grocery store that paid $10 an hour and had benefits. However, the hours at that job were reduced, and she turned to W-2 to try to find more stable employment.

With the exception of the grocery-store job, most of her employment had been part time and paid badly. Asked the reason for her job changes, she replied, "I would say the wages, because when I started off working third shift I made like $5.15. And then at the end when I left, I was only making $6.15." In addition, few of these jobs offered benefits.

Megan's employment history is typical for low-skilled workers. The majority hold multiple jobs. They cite numerous reasons for changing employers, usually the search for better wages, benefits, and hours. Only 41 percent of the low-skilled workers in the Social Network Study had ever held a job that offered health insurance. As with Megan, family situations also factor into the decision to leave jobs. In the Social Network Study, 32 percent of job departures were due to pregnancy, 25 percent due to child-care or family problems, 35 percent because the work was part-time, and 34 percent because the business closed.

As observed in other studies (Stack 2001), many low-skilled workers of color are assigned to evening and night shifts. As Hull (1992) illustrates in her study of women working in the nighttime check-processing operations of banks in California, women in late-night jobs have trouble finding public transportation and child care, particularly in Kenosha, where public transportation stops after 7 P.M. In many cases, relatives provide evening child care.

Low-skilled workers particularly value employers who understand their child-care needs and offer child-friendly work environments. For example, Megan said of one job, "The hours were good because it fit with my schedule, and they would let me come in on Saturdays and bring my son with me." However, employers' flexibility in such matters varies greatly.

Note that when Megan was passed over for a promotion she quit a good job rather than complain to someone higher in the organization. In hindsight, she commented, "I just wish I would have thought about it and got a transfer to another store, but I was mad and frustrated." A tendency among low-skilled workers to leave a job rather than try to resolve a problem is often a cultural response to the power hierarchy of many low-skilled workplaces. Workers like Megan seldom develop trusting relationships with anyone outside their immediate work area. They often experience management as capricious and unfair, as in the case of this manager, who promoted his girlfriend over Megan. A chain such as the drugstore Megan worked for at the time would have a personnel office to handle situations of this kind, but most employees would not even be aware of a grievance process. Even if they knew that they had options, many low-skilled workers would be afraid to complain, believing that a customer's or supervisor's version of events would be believed over theirs. Similar stories are common in communities of low-skilled workers. Particularly in a booming economy, low-skilled workers learn that it is easier to quit and find another job than to complain and risk being fired or given a poor reference.

Megan supplemented a meager income and lack of benefits with welfare. She reported that she had been on some kind of assistance—primarily a medical card—since she had become pregnant with her son. In those nine years, she received cash assistance between jobs, food stamps, and Section 8 housing in addition to the medical card. When interviewed, she was serving in a community-service job while completing a GED and looking for more permanent work. She lived in Section 8 housing with her son and 18-year-old brother. She still maintained close contact with her family.

Megan had not graduated from high school because she was given an incomplete in one class. She was preparing to complete her GED exam in 1999. She did not report any plans to continue education after that. Megan's limited interest in education is not typical of low-skilled workers. Like Chrystal, many had been in multiple training programs. They sought additional education as a way out of repeated low-skilled employment. However, even after multiple training programs and completing college, low-skilled workers were likely to remain in low-skilled jobs.

The primary factors keeping low-skilled workers in unstable jobs that did not support their families were the limits of local labor markets and the experience of their social networks. Low-skilled workers were rich in social capital and energetically used these resources to find work. In the Social Network Study, 70 percent had found jobs through family or friends. Low-skilled workers also reported using contacts from faith communities and social service agencies, but these networks were not able to move them into more stable work. Stack (2001:184) reports identical patterns in California.[5] As with social networks, low-skilled workers turn to employers they know to find work. A full 50 percent of low-skilled workers in the Social Network Study found jobs by walking in and asking; most of these jobs were in retail or fast-food restaurants. One low-skilled worker reported that her friends sought work by going to the mall and filling out applications. Such behavior cemented the pattern of chronic low-wage employment.

Low-skilled workers have a strong work ethic, starting as children or teenagers and persistently moving from job to job trying to make ends meet. In some cases, family members hold multiple jobs in an attempt to reach their desired lifestyle. However, the kinds of jobs held by low-skilled individuals—retail salesperson, laborer, data-entry clerk, nursing assistant, child-care aide, food-service worker, security guard, and secondary-sector factory worker—do not offer enough wages, benefits, and stability to allow these families to save for the future. In hard times, they turn to welfare for support. Even when working, they supplement meager earnings and limited health-insurance benefits with public assistance.

The educational experience of low-skilled workers varied widely, from high school short of a diploma to a four-year college degree. The majority of the low-skilled workers encountered throughout my research projects in all three cities valued education, seeking training programs in an effort to get a better job. However, they continued to find themselves in the low-skilled labor market because of their lack of experience in non-low-skilled work and of social capital connections outside of the low-skilled, primarily secondary-sector workplaces.

Given their tendency to work whenever they can, low-skilled workers are not likely to hit the TANF lifetime limits quickly. In a good economy, as in the

first five years of TANF, many leave the welfare rolls with assistance toward another job. Improved health-insurance programs such as CHIP help these families with health insurance, but, given the low income levels for these programs
in many states, these families can soon earn enough so that they no longer
qualify.

Given the inevitable swings in the economy and the instability of low-wage
work, low-skilled-worker families are likely to continue to cycle on and off
welfare unless TANF programs or additional income supplements can offer an
alternative. These families are likely to start hitting TANF limits approximately
10 years after their TANF clock started ticking.

STABLE-WORKING-CLASS/DISPLACED WORKERS

Stable-working-class/displaced-worker families include at least one adult
worker who spends most of his or her career in jobs that pay family-supporting
wages and offer a comprehensive benefits package, including primary-sector
factory work, skilled trades, clerical work, and skilled blue-collar jobs in government such as police and firefighters, postal workers, and front-line income
eligibility workers. Workers in these families tend to find employment in the
primary sector or government, in unionized jobs, or both. They tend to remain
in one job for long periods of time. Research in the three cities revealed two
types of stable-working-class/displaced-worker families. Particularly in communities of color, representing people kept out of good jobs by discrimination
in earlier generations, some families were first-generation stable working class.
Like Jeff, profiled in the previous chapter, others came from multigenerational
stable-working-class families.

The distinguishing feature of stable-working-class/displaced workers, both
men and women, is strong closed social capital networks connected to well-
paying jobs. These families are least likely to access government services until
economic conditions demand that they seek help, and least likely to deviate
from traditional patterns for education.

Xavier and Maria represent one pattern for first-generation stable-working-
class families. Xavier and Maria were middle-aged Texas-Mexicans from
Kenosha with three high-school-aged children. They are fluent in both English
and Spanish. They were migrant farm workers recruited out of agricultural
work by a Latino social service agency.

Xavier learned about his first stable-working-class job at "the Motors" from
a friend, who told him to apply through the migrant social service organization. Connections through work led to a second factory job when the auto
manufacturing plant began to lay off workers. Xavier told us he had worked
for the auto plant for almost three years: "They were laying off a lot of people
so they told me they were hiring in Waukegan [Illinois] in another company

and I went there and they told me they could hire me if I quit [working at the auto manufacturing plant], and I worked there for three years." When this job ended, he worked at a secondary-sector meatpacking company that hires many Latinos. Although he found that job through a newspaper ad, it is likely that he knew about this factory from ethnic networks. He worked there for 10 years, constantly looking for more stable work. A friend referred him to another primary-sector factory, where he has worked ever since.

Maria began working part-time in social service agencies through contacts in the migrant community. The director of one social service program told her about jobs at the electric company, where she has remained.

Xavier and Maria used welfare twice in their adult lives. When they first arrived in Kenosha, they used some public and private social service agency support until they found jobs. They also used welfare after Xavier was laid off by the second auto manufacturing plant. At that time, the Kenosha economy was so poor that he had trouble finding work. Maria recalled that welfare "was helpful. At the time. We could move forward. It was not something one could live on well. It helped you manage through bad times, but it was embarrassing." After Xavier found work again, the family went off public assistance and have not used it again.

In many ways, Xavier and Maria's experience is typical of the first-generation stable working class. Early in the twentieth century, manufacturers recruited people from Europe transitioning from agriculture to factory work (Thomas and Znanieki 1912; Liebson 1980). As part of the great northern migration, African Americans moved from the rural South to northern cities in search of work.[6] Although many African Americans faced discrimination in the North that led them into service-sector jobs (Lieberson 1980), during and after World War II northern primary-sector companies began to actively recruit African Americans for stable-working-class jobs (Wilson 1978:66–67). Ethnographic research in both Philadelphia (Goode and Schneider 1994:151–154) and Kenosha (Schneider 2001:17–19) showed that companies actively recruited first African Americans, then Latinos, to meet affirmative action goals. Even with widely reported ongoing workplace discrimination (Bodnar 1983:239; Lieberson 1980; Goode and Schneider 1994:151–154; Wilson 1978:76–78), some African Americans and Latinos across the country were able to move into the stable working class.

Like Xavier and Maria, most of the African American and Latino stable-working-class families found jobs in large manufacturing plants through word-of-mouth recruitment via closed social capital networks. Although formal recruitment strategies by companies or through social service organizations served as the initial social capital connection to stable-working-class companies, referral through friends and family soon supplanted institutional ties as a way for workers to find stable-working-class jobs.

Xavier and Maria's experience is unusual because of their connection to a social service agency. Most stable-working-class and displaced workers have little connection to nonprofits providing these kinds of services. This is particularly true for those in the multigenerational stable working class, who rely primarily on friends and family to find work. John, profiled in chapter 1, is an example of this tendency. Despite the fact that John had access to a social service agency to help him find work, he found his next job through his personal connections.

The migrant social service agency that helped many Latinos find work is different because it served much more as a social center for Latinos in Kenosha than other social service agencies. The boundaries between closed social capital network referrals and social service agency placements were blurred in this instance. Very few Latino migrants at that time would go to a white-dominated agency for help finding work.

As research on the multigenerational working class shows (Bodnar et al. 1983; Gordon et al. 1982; Lieberson 1980), generations of established working class young people, like John, used connections to find work. Jeff's work history shows what happens to the multigenerational working class in a changing economy. He had experience and training in high technology and machinery repair but was unable to find stable work.

Jeff anticipated relying on the same strategies that his parents had used to find work. He chose not to pursue work in the police department like his parents but initially used other closed social capital networks—friends and family—for example, his grandparents told him about a job in Atlantic City, and he did construction work with a series of friends. By the time he left the Air Force, however, these connections had dried up as a result of changes in the economy. The Veterans Administration steered him to his first postmilitary job, but he found all his subsequent positions through the newspaper. He found that he had no social capital to rely on because he had moved into fields in which his networks had no experience or connections. After he ran through his unemployment benefits, his family spent a brief time on welfare until he found his next skilled blue-collar job.

Displaced workers in Philadelphia in the Social Network Study followed similar patterns after large employers left, moving among lower-paying factory or blue-collar jobs as the labor market collapsed. Others moved into secondary-sector jobs available in their neighborhoods. Just as Xavier had taken a job in the secondary-sector meatpacking plant when Kenosha hit an economic downturn, stable-working-class people sometimes turned to similar, but less well-paying, jobs in secondary-sector firms.

Both first-generation and multigenerational stable-working-class families find jobs that pay reasonable wages, and they stay at the same employer for long periods of time. Most such families in Milwaukee and Kenosha had worked in jobs paying more than $11 an hour and remained with the same employer for ten or more years. Both the Rapid Attachment Study and the Social Network Study focused on displaced workers: stable-working-class people like Jeff who had been downsized in the new economy. Since many older displaced workers retired or were exempt from welfare-to-work programs, both studies primarily included the most vulnerable, younger members of the stable working class.[7] Nevertheless, 34 percent of the displaced workers in the Social Network Study had stayed at a job for more than five years; 26 percent of them had earned more than $11 an hour and 15 percent had earned $9 to $11 per hour. In the Rapid Attachment Study, 19 percent of the displaced workers had held a job paying $11 per hour or more and 28 percent had earned between 9 and 11 per hour. Fifty-two percent of the displaced workers in the Social Network Study had held a job that provided health insurance.

Although these percentages may suggest unstable employment histories in comparison with those of the unionized factory workers earning more than $15 an hour with full benefits, these displaced workers fared much better than people in the low-skilled worker category. Less than five percent of the low-skilled workers in either study had held a job paying $11 an hour or more. Only 15 percent of the low-skilled workers in the Social Network Study had worked at one company for more than five years and only 41 percent had ever received health insurance.

Most stable-working-class jobs were found through closed social capital networks of friends and family. In the Social Network Study, 65 percent of stable-working-class/displaced workers had found work through friends and family. These people stay at jobs until companies close: 41 percent of the displaced workers in the Social Network Study left a job for this reason. When the labor market changes, displaced workers are often at a loss to develop new networks. This led to difficult choices as families were forced to decide whether to take multiple low-skilled jobs or use welfare while continuing to look for work offering pay and benefits similar to those of previous positions.

Stable-working-class families turned to public assistance when they found themselves unemployed after long periods. The first-generation stable working class generally sought help from welfare first for two reasons. First, like Xavier and Maria, they came from rural agricultural backgrounds or low-skilled families that had a history of using public assistance. Although ashamed to use government aid, they knew how to access these systems and realized that their networks would not look down on them for seeking welfare. Second, these families had fewer resources to fall back on because they had been in the stable working class for a shorter time and had had less time to save.

Older members of the multigenerational stable working class relied on unemployment, savings, family, and friends before seeking public assistance. These long-term workers were more likely to qualify for displaced-worker programs that also provided additional income and training for which low-skilled workers or stable-working-class people might not qualify. For example, Jeff never had access to displaced-worker programs because his secondary-sector workplaces did not fit the federal government's criteria that would trigger these extra benefits.

Most in the multigenerational stable working class found it difficult to seek welfare. Jeff explained, "It wasn't a choice that we wanted to do. Maybe it was stereotypes. Like you're being lazy or not trying." They often followed others in their social networks to the public assistance office. John reported, "One of my wife's friends, she was on it."

Although displaced workers were less likely to turn to public assistance than any other group, they did find their way to the welfare office when in need. A full 56 percent of the stable-working-class/displaced workers in the Social Network Study had used public assistance at some point in their lives. Other people in this group who tried to access public assistance discovered that their assets disqualified them.

Stable-working-class families use their closed social capital networks, access to union apprenticeship programs, and military technical training to find stable jobs offering family-supporting wages and benefits. Closed social capital networks are the most frequently used resource for employment. Cultural capital socialization into stable-working-class jobs also helps multigenerational stable-working-class people find work. Despite a dearth of stable employment, working-class young people like Jeff knew how to find jobs paying decent wages.

Despite strong work histories, stable-working-class people become displaced workers when the primary-sector employers leave town, because their social networks all share similar strategies for finding work. With whole neighborhoods out of work, people had no friends or family who could help them find another job. Because displaced workers had developed lifestyles based on stable income, they were often reluctant to take the low-paying, unstable jobs available in the expanding service sector. As Zippay (1995) notes, these people can become discouraged, relying on welfare for income for a long time. However, as my various studies demonstrate, displaced workers are often easiest to place in employment. Most of the displaced workers who used welfare as adults in these three cities had accessed the system only once in their careers.

RISING EDUCATED MIDDLE CLASS

Families in the rising educated middle class differ from the stable working class in their emphasis on education and an ability to develop bridging social capital into other communities. They have at least one adult member with a college education and professional employment. Children are also headed toward college and professional careers.

They also differ from the multigenerational middle class, in two ways. First, these families have fewer social and economic assets than the established middle class. This means that they have fewer people in their closed social capital networks to turn to for advice, connections to jobs, and models for life choices. It also means that these families are far more vulnerable in difficult economic times owing to limited savings and family resources.

Second, families in the rising educated middle class are more likely than the multigenerational middle class to engage in bridging social capital behavior. In this era of class-segregated suburbs and gated communities, the multigenerational middle class tends to be more socially isolated from people of different backgrounds than any other group in U.S. society.[8] Like the employers in recent studies of hiring practices (Holzer 1996; Moss and Tilly 2001), multigenerational middle-class people tend to perceive people from lower-class backgrounds from the vantage of their power-dominant positions.[9]

Lydia's family was typical of the rising educated middle class. Lydia and Juan are middle-aged American-born Latinos from Kenosha with three young adult children. Lydia is the daughter of Mexican migrants and the only person in her extended family to have attended college. Her husband has a welding certificate from the local technical college but works at the secondary-sector meatpacking company in Kenosha that employed Xavier. Lydia is a teacher with a bachelor's degree from a Wisconsin college. Her oldest daughter is currently attending college.

Lydia began to develop bridging social and cultural capital as a child through her work as a teacher's aide in a social service program run by a church coalition for migrant children. The family had formed earlier connections to citywide social service agencies because an aunt had tuberculosis. These positive interactions with whites helped Lydia develop bicultural behaviors and a comfort with diversity early in her life.

She received little encouragement at school to attend college. Following the cultural patterns established in the Kenosha migrant community as they transitioned into Kenosha's stable working class, she planned to obtain clerical training and move into a secretarial job.[10]

Lydia applied for college by accident, as a result of taking college-preparatory classes with college-bound friends. As in many small cities, Kenosha's high schools include a mix of students from different race, ethnic, and class backgrounds. Most Kenosha schools had ability tracks—Lydia was placed in classes with white, middle-class, college-bound peers, and she developed cultural capital needed for college and professional employment through these connections and experiences. But, lacking the money, she had no college plans herself. She recalls:

It was my best girlfriend from high school, she went to the teachers' college and she called me up the day that you had to take the test to get in and she said, "Come with me, I don't want to go alone." So I was just sitting there waiting, and the lady's passing out the papers and she says, "How about you?," and I say, "No, no," and my girlfriend says, "Go ahead, take it, you're not going to do anything." So I took the test and I filled the application. And I figured "who cares," and two or three weeks later a letter came in the mail from the teacher's college.

The college accepted her and offered financial aid. While in college, Lydia held a series of jobs with citywide social service agencies working with the Latino community. These bridging ties cemented a lifelong career working between the mainstream and Latino communities. Much of her teaching experience includes special programs for Spanish-speaking students in addition to her regular teaching activities.

Even though Lydia's husband holds a low-skilled job, the family values education and stresses bridging opportunities for their children. She belongs to one of Kenosha's established white Catholic churches instead of the congregation serving most stable-working-class and migrant Latinos. Lydia has a commitment to bicultural lifestyles and maintains ties to the ethnic community, but both she and her children lead English-dominant lives among whites with similar class backgrounds and interests. Her husband, on the other hand, remains tied to the Latino community. His English is limited, and he attends the Latino Mass at Annunciation, the parish serving Kenosha's Spanish-speaking community.

This family is similar to many in the rising educated middle class in several ways. First, as reported in an earlier study (Schneider 1986), some two-parent households in the rising educated middle class include one member who works in either a stable-working-class or low-skilled job. Among first-generation college-bound people of color, women were more likely to finish college and enter professional employment than men.

The worker-type identity of the family stems from the support given by the non-college-educated member to the person in professional employment. Note that Juan obtained a welding certificate at the local technical college. Even though this program targeted him for a stable-working-class job that he never held, it shows an interest in education. He supported the educational aspirations of his children as well as his wife's career.

Although this family pattern was observed often in the interviews, it was not the only pattern for those in the rising educated middle class. This research also included single-parent families as well as two-parent households in which both partners had finished college and worked in professional jobs.

Lydia's experience is also typical in that bridging people and institutions encouraged her to continue her education and move into professional work. The same encouragement from connections with bridging ties helped many people move toward college. Several leaders in the African American community recalled that white teachers or family employers provided mentoring and encouragement to seek college education and professional employment. Community-based organizations and faith communities that focused on the ethnic community also played a prominent role in encouraging further education.

Bridging experiences like these provide opportunities to develop cultural capital necessary to thrive in college and professional workplaces. These opportunities arise in a variety of ways. As with Lydia, some result from placement in ability tracks with middle-class students. The military also serves as an effective means of expanding cultural capital. In other cases, people were in after-school programs with people from different backgrounds and thus developed new cultural capital attributes. The after-school programs included both programs with children from different class and race/ethnicity/nationality backgrounds and those exclusively for one group, intentionally pairing young people with mentors who were professionals. Organizations such as Big Brothers/Big Sisters and for students of color that include ongoing interactions with professionals from the same group were often mentioned in the narratives of people in the rising educated middle class.

In all cases, experiences that provided the opportunity to successfully develop new cultural capital shared two characteristics. First, these were long-term interactions with people who were different from the participants. Short-term programs, for example, motivational lectures by professionals, rarely had the same effect.

Second, in these settings, participants either mingled as equals or were treated as potential equals. One Kenosha African American in the rising educated middle class came from a low-skilled worker family—his mother worked as a maid in a white, middle-class household. Her employer took an interest in this bright child and encouraged him to go to college, providing ongoing advice.

Like Lydia, many people in the rising educated middle class do not move into lucrative careers. Working as teachers and social service professionals for nonprofits and government, they are paid low wages and vulnerable to shifts in funding. Similar profiles were described in the Rapid Attachment and Social Network studies. Only one rising-educated-middle-class person in each of these studies had earned over $11 an hour.

Others began in highly paid professions but found that they lacked social capital networks to find jobs when companies closed. For example, Mark was an African American in his late thirties from Philadelphia. His wife was also a college-educated professional but worked part time to care for their six young children. The family relied on public assistance for health insurance, food stamps, and some cash support for several years while he transitioned to another career after being downsized by a high-technology company.

Mark comes from a stable African American working-class background in Philadelphia. Like Lydia, he did well in school and entered college to study electrical engineering. He completed an associate's degree and needed one more semester to obtain a bachelor's degree. After completing his associate's degree, he started work with a major communications company, staying at that firm for fourteen years until it closed its Philadelphia operation. Even though his talents were recognized, he was not included in the networks of the workplace. He observed:

> To get hired at [that company] you had to be a top student. Okay, so all of this was good. Right, so me and them two white boys [were hired at the same time]. But you don't treat me like a white boy. I stayed in my office for six months studying engineering. Nobody come by, say hi, nothing like that. They didn't do that with [the white employees].

The whites developed strong social capital ties in the office, but Mark did not. His peers were promoted in two years, whereas he waited six years to become a senior technical associate. Although he trained many people, he was passed over for promotion and eventually let go when the company downsized. Lacking connections, he was unable to find work in his field.

Other people on welfare from the rising educated middle class told similar stories of workplace discrimination that made it difficult to develop bridging social capital. Some, however, did develop strong social capital ties with peers of other races, which helped them progress through the workplace. For example, Karen, an African American professional, described how her white coworkers and superiors helped her adapt to new work situations. She encountered resistance from white, unionized line workers in a social service office. Rather than assume that problems were her fault, her peers and supervisors helped her acculturate. With support from other professionals in her workplace, she rapidly rose to leadership positions in the government office where she worked.

Families in the rising educated middle class show a tendency toward flexibility, an ability to bridge in contexts with people from other races and classes, and strong social network supports from their closed social capital networks. Encouragement from people in the closed social capital networks of their youth from either stable-working-class or low-skilled-worker backgrounds proved a critical ingredient of future success for many. As Lydia put it, "[My mother] told all my brothers and sisters, she told my dad. The whole neighborhood, her coworkers, and all my girlfriends. So after a while I got used to hearing, 'You're going to college? You're going to be a teacher? Oh, we knew you were going to be a teacher; you're so smart.'"

One factor that distinguishes the rising educated middle class from other types of families is strong social capital support, both within their closed networks and from bridging individuals and institutions. Limited-work-experience and low-skilled workers also value education but were unable to translate education into professional work. Families in each worker type relied on closed social capital networks to meet basic needs. The ability to develop bicultural social and cultural capital is a key stepping stone into the rising educated middle class. This same factor was reported in other studies (Lopez and Stack 2001) as making a difference.

Support from less educated family and friends helped these people in the rising educated middle class ignore pressure from others in their communities to remain in the low-skilled or stable working class. As in other studies (Newman 1999), many in the rising educated middle class remembered others in their closed social capital communities who had derided them for seeking to improve their education or economic circumstances. Some people of color were confronted by community members who accused them of acting white (Fordham and Ogbu 1986). Many also experienced prejudice from multigenerational middle-class people in their workplaces and schools. However, those who succeeded drew on the supporting parts of their networks and their own determination in order to achieve their goals.

Most of the rising-educated-middle-class people in this study also maintained contact with networks of kin and childhood friends who had not risen into the same class. Although their primary closed social capital networks as adults consisted mostly of people from similar class backgrounds, they had not completely left their past behind. They helped lower-income people from their extended networks, but some were selective—setting clear boundaries so that they would not be overwhelmed with requests for assistance.[11]

Many welfare-reform advocates see the rising educated middle class as the preferred future for everyone on welfare. Proponents of higher education, in particular, see education as a way out of poverty for lower-income families. However, as discussed in more detail elsewhere (Schneider 2000) and outlined below, only a few people from other worker categories bridge successfully into the rising educated middle class. The families in this category who are profiled here exhibit a combination of strong individual resiliency, personal talents, and supporting cultural and social capital from two types of networks. In most cases, they have strong supports from within closed networks that value education but consist primarily of people from one race/ethnicity/nationality or another class background, usually a combination of limited-work-experience people, low-skilled workers, and stable-working-class people. Second, they develop long-term relationships with people in the rising or multigenerational middle class who help them bridge into new environments. Sometimes institutions such as schools or social service agencies also provide bridging social capital.

Despite their success, these families are vulnerable in tough economic times because they have limited economic and social capital to rely on in a changing economy. They may turn to public assistance in small numbers during an economic crisis. However, their stay on welfare is likely to be brief, as they have the tools to move back into professional employment.

MIGRANTS AND REFUGEES

Migrants and refugees comprise four groups: legal immigrants, undocumented migrants, refugees, and Puerto Rican citizens. In the United States each has a different legal status that affects access to government resources and social services. However, all four groups share two attributes: English is not their native language and they have similar social capital patterns for locating work and other resources.

Refugees Refugees are resettled through a web of social services and immigrant-community connections. Social service agencies serve as formal sponsors for refugee families, offering adjustment services to locate housing, provide English lessons, and help refugees find jobs and other resources under contract to the U.S. government. Refugees are also eligible for welfare regardless of family structure for a period of time after arrival and are connected to several other government-sponsored social service systems. Some refugees are also sponsored by relatives, friends, or faith communities in the United States, providing a second set of potential social capital resources (Schneider 1988).

Finally, even when not formally sponsored by someone from their community of émigrés, refugees quickly connect with communities of their compatriots in this country that aid them in locating work and housing and meeting other needs. These émigré communities usually serve as closed social and cultural capital communities for new migrants, regardless of their legal status (Portes and Stepick 1993; Portes and Sensenbrenner 1993).

Li Tran, an accountant from Vietnam, came to the United States as a refugee. He has the equivalent of a bachelor's degree from his country and had worked as an accountant for many years before migrating. He is a second-wave refugee, brought to Philadelphia by relatives who had come earlier. He and his family were resettled through the combined efforts of his relatives and the faith-related social service agency that sponsored the family.

Li Tran had been in the country several years before entering a mandatory welfare-to-work program operated by Citizens United. He had been studying

American accounting practices and English at the local community college but was shy about speaking English. Counselors at his welfare-to-work program found that he was able to communicate well enough in English to hold a job in his field. He relied exclusively on the refugee community for advice and supports. He was only comfortable volunteering at a social service agency that had an Asian unit and strong ties to Vietnam. He refused to go to job interviews because he "didn't know those people."

Li Tran's discomfort working outside of organizations associated with his country of origin or other than where others of the same nationality work is common among newcomers to the United States. Emigrés rely strongly on closed social capital networks and familiar cultural capital to meet their needs. Particularly when resettled in communities where their neighbors may be hostile to newcomers, émigrés may be shy with strangers, based on reports about some U.S. citizens.[12]

Although many people identify the inability to speak English as the prime reason that newcomers have trouble finding work or otherwise integrating into the United States, my earlier research suggested that perceived language ability was far more important than actual facility (Schneider 1988). Newcomers who had social capital links to workplaces found jobs regardless of their language. For example, one established Kenosha resident said that his mother, who never learned English, successfully used networks in the émigré community:

> We knew a Lithuanian who worked at this place who knew this other Lithuanian who worked at this other place, and you could always get in. It was like a buddy system. My ma never spoke English, but she always had work, usually because there was a supervisor in that business who spoke Lithuanian.

The same pattern continues today. People can manage in U.S. workplaces if they have others who can translate and explain work processes. On the other hand, newcomers like Li Tran observe correctly that monolingual U.S. residents can be intolerant of émigrés who speak with an accent or have poor grammar, even if they can communicate in English (Schneider 1997b; Schneider 1988; Goode and Schneider 1994). To protect himself from embarrassment or negative experiences, Li Tran restricted his employment options to places where he knew he would be accepted regardless of his nationality or ability to speak English.

Legal Immigrants Legal immigrants are brought to the United States by a sponsor, usually either a relative or an employer. Immigrants sponsored by family members have instant social capital networks through their sponsor's ties to the émigré community and often become involved with faith communities or community-based organizations associated with the same community. Some immigrants who are sponsored by employers first come to the United States as foreign students, developing connections to mainstream employers through internships or work experience. These individuals often have connections to people in their employment networks as well as the community. Legal immigrants have always had limited access to government benefits in the United States, and were barred from using TANF and related programs under the 1996 reforms. Their lack of access to government assistance makes émigré-community social capital resources even more important.

Assan is a Nigerian legal immigrant currently living in Milwaukee. He came to the United States in the late 1980s. Fifty years old when interviewed, he had recently brought his wife and youngest daughter, age ten, to the United States. He speaks English fluently but with a Nigerian accent. He first lived in New York, where he worked as a cabdriver and shipping clerk for four years. He also took courses in computer repair. He had completed high school in Nigeria. In Milwaukee, Assan has held a series of clerical jobs found through a temporary agency. He wants to find stable work, and is primarily looking for jobs through friends. Most of the resources he uses come from the Nigerian community in Milwaukee.

His wife had completed college and has a certificate in health care. She was just beginning to look for work in the United States. His daughter attends a local Catholic school and participates in an after-school program run by Neighborhood Settlement House.

Assan's experience illustrates several work strategies observed among migrants and refugees in all three cities. Driving a cab is a common avenue to employment for stable-working-class or middle-class émigrés. Emigrés learn about cabdriving opportunities through others from the same country. The Social Network Study found that 87 percent of immigrant/refugee families found jobs through family and friends.

Assan's unsuccessful attempt to become a computer-repair technician is also a common occurrence. The Social Network Study revealed a pattern of émigrés taking high-technology repair courses that never led to work in that field. In addition to lacking work experience in a high-technology trade, Assan also had no social capital connections into firms that hired such people. Thus, training went unused.

We found many immigrants in both Kenosha and Milwaukee who used temporary agencies to find work, but only because they followed friends and family members there. In one city, undocumented workers used a temporary agency because they knew from word-of-mouth referrals that this agency did not check employment documents carefully or ask for Social Security numbers. This allowed people who were not permitted to work in the United States to nonetheless locate employment easily.

Undocumented Workers   Undocumented workers have come to the United States without legal work papers. Some sneak across the borders of Canada and Mexico, and many more are tourists or foreign students who overstay the time limits of their visas or work in the United States although not officially allowed to do so. Employers are required by U.S. immigration law to make a good-faith effort to check the documents of employees after hiring them. However, the employer is not held liable if the employee provides false documents. Undocumented workers in émigré communities easily learn where to obtain false documents and which employers do not comply with immigration laws. Although security measures enacted after the September 11, 2001, bombing of the Pentagon and the World Trade Center are likely to make finding work more difficult for undocumented migrants, employment will continue to be available because many businesses need migrant labor and welcome this readily exploitable labor force (Sassen 1998:45–49).

Yolanda and Angel are undocumented Mexican migrants in Kenosha. Now in their early 30s, they have two school-aged children and a new baby. Yolanda completed ninth grade in Mexico, and Angel has completed high school. Yolanda speaks only Spanish; Angel speaks English and negotiates English-speaking systems for the family.

Angel arrived in the United States first, approximately eleven years ago, following brothers who had migrated earlier. He first worked as a gardener, then as a dishwasher, and currently is employed at the meatpacking plant that hires many Latinos. These jobs all pay poorly and do not offer health insurance. He told us that he finds jobs "through friends and acquaintances. They tell you where they work and when they are hiring." He sometimes goes to the temporary agencies but said, "Some people find jobs through the agencies, but I never have."

Besides the new baby, Yolanda takes care of one of her brothers' children. Three brothers share the household with them, one who recently arrived from Mexico. Most of their social supports come from family and Mexican migrants.

This household has an ambivalent relationship with social service agencies. In years past, there was a Latino faith-based organization associated with a church that would provide support. Angel explained that "there was a *padrecito* ["little priest"] who would help. But now he is not there any longer. He used to help people a great deal and through him people would find jobs. He used to take you, help you fill out the forms." Yolanda tried to obtain help through another faith-based project for pregnant women but found that she did not qualify. They have had difficulty with health services and other systems because she does not have a social security number. They currently have no health insurance. Yolanda summarized the situation:

We work and we pay taxes, but we do not get any services. That is a problem one has for not having a Social Security number. But one is paying all the same. When I applied for Medicaid they told me that if we had income they would take it away. The baby is a citizen, but they told me that I should be working and bringing income.

Yolanda and Angel's situation highlights the complications of the 1996 TANF law as it relates to immigrants. As undocumented newcomers, the adults in this family have no rights to government aid, and it is unusual that they attempt to access social service systems at all. They trust Kenosha's welfare system somewhat because the city has contracted with a community-based organization to do outreach on Medicaid for the Spanish-speaking community. However, the outreach workers confused requirements for TANF and Medicaid when communicating with Yolanda about a medical card for the baby. This family should be eligible for Badgercare through the CHIP system. As outlined in chapter 2, there are no work requirements for Medicaid. However, the outreach workers told Yolanda to go to work, a standard diversionary message under TANF.

Social service agency contacts for most migrants, regardless of their legal status, were mediated through the émigré community. Church-based missions served as the connector to social service organizations for many newcomers. Angel and Yolanda used such systems. Community-based organizations for émigrés also facilitated entry to other systems.

Non-English-Speaking Citizens   Most of the citizens in the migrant and refugee worker category were Puerto Ricans. Puerto Ricans have been U.S. citizens since the Jones Act in 1920. Poor economic conditions on the island have brought many people to the mainland in search of work. As citizens, Puerto Ricans are eligible for welfare, and many poorer people learn how to access government assistance systems before migrating. In large cities, many low-skilled Puerto Rican newcomers move into impoverished or changing neighborhoods where they also turn to public assistance for support. However, like low-skilled people born in the United States, many Puerto Rican citizens also find work and seek educational opportunities to improve their circumstances.

Jaime came to the United States after completing high school. When interviewed, he was in his early twenties and married, with two children under the age of five. He had worked in a factory in Puerto Rico for a few years after high school before being laid off. He spoke no English when he came to the mainland. Realizing that he needed further education and facility in English to succeed here, and unable to find work, he went on welfare and enrolled in courses on repairing electronic equipment and in ESL at community college.

Jaime entered Citizens United's mandatory welfare-to-work community service program and was initially placed as a janitor at a nonprofit organization in a Puerto Rican–dominant neighborhood. As his English improved, he asked to be transferred to another organization where he could get experience doing something other than manual labor. The agency placed him as an intern in a housing counseling program. He excelled as a bilingual counselor and was eventually hired by the agency. Seeing the opportunities available in social service work, he changed his major at the community college and planned to pursue a four-year degree.

Jaime's story is similar to that of other émigrés in the rising educated middle class, regardless of their legal status when they enter this country. However, as a citizen, Jaime had advantages that Assan and Li Tran lacked. Jaime came from a U.S. colony with strong, long-standing ties to the United States. His cultural capital thus included familiarity with welfare, U.S. educational systems, and social service agencies. He also had access to a wider array of government aid than Assan did. His decision to use public assistance, government educational programs, and other services stemmed from his own previous experience and the cultural capital familiarity with such systems in his closed social capital community.

The networks of the Puerto Rican community in Philadelphia included many people who bridged into communities of more established U.S. mainland residents, including people of different races. Compared with Assan and Li Tran, Jaime would receive more encouragement from people in his closed émigré community to branch out through education and work experiences outside of émigré networks. His willingness to bridge through community college and internship placements eventually led to a successful career in nonprofit service.

Jaime also spoke a language much in demand in Philadelphia. Although people from Africa and Asia, like Assan and Li Tran, also lived in Philadelphia (and in the Wisconsin cities), Spanish was the other major language used in the city. Jaime thus had entree into more jobs than would émigrés from countries with a smaller population in that community.

Summary and Policy Implications   Reliance on social capital networks in their community is the distinguishing factor for new émigré families. Cultural capital for adults comes primarily from other émigrés. Adults use social capital from the émigré community to locate jobs at places that employ others from the same country. They maintain homeland culture in mixed workplaces in this way. Emigré faith communities and community-based organizations also provide opportunities to maintain homeland culture and develop ethnic identity.[13] Children are more likely to develop bridging social and cultural capital, becoming translators between communities as they are socialized through school, peer relations, and other interactions.

Given the legal barriers for all newcomers except citizens and refugees to access government aid, post TANF, few migrants use government social service systems. Immigration literature highlights the fact that most migrants use few government services regardless of their legal status. That said, as for Angel and Yolanda, TANF has created additional hardships for economically marginalized migrant families who might otherwise access needed social services.

POLICY IMPLICATIONS

Taken together, individual career trajectories and family survival strategies suggest two general policy implications:

1. Support, employment, and advancement programs should be tailored for each family type. Families in each group have different resources and needs. Policy initiatives should be designed to allow flexibility for each type. Individual plans, as required by TANF, should be further tailored to meet family needs.
2. Initiatives to move families from poverty to economic self-sufficiency should include the development of social, cultural, and human capital.

Careful review of individuals' experience reveals that families' economic strategies are profoundly influenced by the labor market and social capital resources. In a good economy, even people with limited work experience can be helped toward employment given enough time and social and institutional supports. Different family types will need various kinds of supports in a bad economy. Comparisons across family categories show similarities and differences in the approaches families take with problems of adult education, child care, and relationships with social capital networks. The next chapter uses this typology to compare family strategies across groups.

CHAPTER 8

Comparisons Among Worker Types

Jeff, Sam, Sandy, Martha, Chrystal, and Margaret all participated in Citizens United's welfare-to-work program. In many ways, Jeff and Sam had similar education and career trajectories: both had finished high school and one year of technical college in the military. Both had wives who chose to stay home to care for young children. Both ended up on welfare for short periods of time when the Philadelphia economy turned sour in the early 1990s. Yet their work experiences were very different. Jeff, from a white working-class background, found decently paying skilled blue-collar jobs through the newspaper and family connections. Sam, an African American from the rural South, worked as a maintenance man and in other low-paid service-sector jobs.

The four women were all African Americans with high-school diplomas from the Philadelphia school system. All lived in neighborhoods that included both poor families and the working class. Only Chrystal was a single mother when she entered this welfare-to-work program. Despite these similarities, these woman had very different career and training paths. Sandy and Martha received quality secretarial training early in life and had well-paying clerical jobs. Both stopped working when their children were born. Both families turned to welfare during the economic downturn of the early 1990s. Both women performed community service when required by the welfare-to-work program as a way to return to the workforce, and both quickly found work through their welfare-to-work program. Sandy chose to remain an administrative assistant, learning word processing on the job. Martha pursued her dream of becoming a social worker, with the help of the agency that hired her.

Chrystal and Margaret had less stable careers and did not find jobs through Citizens United's program. Chrystal had started to work during high school and held a string of low-skilled jobs, including nursing assistant and housekeeper, before taking a clerical course at the community college. She also relied on welfare between jobs. Although she probably found work after leaving the Citizens United program, the agency was unable to place her in a clerical position in the 90 days allocated to help participants find jobs.

Margaret was functionally illiterate and had a host of family and personal problems that made it difficult for her to work. She had never held a job and had trouble fulfilling the community-service obligations of her welfare-to-work program. She stayed in the Citizens United program for three years, then spent another three years in a second TANF program before being placed in her first paying job.

The previous chapter described five worker types. This chapter compares different family strategies for work, education, and child care across families in each worker type. The chapter then describes the role of closed and bridging social capital for each worker type. Finally, I use data from the Rapid Attachment Study to examine the responses of the various worker types to work-first TANF programs. The chapter addresses the following questions:

- Do various family types approach needs for child care, education, and assistance from institutions differently?
- What is the role of bridging and closed social capital in economic strategies for various kinds of families?
- How do different family types fare in work-first programs?

COMPARISONS OF WORK HISTORY AMONG DIFFERENT FAMILY TYPES

Families are assigned to different worker types based on the employment experience of adult workers. Contrary to the stereotypes of welfare recipients as lazy or lacking a work ethic, family portraits for all five groups show that most households are engaged in productive labor to fulfill family needs. Limited-work-experience heads of household may rely on government aid to pay for basic necessities, but they fulfill much-needed caregiving roles for their extended families and others in their closed social capital networks. Although some limited-work-experience adults face significant personal barriers to finding and retaining jobs—for example, addiction, health problems, disability, and domestic violence—these challenges alone did not place a family in this category. Family members in all five worker types had these problems.[1] However, people with multiple barriers in other groups had more social and economic resources to provide sources of income other than welfare.

Limited-work-experience and low-skilled workers are generally the most economically vulnerable families because heads of household rely for subsistence on either limited government benefits or a combination of government aid and low-paying work. Families tend to live at or near the federal poverty level, and their incomes are generally far below the median household income for their community.[2] International policy scholars tend to use half of median household income as a measure for poverty (McFate et al. 1995); by using this standard, most families in these two groups would qualify as persistently poor. Because neither low-wage jobs nor welfare provides enough income to save for a better future or hard times, these families have no alternative to government aid when between jobs.

All five worker types rely heavily on social capital to locate work. Differences in career trajectories between individuals often depend on the resources available through either their social networks or their institutional affiliations. Social capital combines with cultural capital to influence individual outcomes For example, compare Maria, Martha, Chrystal, Anna, and Sandy, all of whom had completed solid clerical training. Maria, Sandy, and Martha all relied on social capital networks through their schools and closed social capital networks to find well-paying clerical jobs early in their adult work life. Both Sandy and Martha stopped working to raise their children, reentering the workforce with the help of social capital connections from a welfare-to-work program that placed them in internships at likely employers. Both women possessed bicultural social capital that impressed the nonprofit agencies that hosted their mandatory community-service internships, which led to job offers. In both cases, employers were willing to improve human capital skills to enable each woman to pursue her career objectives.

Chrystal and Anna, on the other hand, had good human capital skills but lacked the social capital connections and work experience needed to locate jobs that used their clerical skills. Anna, as described in chapter 1, had mainstream work experience as a sales clerk in a department store and had bicultural social skills similar to those of Maria, Sandy, and Martha. After deciding not to use the social capital of the welfare-to-work program, she returned to previous social capital networks that placed her back in a low-skilled job despite her improved educational credentials. Chrystal lacked both the social and cultural capital expected in clerical workplaces and as a result was unable to locate employment.

Social, cultural, and human capital combine with policy and macrostructural factors to influence individual career histories. Comparing Jeff and Assan highlights these differences. Both men have training in high-technology maintenance and repair. Only Jeff was able to find a job related to his training; his positive experience resulted from a combination of institutional social capital and public policy. His training came from the military, and as a veteran he had an advantage—conferred by formal public policy—in finding a job that used his skills. Veteran status thus serves as an institutional social capital link for people who served in the military. Because most of the companies that hired him had military contracts, his veteran status created institutional trust

that suggested that it would be easier to get a security clearance for Jeff than for someone who was not a veteran. In addition, some military contracts require that workers in sensitive positions be U.S. citizens, an advantage that Jeff had over Assan.

In contrast, Assan lacked both social capital and the policy-defined preferences to get work in his field. Although the quality of Assan's training is hard to assess, he did not mention any effort by the training agency to place him in a related job. Finally, like Jeff, he had no personal social capital networks to help him find lucrative work in his field.

Families in the rising educated middle class rely most on social and cultural capital developed outside of natal closed social capital networks, combined with related work experience. Comparing Sam and Mark demonstrates the importance of these factors. Sam had some college education and aspired to enter the rising educated middle class as a social service worker and nonprofit director. However, he lacked the social capital to gain entry into social service jobs, and employers would not consider him for these positions because he did not have previous work experience in this field. He also spoke and wrote in black English, causing him to do poorly in interviews; his communication skills indicated that he did not have the cultural capital expected by employers. Mark grew up in an integrated stable-working-class and middle-class neighborhood and attended integrated schools. Home and school provided bicultural cultural capital, and college social capital helped him move into professional employment.

EDUCATION

Family type is determined by work experience, but comparing families on such issues as education and child care reveals both similarities and differences across groups. I discuss Philadelphia's adult-education patterns in detail in another article (Schneider 2000). Research in Milwaukee and Kenosha yielded similar results. Here, I briefly outline differences among family types regarding education and training programs for adults.

Most research on poverty stresses that a high-school diploma is a basic criterion for success in the today's labor force. While ethnography in these three communities supported the need for people to acquire this basic credential, a high-school diploma alone did not determine worker type. In the Social Network Study, with the exception of the rising educated middle class, all groups had relatively the same proportions of people who had finished a high-school diploma or GED. People were as likely to find low-skilled worker or stable-working-class jobs whether or not they had graduated from high-school. Although African Americans were more likely than whites to leave high school before finishing their degrees, many later completed GED programs, yielding the same percentage with a diploma. Only 47 percent of Latinos had completed high school. Instead, social capital combined with human capital to determine worker type.

Most adults had had some form of education after leaving high school. Table 8.1 shows educational experience for the three statistical studies. At least half the people in each study had participated in a post-secondary-education program. Like others profiled throughout this book, many adults took multiple programs in an effort to better their economic circumstances. Although the desire to improve human capital skills persisted across worker types, people in each category chose different kinds of educational programs and had varying levels of success translating training into better jobs.

TABLE 8.1 EDUCATION

	Social Network (%)	CWEP (%)	Rapid Attachment (%)
Had high-school diploma or GED	68	52	54
Attended a training program	83	59	49
Attended college	16	7	9

Sources: Social Network, CWEP, and Rapid Attachment studies.

STABLE WORKING CLASS

Men and women in the stable working class had different approaches to post–secondary education. Men in primary-sector unskilled positions relied on union seniority as a source of promotion. Male stable-working-class/ displaced workers were the least likely of the worker types to seek post-high-school training. The only training programs reported for this group were apprenticeships before starting work associated with unions or the military, like Jeff's technical training. Displaced male workers were often funneled into training programs after their primary-sector workplaces left town but found that these short-term programs would not return them to well-paying jobs (Schneider 2000), or they were reluctant to return to school because of cultural antipathy toward higher education (Dudley 1994).

Older unskilled blue-collar workers, in particular, had little inclination to return to school, particularly when the training they were offered led only to low-paying jobs. Construction work, considered a preferred training option for unemployed workers, is seldom a viable option in communities with large numbers of displaced workers because the building trades in deindustrializing communities often have too many applicants. Men who, like John, had limited literacy were particularly reluctant to return to school.

Recognizing this problem, staff at Citizens United started placing these men in community-service building-maintenance positions at nonprofit agencies. These jobs require some mechanical or building skills but not the level of training expected for the unionized skilled trades. Most had mechanical experience through either work or home, and these jobs paid better than other service-sector options. A number of these displaced workers were hired by the agencies where they volunteered or used this new experience to find similar work elsewhere.

Stable-working-class women, on the other hand, used clerical training throughout their careers to gain entry to stable jobs with benefits and to upgrade skills. The Social Network Study showed that these individuals combined training with similar work to rise in their professions. A full 29 percent of those taking clerical training found related jobs, the largest percentage for any type of training program. As with Maria's secretarial certificate, clerical training led to secure work. However, clerical programs led to an upward career trajectory only when combined with related work with a future. Both Sandy and Maria were able to enhance skills once they had proved themselves in earlier clerical positions. In many cases, women with stable-working-class clerical careers either held clerical jobs before obtaining post-secondary training or had internships that socialized them to the cultural capital needed to succeed in primary-sector clerical work. During economic downturns, these stable-working-class women were highly valued as prospective employees in the nonprofit sector and the secondary sector because of their skills and professional office demeanor.

Examination of stable-working-class training strategies suggests that this worker type uses training most effectively if it directly relates to paid work experience. Strong social capital ties to stable workplaces set these individuals on the path toward family-supporting employment. Training enhances already established connections to preferred workplaces.

LIMITED-WORK-EXPERIENCE AND LOW-SKILLED WORKERS

Limited-work-experience and low-skilled workers lacked this crucial connection to workplaces offering family-supporting jobs. They sought training more frequently than any other group and benefited the least from their education. Three factors accounted for the failure of training to turn into lucrative work.

The first involved the nature of the training. Cultural and economic capital determined the kinds of programs sought by limited-work-experience and low-skilled workers. Like Jaysa's day-care training program, Chrystal's nursing assistant program, and the numerous food-service and short-term clerical programs completed by other limited-work-experience and low-skilled workers, these programs trained people for jobs with low wages, part-time hours, and no benefits. The vision of appropriate training was shaped by the experience and advice of their social capital networks. For example, in the cases of both Jaysa and Chrystal, they sought training in a particular field based on advice from family and friends.

The second factor involved the quality and goals of the training program. Financial factors loomed large in selection of schools: trade schools and community colleges advertised the availability of federal student-aid packages to pay for education. Lacking cultural capital that provided a concrete understanding of how to evaluate a school, people were unable to judge the quality of programs.

Others taking training programs through the official JTPA system found that many programs also had limited placement goals based on policy requirements. For example, I found that many agencies, faced with performance-based contracts to find jobs for their participants within 90 days, placed their better graduates in positions related to their training—jobs with a future—and then did their best to place less marketable candidates in any job that met their contract criteria.

The final factor involved social and cultural capital needed to translate training into jobs. Many limited-work-experience and low-skilled workers finished training, but could not find someone who could help them locate appropriate

work. As with Sam, social service agencies were unable to help when participants lacked appropriate cultural capital for clerical or professional jobs.

MIGRANTS AND REFUGEES

Training patterns for migrants and refugees depended on the social, cultural,
and human capital of the émigré community. Just as Assan was unable to use
his computer training, many immigrants were unable to translate training
into jobs. Immigrants were most likely to rely on friends and family as resources, and formal training programs had the most difficulty placing them in
related employment. On the other hand, as demonstrated by the stories of immigrant children who, like Lydia, moved into the rising educated middle class,
the resources of the immigrant community can provide supports to enable
finishing college and finding professional employment.

Middle-class émigrés relied on their previous educational experience and
nationality-based community networks to identify educational opportunities.
These included networks in their countries of origin tied to particular colleges.
These educational institutions provided social capital toward professional careers. Middle-class émigrés unable to translate their own education into similar jobs used their previous experience to guide their children's education.

THE RISING EDUCATED MIDDLE CLASS

Rising-educated-middle-class children like Lydia change their vision of possible futures through experiencing different cultural expectations from friends
or mentors. They receive support and mentoring both within and outside of
their closed social capital networks.

This does not mean that children from other types of families do not desire
a college education and professional careers. To the contrary, many children in
low-skilled and limited-work-experience families wanted to become lawyers,
doctors, or engineers or work in other professional occupations. These dreams
were dampened by poor schools, limited counseling, and lack of appropriate
mentors.

POLICY IMPLICATIONS

The differences in the role of education for each worker type highlight the
need to combine skills training with related work experience, mentoring, soft-
skills training through modeling and other mechanisms, and efforts to build
social capital between employers and prospective employees. Social capital can
be developed by the institution on behalf of their trainees if cultural capital

factors are included in the educational program. Activities such as internships and partnering of trainees with established people at the work site help foster new individual social and cultural capital for people entering new fields.

CHILD CARE AND CHILDREN'S ACTIVITIES

Social capital involves much more than simply referral to jobs. In many cases, informal resources for child care, transportation, and emotional support make the critical difference between an individual who can survive in the labor market and one who chronically loses jobs. Edin and Lein (1997) and Dodson et al. (2002) document these factors for low-skilled workers. This research highlighted the same factors for all working people. People who had family to provide backup child care and transportation were much more likely to establish stable careers.

Comparing Sandy with Margaret shows how social capital supports for child care make a difference. One of Sandy's "good work qualities" was her reliable, on-time attendance at the workplace. Sandy had a preteen daughter and two grade-school-aged sons. The children would always call in after school, and Sandy never seemed to have trouble with child care. Childcare support was provided by relatives living nearby, her husband, and her daughter.

Margaret, categorized under limited work experience,[3] had none of these supports. Instead, she was expected to provide care for a disabled husband and several grade-school-aged children and to support other relatives. As a result, she was constantly late for work and sometimes missed it altogether. Internship supervisors were not impressed.

Margaret's story reveals that the needs of social networks often placed low-income workers in positions where they were constantly torn between work and family. In particular, many of those with limited work experience had rich social networks, but their obligations to kin and friends often prevented them from locating or keeping stable jobs. Employers in both Philadelphia and Wisconsin complained repeatedly about employees who failed to show up because a family member was sick or needed help. Enforceable trust was broken by the competing demands of social capital exchange from individuals' community networks.

Child-care arrangements affect both the employment choices of adults and children's future options. As Dodson et al. (2002) observe, former welfare recipients have difficulty managing child care to fit employers' schedules. Particularly in communities where everyone works multiple jobs or has other caregiving responsibilities, parents have trouble finding backup child care that meets their needs. The quality of paid child care often depends on ability to pay, meaning that low-income parents may seek less stable family caregivers if they cannot afford quality care. The free programs of good quality, like Head Start, are available only to families that meet needs-based criteria, meaning that many working poor families may not qualify.

As children get older, the choices become even more difficult. A comparison of after-school programs across the three communities revealed uneven availability of activities and formal programs. The rising educated middle class, who could afford to pay for a variety of enrichment programs, had many more options than other groups and tended to involve their children in more activities. Particularly in poor neighborhoods, some children had few alternatives to the streets (Furstenberg et al. 1999). Family oversight offered the only adult supervision in some neighborhoods. Opportunities for these children to become involved in after-school enrichment programs depended on their parents' ability to pay and availability of an adult to manage transportation to programs in other parts of the city.

As designated caregivers, limited-work-experience individuals are least likely to look for child care outside family circles. For example, Jaysa reported that she simply did not trust anyone else to care for her children. She started to work only after her children had entered school, taking a job that allowed her to be home by the end of the school day.

Low-skilled workers, immigrants/refugees, and those in the stable working class and rising educated middle class all rely on similar systems to care for children. Family members are often the first resource, and grandmothers and other family members serve as primary caregivers or backups when formal systems fall through. Low-skilled workers are less likely to use formal center care because of the cost and concerns about the quality of care. Yolanda's staying home to care for her brother's children was representative; it is often easier to become the household child-care provider than to pay for day care and work at a low-skilled job. Single parents like Jaysa and Megan have fewer options. Megan relies on her mother and a cousin as backup caregiver for her school-aged son, who also participates in an after-school program. Child-care systems seem to be less reliable for low-skilled workers than for the stable working class (Dodson et al. 2002).

Many children in these studies, in all family types, participate in youth programs. These programs are often the first source of social and cultural capital models outside of closed social capital networks that have long-term implications. As earlier research in Kenosha shows (Schneider 2001), youth programs that foster bridging social and cultural capital can prove a key catalyst toward attaining rising-educated-middle-class status. On the other hand, youth programs can also foster closed social capital. For example, Kenosha had two youth programs: one serving mostly African Americans and the other whites. The adult social and cultural capital developed in these organizations continued throughout the participants' adult lives. Church youth groups were a major resource for many children. As discussed in chapter 11, these programs could produce closed or bridging social and cultural capital or a combination of the two.

A comparison of child care and youth programming reveals that policy makers need to pay attention not only to the availability and cost of care for children but also to their compatibility with families' work schedules and goals. Since children's care arrangements combine with school to affect lifetime career trajectories, the ability of programs to help children build social, cultural, and human capital skills appropriate to the community is also important.

Bridging and Closed Social and Cultural Capital

Families from all groups rely on closed social capital to meet their needs. Families with changed economic circumstances are more likely to engage in bridging behavior. Interviews reveal differences in the ways that the stable working class and rising educated middle class bridge into different systems.

The Stable Working Class

People tend to move into the stable working class as a group. For example, Xavier was encouraged to apply for his various jobs through the Latino social service organization and his friends. Others reported that they started work in stable factories because friends and family had heard that positions were available. These social capital resources set off a chain reaction as more and more people from the same communities seek work in these factories. For example, Xavier reported finding employment in a stable factory in this manner: "A friend told me they were hiring, and it took about one year to get in there."

Once employed, people newly in the stable working class develop bridging social capital through their workplaces, unions, and the schools and sports clubs their children attend. For example, one study in Miami found that Cuban dominance in the building trades started when Cubans gained access to the closed white social capital networks that dominated construction by intermarrying with whites from similar class backgrounds (Stepick et al. 1997). White relatives helped Latinos find jobs in construction, and the Cubans in turn helped their countrymen find jobs at the same firms. Earlier research in Philadelphia showed that both children and adults developed bridging relationships with people from other groups in schools, workplaces, and neighborhoods (Goode and Schneider 1994; Schneider 1997b). Cultural capital based on work and organization activities develops over time. The new connections evolve into new closed social capital networks.

When factories leave town, communities of displaced workers fall into low-wage jobs or shift, often together, into comparable jobs in the service sector. In neighborhoods where the low-skilled working class and stable working class live next to each other and attend the same schools, young people are likely to turn to their peers from different worker-type backgrounds to find work. Social and cultural capital combine to cement already existing closed networks.

RISING EDUCATED MIDDLE CLASS

Those in the rising educated middle class are more likely to develop bridging networks as individuals, but with the support of preexisting closed social capital networks. For example, one African American woman working in a small community hostile to people of color recalled going home to her family and friends in a neighboring state every weekend for several years to find the supports she needed to continue working in the new community.

When the rising person's initial networks are not supportive, people often develop new closed social capital networks among people like themselves as a supportive base for their lives in bridging situations. For example, the African American professionals in Kenosha founded a club that meets regularly to offer social supports and social capital resources for jobs and other needs. Because many of these rising-educated-middle-class people have few social capital resources among their families, the club becomes a new closed network for people who are often the only person of color in their workplace. The club also provides alternative social and cultural capital to the networks that these individuals developed as children.

In some cases, schools serve as bridging institutions, as for Lydia and Mark. Lydia developed bridging friendships through school. In other cases, faith communities, community-based organizations, and citywide social service agencies provide bridging opportunities. The rising educated middle class are also more likely to turn for advice and information to citywide resources, including newspapers, professional organizations, and government services. Already comfortable in bridging institutions, they are more likely to trust advice from citywide resources. For example, they often spoke of finding resources by using the Internet, government, or nonprofit referral systems, or the yellow pages. Comfortable in mixed class and race/ethnicity/nationality settings, they felt they had the skills to use middle-class, mainstream resources and accurately compare options for child care, training, and other needs.

Each worker type used closed social capital networks to meet most needs. Some groups and individuals were more successful than others in developing bridging behaviors. Comparing family strategies highlights the fact that both bridging and closed social capital are necessary to survive in today's multicultural environment.

WELFARE REFORM AND WORKER TYPES

How do these different kinds of families fare in the current welfare-reform climate? As discussed in chapter 2, welfare reform presumes that poor families simply need to find work to become self-sufficient. The Rapid Attachment Study, an analysis of the administrative data from one of Pennsylvania's pilot welfare-to-work programs, shows how families respond.[4] The study consisted mostly of women who had never married. Eighty-six percent of the people in the program were female, 68 percent were single, 8 percent were currently married, and the rest were separated or divorced.[5] The majority had small families—66 percent had two or fewer children. Forty-nine percent were the only adult in the household, 26 percent lived with another adult, 8 percent were teen parents with no adult in the household, and the remainder lived in households with more than two adults. Sixty-four percent said that their housing was stable.

The wages and benefits for all the people in the Rapid Attachment program were very low. Only 17 percent had earned between $7 and $9 an hour at any point in their career. Six percent had earned between $9 and $11, and only 4 percent had ever held a job that paid more than $11 an hour. Given these low wages, employment provided little means to support a family and seldom enough to save for hard times.

The Rapid Attachment Study encompasses a more vulnerable population than the families in the other studies, but the diversity it shows in worker types is similar to that in other research. Twenty-three percent had worked in data-entry or clerical jobs in the Rapid Attachment program. In addition, 11 percent of the participants had worked in professional or professional entry-level jobs such as social worker, caseworker, or nurse.

Rapid Attachment Study participants were categorized by worker type based on work experience, wage progression, and education.[6] Unfortunately, because the database did not include information on dates of employment, I was unable to measure the duration of employment for program participants in this study. For this reason, this analysis divides the population of low-skilled workers into two groups. *Low-skilled workers with three to five jobs* fits the profile of most low-skilled workers, the long-term welfare cyclers who make up the bulk of the population on welfare. The *low-skilled workers with one or two jobs* consists primarily of people with low-wage work in the service sector, like other low-skilled workers—however, given the large number of clerical and

TABLE 8.2 WORKER TYPE BY EMPLOYMENT HISTORY (%)

	Limited work experience	Low wage workers, one or two jobs	Low-skilled workers, three-five jobs	Displaced workers	Rising educated middle class
	$N = 124$ (17%)	$N = 424$ (59%)	$N = 92$ (13%)	$N = 58$ (8%)	$N = 20$ (3%)
Ever held job as					
Cashier	0	18	29	5	5
Clerical/data entry	0	22	48	33	40
Housekeeper	0	19	22	14	10
Sales	0	13	28	9	25
Restaurant	0	17	29	9	5
Factory work	0	17	28	12	20
Professional entry-level	0	7	5	52	85
Professional	0	0	0	57	30
Ever earned					
Less than $5 an hour	0	79	96	62	85
$5–7 an hour	2	33	67	59	50
$7–9 an hour	0	14	26	48	50
$9–11 an hour	0	4	2	28	35
>$11	0	2	3	19	5
Company relocated	0	4	12	19	20
High-school diploma	29	53	77	76	65
Attended college	6	6	10	0	100

Source: Rapid Attachment Study.

factory workers in this group, a few displaced workers who held jobs in the secondary or nonprofit sectors of the economy may also have been placed in this category. Since the Rapid Attachment program included few immigrants and refugees,[7] I do not include that worker type in this analysis.

Table 8.2 shows employment experience and educational information for participants in the Rapid Attachment study. The kinds of jobs held by people in this program were very similar to those of people in the other studies. However, more Rapid Attachment Study participants held jobs such as housekeeping that could be in the informal economy than in any other study. Only the displaced workers showed a wage progression throughout their careers.

Informal economy refers to a variety of economic strategies based exclusively on "under the table" cash or barter payments that are not reported to government. These include many income strategies similar to those in such mainstream occupations as housecleaning, building trades, car repair, beautician work, and sales of Amway, Avon, or other products obtained in a variety of ways. In the informal economy, people work out of their homes or as independent contractors strictly for cash or trade. Informal economy income sources also include illegal businesses, for example, dealing drugs, fencing stolen goods, and trading commodities obtained through welfare.

The rising-educated-middle-class people in this program differed from participants like Lydia, Karen, Paul, and Mark because all the people in this category in the Rapid Attachment Study began college and middle-class jobs later in their lives. The work histories of these individuals are more similar to those of Martha and other women who started out in displaced-worker or low-skilled jobs and decided to pursue college education and professional employment later in their careers. As documented in table 8.2, these people began their careers in a range of jobs, most earning low wages before returning to college. At the time that they were in the Rapid Attachment program, they had just begun work in professional or professional entry-level jobs. This explains why only 5 percent of the people in this worker type had earned more than $11 an hour and only 30 percent had held a true professional job.

Data on placement status were missing for 28 percent of the participants, or 202 people. Presumably, many of these individuals were current participants in the program. Of the remaining participants, 47 percent were placed in jobs, 46 percent were not placed, .2 percent quit for health reasons, and 7 percent quit for other reasons.

FACTORS INFLUENCING SUCCESSFUL COMPLETION AND DROPPING OUT

The percentage of people placed varied by whether a person had a high-school diploma, degree of social isolation, and worker type. Fifty-five percent of those with a high-school diploma found jobs compared with 36 percent of those who did not have this credential. Eleven percent of those without a high-school diploma quit, versus 5 percent of those with a diploma.

College education related to both placement and quitting the program. Sixty-four percent of those who had attended college were placed, and 18 percent of this group quit. It is no surprise that people with better human capital skills would more easily find jobs. The high quitting level for this group may be attributable to cultural clashes between program assumptions and the abilities of these individuals. For example, Sam, a participant in our welfare-to-work program, told me that his wife, who was enrolled in Training Solutions's rapid-attachment program, planned to "go out and get any job" to keep the agency from bothering her. "It's just a joke," he told me. Participants are told about "showing up on time and how to do résumés. She knows how to do that." Sam and his wife felt that Training Solutions showed disrespect for their clients by assuming that they did not understand mainstream work habits. Similarly, college-educated people may feel humiliated by programs that presume that participants lack basic social or work-readiness skills. This finding suggests that designing individualized programs based on ability would be most appropriate for this population.

Social isolation was a key factor in the rate of program completion. Most socially isolated individuals came from limited-work-experience environments; 43 percent of those who quit were categorized as socially isolated. Only 34 percent of the people who were socially isolated were placed in a job.

Displaced workers were most likely to be placed. A full 69 percent of this group found jobs, whereas only 30 percent of those with limited work experience were placed. Those with low-wage work experience fell in the middle: 47 percent of those who had had one or two jobs and 52 percent of those with three to five jobs found work.

People with work experience in several key occupations were also more likely to be placed. Fifty-nine percent of those with clerical work experience, 55 percent of those with sales experience, 68 percent of the professionals, and 61 percent of those with professional entry-level experience were placed. Better placements in these categories were the result of both higher skill levels among these individuals and the availability of more jobs in these categories in the Philadelphia labor market.

However, when evaluated through analysis that compared many attributes, none of these variables proved statistically significant in determining who was placed by this program.[8] Only two factors were statistically significant: the number of questions answered on the TABE math test and being a displaced worker. The TABE (Test of Adult Basic Education) is a widely used standardized test to determine basic math and reading ability.[9] Background experience and education play a limited role in determining who finds work via a rapid-attachment program.

CHARACTERISTICS OF JOBS FOUND THROUGH THE PROGRAM

These various characteristics play an even more complicated role in the kinds of work found by participants. Fifty-six percent of those placed found full-time jobs (35–40 hours per week) and 44 percent found part-time work. Twenty-seven percent of the jobs were for 20 hours a week or less. Thirty-three percent of the jobs offered health insurance from the start, and another 7 percent provided health insurance after several months; the majority of those placed relied on Medicaid. The average wage was $7.09, with a minimum wage of $4.25 and a maximum of $17.63.

Table 8.3 lists the primary types of jobs found by program participants. As in their previous work experience, many found employment in clerical jobs and as nursing assistants. The same occupations seen in the list of previous employment appear, but many jobs are less important. Far fewer people were placed in jobs as cashiers, in housekeeping, in factory work, and in restaurants. Only one person found a professional job while in this program.

These similarities and differences reflect a combination of previous work experience, the nature of the local labor market, and the placement strengths

TABLE 8.3 MAJOR PLACEMENT JOBS

Job Title	%
Cashier	8
Data entry/clerical	19
Nursing assistant	14
Child care	5
Housekeeper	5
Security guard	1
Sales	7
Factory work	4
Maintenance/construction	4
Restaurant	5
Other	25

Source: Rapid Attachment Study.

of the agency. Work experience played the biggest role. Sixty-one percent of those who were placed in clerical work had worked in computer or clerical jobs in the past. Most of those with health-care experience found work as nursing assistants or in child care. Forty-four percent of the nursing assistants had worked in health care in the past. Thirty-six percent of those who found work in child care also had a health-care background. Forty-seven percent of those who found sales jobs had sales experience. People with factory experience found jobs as security guards (100 percent), factory workers (44 percent), and factory drivers (50 percent). Thirty-one percent of those placed in restaurant jobs had worked in a restaurant before. Only two placements—as a cashier and a housekeeper—had no relationship to previous employment.

Table 8.4 summarizes the types of jobs found through this program and the average wage for each. The majority found work in the service sector (cashier, restaurant, sales), the helping professions (nursing assistant, child care, teacher's aide), and clerical jobs. The quality of the jobs found through the program did not match that of the jobs previously held by the program participants. In fact, the results of the Rapid Attachment Study suggest that quick-placement programs may hinder the chances of displaced workers and the rising educated middle class regaining their previous economic status. Most of those with professional and professional entry-level experience found work in clerical, sales, or helping occupations. These results highlight the fact that, under time pressure, people with good experience will end up in low-paid, no-benefit, secondary-sector jobs.

Participants with various characteristics reacted differently to the rapid-attachment program. The wages and hours for people of different worker types had no relationship to previous experience or worker type. Overall, displaced workers and those in the rising educated middle class earned about one dollar more than the others, with a median wage of $8 per hour as opposed to $7 for other groups. However, a close look at the job-type characteristics reveals that most displaced workers and rising-educated-middle-class people were taking jobs that either were part time or had no insurance. None of the displaced workers found full-time clerical work with insurance, the kind of employment held by many displaced workers before losing their stable jobs. Thirteen percent took clerical full-time jobs with no insurance, 22 percent took blue-collar part-time jobs with insurance, 13 percent took other part-time jobs with no insurance. The strategy seemed to be to take the job that was easiest to find, which often meant not getting the most stable, family-sustaining employment.

Work-first strategies largely returned low-skilled workers to the same kinds of jobs they had held before entering this mandated program. Many of these jobs were part-time, with no insurance.

Those with limited work experience or only one or two low-skilled jobs found work in part-time helping professions and blue-collar part-time jobs

TABLE 8.4 PLACEMENT JOB CHARACTERISTICS

Job Type	%	Average Wage ($/hour)
Service-sector, full-time, insurance	2	7.59
Service-sector, full-time, no insurance	6	5.28
Service-sector, part-time, no insurance	12	6.00
Clerical, full-time, insurance	4	8.71
Clerical, full-time, no insurance	9	8.09
Clerical, part-time, no insurance	6	6.39
Helping professions, full-time, insurance	2	8.02
Helping professions, full-time, no insurance	6	6.25
Helping professions, part-time, no insurance	16	6.36
Blue-collar, full-time, insurance	6	6.30
Blue-collar, part-time, insurance	6	8.30
Blue-collar, part-time, no insurance	19	8.16
Other, part-time, insurance	2	10.36
Other, part-time, no insurance	4	6.90

Source: Rapid Attachment study.

Service-sector jobs include sales, cashier, and restaurant work. *Clerical* includes data entry. *Helping professions* include limited-education jobs working with people, e.g., nursing assistant, child-care worker, teacher's aide. *Blue-collar* includes security guard and maintenance/construction and factory work. *Other* includes jobs listed as *other* and one professional position.

with no insurance. Twenty percent of the low-skilled workers with one to three jobs found helping-profession part-time jobs, and 19 percent found blue-collar part-time jobs. Forty-two percent of those with limited work experience found work in these two categories (21 percent for each category). None of those with limited work experience found jobs with insurance. The most vulnerable program participants often found work in the worst jobs.

However, many of the most secure, well-paying jobs went to those with only one to three low-skilled jobs. Seventy-nine percent of those in clerical, full-time jobs with insurance and 83 percent of those in helping-profession jobs with insurance fell into this category. Since one would ordinarily expect the displaced workers to get these better jobs, another principle may be operating here. Ethnographic work with program participants suggests that these individuals may have avoided taking the less stable employment because of the potential lack of wages and benefits. Since they were more likely to rely on the agency for placement than the displaced workers, the rising educated middle class, or those with more work experience in low-skilled jobs, they may also have benefited more from the program's priority to find full-time work with insurance, compared with those who had better personal resources. Thus, a few of the more vulnerable participants with some work experience actually found better jobs through the rapid-attachment program than they had held previously. It is important to note, however, that only 9 percent of the people in this worker-type category found these stable jobs. In most cases, rapid attachment meant quickly finding unstable, secondary-sector employment.

The Rapid Attachment Study suggests that these programs do not draw on the strengths of the more stable families or make up for social capital weaknesses among people out of work. Instead, work-first initiatives lead to quick and often inappropriate placements. Work-first strategies are generally based on the presumption that welfare recipients lack work experience, and that finding any job will lead to long-term economic success. However, as analysis of individual work history shows, these people lack connections to stable jobs, not work experience. This research suggests that finding good jobs takes a combination of time, appropriate education or skills, previous work experience, and connections. Experience with rapid attachment suggests that other work-focused strategies may have better long-term results.

POLICY IMPLICATIONS

Discussions of education, child care, and responses to work-first programs show that families consider the needs of the entire family when developing strategies for one member. Families' responses also reflect the resources available based on their closed social capital networks and ability to bridge into other communities. Two policy implications arise from this discussion:

- Welfare-to-work strategies need to address the needs of entire families, not only working-age adults. A family's choices depend on the needs and goals of various members. Designing plans that address all these diverse needs is much more likely to lead to economic stability than programs aimed simply at finding work for the head of household.
- Since people rely on their closed social capital networks and communities to meet their needs, successful welfare-to-work strategies should focus simultaneously on individuals and their communities.

SUMMARY

Comparisons across groups show that family survival strategies involve inter-meshing of human, social, cultural, and economic capital. While all five family types valued education, each saw adult education as playing a different role in career trajectory. Limited-work-experience and low-skilled workers hoped education would lead to stable jobs, but they were repeatedly disappointed in this goal because they lacked the social and cultural capital to benefit from their training. The stable working class and rising educated middle class, on the other hand, were better equipped to make wise educational choices and use education to advance their careers because they developed social and cultural capital that helped them choose appropriate training and find related jobs. Migrants and refugees had a wide array of resources that led to various outcomes.

Child-care strategies were similar across groups. Here, economic capital and family structures influenced choices more than social and cultural capital.

All families use closed social capital resources to achieve their goals. Each family type responds differently to bridging opportunities. Ability to cross boundaries depended on trusting people from different groups. People in the rising educated middle class were most able to develop trusting relationships across class boundaries because of positive encouragement by people from different groups and leadership opportunities at an early age.

Rapid-attachment programs helped families get back into the labor force, but they did little to help these families find stable, family-supporting jobs. Pressure to find work quickly led even the most employable people into low-wage service-sector jobs. Instead, employment strategies targeted to particular strengths and weaknesses benefit families the most.

PART II
SOCIAL CAPITAL AND
COMMUNITY CONTEXT

The first half of the book describes five factors that influence implementation of social welfare policy in Philadelphia, Milwaukee, and Kenosha. In these three cities, organizations and individuals using the public assistance system encounter local policies that tailor federal regulations to fit state and local philosophies and conditions. Wisconsin uses a geographically based, hierarchical model focusing on work to make public assistance users more similar to the working-class populations in each city. Pennsylvania's program offers more options and mixed messages, also working more closely with local providers to develop policy strategies.

Policy encounters nearly identical organizational types, implementation systems, labor markets, and worker types in all three cities. Organizations fall into the categories of citywide institutions, community-based organizations, and faith-based organizations because they are oriented toward different constituencies. Citywide institutions connect to people and institutions concerned with a given social problem; community-based organizations look toward their mission-defined community; and faith-based organizations focus on the founding religious body for resources and direction. Each draws on social capital from those constituencies.

Organizations function within four interlocking systems: the official welfare system, the ancillary services system, the community-based system, and the faith-community system. Social capital networks within each system influence policy implementation in each locality. Although organizations need to connect with other institutions offering complementary services in that city, relationships crossing systems of organizations are often idiosyncratic.

The labor market in the three communities presents challenges to government policies and organizations attempting to move families out of long-term poverty. The bifurcated labor market offers plentiful jobs but fewer opportunities that pay family-supporting wages with benefits. As a result, welfare caseloads have fallen, but many families remain in poverty.

Families rely on their social capital to navigate social service systems and the labor market. Examination of worker types indicates that, although human capital makes a difference, often the determining factor in individual career trajectories is a family's social capital resources.

Taken together, these chapters show individuals and institutions negotiating systems based on global economic systems, regional cultural cues, and state and national policies. However, each family must access systems through particularistic social capital mechanisms. Resources include family, friends, community, social service organizations, churches, and government. Organizations function in the same kind of localized social capital systems.

People and institutions access social capital in specific contexts. Part II begins with a careful look at the role of several relevant environments on social capital development and use in light of welfare reform. I use the case examples introduced earlier in book, as well as a few new ones, to examine social capital in each context. The appendixes provide a quick reference to the case examples. Appendix B lists all the organizations and churches profiled in the book. Appendix C provides information on the key individuals and families.

Chapter 9 examines the ways families use social service organizations to meet their needs. How do families conceptualize social service agencies as potential resources, and how do individual connections to organizations influence the role of these institutions for families? How does an organization create social and cultural capital for its participants? Do organizations create closed or bridging social capital, and, if so, why, and how does this process work?

Chapter 10 places organizations in the context of their social capital resources to examine the impact of welfare reform on different organizations, focusing on two aspects of organization behavior. First, it looks outward at the way that organizations use their social capital to gain funding and other needed resources. The relationship of each organization to the interlocking service-delivery systems become particularly important in understanding this process. Second, it looks at mission focus and management structures as they influence the way that specific organizations carry out welfare programs. What role does an organization's social and cultural capital play in its ability to carry out its mission and program goals?

Chapter 11 asks the same questions of faith communities. Through an examination of activities within congregations and the communities they create, the chapter describes how social and cultural capital and community develop in congregations. Looking at the issue of faith-based social welfare provision, this chapter discusses important differences between church congregations and nonprofit organizations as entities offering formal programs.

The final two chapters explore the interactions of various organizations in implementing social welfare policy in these three cities. Chapter 12 focuses on service delivery as well as the interaction among congregations, nonprofits, and government. This chapter examines the flow of individuals among these institutions and the role of individual social and cultural capital in expanding community. Chapter 13, on advocacy and social change, considers the role of social and cultural capital in the development and success of advocacy coalitions.

The concluding chapter brings together common themes throughout the book to propose a social welfare system that reflects the importance of social capital in welfare reform.

CHAPTER 9

Social Service Agency Use and Social Capital

Scholars of civic engagement often see nonprofit organizations as venues for developing social capital, political participation, and community (Putnam 1995; Berger and Neuhaus 1977; Hunter 1974). In this model, nonprofit organizations are embodiments of community spirit. Organizations are participatory institutions in which people both give and receive services. This first model most closely fits organizations created to serve one closed social capital community through recreation, political activity, or services. For example, an Elks club may offer a gathering place for community members. In addition to participating in its activities, members sometimes volunteer or work at the organization. Putnam (1995, 2000) sees the demise of these institutions in the United States as a sign of declining social capital because people now have fewer opportunities for face-to-face interactions in which to work together to improve conditions in a locality.

Other scholars see government contracting as turning nonprofits into agents of government. This view also envisions nonprofits as institutions created by and for local citizens to assist one another (Smith and Lipsky 1993). However, in this second model, social service agencies have lost their connection to the people they serve, becoming merely places to obtain services without community input or oversight. The social-service-agency-as-arm-of-government model sees organizations as losing their connection to the local community as government contracts replace private funding. One extension of this view is that nonprofits no longer control the way they provide service. In addition, volunteers and other local people are less likely to participate in helping one another as organizations substitute paid staff for volunteers. As in the first model, nonprofits no longer serve as venues for community.

The history of several of the nonprofits profiled here partly supports this view. For example, Neighborhood Settlement House and Latinos United both started as community centers that involved both elites and community residents working together to meet community needs. The youth and adult improvement programs that these organizations originally created served a broad range of community residents. Programs also included much volunteer involvement from residents as members of both the board and the staff. Although the board, staff, and participants did not all come from the same closed social capital networks, they had enough common ground to work together toward similar goals. Both organizations fostered bridging relationships among staff and participants.

However, as the focus of each organization changed to working more with categorically needy populations and the original population of the founding community became more economically stable, linkages among participants, staff, and board became more attenuated. Still, each organization involves community residents as both receivers and givers of service. The boundaries between participants, staff, and board were renegotiated in this process. For example, Neighborhood Settlement House was initially chartered as a member organization, and its program participants are still charged a nominal fee to join.[1] However, given the current paternalistic vision of program participants, these fees are now considered a token to instill the values of civic participation and mutual responsibility in program participants. The board recently deleted the line *and members* from the by-laws with the rationale that the settlement house had no members involved in governance. No one on the board or management staff thought to ask the board member who was an active organization participant/member, but not present for the vote, whether she or any other of the actual "members" approved of this change.

Despite the change from community-based voluntary organization to professional agency, each of these organizations still serves as a community center and a place where some of its participants could develop social capital. This was also true for most organizations except the large, citywide social service institutions. Particularly in impoverished neighborhoods, social service agencies combine with faith communities and family networks to offer alternatives to often dangerous streets. However, social capital means relationships that help people find resources to meet their needs, not civic engagement. Developing community and becoming involved in sustaining that community may be one by-product of social capital development through organizations. Families also actively volunteer at organizations in a variety of roles.

This chapter explores the different ways that families use social service agencies to meet multiple goals. Participants choose the impact of an agency's programs on their social capital development. The difference in how participants define community and social capital for themselves becomes a key factor in understanding the role of social service agencies in welfare reform. The chapter addresses the following questions:

- How do families use agencies to meet their goals?
- Do families use social service agencies as avenues to social capital and community?
- Does the referral structure of the agency influence how people use it?

- Do families of different worker types use social service agencies and government differently or look toward different organizations for assistance?

Use Patterns and Social Capital

Both community and social capital are created through participation in ongoing activities. Simply belonging to an organization or living in a neighborhood does not constitute community or social capital. Community and social capital also involve both affective and instrumental supports. This section explores the ways individuals use social service organizations to build social capital and meet instrumental needs.

Examining family strategies revealed two patterns. Some families use a single organization or a small group of linked organizations to meet their needs. These families developed a strong commitment to these organizations, fostering social capital and community through involvement in activities. Participation in social service agencies became a significant component of closed social capital development. I call these *agency-focused families.*

Other families developed closed social capital through either faith communities or individual networks, using organizations as a tool to address certain needs. These individuals participated in disparate organizations with different goals. Sometimes either members of individual networks or other institutions would serve as a referral mechanism to social service organizations. The organization was not a source of community and seldom became a long-term social capital resource. These are labeled *instrumental-need-focused families.* I use examples from Neighborhood Settlement House to illustrate the two family types.

Agency-Focused Families

Neighborhood Settlement House became the source for friendships, civic activity, employment, and instrumental goods and services for some families associated with the organization. These families helped shape the agency's culture and focus because they recruited additional participants as well as the people who come to the town hall meetings that determine the direction of the organization. The settlement house now serves a largely African American, low-income population because they are the community most visible to the organization. Its expectation of appropriate clientele contributed to determining the target population, but then the dynamic between organization and participating community took over to cement the organization's role in the community as the locus for both recreational and social service supports for low-income African Americans.

Agency-focused families became a core group of participants and volunteers at the organization. Various family members used multiple programs there. In addition to receiving services, these participants also volunteered to assist at events, serve on the board, and help operate programs. The agency also hired some members of these families as staff.

This core group shared several characteristics. The majority were single parents who were dependent on welfare or had low-paying jobs. Many either had health problems themselves or had relatives with health problems that required extra care. These family dynamics limited their ability to hold paying jobs and led them to seek social services. Some were long-term residents of public housing. Education level varied across this group, but the majority lacked the cultural and social capital to succeed in white, "mainstream" workplaces (Fernandez Kelly 1995; Schneider 2000). Although members of this group developed strong and active organizational lives within the housing project and Neighborhood Settlement House, few had many ties outside these communities.

Sally is a leader of this group. She has much more leadership involvement in the organization than other core group participants, but in many ways she is typical of them. She is an African American single parent with two children and three foster children. She has been disabled since high school and has a developmentally disabled son. Despite these problems, she has completed two years of college and worked as a printer for six and a half years before focusing on caring for her disabled child. She has lived in public housing for more than twenty years. For most of her life she has survived on a combination of part-time work,

AFDC, and SSI. She is currently supported by a combination of SSI, a part-time paid position with the housing authority, food stamps, and Medicaid.

Although Sally relies on government support, she is hardly the stereotypical welfare mother spending her time watching soap operas. Instead, she is an active volunteer for both the housing project and Neighborhood Settlement House. Her family uses multiple programs at the organization as well. She describes her early relationship to Neighborhood Settlement House as follows: "The atmosphere was friendly, welcome. The [workers] let me be involved in almost everything I wanted to volunteer in. My son goes there. My girlfriend works there." Sally's story shows how social networks led her to the center. She then relied on these networks to find services and develop a meaningful volunteer career. As is typical of social capital, her relationship with the center involves reciprocity and trust. She has also created a cohesive community of friends and resources that provide both instrumental and affective supports.

In the fifteen years that she has been involved with the center, Sally has both used services and provided network entry to others now in the core group. This includes referring people to services, involving them in volunteer activities, and encouraging others to use the resources of the organization. She also serves as a key link to other organizations that seek to help residents of the Uptown housing project through Neighborhood Settlement House. For example, she was the contact person when a church developed outreach activities for the housing project.

Sally has extensive knowledge of Uptown, organizations that serve her community, and Neighborhood Settlement House but is not very knowledgeable about the wider neighborhood beyond a few blocks from Uptown. For example, when I asked her to lead a van tour of the neighborhood, she could talk at length about the organizations directly tied to her world but could answer few questions about parts of the neighborhood or institutions outside her social community. Asked about businesses, she said only, "They don't hire many Uptown residents." The same was true of the white people living a few blocks away; she had no idea how much the houses cost, where people worked, or why they had little to do with Neighborhood Settlement House.

Sally's world view is based on focused experience in a closed social capital network that consists primarily of other low-income African Americans. She has no involvement in a faith community, and her volunteer activities, access to social services, and social ties are centered on this agency. Like others in the group who use multiple services, Sally in many ways epitomizes the ways that these Neighborhood Settlement House participants creatively used the organization as a source for community and social capital.

In other cases, people in the core participant group were hired by the organization, as Jaysa was. For these people, Neighborhood Settlement House became a source of employment as well as social service. A number of community residents were employed in the agency as day-care or youth aides, as receptionists or in other low-level jobs. However, the agency provided little additional training for these low-level staff, and many remained in the same job for many years.

This core participant and staff group developed social capital links that allowed them to fulfill instrumental needs. Although Neighborhood Settlement House attempts to inform all participants about available services through fliers and informational orientations, many program participants remained unaware of the full array of offerings. The problem stemmed partly from the building's physical layout, which was a maze of corridors. The fact that there was no welcoming receptionist or formal intake process to tell people about available programs added to the confusion. Newcomers had no easy way to learn about the organization.

Instead, people connected to Neighborhood Settlement House through referral to a specific program or word of mouth from someone already involved. If people connected to the core participant group through either staff or other participants, they found themselves in a rich network that would guide them through the organization maze. Closely connected to staff, they learned about special events in addition to the full range of social services. For example, one program director complained that when school supplies were donated for participants in one program, before the staff could give the supplies to the intended recipients, others were asking for them—community-based staff members had already reported the gift to the core group, who had spread the word among their friends.

Some of the W-2 recipients placed at the agency for their required community-service became part of this closed social capital group. Some were quickly adopted by the established core group. Others developed social capital links through friends in the community-service program who had developed links to the core group. All these women shared cultural assumptions similar to those of the older core group members.

The existence of this core community was not lost on other people who used the organization or lived in Uptown, and accusations of favoritism were made. Thus, close social networks led to barriers between members of the closed social capital core group and other participants.

For both core group staff and program participants, Neighborhood Settlement House became an inclusive community where all their needs were met. This core group circumvented the formal goals and hierarchy of the organization for their own purpose. Ironically, the people who best fit the integrated-services model of the organization were least likely to meet the mission goals of self-sufficiency. Rather than passive recipients of paternalistic service, they are active forces in the organization who make full use of available resources.

However, their community and social capital networks are relatively closed to outsiders. They also have formed a community that allows them to remain within their established social world. In making full use of Neighborhood Settlement House's resources, they have circumvented the need to build bridges into other organizations or communities.

This pattern of closed social capital through organizations effectively fulfilled social and instrumental goals for these families. Although the basis of this particular network is a social service agency, it is similar to closed social capital networks using a few agencies typical in immigrant communities or closed communities of color.

For example, the core group that developed Latinos United was part of a Mexican migrant community in Kenosha that relied on a closed social capital network based in this organization, a migrant worker organization, and two churches. A whole generation of Kenosha's Latino families oriented their social capital networks around this small group of institutions. However, in this case, the institutions arose out of preexisting social capital networks in the migrant community rather than the organization's becoming the source of social capital and community. Families knew one another from their home base in Texas; they had migrated to Kenosha together. However, as important links to employers and other aspects of white Kenosha, these institutions became critical bridging social capital resources as well as venues for developing closed social capital and community. Families considered them part of their social capital repertoire of resources.

As the first generation of Kenosha Latinos became established members of the stable working class, they gave back to this core community by serving on Latinos United's board. In many ways, board involvement recreated the earlier sense of community as these families worked closely together to keep the organization functioning. Fund-raising events and use of the organization's facilities for family celebrations also preserved the earlier sense of community center for established Texas-Mexicans.

As both the organization and the community changed over time, Latinos United became less of a source for community for its participants. Program participants are now likely to use the organization for instrumental needs but develop social capital and community elsewhere. As one board member observed: "It's not so much that they're all migrant workers anymore. . . . I think in the old days [Latinos United] served just Mexican Americans, and over the years it has evolved to a agency that helps anybody who walks through the door."

This change in constituency occurred for two reasons. First, the organization no longer offers opportunities for participants to work at the agency or contribute to its planning. Thirty years ago, as with Lydia, these organizations regularly employed program participants. Now employees come from the pool of established Latinos and outsiders offering particular skills. Recipients of service are new migrants or low-income Kenosha residents, a diffuse group of people from several communities. Staff and participants come from different closed social capital networks. There is less opportunity for the new participants to use the agency as a source of community because of these social capital barriers between them and the staff.

The second reason for this change involves the nature of services. Latinos United still offers many of the core services that it did when it was initially founded, for example, ESL, translation services, and the food pantry. However, these services are now seen as providing assistance to the needy rather than helping members of "our" community. In addition, funding comes primarily from government contracts for energy assistance, gang prevention, and antipoverty programs serving all Kenosha residents. The Mexican migrants are just another group receiving service. Recognizing this change, participants now see Latinos United as a resource for fulfilling instrumental needs for families whose major social capital networks exist elsewhere.

INSTRUMENTAL-NEEDS-FOCUSED FAMILIES

Differences in the closed social capital networks of agency staff and participants are only one reason that families would use agencies exclusively to meet instrumental needs. Even when families come from the same community as the agencies they use for services, they often seek social capital elsewhere.

The household of Assan, the Nigerian immigrant profiled earlier, is one example of a family that uses institutions for instrumental needs. Assan's primary social capital networks are focused on the émigré community. He has gone to Neighborhood Settlement House for assistance in paying high utility bills and has enrolled his daughter in the after-school program. However, he regards the agency as existing primarily to fulfill instrumental rather than social capital needs: "The purpose of the center should be to help people living around the neighborhood, like for job placement, assisting them in whatever area they have difficulties in."

Most families that use social services only to fulfill instrumental needs have strong social capital networks elsewhere. They find out about agencies through either these social networks or formal institutions. For example, Assan found out that Neighborhood Settlement House had a program to help with utility costs through the utility company.

Although families that use agencies as a center for social capital tend to belong exclusively to one closed social capital network, families that use agencies for instrumental means reflect either exclusively closed social capital or closed social capital combined with bridging tendencies. Rising-educated-middle-class families are most likely to seek a range of different agency supports to meet needs. However, low-income and limited-work-experience families may also use multiple agencies for resources. For example, one Kenosha family explained how they used most of the safety-net programs available through social service agencies and churches to meet instrumental needs. Most referrals came from other agencies, demonstrating social service agencies' use of their social capital to help families fulfill instrumental needs.

Summary

Both agency-focused and instrumental-needs-focused families use social service agencies to meet their needs. The difference between the two types of families stems from their relationship to the organization and their links to other agencies. Agency-focused families see themselves as participatory members of an institution, becoming involved in several aspects of organization activity: receiving service, volunteering, recruiting other participants, and sometimes participating in planning or governance. They develop friendships and closed social capital through involvement in agency activities.

Instrumental-needs-focused families, on the other hand, tend to use one program for a short period of time. Even when these families use the same agency more than once, as when Assan sent his daughter to the Neighborhood Settlement House's after-school program, the family concentrates on the need fulfilled by the organization—in this case, help with homework. Assan could have chosen another resource for this service if one was available; he feels no allegiance to the agency. These families are much more likely to use multiple agencies with no connections to one another to meet family needs. Referral to agencies come from multiple sources as well. Does orientation toward an agency affect a family's economic progress?

Family Economic Change and Agency Use

W-2 potentially fosters change in the economic circumstances of families through its emphasis on work. However, in studies of low-income families leaving the welfare rolls, many did not dramatically improve their income (Acker et al. 2002; Wiseman 1999). Analysis of family survival strategies reveals that those that intentionally use institutions as part of their bridging strategy are most likely to move into stable income brackets.

Families that focus exclusively on social service organizations in one closed social capital network have limited opportunities in a changing economy. In one example of this tendency, those who use Sunrise, the homeless shelter in Kenosha, develop a rich resource base relying on a combination of safety-net providers and personal networks. A group of women came to Sunrise through common closed social capital links in the African American communities of northern Illinois and Kenosha. They formed stronger friendships while in the shelter program, and they added other shelter residents with similar cultural capital to their network. Once the group found housing, they continued the closed social capital networks developed within the agency, helping one another to find child care, jobs, and other resources. The agency had become their community, fostering social capital links that lasted after they had left the shelter.

Unfortunately, these links were circumscribed by the resources available among the limited-work-experience and low-skilled-worker relatives who had initially told these families about Sunrise. Social capital links may have expanded to include other individuals in the shelter, but these people belonged to the same closed social capital networks in the broader Kenosha community. As a result, these former shelter residents had limited success changing their life circumstances significantly. Their reliance on newly formed social capital with resources similar to those of their previous networks kept them in poverty despite the efforts of the agency and government to improve their conditions through advice about job hunting and other economic strategies.

Advice from agency staff offered middle-class cultural capital but not the social capital referrals to turn strategies into different resources. These women lacked either the human capital or the social capital to find jobs that paid more stable wages than their previous employment had. They lacked the income to obtain housing in better neighborhoods or higher-quality day care for their children. After having limited success using agency advice, these women decided to rely on one another rather than on the official helping systems available through Sunrise and the W-2 agency. When people continue in the same worker type despite their best efforts to change their economic position, available social, cultural, human, and economic capital combine to influence long-term strategies. Like other instrumental users of social services, these women continued to use government and social service agencies on a regular basis to meet their needs. However, their social capital came from their community-based resources rather than agencies.

The stable-working-class families who developed strong social capital links to one employer, the union hall, one set of youth programs, and their faith communities similarly found themselves without useful resources when the economy changed. These families used a different set of closed social capital networks to meet their needs. Their networks led them to either leave Kenosha or search for jobs in line with their previous experience. When these networks failed, some of the family members slipped into the ranks of low-skilled workers or, discouraged, stopped looking for employment altogether.

In contrast, families that drew resources from a range of institutions and developed bridging social capital were able to move into more stable opportunities. Martha, the rising-educated-middle-class African American woman described in chapter 1, is one example of this tendency. Other families in the rising educated middle class, as well as low-skilled workers and welfare-dependent families that moved into the stable working class, show similar patterns.

Comparing Jaysa with Martha illustrates the difference that bridging use of agencies makes. Jaysa turned to government for financial support in raising her children. A welfare-to-work program placed her at Neighborhood Settlement House, where she found both instrumental and social capital supports. She now relies on this one agency to meet most of her needs, usually using other social service organizations only through agency referrals. She has not actively sought support from different kinds of organizations to improve her economic condition. Jaysa's use of social services consists of relying on organizations that are already connected to her closed social capital community and that do not encourage her to expand her horizons. As a result, she is likely to remain a low-skilled worker for the remainder of her career.

Martha comes from a neighborhood similar to Jaysa's, but she envisioned opportunities differently. She initially sought clerical training from a local community college, which led to work in that field. Expanded cultural and social capital on the job encouraged her to pursue additional college education and enter social work. She specifically sought placements in the welfare-to-work program that would further these goals. This strategic use of social service agencies, education, and personal resources has included numerous bridging experiences. She relies on workplaces to help her locate appropriate social services and schools, recognizing that these institutions as creating bridging opportunities that will expand cultural, social, and human capital. Agencies are one component in her long-term strategy.

AN AGENCY'S ROLE IN DEVELOPING CLOSED OR BRIDGING SOCIAL CAPITAL

These examples of the ways families use social service agencies suggest that individuals hold control over the role of organizations in their lives. Different participants may use the same organization as either their primary resource for social capital and community or as a means to fulfill instrumental needs. In fact, a much larger percentage of Neighborhood Settlement House's participants fall into the second category. The same is true of other organizations.

That said, agencies do play a role in developing either closed or bridging social capital. Neighborhood Settlement House intends to serve as a one-stop

shop serving all the needs of its participants. It is no surprise that some participants use the organization in this way. In contrast, Citizens United tries to
bridge participants between organizations. As a center-city institution, one of
its missions involves bringing together community-based organizations to address social problems. The direct-service programs introduce participants to a
wide range of programs and opportunities. Attempts to place participants in
neighborhoods other than where they live are designed to help participants
become comfortable in other parts of the city. As with Neighborhood Settlement House, participants react in different ways. For example, as a community-
service job placement, Javier was initially employed by an organization near
where he lived. He used this opportunity to become more active in the neighborhood and the antidrug activities that his placement organization sponsored. He expanded already strong neighborhood-based social capital through
this experience. At the same time, Javier also became involved in citywide political work, using opportunities offered through Citizens United.

On the other hand, some participants use the same bridging opportunities
through organizations without expanding community involvement. Mark
also used the resources available through Citizens United to change careers.
These included pursuing educational and volunteer opportunities. However,
these resources were used in strictly instrumental ways, while social capital remained elsewhere.

POLICY IMPLICATIONS

Agencies can offer opportunities to build bridges through referral to other
agencies, programming that builds bicultural behaviors, and mentoring programs. An earlier study suggests that these kinds of activities for children are a
major factor in families' entry into the rising educated middle class (Schneider
2001:84–85). However, analysis of the ways people use organizations suggests
that agencies can only offer alternatives to families, in the hope that they will
make full use of available resources. Programs like Citizens United's welfare-
to-work program create a culture that encourages participants to cross boundaries. These types of programs may ultimately have more success in fostering
bridging social capital than those designed primarily as the intermediary with
mainstream institutions. However, no single model succeeds in building
bridging social capital, given the importance of individual agency in social
service outcomes.

Nevertheless, welfare-to-work programming would do well to foster bridging behavior among their participants. This includes widening the vision of
possible resources for their program participants and encouraging people to
use other organizations. Although participants can still develop strong community and closed social capital networks within one organization, promoting

wider horizons benefits both the individual and the organization in the long run. Compare Sally to Javier. Sally is active in the housing development and Neighborhood Settlement House, but unable to work effectively outside her closed community. Javier, on the other hand, has become a more active participant in his neighborhood after participating in the Citizens United program that encouraged him to develop citywide networks. He has also maintained contact with Citizens United and other institutions that he encountered through that experience. Bridging social capital strengthens all the constituent institutions.

Agency Strategies and Participant Base

An agency's programmatic agendas can influence the kinds of social capital that participants develop. In addition, government referral systems influence, to a degree, who uses an organization. As demonstrated by the analysis of different agency use patterns in Neighborhood Settlement House earlier in this chapter, although the mandatory programs can connect participants to other programs in the organization, this does not always occur.

The same patterns can be seen in other organizations. For example, Citizens United's programs included a mandatory welfare-to-work program and an adult basic education program. The welfare program drew only people referred by the Private Industry Council or the Department of Public Welfare. These participants came from throughout Philadelphia and had no prior links to the organization. Once involved in the welfare program, some enrolled in the adult basic education programs as either students or teachers.

The adult basic education program, in contrast, drew its volunteer tutors and students from the neighborhood organizations that hosted the programs and the Mayor's Commission on Literacy. These populations came to Citizens United through social capital links in these two very different types of organizations. The community-based referrals tended to differ by neighborhood, reflecting social capital links to partner organizations. This resulted in several largely separate participant groups. The agency's funding and partnering strategies thus largely determined who came in the door. Individual social capital links were weaker than for Neighborhood Settlement House but did influence who participated somewhat.

Neighborhood Settlement House also exhibits a referral system whereby needy participants from other neighborhoods refer friends and family from their closed social capital networks. This pattern also appears in other organizations. For example, Sunrise developed a steady stream of shelter residents from northern Illinois. These participants came to the organization via word-of-mouth referral by friends and family living in Kenosha.

SUMMARY

Examination of agencies' referral patterns suggest that, after initial referral to the organization, individual choice and pre-existing social capital networks take over to determine how families use organizations. The differences in use stemmed primarily from two factors. First, families who developed strong social capital links with other participants shared similar cultural capital with them. Second, these families had not developed strong closed social capital networks through other institutions. Families with strong ties elsewhere sometimes used social service agencies as sources of bridging social capital.

USE OF SOCIAL SERVICE AGENCIES AND WORKER TYPES

People can connect to social service agencies in two additional ways: as either givers or receivers of service. Although families in need were most likely to benefit from social service organizations as program participants, many more families both used services and contributed as volunteers or in fund-raising efforts. Families in every worker category served as both givers and receivers of services. However, comparisons across family types show that different worker types access varying kinds of social service agencies and government. People in different categories may also use agencies for different reasons and experience agency service differently.

LIMITED-WORK-EXPERIENCE AND LOW-SKILLED WORKERS

The types of social service agencies used by families varied widely by family type. Low-skilled workers and limited-work-experience families used safety-net systems most frequently, considering them part of their base resource systems. These included food pantries, clothing programs, and training programs, in addition to formal government systems. People of color, particularly African Americans, were most likely to use these systems. For example, the Social Network Study found that 23 percent of African Americans, 24 percent of Latinos, and 20 percent of Asians, but only 9 percent of whites found a training program through a social service agency. African Americans were most likely to find multiple programs through official agency referrals. These low-income families also received holiday assistance from social service agencies and faith communities. Like Jaysa, who volunteered at Neighborhood Settlement House, low-skilled families both gave to and received from these systems.

While many low-skilled and limited-work-experience families disliked the bureaucracy—and the often rude treatment they received at the hands of government workers—they regularly sought support from government when in need. Using government assistance was part of the cultural understanding of how one survived given the realities of limited savings and poorly paying jobs. These families also had cultural resources that taught how to navigate government systems. Social capital resources in these communities included knowing where to turn for assistance.

Unfortunately, these closed social capital networks were also likely to spread misinformation on program rules, available benefits, and so forth. For example, low-skilled workers in Kenosha spread rumors that people attending community college were not eligible for child care because of TANF work rules. While many full-time students had trouble qualifying for this assistance given W-2 priorities, people working and attending school part time could get child-care assistance. However, many people didn't apply because they trusted their network's understanding of government rules.

STABLE-WORKING-CLASS/DISPLACED WORKERS

Stable-working-class and displaced-worker families seldom used safety-net programs unless in dire need. The same was true of government programs, partly because their greater assets disqualified them. However, stable-working-class people participated in these programs regularly as volunteers and through contributions. For example, most of the people serving at the soup kitchen and donating in-kind goods to Sunrise are in the stable working class. These families also participate in a variety of youth programs. Unions and other clubs provide social capital resources for adults.

The stable working class are by far the most insular group when it comes to government and social service agency assistance. In part, this comes from bad experiences that some have had trying to seek assistance in the past. As I document in another article (Schneider 1999b), working-class people who have become unemployed repeatedly report that they are turned away when they seek aid from government and social service agencies because previous income and assets make them ineligible. These negative experiences are shared within closed social capital networks, leading many to simply not bother with the government or the government-funded safety-net system. In addition, because community culture places great value on self-support, many people choose to avoid the stigma of social welfare assistance.

MIGRANTS AND REFUGEES

Migrants and refugees rely on community-based organizations associated with their country of origin for supports. For example, Lydia's family relied on the migrant social service agency for assistance, and Angel and Yolanda used Latinos United when in need. As for Angel and Yolanda, faith-based organizations provide another avenue to resources or information. These organizations may help newcomers to the mainland United States access government or mainstream social service agency programs.

The relationship that immigrants and refugees have with government is based on their legal status in this country. Puerto Rican citizens may access U.S. government social welfare systems in Puerto Rico and use similar systems here. They also rely on community-based and social service agencies for help, based on previous experience or on knowledge of these systems among more established people in the closed social capital networks of the communities where they live now. Refugees may use government assistance when they first arrive in this country and, depending on their economic circumstances here, may come to rely on government systems. However, these experiences are often mediated through the social service agency that resettles them or community-based organizations serving these communities. Legal immigrants are far less likely to use government aid, and undocumented migrants are least likely of all.

The Rising Educated Middle Class

Families in the rising educated middle class participate in the same systems. However, as illustrated by Lydia's becoming an assistant teacher in the local community-based organization, they are more likely to move into leadership positions in community-based organizations at a young age. These bridging experiences are often the first step to movement into professional careers. As adults, the rising educated middle class are more likely to judge social service agencies by their ability to provide their children with bridging resources. For example, Lydia pays close attention to activities in her children's schools. Another rising-educated-middle-class parent raised concerns about the quality of a youth program serving mostly low-skilled and stable-working-class youth.

People in the rising educated middle class also serve as volunteers and board members for community-based and citywide social service agencies. In fact, bridging individuals are likely to be overcommitted, as many organizations seeking diversity on their boards ask them to serve. For example, one African American leader in Kenosha served on more than twenty boards and was regularly asked to represent her racial group at yet another community forum. Other community leaders of color reported similar experiences. Earlier research recorded identical patterns in Philadelphia (Goode and Schneider 1994).

Policy Implications

Comparing these five groups on bridging behavior reveals some important differences related to use of various social service and government systems. Although everyone but the stable working class is willing to turn to government or social service agencies when in need, middle-class people experience mainstream resources very differently than those with less economic power and social capital connections among those providing service. The rising educated middle class are often the peers of those providing social service because they work as professionals themselves. They expect equal treatment and may be treated better than their less advantaged peers.[2] As they did for Lydia, social service agencies and government have provided important, positive supports in the past. When government or social service experiences are negative, the rising educated middle class know how to effectively file complaints or seek changes in the system (Lopez and Stack 2001). They vote, run for office, serve on boards, and have no problems calling a supervisor when they need to. They are also more likely to experience better service because they may have social capital ties to needed services and are more likely to use systems designed for the entire community, such as educational referral systems, than the needs-based systems designed for the poor.

Although low-skilled workers and people with limited work experience are even more likely to use social service systems, they experience them very differently because their economic circumstances dictate different power relations to these systems. They also often experience different systems than those with more stable incomes. People in these groups must depend on the good will and quality of often overworked front-line workers to gain assistance. They have little power in relationships with agencies and often see themselves as victims of capricious systems. As the literature on welfare use documents, these concerns are often well founded (Kingfisher 1996; Susser 1982; Susser and Kreniske 1987). Although people in these groups have social capital resources that help them know where to apply for aid, they seldom have social capital relationships with anyone working in a service-provision capacity in government. Their cultural capital may also clash with that of the social service agency or government worker. They may have friends who work or volunteer at community-based social service agencies, and often consider these organizations first choice for some kinds of assistance. Low-skilled and limited-work-experience families also use social service agency workers at community-based organizations as bridging agents to deal with government.

Also, low-skilled and limited-work-experience families often lack the cultural knowledge and social capital contacts to accurately evaluate an array of available resources. Like the numerous Social Network Study participants who chose low-quality training programs from advertisements on the subway or television (Schneider 2000), these people have no way of knowing whether a training program will live up to its claims. Their limited financial resources also play a key role in choices. For example, one rising-educated-middle-class woman from Kenosha initially hesitated when her middle-class coworkers suggested that she obtain advanced education because, she explained, she "had no money." She agreed to take advanced training only when, through her workplace, she received help in funding her training and another coworker decided to enroll in the same program (Schneider 2001:13). By providing both economic capital and social capital to a promising low-skilled worker, these instrumental bridging supports made the difference between continuing life in low-skilled jobs and moving into the middle class.

Comparing reactions to social service systems among these family types reveals problems with current public policy tendencies to use vouchers and other market-based systems to provide resources to the low-skilled workers and limited-work-experience families that more often use these systems. For example, the Workforce Investment Act expects people to choose training programs from an array of programs available in one-stop shops. Government-sponsored child-care systems and school-choice vouchers work the same way. People of the rising educated and established middle class have the skills to evaluate these options, but this is far less likely to be the case for regular users of these systems.

Families with limited incomes also have limited options because they lack the economic capital to choose more costly services or programs. For example, poor families facing high copays for center-based day care are more likely to choose home-based care partly for this reason. The same is true for children's schools. Although these programs may offer more options to low-income families than they did previously, they do not give these households the same options that more affluent community residents have.

The same is true of stable-working-class families who now access educational services much more often as they attempt to adapt to the new economy. For example, working-class students in several classes I taught that primarily served the children of displaced workers told me that they were attending college only because school counselors did not suggest other options.

The Racine school district offered another path, through a program linking students to internships in the skilled trades. Recognizing that many skilled workers would be retiring without replacements, this program offered an alternative to college that led to lucrative employment. Like other successful skilled trades programs, this one included strong institutional social capital links to unions and employers that could offer real jobs to successful graduates.

To use government or private-sector educational services effectively, people need to develop the social and cultural capital skills to evaluate choices. For example, WIA centers could train community-based organizations to help people better evaluate educational options or develop mentoring programs using people working in various fields to assist applicants in choosing appropriate programs. These aid initiatives would need to include continuing assistance to help people moving into careers outside the experience of their social networks complete applications properly and successfully complete their course of study. The Workstart program of the CWEP and similar programs provided a more comprehensive curriculum to help people clarify goals and identify future directions. In addition to Workstart, CWEP hosted Community College of Philadelphia courses at their Kensington-based center, facilitating the move toward college by offering the classes in a familiar setting. In each case, an individual needing assistance in deciding on a career path or educational options would have someone not affiliated with a training program to provide guidance.

Policy Implications

Neighborhood Settlement House represents one kind of one-stop shop, an agency that offers a range of programs under one roof. Examining the ways participants use this social service organization and others like it shows that multiservice centers may succeed at providing wraparound services for people involved in the program. However, these institutions equally run the risk of hindering attempts to move participants toward self-sufficiency outside this closed social capital community because all needs are fulfilled in house. Another policy strategy involves using vouchers or advertising a one-stop-shop's range of programs as a mechanism to fund a wider range of choices for a given service. Analysis of the ways families from different worker types use available resources suggests that this strategy may have advantages and disadvantages. Although participants are no longer restricted to referrals through government or another organization, they may not have the resources to adequately evaluate or pay for some options. These observations highlight several policy implications related to current policy strategies regarding social welfare provision:

- Voucher and one-stop-shop initiatives will be effective only if participants have the education to adequately evaluate program choices. To serve a range of potential participants, materials should be designed for several audiences and appropriate counselors available to interpret options.
- Voucher programs need to provide sufficient funding so that low-income families can access a full range of programs. Copays need to be sufficiently low that they do not compromise a family's ability to meet basic needs.
- Because most families learn about social services available from government or nonprofits through closed social capital networks, providers should use networks of participants or venues that serve as closed social capital communities for target populations—such as community-based institutions, faith communities, and employers—to explain their programs and advertise for services.

- Agency officials and policy makers should be clear about the goals of wraparound service programs. If these programs are designed to help participants navigate a wider arena of employers or services beyond the local community, programs need to offer culturally appropriate mechanisms to build bridging social capital.
- Families from all worker types both give and receive services. Often volunteer opportunities turn into paying jobs or help people determine career paths. Organizations would do well to recognize this dual role of the people served by the organization and encourage opportunities for participants to both serve as volunteers and play a role in agency planning and governance.

Summary

This chapter describes how participants' decisions heavily influence how people use social service agencies. Both an individual's social capital resources and institutional referrals bring people to institutions. Participants then choose whether to use the organization as a source for social capital and community or as a place to simply fulfill instrumental needs. People are most likely to use organizations as sources of social capital and community when their cultural capital matches that of other participants. Although an organization's recruitment strategies and program design play a role, its control over outcomes is mediated through participant behavior.

Families of the various worker types use institutions and respond to programs in different ways. Their decisions are heavily influenced by the experiences of people in their closed social capital networks with similar institutions and government programs. Welfare reform changes current assumptions about social service use by altering the kinds of organizations that provide service, funding structures, and the rules an agency must follow to provide service. However, agencies have changed some of their programs in response to welfare reform. The next chapter looks at the impact of welfare reform on the organizations providing service.

CHAPTER 10

Agencies and Social Capital

Families use social service agencies to meet a range of instrumental and social needs. Government increasingly turns to agencies as partners in implementing social welfare policy. In both cases, agencies become mediating structures, providing centers to implement policy, develop community, foster social capital, and access resources (Berger and Neuhaus 1977). How do agencies accomplish these multiple goals? This chapter looks inside agencies to examine the different kinds of social capital involved in service provision after welfare reform.

Social service agencies maintain a multiple focus on two types of constituencies: 1) their funders and partners and 2) the people who use their services. For agencies offering social welfare services, these two stakeholder groups often come from very different closed social capital networks. Part of an agency's mediating role involves negotiating between these two groups. As the case examples below illustrate, the strength of an agency's clarity about its mission and the quality of its management structures influence its success in serving both constituencies. Successful agencies use their social capital resources to meet the needs of the people they serve. The case examples below illustrate several strategies used by agencies to successfully fulfill their mission in an era of welfare reform. This chapter focuses on the way nonprofit agencies interact with their funders and adjust their operations given TANF.

Social service agencies considered successful among their peers and funders were able to demonstrate to their funders that they accomplished the service-provision goals stated in their missions. For agencies involved in providing social welfare services, these goals included the outcomes specified by government contracts or identified in grant proposals. At the same time, agencies were expected to meet the needs of the people served by their programs. The goals and desires of program participants may not necessarily match those of funders.

An agency determines its own strategy to address the general goal of economic self-sufficiency as it implements its mission and program. The agencies in this research that were most successful in helping their participants move toward their goals kept in mind both funders' expectations and participants' needs when clarifying their mission and developing programs. Agencies served as bridges between the cultural expectations of funders and those of

program participants. These organizations paid close attention to the economic strategies used by their program participants but mapped their own
plan to help participants negotiate the mainstream economic and policy structures of their community, based on a combination of organization philosophy
and the experience of their board and staff. The most successful social service
organizations also drew on research related to the problems they attempted to
address in formulating policy and programs. They then negotiated with government and other funders to carry out that plan. The needs of the constituencies of funders and program participants were necessarily intertwined.
This chapter addresses the question of how agencies use their social capital to
fulfill their mission given welfare reform. It looks at three aspects of agency
behavior influenced by welfare reform: 1) funding strategies, 2) mission implementation, and 3) staff interactions with government and other key stakeholders. Recent reports on welfare reform suggest that nonprofits experience significant stress as agencies respond to government policy (Abramowitz 2001).
My research suggests a more mixed picture. Two factors—the size of an agency
and the nature of its connections to the three social service systems described
in chapter 4 (government-contracted services, ancillary services, and community-based systems)—influence the impact of welfare reform on individual
organizations.

Chapter 3 identifies three types of organizations: citywide, community-
based, and faith-based. Citywide and community-based organizations are further categorized by size. All the faith-based organizations in this research were
directly tied to church congregations and are discussed in chapter 11. This chapter looks at agency strategies for different types of citywide and community-
based organizations. Appendix B provides a description of agency types and
examples.

FUNDING

Welfare reform potentially affects the budgets of social service agency in two
very different ways. Proponents of government contracting see social service
agencies as benefiting from devolution of government services onto nonprofits. As scholars of the nonprofit sector note (Salamon 1995; Smith and Lipsky
1993), government funding has fueled an increase in the scope of the nonprofit
sector. On the other hand, some researchers of nonprofits' response to welfare
reform portray devolution as hurting social service agency funding through
three simultaneous mechanisms. First, social service agencies find themselves
providing more unsubsidized services because government is no longer offering supports to low-income families (Horten et al. 2001; Abramowitz 2001;
Fendt et al. 2001).

Second, changes in funding structures mean that agencies have less money (Horten et al. 2001). For example, agencies providing health care under Medicaid managed care receive payment only if they can verify that the patient is registered with that particular agency. Per-capita payments may be much lower than previous fee-for-service payment structures.

Agencies that previously received payment for each participant regardless of outcomes under fee-for-service contracts find that the fee structure is different under the performance-based contracts now preferred by many government agencies. Under a performance-based contract, the agency gets partial payment for accepting a participant but receives full payment only if the participant meets a contracted goal. For example, the agency may get final payment only if participants complete a welfare-to-work program, find a job, and remain employed for 90 days. Agencies thus have more risk and may not receive final payment for some participants until long after they have left the program or full payment for participants who quit or do not find jobs after completing the program. Agencies with tight budgets or that have participants who may not fulfill the program's goals find themselves at risk of losing money on their programs, exacerbating budget deficits.

The third mechanism by which welfare reform may affect funding is the additional work created for agencies with no means for compensation. For example, Horten et al. (2001) found that agencies spent many uncompensated hours serving as advocates for their program participants and negotiating with their funders. Abramowitz (2001) reported that staff spent time educating participants about TANF without funding to do so.

The research on the social service agencies in Philadelphia, Milwaukee, and Kenosha confirmed that all these outcomes occurred. However, the nature of the impact of welfare reform on any given agency depended on the size of the organization and the types of services it provided.

LARGE CITYWIDE SOCIAL SERVICE AGENCIES

Because larger organizations tend to have stronger links to government, social capital influenced the impact of welfare reform on these organizations. Welfare reform increased opportunities for large citywide nonprofits. As established providers of social welfare services under contract with government, these agencies used their preexisting social capital to expand already existing services. For example, Faith in Action increased its income share from the Pennsylvania Department of Public Welfare from 20 percent in 1995, the year of its first welfare-reform contract, to 25 percent in 2000. During this period, the overall agency budget increased from $29,179,000 to $35,827,000, with the Department of Public Welfare contracts accounting for the largest increase from any funding source.

Involvement in welfare reform led to initial increases in staff. Project Connect staff tripled in size as Faith in Action shifted their welfare-reform initiatives from pilot projects to mandatory services for all TANF recipients. As welfare caseloads fell and Pennsylvania developed new strategies to better serve its welfare population, Faith in Action contracts followed suit. The agency continues to provide rapid-attachment services and gradually added new programs for retention and outreach from 1998 through 2000.

Faith in Action's participation in welfare reform originated from a clear strategy to build on preexisting social capital to expand services. In the 1996 annual report, the executive director explained:

> I have concentrated on solidifying existing relationships with funding sources as well as forging new ones. This power base, which includes appointed and elected officials in Washington, Harrisburg, and the Philadelphia region, holds the key to enhancing [Faith in Action's] role in helping thousands of people each year. Rest assured that these groups know about [Faith in Action's] vital importance as a major provider of skills training, rehabilitation health, and other services.

As a key participant in the contracted services system, Faith in Action maintained visibility both in government circles and among groups of agencies providing various services. As the executive director reported, this was part of a deliberate strategy to use relationships to influence service provision in this community. Social capital development paid off in additional government contracts.

Despite TANF's increased role in welfare reform, TANF-related services represent only part of Faith in Action's activities. The Employment and Vocational Counseling budget rose from 12 percent of the direct program outlays in 1995 to 14 percent in 1998. This proportion of the outlay budget declined to 10 percent in 2000 as the welfare caseload dropped in Philadelphia. Together with education, training, and vocational assessment, career-development programs held steady at a little below one-third of programmatic spending. More costly rehabilitation services remained the major source of income and spending during this time. Welfare was only part of a mixed mission for this organization.

In contrast, welfare became the major activity for Community Solutions as the agency expanded its Family Support Act contracts to become a W-2 agency. In addition to significant budget expansions, welfare reform led to the acquisition of new sites, addition of staff, and expansion of relationships with smaller organizations such as Neighborhood Settlement House and Empowerment Education. As outlined in earlier chapters, this agency used its social capital to obtain and maintain contracts. One state administrator commented that Community Solutions was particularly adept at using the political situation in Milwaukee to benefit the agency.

SMALLER NONPROFITS

Welfare reform had mixed results in smaller organizations. The nature of social capital relationships with funders and other agencies made a difference for these institutions. In the most positive example, subcontracting as a W-2 agency under Community Solutions transformed Empowerment Education from a tiny, mostly volunteer operation to a formal multiservice organization. Most agency funding comes from the W-2 contract. As funding has increased, the agency has also expanded its social capital ties. Before its connection to Community Solutions, the organization remained isolated even from other adult basic education providers. This situation has altered dramatically as its key partner drew Empowerment Education staff into its evolving welfare-reform-related coalitions. The organization now has a positive reputation throughout the city as a W-2 provider.

In contrast, welfare reform created a financial crisis for Citizens United. Pennsylvania's TANF program initially did away with the community-service program that covered salaries for two-thirds of agency staff. Strong social capital ties meant that the agency knew about impending changes and had already moved to find new partners to replace this funding. However, government was slow to process contracts, leaving the agency without this key funding source for over six months. The agency found that it had less control over service-provision strategies in the new partnership it developed with FUTURE, a for-profit provider with a commonwealth contract for RESET—after a difficult partnership to provide rapid-attachment services, the organization was able to use its social capital to regain a contract to provide its community-service program.

Shifts in public policy meant both expansions and stresses for other organizations. As was typical of safety-net providers of such basic needs as food and shelter throughout the country (Fendt et al. 2001), Sunrise and Neighborhood Settlement House reported critical expansions in use of their food pantry. Sunrise's executive director reported:

> We have spent more and more money this year since the summer on purchasing food. Much more money than we have in previous years. That's just because the support we get from the community has remained steady, and it probably has even gone up, but the numbers [of users] have increased so dramatically that we can't meet that need.

Although shelters and feeding programs saw increased need and strained resources, Sunrise was able to expand other programs as welfare reform developed. The organization is a faith related institution founded by local churches and the only homeless shelter in the area. It has always had contracts with Kenosha Country to provide shelter services but has been able to build on this existing relationship with new contracts. The organization maintains close ties to the Kenosha County Job Center because many shelter residents use W-2. The organization recently received a faith-based-initiative contract to expand its counseling services for the homeless.

Neighborhood Settlement House presented a similarly mixed picture. Welfare reform strained the food pantry and increased uncompensated care at the health clinic by 50 percent. However, through its contracts with Community Solutions, Neighborhood Settlement House experienced a significant budget increase to provide W-2-related services. The Community Solutions contracts contributed to general overhead and facilities costs, benefiting the general programs of the agency.

RELATIONSHIP TO SERVICE-DELIVERY SYSTEMS AND FUNDING

This difference in impact on smaller organizations comes from their relationship to the three service-delivery systems of the official welfare system, ancillary service system, and community-based system. Faith in Action, Citizens United, Empowerment Education, and other agencies that were tied to the official welfare systems were directly affected by TANF because funding for their programs was tied to it. Over time, all these agencies were able to expand their programs because of increased funding available to social service agencies under welfare reform. These agencies succeeded in expanding their TANF-related programs because of their social capital connections to funders or larger social service agencies.

Agencies involved in the ancillary system experienced funding strains under TANF as they sought to address the unexpected consequences of welfare reform. Particularly hard hit were the organizations providing food, shelter, health care, and other basic necessities because people who were no longer receiving cash assistance, food stamps, and Medicaid turned to the agencies in larger numbers.

Neighborhood Settlement House, Sunrise, and similar organizations were attached to both the official welfare system and the ancillary service system. Note that both organizations experienced strains in their safety-net programs. Food pantry use rose for both organizations; Neighborhood Settlement House saw increases in uncompensated health care, and Sunrise reported jumps in shelter use. However, both agencies were able to expand their welfare-to-work contracts.

Organizations primarily attached to community-based systems felt more indirect effects of TANF implementation. Connections to the formal welfare service-delivery system also influenced the impact of welfare reform on these smaller community-based agencies. Latinos United reported little impact on its budget by W-2. This organization offered a range of services to the local Spanish-speaking population, but its funded programs were less related to welfare reform. Although W-2 did have an impact on service provision because Latinos United hosted Medicaid outreach through colocation of Kenosha County staff at the organization, welfare reform did not influence agency funding. The host relationship in this case consisted solely of providing office space to county staff.

AGENCY RESPONSES

Analysis of the impact of welfare reform on funding for these various agencies suggests that an organization's social capital ties and size influence the effect that shifts in government policy will have on its budgets. The largest organizations with the strongest social capital ties to government benefited the most from welfare reform. Small organizations that relied on welfare-related contracts for most of their budget were hurt the most by sudden policy changes. Citizens United is one example, although social capital ties eventually enabled it to replace lost funding.

Organizations offering safety-net services previously provided through the AFDC package of food stamps, cash assistance, and medical assistance experienced the most sudden upswing in new need, as former AFDC recipients struggled with policy changes. The social capital connections to government focused on employment and training that most TANF providers relied on to gain contracts offered no new mechanisms to cover these needs. The social capital ties for these ancillary systems were different than for TANF, creating a social capital gap just like the resource gap experienced by program participants. Because previous policy had designated government the primary provider of these basic needs, the employment-focused agencies offering welfare services had not developed social capital ties to food pantries and providers of health care for the indigent. Although government often provided lists of safety-net providers as part of the diversion strategy, contracted agencies generally did not have strong ties to these organizations. They faced the choice of fostering social capital ties with these increasingly strapped ancillary service organizations or changing policy.

Agencies responded by drawing on community social capital resources through ties to network organizations, faith-based organizations, churches, and local politicians to create pressure to increase food stamp and Medicaid outreach in addition to seeking additional resources. These strategies are discussed in more detail in chapter 13. There was political pressure to reconnect the safety-net aspects of welfare to employment-driven welfare reform. As the pressure mounted nationally, both Pennsylvania and Wisconsin took steps to improve food stamp and Medicaid enrollment.

In each of these case examples, welfare-related services accounted for only a portion of agency budget and activity. Increased funding significantly impacted on the programs of some agencies—Community Solutions, Empowerment Education, and Citizens United—but had little effect on others. How did agency mission shift as funding patterns altered? The next section addresses this issue.

MISSION

Agencies are challenged to maintain their missions in the face of government contract expectations (Smith and Lipsky 1993). Nonprofit scholars speak of "mission drift," in which where organizations lose track of their original missions as they seek to please funders that have other goals. In the worst cases of mission drift, organizations have no cohesive philosophy or service-delivery plan; instead, they keep changing their constituency and goals in an effort to maintain funding. Often the quality of service suffers as a result of this lack of planning.

The nonprofits with government contracts that I worked with in Philadelphia, Milwaukee, and Kenosha clearly weighed the relationship of welfare-related programming to their mission before applying for funds. In each case, agencies chose to engage in government contracts in order to best fulfill their mission. For example, an administrator of Neighborhood Settlement House, which was chartered to help its community residents become self-sufficient, noted: "We had a strategic plan about the same time and then out of the strategic plan and the town hall meeting we looked at, [we decided to get involved with W-2] and I guess if there is a basic rule at all, as far as I'm concerned, if [welfare reform is] affecting the people in the neighborhood and the residents that we are serving, then we need to get involved in it or we need to provide the service."

The mission of Neighborhood Settlement House served as the mandate to move into welfare services, and the agency chose to subcontract with Community Solutions for this reason. However, this decision was made only after six months of meetings and deliberations. Other agencies reported similar processes.

After engaging in government contracts, agencies focused on maintaining their ethos and mission-based service expectations given the parameters of government service. For example, Citizens United initially agreed to offer a mandatory government program only if they could design the program based on its philosophy. Faith in Action became one of Philadelphia's largest TANF service providers because government wanted the agency to use its established model to serve welfare recipients.

Neighborhood Settlement House continued to be ambivalent about changes in agency "feel" under the W-2 program. The organization prided itself on providing a comfortable environment for community residents. The agency was concerned that bringing in mandatory participants for W-2 would change the atmosphere. As the contract was implemented, tensions arose among Neighborhood Settlement House, Community Solutions staff, and county government public welfare workers stationed at the community-based agency. Major issues centered on a clash of cultures: Neighborhood Settlement House expected staff to help people whenever they needed it and in all possible ways, whereas Community Solutions and government workers required firmer boundaries. Government workers, in particular, kept clients waiting; Neighborhood Settlement House felt that leaving people in the waiting room for long periods destroyed the friendly community feel.

In a meeting to address issues, the executive director began by saying that Neighborhood Settlement House was "here for over 40 years before W-2 and, while W-2 may not be here in a couple of years, we will." This was a strong statement that the agency had no intention of changing its core values for these partners; its goal was to maintain its mission and ethos regardless of the W-2 contract. These issues were never completely resolved.

Other organizations also tried to imprint their philosophy on government programs. This strategy was accepted—even encouraged—in Pennsylvania, where contracted programs were seen more as partnership with social service agencies. However, Wisconsin tried repeatedly to enforce government goals with unwilling agencies. A faith-based leader involved in monitoring TANF implementation in Wisconsin reported the following exchange:

> The state of Wisconsin runs the show. [The W-2 agencies] are merely—and I don't mean that in a pejorative manner—merely contractors who implement a state program. [The agencies] don't see it like that. They see it that they run this program, and they know how to run this program, and nobody, including the state, understands the nuances of running this program. And nobody should tell them what to do. As a matter of fact, [a monitor] chewed them out at one of these meetings, 'cause they were complaining about having no voice in setting policy. And she said, "You don't make the policy, you implement the policy, that's your role."

Mission and Social Capital

In both states, social service agencies felt differently. Their role as community providers entailed implementing programs in a way consonant with their missions. Organizations used their social capital to influence the policy-implementation process. As observed in other studies (Couto 1999:256), organizations used their links to government and other nonprofits to share their message about appropriate service provision. In many cases, this use of social capital was explicit. For example, executive director of Faith in Action reported in the annual letter for 1996:

> We also have initiated collaborative meetings with other social service providers. Today, we look to each other as allies. We can work together to educate public officials and to encourage them to work with us as partners to enhance the region's social fabric and economy. By creating a synergy with other providers, we bring the needs of every client to the minds of policymakers.

Although individual agencies' missions differed somewhat, organizations used "strength in numbers" and the trust that they had developed with government to use policy to best fulfill their missions. Government contracts became one means to succeed in meeting agency goals. By attempting to "bring the needs of every client to the mind of policymakers," as Faith in Action's executive director put it, agencies sought to strengthen the partnership between social service agencies and government to provide social welfare services. As "street level bureaucrats" (Lipsky 1980), they used their role as policy implementers to change the nature of service provision. This led to a diversity in on-the-ground program ethos that was clearly visible to evaluators and participants alike.

This adherence to agency mission persisted even when a government contract changed the services provided by an agency. For example, by developing a relationship with Community Solutions, Empowerment Education was led into government contracts that expanded programming from GED courses to include welfare services and child care, but it retained its goals to "to help people make that transition educationally and financially out of poverty." In fact, the new contracts enhanced the agency's ability to fulfill these goals.

STATE RESPONSES

Taken together, analysis of the relationship between social service agencies and government showed that these organizations kept careful track of their fundamental mission while engaged as government contractors. However, the two states responded differently to these efforts to maintain mission-based control over service delivery. Pennsylvania welcomed individualized agency plans as long as the organization was able to meet its contracted goals. In fact, the commonwealth sought out creative programs with a reputation of providing quality, sensitive service to program participants. Wisconsin, on the hand, attempted to impose the state's philosophy of welfare reform on organizations by micromanaging contracts, audits, and other control mechanisms. Although Wisconsin officials stated that they wanted program diversity that fit local needs, their management process supported only variations in service-delivery structure that fit the state's model. W-2 providers with different strategies faced an uphill battle to maintain organization goals.

For example, the mission of the Kenosha W-2 agency was based on the ideology that welfare recipients and other Kenosha residents should receive identical services. The agency ran afoul of Wisconsin auditors because they were too creative in their use of government funds to support their package of programs for all Kenosha residents in need. W-2 funds, which accounted for a significant portion of agency revenue, could be used only for participants who fit the narrow needs-based criteria for TANF. Despite Kenosha's well-deserved reputation as a leader in work-first programs, Wisconsin officials chose to use the agency as an example to ensure that TANF organizations followed state guidelines for welfare reform. Auditors accused Kenosha of using funds for community-support activities outside of the W-2 contract. The audit revealed an agency attempting to reconcile organization mission with government funding criteria, not misappropriation of funds to benefit individuals or wealthy county citizens.[1]

Nevertheless, the audit became public, leading to a change in leadership and significant program cuts when Kenosha lost funds because of small W-2 caseloads in the second contract. As a result, Kenosha changed some of its contract relationships, reduced frequency of some services, and cut others altogether. The agency was able to maintain its program goals only because it earned community-reinvestment funds, which it could use any way it wanted, through its success in placing people in jobs.[2] The agency continued to be turned down for additional funding for their programs despite an increase in caseload. A Kenosha administrator reported:

> [In] this last contract period, there was a contingency fund established for agencies if they ran short of programmatic dollars, and we made two valiant attempts to access that money and were turned down by the state. We were not real happy about this because our understanding was if you met the conditions of the contingency fund policy you'd be able to access the money and we were unable to. The first proposal had to do with the kinds of people we found ourselves providing services to, people with lots and lots of barriers. When they sent it back to us they said there are lots of people dealing with barriers; the policy says you have to have an emergency beyond your control and another criteria. Then, lo and behold, we had a crisis beyond our control, the unemployment rates began to incline up and up and up in this area. . . . And we presented our second request and they acknowledged it was a valid request, we had met all the criteria. However, they were in a budget-crunch situation and advised that we try to find other funds ourselves.

This example shows an organization struggling to maintain its mission-based program despite lack of support from its funding source. Limited social capital connections to the state exhibited by this example were further weakened when the administrator of the Kenosha County Job Center, who had strong social capital ties to Wisconsin TANF administrators, lost his job in a change of administration. Fortunately, the job center was able to increase W-2 funding in the next contract owing to rising caseloads as the economy declined. Kenosha has maintained its mission-based philosophy and general program goals despite these funding problems. However, since the audit, the agency has not entirely returned to its previous staff levels and program design.

Organizations used their social capital to facilitate their goals of mission-based service. For example, Faith in Action endeavored to strengthen social capital relationships with both government and other social service agencies, and Community Solutions used political connections to maintain their program goals. The tension created by government contracts affected the manner in which services were performed more than they did the base goals for service.

Although issues such as agency atmosphere and quality of service are linked to mission, these are distinct parts of agency management. As discussed in the next section, an agency's philosophy influences the ways in which it negotiates partnerships with government on a daily basis. Government contracts challenged the means rather than the ends of service provision. Agency mission remained firm despite shifts in policy.

AGENCY MANAGEMENT ISSUES AND STAFF INTERACTIONS WITH GOVERNMENT

Through focusing on moving welfare recipients into employment, TANF created new roles for both agencies providing services directly tied to welfare and those offering ancillary services. Three patterns emerge from research throughout the country that were similar to the experience of the social service organizations in Milwaukee, Kenosha, and Philadelphia. First, TANF changed the nature of welfare provision by shifting aid from cash assistance for needy families to employment assistance for needy adults. Second, TANF created larger facilitator roles for social service agencies as they became mediators between government and their program participants. Third, TANF changed the nature of the clients served by some agencies as well as the kinds of services provided.

CHANGING STAFF ROLES

By shifting front-line welfare workers' primary activities from determining eligibility for benefits to welfare-to-work case management, TANF altered a key component in welfare provision. In many states, the same government eligibility workers who had determined eligibility under AFDC served as TANF case managers, adding duties to already overwhelming caseloads (Morgen 2001; Lurie 2001). Government managers were challenged to change the culture of the welfare office, as noted by Pennsylvania policy makers in chapter 2.

Both Pennsylvania and Wisconsin avoided role conflicts and shifts in duties through contracting. Although Pennsylvania maintained a case-management system in the welfare office, social service agency contractors such as Faith in Action and Citizens United were responsible for employment-related counseling and activities. Department of Public Welfare workers still played a role in communicating TANF goals, but their primary job consisted of referral, determining eligibility, and dispensing benefits. Further division in the welfare offices between income eligibility workers and employment and training specialists also helped to limit role confusion.

Wisconsin devolved casework roles further through the W-2 agency contracts. Each county had its own structure. Kenosha had county government as the prime contractor, but the structure of the Kenosha County Job Center combined government, nonprofit, and for-profit organization staff under one administrative umbrella. In Kenosha, the FEP team that worked with each participant included both government employees and nonprofit agency caseworkers. The government eligibility workers kept their previous role of determining eligibility for food stamps, Medicaid, and other benefits, while the nonprofit agency employees were responsible for job placement, child care, and other welfare-to-work matters. This team approach limited the ability of one worker to determine case outcomes and fostered more integrated service.

Milwaukee made the five nongovernmental agencies with W-2 contracts responsible for each case, but gave the county the contract to determine eligibility and process claims for food stamps, Medicaid, and child care. Milwaukee county employees were colocated at the various W-2 agencies to provide these services. Even though social service agency employees and government staff worked at the same offices, they did not develop the team approach achieved in Kenosha. Instead, the more customer-service-oriented agencies were constantly challenged by the bureaucratic, union-driven behavior of these government workers. For example, the county worker supervisor stationed at Neighborhood Settlement House insisted that the agency go through official channels whenever they had a concern about worker behavior, by reporting concerns to the prime contractor (Community Solutions), which could then talk to Milwaukee Department of Public Welfare management. She insisted that her workers follow the protocol for their work established in the union contract. As both the state and agencies acknowledge, the W-2 contractors failed to develop a good relationship with the county, leading to resolution to few of these conflicts.

THE ROLE OF MANAGEMENT STRUCTURES

Managing the relationship among staffs from different agencies at community-based sites became a particular issue for both Neighborhood Settlement House and Empowerment Education. Negotiating the different cultures of government agency, prime contractor and subcontractor was the greatest challenge. The differences between these two agencies and Community Solutions's main office show how management ethos makes a difference in service provision.

Community Solutions   A field-worker at Community Solutions's largest office observed:

> Every Thursday that I came to this agency before the W-2 deadline, things were always chaotic. You found many of the clients arguing with the receptionist desk because they have been waiting on their FEPS too long. When you seen the FEPs, they were taking their breaks with no hesitation. Sometimes you found FEPs taking a lunch and had clients waiting on them. I

thought this was very disrespectful. On average the phone would ring ten times a minute. Many clients had complaints of trying to reach their FEPs and the FEPs not returning their phone calls back. Clients would come in without an appointment with their FEP because the FEP didn't call them back and they were making sure that their benefits wasn't going to be affected.

This large, busy office displayed many signs of overcrowding and limited staff management. Although Community Solutions presented itself as a client-focused program, it experienced high staff turnover and the quality of FEPs was uneven. The agency also transferred staff between offices, adding to existing continuity problems. For example, one FEP placed at Neighborhood Settlement House developed a good relationship with both her clients and the host site's agency staff. When she became an advocate for additional funding and support at Neighborhood Settlement House, she was transferred to another site.

Some of the problems witnessed by the field-worker quoted above were due to high caseloads and limited training time at the beginning of the program. One FEP interviewed at this stage reported caseloads of between 60 and 160 families, much higher than anticipated and well above social work standards.[3] Although Community Solutions's caseloads continued to be high, they resolved some of the staff training problems by spreading older employees throughout the sites to help train newer caseworkers.

Nevertheless, the chaotic ethos of the main office remained. One program participant compared this site with the Neighborhood Settlement House site a year later:

> Over here [at Neighborhood Settlement House] you get waited on right away; over there [at the larger Community Solutions office] it takes a while for you to get waited on. And then they make an appointment for you to come in, then they maybe won't see you, they'll say they're in a meeting and it takes a long time again. So, then they tell you to come back again, so I keep on coming back and back.

Neighborhood Settlement House   Neighborhood Settlement House's executive director paid particular attention to waiting times for W-2 participants served at the agency. This hosting agency tried to persuade Community Solutions and county staff to adhere to agency style, with limited success. The organization was able to control waiting times but not change the appointment policy or create more of a customer-service orientation among the county employees. The settlement house's leadership was reluctant to push its funding agency for changes. Eventually, Community Solutions staff stationed at Neighborhood Settlement House went to higher-ups at Community Solutions to seek changes.

This is an example of an agency that has strong relationships with its prime contractor but is afraid of disturbing the trust between them by pointing out problems. Numerous staff members commented that the executive director was afraid of upsetting key Community Solutions staff. Community Solutions staff stationed at Neighborhood Settlement House continued to reassure the agency's leaders that the relationship would survive complaints. When Neighborhood Settlement House failed to ask for needed changes, Community Solutions used social capital ties within the organization to speak to management.

Neighborhood Settlement House had one employee responsible for all the community-service job placements at the agency, often a caseload of over 300 people. She also served as a liaison to Community Solutions and had other duties as well. Management was limited, and this employee often felt overburdened.

With little oversight and sometimes no training for their positions, participants in the community-service job program had poor attendance records and sometimes complained about their jobs. However, other people placed by the program were able to acquire new work experience and were hired by the agency.

Empowerment Education   Empowerment Education practiced stronger management than either the Community Solutions main site or Neighborhood Settlement House, with better results. The agency kept close watch on both the employees from other organizations stationed at the site and the welfare recipients. Empowerment Education established the atmosphere and reinforced its organizational style among all employees stationed at that site regardless of their official employer. A key employee said:

> I love our county workers. They are the best. They are so good, they are so helpful, they are wonderful. But I'm not going to take any crap from you because wherever you came from, you're going back because you have to fit my agency motto and I'm sorry, that's the way it is.
>
> What happens is, we don't hit people. We are old hippies. We're pretty mellow. They come in and we say we're going to give you all the respect that you deserve. We're gonna be nice to you, we're going to nurture you, we're going to give you cookies. We're going to give you rugs. We're going to let you do anything you want, as long as you help people and you are nice. I'm sorry that's it. So far people have been really great.
>
> I can ask our SSPs [county workers] to do anything. Our relationship with our FEPs—our FEPs will do anything for us. If I have a participant and

I say this person got really ripped off here, this is not right, she should have not been sanctioned for these hours, they go in and put a clause in. They know that it's right, that I'm not just saying it as a favor to someone but because it's right because that's how our agency is built.

Unfortunately, our model does not work for everyone. We had some FEPs that had to go. . . . We did have one woman who was here less than 36 hours. She was not nice. She slid a very derogatory memo under my door, listing about 15 things that she did not like about being here. She was just not going to fit in because she didn't want to.

I'm pretty much dealing with [management on site]. To be at an outstation you really have to be independent and you have to have a work ethic. We really go out of our way to include all of our staff. I mean, if you walked out there you would not know who's a state worker, who's a county worker, who's a FEP. They kind of go mental every once in a while, and usually it will be their peers who will correct them. I never have to go out and say, "Come on, you guys." They know that they don't want to be transferred.

Summary   Comparing these agencies shows that clear, mission-based, on-site management influences service provision. Other scholars note similar trends (Wagner et al. 2001). Empowerment Education and the Kenosha County Job Center are able to create a seamless, integrated services model through a philosophy of team service and a strong management ethos that enforces a particular type of service provision based on agency philosophy. Service provision at Neighborhood Settlement House and Community Solutions was more chaotic owing to weaker management oversight.

In each case, management attempts to convey agency mission through its service strategy. Kenosha focused on work-first orientation with supports for participants in order to meet their employment goals. Despite limited management oversight, Neighborhood Settlement House created a more customer-oriented flow through their office. This agency had less success in enforcing its mission and culture among the employees from various organizations because upper management was spread too thin to provide sufficient oversight of relevant employees. This failure stemmed from the leadership's philosophy of doing more with less rather than from lack of social capital links. The leadership chose not to use its social capital to improve W-2-related services until a crisis developed.

Empowerment Education most clearly achieves its mission-driven quality goals by asserting its authority to manage operations on site. Unlike Neighborhood Settlement House, it chose to limit the kinds of services it offered in order to have a staff large enough to manage each program effectively. This paid off in high regard for the agency.

FACILITATOR ROLES FOR AGENCIES

Regardless of the form of TANF service provision, communications with welfare service providers became a problem in all three cities. Although communications with AFDC offices were often reported as equally troublesome, the possibility of sanctions and time limits added urgency to the need to reach caseworkers. Telephone communication were described as problematic in all sites. For example, , one ethnographer in Milwaukee reported:

> [A W-2 recipient] also said that it was very difficult to resolve the problem with her check being stopped because nobody ever answers the phone [at Community Solutions], that you can only leave messages on the voice mail. I wonder if this is a policy. I know at [another W-2 agency], voice mail was an avoidance technique and one that makes callbacks problematic since participants are mobile and phoneless in some cases.

Organizations tried various ways to solve communication problems, with little success. Philadelphia's welfare offices created a voice mail system when people complained that workers focused on serving clients at the office rather than answering the phones. Kenosha developed a write-in system and tried to educate clients about leaving phone numbers and callback times. Often ancillary agency staff or contracted agencies like Neighborhood Settlement House tried to reach caseworkers when program participants could not get through—sometimes these professional intermediaries had more success than low-income clients.

The dual case-management system in Philadelphia, with both the Department of Public Welfare and contracted agencies maintaining case managers, allowed contracted agencies such as Citizens United to serve as advocates for their program participants. The Department of Public Welfare facilitated this relationship by appointing a liaison with each agency. This individual developed the social capital that enabled easier problem solving. Citizens United's case managers first tried to empower participants to talk with their caseworker; if it didn't work, the liaison or her manager was asked to look into the situation. Sometimes the case managers tried to contact a Department of Public Welfare caseworker directly.

Ancillary agency staff in both Kenosha and Milwaukee played similar roles. The counselor at Sunrise coached program participants on the process of applying for W-2. This became particularly important when staff at the Kenosha County Job Center denied eligibility for benefits or gave erroneous information. On several occasions, this caseworker called the W-2 agency to resolve problems. Neighborhood Settlement House social workers reported that they held training sessions for W-2 recipients placed in community-service jobs at the agency. These sessions were intended to empower welfare recipients to talk with their caseworkers and to provide information on welfare reform.

Because front-line workers had so much discretion in determining TANF participants' activities and benefits, neither the organizations offering related services nor low-income families could depend on clearcut rules to determine who qualified for welfare. This created a great deal of confusion for participants. Helping participants deal with problems related to TANF created extra work for agency staff in these communities, as in other parts of the country (Abramowitz 2001; Horten et al. 2001). Staff at many agencies reported that participants' concerns about W-2 seeped into their programming. One Neighborhood Settlement House staff member said, "Sometimes the participants come and they'll say they had some problems with the FEP, they be really, really keyed up and they might explode on you. So I think you have to learn how to be very, very tactful."

Agency staff felt that TANF complicated their jobs by adding unfunded mandates to educate program participants about welfare reform. In many cases, such programs as the food pantries and health clinics cushioned the impact of changes in government policy on low-income families. In other instances, as when staff from Empowerment Education and Sunrise intervened to assist their clients, social service agencies served as buffers between government and the people who used their agency. These additional activities on behalf of welfare recipients were placed on top of the staff's other duties. As exemplified by the Neighborhood Settlement House staff person who had to change discussions in her workshops to accommodate participants' concerns with W-2, welfare reform shifted the focus of agency programming. These changes created more stress for staff.

Changes in Participants and Programming

A number of agencies reported that their participant base included more hard-to-serve families after TANF was implemented. This trend echoed experience in other cities (Bischoff and Reisch 2000; Abramowitz 2001). For example, Sunrise found that the families entering the shelter in recent years had more difficult problems and a harder time finding housing. To accommodate these changes, the agency extended the length of time that people could stay in the family shelter from 30 to 45 days.

Neighborhood Settlement House also reported people with more difficulties in some programs. Agencies speculated that this shift was due partly to the fact that many of their regular clients were less able to use agency services because of increased work hours. Other organizations found that they needed to refocus programs to address needs created—and unmet—by welfare reform. For example, Latinos United became an outreach center for Medicaid when many low-income Latinos eligible for the program lost assistance because of misunderstandings about whether the citizen children of immigrants still qualified for aid.

Other organizations shifted or changed their programs to address the TANF employment focus. For example, many of the community-service job participants at Neighborhood Settlement House needed GED training but were required to spend four to six hours a day in a community-service placement. The agency shifted the times for the GED program so that they could both fulfill this obligation and continue their education.

Faith in Action added several outreach and retention programs in response to additional Pennsylvania Department of Public Welfare requests for proposals. The agency paid close attention to the evolving needs of the people served by the organization and new contracts available through TANF and related programs. While maintaining the general mission focus, the organization chose to expand into programs for new populations and develop new service-delivery models to best achieve its goals.

Agencies also debated their role in serving all community residents given increased need due to welfare reform. At Neighborhood Settlement House, concerns centered on the day-care program, one of the better-known subsidized programs in the city. It always had a waiting list and sent many families to the home care providers under its auspices. The staff at other programs in the agency, including Community Solutions, expected that W-2 program participants would be able to place their children in this program. However, space was often not available. This raised debate over whom the agency should be serving and why. The day-care director saw her program as serving the entire community that used the agency on a first come, first-served basis. Staff involved with the mandatory programs felt that the most needy should be served first. This issue was not resolved, but it highlighted shifts in this organization from a community center to one serving populations at greater risk. The same debate surfaced at other organizations facing funding cuts as both foundations and government put more capital into programs for lower-income families.

Shifts in the kinds of people using an organization and concerns about appropriate agency populations speak to issues of mission and the role of agencies in family survival strategies. If social service organizations serve only families leaving the welfare rolls, they lose their capacity to serve as centers for development of social and cultural capital for others in the community. Over time, these shifts can alter the nature of the agency as the participant base shifts. This, in turn, further impacts on who comes in the door for service.

Policy Implications

Analysis of agencies' responses to welfare reform suggests that subcontracted agencies can produce higher-quality service as partners with government than the traditional public bureaucracies. However, as the cautionary examples of chaotic service at some agencies demonstrate, that partnership needs to stress both cost-effectiveness and quality. Government should set standards for program provision but respect the differences among localities and different organizations. The following specific recommendations come out of this research:

- Government contracts need to provide adequate funding for sufficient staff, adequate training for staff, and sufficient management at contracting agencies.
- Contracts should stipulate caseload and supervisory ratios as well as minimum qualifications for case-management staff. Given the communications and staffing problems evident at most agencies due to limited funding, government needs to seek advice from social work and other professional associations to determine adequate staff/participant and staff/supervisor ratios. Minimum qualifications should be established through consultation with a range of experts and agency administrators.
- Although performance incentives—for example, the surplus or profit allowances and community-reinvestment funds in the Wisconsin contracts—successfully encourage agencies to meet contract goals, current performance-based contracting systems have deleterious effects on smaller organizations. As detailed elsewhere (Schneider 1999a), the small to midsized organizations involved in performance-based contracts faced choices of whether to "cream" (select only clients who could meet program goals), force their participants into inappropriate placements, or lose money. Organizations without large revenues from other sources can face budget deficits that could jeopardize the agency. To encourage smaller organizations and those serving clients with greater barriers to economic self-sufficiency to engage in government contracts, government needs to modify contracting systems to support quality work in all organizations.
- Government contracts with local social service agencies should respect the mission-based strengths of their contractors by encouraging them to maintain mission-based differences within general policy guidelines.
- Both government and social service agencies should explore more effective ways to improve communications between program participants and organizations providing government benefits. Since welfare reform, problems connecting public assistance recipients with their caseworkers have

increased in all three communities. Given work schedules, lack of telephones, and other problems, communications issues are not easily remedied. Communications patterns are also community-specific, meaning that solutions that work in one locality may fail in another. Identifying effective practices through research on this issue and offering contracts to improve communications might help to alleviate this problems.

- Government needs to provide funding for ancillary services, advocacy by ancillary agencies on behalf of TANF recipients, and community education through increased contracts to agencies in the ancillary services and community-based provision systems.
- Improving social capital relationships among the official welfare system, the ancillary system, and the community-based system would also help mend gaps in the safety net that have developed with employment-focused welfare reform.

Summary

Comparing families with institutions shows that similar factors benefit both. The organizations that, like Empowerment Education and Sunrise, expanded their social capital networks and developed flexibility to address the changing policy and funding context succeeded in improving their position and developed stronger programs for their participants. Large organizations like Faith in Action were already in a similar position. Organizations lacking these attributes have a more limited, or less successful, role in welfare reform.

The strength of the contracting system is the diversity of programs available through organizations with missions to serve people in their local communities. Ability to develop programs for different populations is another benefit of social service agency provision of government-funded programs. Even the large agencies, like Faith in Action and Community Solutions, develop smaller, tailored initiatives. Fostering this diversity through broadly defined requests for proposals that encourage creativity, as Pennsylvania did, rather than micromanage TANF providers, as Wisconsin did, better achieves this goal.

The interplay between an agency's approach and the way individuals use organizations suggests that social service agencies are an important component in family survival strategies. Looking at the life histories of families also suggests that the agencies are only one component in family social capital resources. In many cases, faith communities serve as a much more relevant source of social capital and community. The next chapter examines these institutions.

CHAPTER 11

Faith Communities and Social Capital

In the three cities studied, faith communities served as sources of material assistance, instrumental guidance, community, and spiritual support for most families. As also seen in other studies, congregations provided a second set of resources beyond the formal social service agency system for families in need regardless of their affiliation with the congregation (Cnaan et al. 1999; Cnaan 2002; Ammerman 1997; Edin and Lein 1997). Congregations also provided instrumental supports to their members and encouraged them to connect with other organizations.

Church social welfare assistance has drawn considerable attention in policy circles, particularly after passage of the charitable choice provisions in TANF. Religious-based nonprofits and congregations are seen in some policy circles as preferred providers of welfare-to-work programs, substance-abuse treatment, youth programming, community development, education, and numerous other activities that would benefit from a "moral" component or from the community-centered activities of religious organizations (Sider 1999; Carlson-Theis and Skillen 1996; Queen 2000; Sherman 1997).

Congregations are promoted as preferred agencies for social supports for four reasons. First, churches concentrate on the whole person or community in its complexity rather than on piecemeal needs as in many government-funded programs, and are assumed to offer better-quality service because of this holistic approach. Second, proponents view faith communities as providing moral and spiritual guidance supposedly needed by the poor. Third, because churches are enjoined by the Bible to serve the needy, it is presumed that such programs will have more altruistic interests than nonsectarian nonprofits and will be less expensive because they draw on volunteers and other church resources. Fourth, supporters envision faith communities as centers for community, naturally providing social and cultural capital needed by impoverished people. They assume that low-income families lack connections and appropriate values to succeed in jobs and that churches can help them develop the resources that will lead them to self-sufficiency.

This chapter focuses primarily on the last aspect of church social welfare provision. Faith communities are widely described as creating community and fostering social capital (Ammerman 1997; Foley et al. 2001). However, as other scholars recognize (Foley et al. 2001), congregations can foster either closed or bridging social capital. This chapter demonstrates that faith communities usually cultivate community among their members and develop closed social capital networks. These closed networks become sources of instrumental supports, information on jobs and other resources, social supports, and spiritual guidance. Faith communities serve as major sources of cultural capital and sometimes also help develop bridging social capital. However, like social capital, cultural capital developed through faith communities can either help or hinder individuals in their interactions with the dominant culture. I explore the following questions:

- What role does church involvement play in individual lives?
- How do faith communities develop social and cultural capital for their members?
- How and why do faith communities develop bridging and closed social capital for their members? How is cultural capital development through faith communities linked to this process?
- What instrumental supports do faith communities provide for their members and others?
- How are congregations involved in welfare-reform-related service provision?

Faith Communities and Social Welfare

In general, faith communities have three functions:

1. As a spiritual well for participants
2. As a source of community, providing social and instrumental supports to its members and others who seek help, and fostering social and cultural capital among active participants
3. As a source of empowerment and change, both individual transformation and change in an institution or society

Each of these roles takes place within the context of religious faith. Faith communities exist to provide spiritual guidance and nourishment for members of their community and society at large. All other activities are subsumed under the first function. Initiatives that promote community, social capital development, and empowerment arise from efforts to practice God's presence and promote a faith-based vision of individual behavior and a just world. Practical outcomes of church participation cannot be separated from this primary purpose. Discussion throughout this chapter relies on this premise.

Faith communities simultaneously influence individual lives and community-wide institutions. Case studies demonstrate how congregations create community, foster social capital, and provide instrumental supports. Sometimes these efforts can change lives. In other instances, churches maintain the status quo even as they seek to use faith to better their communities.

FAITH COMMUNITIES AND INDIVIDUAL FAMILIES

In all three cities, church involvement loomed large as a source of inspiration, social support, and guidance for individuals. Very few families in these studies fit the profile of "unchurched," morally confused people envisioned by conservative proponents of faith-based social welfare provision. Many families who experienced joblessness or other problems sought support from their faith communities. As in other studies (Cnaan et al. 1999; Chaves and Tsitsos 2000), some of the larger churches hosted Alcoholics Anonymous and related programs. Other congregations used individual counseling and group support to help people address personal challenges. Assistance to individuals and their families was often a side line to incorporating people into the community of the church.

Christina's life illustrates the connections among church, community, social capital, and empowerment. Christina, an African American woman in her mid-thirties, is married and has two teenaged daughters. She finished her GED through a Neighborhood Settlement House program and is employed part time as a bus driver. She intends to return to school soon to obtain a college degree and move into more professional employment.

I first met Christina at a focus group during the Milwaukee phase of the research, where her vitality and presence stood out. She explained that about 15 years previously she had been an alcoholic. However, with the help of her church, she pulled her life together and today her church is very much the center of her life. She attends activities there three days a week and is an active volunteer. There is a strong friendship network in the church; members go out together. There are also events for the entire family. She finds theses activities helpful social venues for her children. Participation in church has empowered her while providing social capital and spiritual supports that enable her to succeed in all areas of her life.

Her pastor stresses both spiritual supports and expected behaviors. For example, she mentioned that he expects parishioners to be punctual. Through this kind of mentoring and behavior modification, the pastor encourages cultural patterns that help his congregants find and keep jobs in the mainstream work world. As in most social capital environments which help build bridges across race/nationality/class barriers, this pastor promotes the cultural capital

required by the white, middle-class mainstream while providing an environment that offers the social capital and spiritual guidance required to survive in an often alienating work setting.

Christina's experience is typical of people who had created stable lives combining work, family, and community. For many such people, the church served two functions. First, it was the source of respite and empowerment for individuals pulled in many directions by unsatisfying work and the demands of family, school, and modern life. Within the church, people created cohesive communities and were empowered by active volunteer efforts that helped sustain and guide the organization, at the same time receiving both spiritual and instrumental support such as food and rent assistance.

The second function served by the church was as a bridge between closed communities and the wider world of work and social service. Faith communities provided networks that led people to jobs and other resources. Some congregations taught through example behaviors that helped people negotiate white, middle-class social service, school, and work environments. These congregations served as key sources of bridging social capital by creating strong communities that foster in-group comfort while encouraging bridging across "communities in themselves" and the wider world (Milofsky and Hunter 1995).

Faith communities accomplish individual change both through intentional activities and as a by-product of people working together. Even for people who were not currently active in church, childhood religious experience played a large role in shaping approaches to daily life. As with Christina's involving her whole family in her church, family social capital networks often centered on religious activities. As children left home and childhood faith communities, they often recreated their relationships to religious institutions in other localities. Examining each component of religious faith in individual families demonstrates why religion is such a potent aspect of social and cultural capital development.

CHURCH AS SPIRITUAL WELL

Religious faith served as a touchstone for all aspects of life for people like Christina. For example, one adult participant in an intensive program that was intended to keep children out of foster care said she needed to "spiritually get myself together" before she would be able to take a job or adequately care for her children. When asked what she meant by spiritual assistance, one women said it was "just help, you know like some people turn to drugs and alcohol, I just go to church." Rachel, an African American low-skilled worker from Kenosha with two adult children, had been active in church as a child but stopped attending when she moved to Kenosha as a young adult. She explained:

> Without church your life isn't complete. You're not there where you should be. One time when I wasn't in church, I knew I believed in Jesus Christ but I knew I had to have church in my life. I wasn't ready to go back to church so I kept it inside me everywhere I go.

Rachel's reliance on religious faith continued despite not having participated in organized congregational activities for more than 20 years.

For many low-skilled workers, religion helped them cope with demoralizing work. People employed as nursing assistants or in menial service-sector jobs talked about praying when they encountered a rude client or bad boss. Some rely on faith for support during difficult family situations. For example, Rachel told us, "I tell you right now, if I didn't have the church in my life I don't know where I'd be. The church has helped me so much, especially with this divorce I'm going through. [If] I didn't have God and the church in my life, I think I'd be a mental case."

People also used religion to decide on a career. This was true of many of the families in the rising educated middle class who worked in social service, education, or other helping professions. Their work choices originated from a religious injunction to serve those in need. Once they were employed in social welfare provision, faith sustained these workers against burnout and provided spiritual and moral lessons to help them make decisions on the job.

Church as a spiritual well places the individual within a larger context. Much of the uplift drawn from connecting to religion in daily life came to religious individuals from a sense of God's presence in every activity. Individuals relied on spiritual guidance through good times and bad. This sense of spiritual support was key in Christina's decision to stop drinking as well as her choices regarding education, marriage, and work. Others reported similar feelings.

CHURCH AS COMMUNITY

The church is the center of Christina's social life. It serves as her base community for recreation, career matters, and many other aspects of daily life. Her experience is not uncommon—particularly in the African American community, church members generally served on several committees and focused their social life on church.

Faith communities became long-term communities for their members. Involved members form the nucleus of church organizational activities and create closed social capital networks that exist alongside the formal administrative structure. For example, James, a long-time member of St. Xavier's parish, a mostly white Catholic church in Milwaukee, said, "I probably have seen close to a dozen priests come and go. It doesn't bother me really. The church is not the priest, he's part of it. All the community, all the parish members are the church just as much as the priest is, if not more so."

Faith communities become community centers for families because they intentionally build community, which is often a centerpiece of church mission. For example, Grace Baptist in Kenosha prints its mission on each weekly order of service program:

> [Grace] is the Church where the neighborhood becomes a brotherhood. We say to all who are weary and need rest, to all who mourn and need comfort, to all who are friendless and wish friendship, to all who pray and to all who do not, but ought to, to all who sin and are in need of a Savior this church opens its doors in the name of Jesus, the Lord says WELCOME!

Like many churches, Grace expands its community by actively recruiting visitors as members. For example, each of our field-workers reported that church members approached them to welcome them to the church. As these students continued to attend services, church members took an interest in their welfare, inquiring about whether they had plans for Thanksgiving, showing concern about school progress, and continuing to welcome them to church. All the African American churches included greeting periods midway through the service that encouraged participants to reach out to the people around them. Coffee hour after church also offered an opportunity to chat and welcome newcomers. Sometimes these overtures turned into direct recruitment tactics. For example, after attending Grace for several weeks, our field-worker reported:

> After the services were over, there were two elderly women who . . . were working up probe questions to find out exactly where was our "church home." My sister explained to them that we did not have a church home. They smiled and said, "Yes, you would always be welcome, but it would be a much better experience if you joined Grace!"

As new people become more involved in the church, the congregation become a place to celebrate achievements and ask for assistance. For example, during the welcome time at Grace one Sunday, a woman stood up and announced that her daughter had just attained a 3.5 grade point average in high school. The pastor congratulated the girl and then asked all the young people who had achieved this average to stand. The same public care for community was expressed for people who were ill or elderly. Several congregations printed lists of people requesting prayers in their weekly service booklet.

Although faith communities can become intensive, not all members are equally involved in church activities. In some cases, changes in degree of involvement stem from community politics. For example, one active member in Faith Temple reported that her daughters resigned from several committees after they were snubbed by longtime members.

Other people reported that they were less involved with their congregations because of work or family commitments. However, even for people tangentially involved in the church, it became a link to a larger community, as it was for Linda, who experienced extreme social isolation. The only family members she talks to are her brother and one sister active in church. Asked whether she had other social contacts, she responded, "Older people going to church. Like this lady right next door . . . her and the lady upstairs from me, they're the only ones I talk to."

Church communities are often linked to family and friendship networks. For example, Rachel found her church through friends:

> Well, I have some friends that go to Faith Temple and they kept saying, "You should go to church with us sometime." So I went and I kept going and I really liked Faith Temple. One of my cousins goes to Faith Temple and we were supposed to go there for Sunday after our [family] reunion and I joined the church that Sunday.

Churches like Grace that became closed social capital communities often became the province of several families. For example, one active Grace member reported:

Marcus is my cousin, his mother [another church member] is my first cousin. [The Pastor's wife] is my sister and this is my other sister. There were originally a family of 15 of us, with 13 still living. Grace is filled with my relatives, and the adult Sunday school teacher is my husband.

Kinship-based communities like this one can limit the ability of a church to reach out beyond the closed social capital networks of existing members. As illustrated by the members who withdrew from committees at Faith Temple, domination of the church by one faction can discourage other members from becoming active participants in the church community. Faith communities do not offer automatic community to everyone who comes in the door. As with social service agencies, some members use faith communities as a source of community whereas others do not fit into the milieu of a particular congregation.

By intentionally creating community, faith communities become centers for the social lives of their members. As Christina's and Rachel's experiences demonstrate, churches serve as the institutional locus for closed social capital networks of family and friends. Churches also reach out to others loosely connected with their membership, as when Linda's neighbors invited her to church. Concerns about school progress, work, health, and other matters were brought up in services as the objects of church benevolence. Through these activities, faith communities served as social capital for their members and others in the community.

FAITH COMMUNITIES AND SOCIAL CAPITAL

Faith communities often served as social capital resources for jobs, educational opportunities, and material supports. Many people had found their first jobs through church connections—they helped Megan, the low-skilled worker profiled in chapter 6, find hers, at age 16. Mary, the limited-work-experience woman described in chapter 1, was only comfortable working in the safe, trusting environment of the church her mother had introduced her to in Kenosha. Others reported that church members told them about job possibilities or provided references.

In some cases, older church members intentionally become mentors for church youth. Karen, active in Faith Temple and a successful government employee, took particular interest in one young woman in her church. She frequently gave her guidance and encouragment to become involved in various activities.

Church members became resources for information on institutions. When asked how they would locate schools, day care, and other supports, people often said that they would ask friends whom they knew through church or their pastor. For example, after a racial incident with the police, one Faith Temple member contacted her pastor for advice. The pastor referred her to a civil rights organization to file a complaint. Negative information traveled through church channels too. For example, much of the reputation of the Kenosha police regarding their treatment of African Americans was based on negative experiences shared at church.

Church social capital and community go hand in hand. Faith communities often become the first resources outside of family networks people turn to for advice, referral, or instrumental supports. The same mechanisms that build community foster social capital. Faith communities encourage intense connections among members. Churches show concern for congregants' lives outside of church activities. Congregations monitor and encourage participation in education, volunteer activities, and other mechanisms that can create trust-based connections that benefit their members. In some cases, faith communities intentionally build bridging social capital by encouraging members to seek resources outside their known networks. For example, several of the churches encouraged congregants to attend college. One listed all the college students in the weekly service bulletin, along with the colleges they attended. Interfaith activities and services with other congregations also built social capital across boundaries.

Most examples of social capital formed through congregations involved links to cultural capital. People were not only referred to jobs but also taught ways to behave. The trusting environment of the church helped Mary develop work skills. Faith-based actions encouraged certain behaviors. For example, Maria reported this link between faith and social networks:

> If we are not on God's road . . . It sustains us, it helps us live a different life. Otherwise we get involved in things that are not conducive [to a good life]. It will help us leave the life we led before. The social life we had was not the kind of life to create a family, you understand? The friends we had then were not very good models for our children.

By changing their social networks through church involvement, this family developed different models and new behaviors. Social capital fostered particular cultural capital.

FAITH COMMUNITIES AND CULTURAL CAPITAL

As well as developing social capital and community, faith communities foster certain kinds of cultural capital through both formal and informal activities. Take, for example, Christina's pastor exhorting his congregants to be on time for events. Many sermons spoke to cultural capital values and behaviors. For example, the Grace Baptist pastor frequently railed against consumerism among his low-skilled worker and stable-working-class flock. These sermons combined biblical messages with modern cultural capital and humor. For example, one sermon asked congregants to focus on the Lord rather than earthly goods:

> Pastor was reading from the 31st chapter, verse 14, from the Book of Jeremiah ("And so I will satiate the soul of the priests with fatness, and my people shall be satisfied with my goodness, saith the Lord"). He then began with the sermonizing of this passage with "Every individual yearns for satisfaction . . . but most are only pacified. Like a baby crying for milk and given a pacifier . . . pacification gives no true benefits, no real fulfillment, no lasting satisfaction . . . infant receives no nourishment from a pacifier. People drink alcohol until they are drunk . . . spend money until they're broke, and they get no lasting satisfaction . . . this world does not have what it takes to satisfy. . . . A good income, a facelift, weight loss, even the human body only pacifies because after a while, the aches and pains come . . . just keep living. . . . Some people are *never* satisfied with the people they have, so they switch . . . never before in the history of mankind have divorces been so high . . . but only Jesus can provide the lasting satisfaction your body needs, the assurance that will satisfy your lonely spirit, only Jesus is able to satisfy."

This sermon contains a number of cultural messages for the congregation. First, the pastor rails against overindulgences and preoccupation with material goods. Second, he preaches constancy in marriage, but his references could be extended to work and other aspects of life. Finally, he tells his audience to focus on faith rather than constantly seek satisfaction.

In some instances, faith communities became centers for passing on ethnic culture. For example, Lydia reported continuing to attend Spanish Mass because "It's been an extension . . . the Hispanic Mass is one way to keep the culture alive in the environment here . . . very, very evident." African American faith communities also promoted cultural pride.

Faith communities can also promote cultural capital at odds with mainstream values or behaviors. For example, Grace Baptist informally promoted a culture of mistrust of outsiders that was common in the closed social capital networks of the Kenosha African American community. Dress-up clothing in certain bright styles among low-income African American faith communities led people without any other models to wear the same kind of clothing for job interviews or in other settings where it was inappropriate. The boisterous involvement in church services, including the call-and-response and movement common in African American services, clashed with expectations of calmness in school settings. In both Kenosha and Milwaukee, African American children were reprimanded in school more often than white children for being too loud or active. School culture clashed with models developed at home and at church.

Service activities fostered a sense of community involvement. A member of St Xavier's parish became active in outreach to the Uptown housing project because:

> [The priest] had made mention many times of this letter from the Bishop and there was one line in there, one or two sentences, about "we need to be more involved in our community, our neighborhood, especially Uptown," and so I think that was kind of a calling to me that if nobody else was really getting involved in Uptown besides St. Vincent de Paul [a lay service organization], maybe I could strike up something with them.

As discussed in more detail later, this call to service led to a congregation-wide outreach to the housing project. This individual had learned the practice of service through earlier involvement in the church. He served as an altar boy and was active in St. Vincent de Paul activities. He also was a mainstay in the fund-raising efforts for the church's school. The cultural ethos of service began within the closed social capital environment of the church and expanded into other activities.

As noted earlier, just as faith communities are centers for community and social capital development, they become a major source of cultural capital. As these examples show, cultural capital is fostered through both formal and informal modeling of appropriate behaviors. In some cases, cultural capital acquired through the church has a positive influence on the lives of congregants outside the church environment. In other instances, church cultural capital is at odds with expectations in other settings.

EMPOWERMENT AND CHANGE

Some academics claim that social welfare initiatives to empower individuals weaken group strategies for social change. These arguments are often linked to the self-esteem movement, described as aligning "my personal goals with those set out by reformers—both expert and activist—according to some notion of the social good" (Cruikshank 1993:235). Self-empowerment and self-esteem are both equated with co-opting "poor people" into the dominant ideology and reform strategies of conservative welfare reform.

Although I agree with critics of the self-esteem movement, research in Philadelphia, Kenosha, and Milwaukee suggests that advocacy strategies that denigrate self-empowerment in favor of group mobilization create a false dichotomy that ignores an important element of enabling disempowered parts of a community to speak for themselves. Empowerment—helping individuals develop the comfort in diverse settings and the appropriate cultural capital to advocate for themselves—is the first step in effectively participating in social change initiatives.

This approach agrees with the concept of "relational empowerment," which describes empowerment as emerging through interaction with others (VanderPlaat 1999:5). Relational empowerment requires the bicultural skills of bridging cultural capital as well as the ability to move beyond closed social capital networks to participate in wider social and policy arenas.

Faith communities fostered both individual and group empowerment by several means. First, ongoing encouragement in church builds confidence and encourages personal growth. Christina's transformation from alcoholic to working woman with professional career plans stemmed from ongoing support through her church.

Sometimes faith communities develop programs aimed at empowering their members. For example, Faith Temple created a Boys to Men ministry specifically designed to create a positive self-image among African American youth. Empowerment was also promoted by encouraging congregation members to vote or otherwise participate in the electoral process. This gradually led to increasing involvement in visible jobs and other leadership roles throughout Kenosha.

Faith communities developed leadership by placing members in active roles in the church. In many cases, young people took church-based leadership roles as teenagers. For example, Rachel reported, "When I was young I loved to go to church, I used to be the secretary and every year they would have two delegates sent to the Sunday School and I went there as the secretary."

A number of low-skilled workers and stable-working-class individuals found a sense of efficacy in church leadership roles that did not carry through to their paid work experience. Rachel worked as a nursing assistant before going on welfare. Maria, also a church secretary, directed most positive energies into church, making it the center of her life. Other people active in closed social capital communities through church showed similar tendencies.

On the other hand, some church-based empowerment activities are intended to propel congregation members into more active roles in the wider community. Karen's mentoring of a young Faith Temple member illustrates this kind of empowerment. Active political participation also helped encourage individuals to engage in social change.

SUMMARY

Often, faith communities developed faith, community, social and cultural capital, and empowerment through the same sets of activities. Congregations fostered change in individuals through two related kinds of activities. Instructional methods, including sermons, Bible classes, ministries, and others, provided one form of individual development. Experiential activities—participation in church ministries, social events with other members, and simply attending worship—equally served to help people become active parts of the congregation community. These activities not only reinforced the formal messages, they also provide another mechanism for socialization, empowerment, and the formation of social and cultural capital.

The kinds of empowerment promoted through faith communities depended on the nature of the institution. Bridging faith communities fostered different kinds of behaviors than more closed communities did. Faith communities also engaged in development of community, social capital, and cultural capital as institutions. I next examine faith communities as institutions.

Congregations and Social Capital

A comparison of the four congregations profiled here shows how the history and ethos of a church influence the kinds of social capital it provides and demonstrates ways that congregations serve the wider community.St. Xavier's is a predominantly white Catholic parish in Milwaukee. It has struggled as the neighborhood has changed from largely Catholic to a mix of religions, and its original population has aged. It has sought to redefine its relationship to the neighborhood and the Uptown housing project on its borders. It represents a closed social capital network attempting to reach out through service.

Faith Temple is a large African American denominational church in Kenosha that has changed from a small, isolated church to one of the city's major bridging institutions. At the same time, it has widened the class range of its congregants to include families of the rising educated middle class. It demonstrates how faith communities serve as bridging forces for their members and a community.

Grace Baptist serves stable-working-class and low-skilled worker African Americans in Kenosha. The church is a spinoff from Faith Temple and maintains closed social capital networks. Grace Baptist's use of social capital to support its members shows how closed social capital networks maintain boundaries.

Annunciation is a Catholic church that hosts the Spanish-language Mass in Kenosha. The Latinos operate a separate congregation within the predominantly white parish, complete with its own social service organization. Examining this congregation shows how a closed social capital community interacts with white institutions and maintains its separate identity.

St. Xavier's Parish

St. Xavier's parish sits on the other side of Uptown from Neighborhood Settlement House. It was built to serve the newly founded community—both the small houses and the housing project. The parish was incorporated in 1956, when many residents were Catholic. The church was built the next year, and the school was established in 1960.

Until the late 1970s, St. Xavier's was a thriving parish. The parish priest said that "at the peak the parish was about 1600 families and [there were] probably about 325 in the school." It was also exclusively white working class. Like the neighborhood, the church was a starter community for young families. The parish priest reported that "in 1961 [this parish], baptized 361 children, and as of this year, 1998, the three largest parishes in the diocese together would not baptize that number of children."

In addition to the spiritual activities of the church and the school, the parish supported active men's and women's groups, Boy Scouts and Girl Scouts, and a variety of other activities. St Xavier's has always been a very giving parish, and remains involved in St. Vincent de Paul activities in inner-city Milwaukee, such as a soup kitchen. The church currently has a food pantry and St. Vincent de Paul clothing and holiday drives for the poor in the neighborhood. It also hosted community activities like a battered women's support group.

At present, the church has about 530 households.[1] An active core of parishioners remains. The archdiocese now allows members who have moved away to retain membership in their home parish, which has kept approximately 10 percent of the more established members in the parish. However, as the numbers have declined, many church activities have been discontinued and others have become more low-key. The decline began in the 1980s, along with racial transitions in its neighborhood. St. Xavier's had lost about 30 percent of its families since 1990, and the church currently has only a few African American members. The school had too few students from the parish to be viable. Given a priest shortage and declining membership, the archdiocese slated St. Xavier's for merger with another parish.

The archdiocese also gave the parish a way out in the form of a renewed mission to minister to the Uptown housing project. Previously, St. Xavier's had largely ignored the welfare-dependent, African American public housing population next door, and the archdiocese suggested that the church develop an evangelizing mission to the housing project and to nonpracticing Catholics in the area. An all parish workshop document on evangelizing included the following message: "Our Holy Father and our bishops are urging EVERY parish to evangelize. And if we do, we will also become a GROWING parish— because people will find the Lord Jesus among us and want to become part of our community."

Although not specifically articulated, the archdiocese was following a philosophy that community organizing through mission outreach activities would help the parish grow (Milofsky 1997:s142–s144). The parish priest and council responded to this enjoinder in several ways. First, they expanded the school population and increased its budget by become a Choice school, under a Milwaukee voucher program that allows parents to send their children to private and parochial schools. The parish also agreed to rent the convent to Neighborhood Settlement House to enable expansion of their day-care program, a move that both raised income and brought more African Americans onto church property. Finally, the parish priest recruited an active volunteer to start mission outreach to Uptown. By late 1999, the school had a stable population and the parish had received its own priest after nearly a year sharing with another parish. However, parish membership remained small and mostly white.

By the mid-1990s, social capital and community worked differently for the three components of church, school, and mission to the Uptown housing project. The church tried to build a stronger community of Catholics from among existing members and friends they might bring into the parish. The parish encouraged community by involving members in more ministries, particularly programs for the needy and the school. The church served primarily as a resource for spiritual guidance and an opportunity for service. One key member described his participation as follows:

> How does the church affect my life? That's quite an involved tangent, most everything I do centers around my spirituality, not so much this church but what I feel in my heart.
>
> *Interviewer*: But it's through a spiritual call, it's not social space.
>
> Yes, absolutely. If I was 10 blocks away at [another parish], I would be as active in that church and/or community, at least I would hope to be if they would accept myself.

As for several other key parishioners, involvement in church mission work becomes a way to express spirituality. Community and social capital networks for this individual were focused elsewhere, particularly on work-based friendships. The same pattern held for many involved in this church. Parents with children in the school concentrated on school-based community. Others simply attended worship services at the church. The congregation itself did not create the kind of strong community and social capital networks that were observed in the other faith communities profiled here.

With respect to social capital, St. Xavier's is an institution that provides resources for its school and other mission activities but creates limited community for parishioners. Even though many ministries are meant to build church membership, most parish members use church social sevice activities to carry out individual religious calls to service rather than create strong closed social capital networks or a community that supports its members. Church may be an important part of parishioners' lives, and probably plays a role in developing cultural capital. Church certainly serves as a spiritual well for members. However, for most members, the faith community does not serve as a center for social capital for work, education, or other aspects of life. Most of the middle-class parishioners have other social networks outside of the congregation that serve this purpose. Instead, church is a place in which to practice faith, develop cultural capital, and participate in voluntary activities that serve a wider community.

FAITH TEMPLE

In many ways, Faith Temple shows tendencies opposite from those of St. Xavier's. This church is a major source of community and closed social capital for its members, as well as providing the spiritual and cultural capital support available through all four churches. By 2000, the African American community in Kenosha was beginning to transform from a passive, closed society to an activist community focused on both empowering members of the subculture and promoting forms of racial equity that welcomed diverse styles. The churches were at the center of this process. As the largest and most politically visible one, Faith Temple epitomized church as a source of community and empowerment. Faith Temple also envisioned itself as a bridging institution, successfully playing this role in Kenosha and supporting its members, who moved between race-based closed social capital networks and the wider Kenosha community.

The African American churches in all three communities maintained their historical role as institutions providing "succor and inspiration for a people struggling both to survive and advance under harsh and changing social circumstances" (Baer and Singer 1992:xi). African American churches served as "public space" (Higginbotham 1997:208) for their members, providing educational support, entertainment, and social activities. As in other African American churches, these congregations reflect dialectical processes between priestly (worship) and prophetic (political and service activities) as well as accommodation to the larger society and resistance to domination by whites (Lincoln and Mamiya 1990:10–16). In contrast to St. Xavier's, African American churches frequently became centers for community and social capital.

Faith Temple started as a home-based mission in 1919. It remained a small mission project, partly under the auspices of a white congregation, until 1943. The church remained a small congregation largely invisible to the white community for many years.[2] Until the 1990s, membership remained at between 65 and 75 families. It had a few part-time ministers who stayed with the congregation for long periods of time.

Faith Temple is one of two large denominational African American churches in Kenosha, and families moved between these two churches for worship and social life. Together, the two churches formed a cohesive closed social capital network and an all-encompassing community. Family social capital for work, housing, recreation, and spiritual support was shared between these two congregations. As several newer African American churches developed, the community widened somewhat. However, most of the stable working class focused on Faith Temple and Zion, the other denominational church.

When Chrysler was the dominant employer in Kenosha, community for most Kenosha African Americans centered on two institutions: their church and the UAW union hall. Although the unions remain important today, the closure of the Chrysler plant in the mid 1980s refocused the community on its churches as the primary remaining institution for all forms of support. The churches now serve as the only centers for community in this small city. The several weak African American social service organizations retain strong connections to the churches and do not serve as major resources for either community or social capital.

Faith Temple began its transformation from a haven for a closed social capital network to a bridging institution when it hired a dynamic educator as its pastor in 1981. The pastor began to transform the small group of "passive, take anything people" that he found at Faith Temple into a dynamic congregation of 600 members. He explained:

> When I came here there was a lot of people who really had the old-time religion. I said there is nothing wrong with old-time religion, but what I said is what you need to have is relevant religion, which will help to empower you and equip you to maximum success. My whole context for the church is that the church would be an empowering agent, that the church would be used to build what I would say is self-independence. You see, you don't need to be dependent on anyone else. You need to be in a situation not only that you feel good, but also that your fullness would be illuminated also.

He strove to involve members in ministries: "We started what we call contact ministry, and that is reaching out to people and also contacting families." Contact ministries led to a number of other initiatives; organized ministries are now available for people of all ages. The goal of these ministries is to build community "so that everybody that comes into the church will be involved in something and somebody will have contact with them."

The church serves as a social capital center for its community. During the year that we observed church services, people frequently received information from other members about jobs and other resources. The women's ministry kept track of families in need so that they could provide for their material welfare. As an institution, church members worked on antiracism campaigns and helped elect the pastor to the school board. The congregation became a forum for a number of other political and social welfare activities.

In addition to the traditional women's ministry, ushers, choir, youth programs, and hospitality, the church includes Boys to Men, African Crusade ministries, Afrocentricity classes, Prison/Jail ministry, Narcotics Anonymous, a Bible studies ministry, Kwanzaa celebrations, and a television broadcast of services. The youth groups, men's and women's ministries, and similar activities combined Bible study with discussion that connects religion to dilemmas at work or home. Activities aim to serve as a spiritual well for church members through exuberant worship services and small group meetings meant to relate Bible lessons to daily life.

Ministries equally attempt to build human and cultural capital and empower members. This led to a large number of young members moving on to college and serving the community as teachers and social service workers and in other capacities. The growing church also drew many of the newcomer African American middle class who had moved to Kenosha as it became a bedroom community for northern Illinois. Several of these newcomers became active participants in the ministries aimed at developing middle-class cultural capital among congregation youth—for example, the Boys to Men ministry, as explained by the pastor:

> We try to teach them various pro-social skills to help empower them and keep them out of the criminal justice system and . . . also to give them spirituality. . . . We teach them communication skills, we teach them social skills, we teach them drug awareness, we also teach them discipline, we teach them conflict resolution.

As my study of Kenosha African Americans demonstrates (Schneider 2001), these church activities were most effective when they were combined with other organizational programs. Church served as a base community for its members, and its lessons reinforce positive messages from other institutions. The faith component added another aspect of socialization that contributes to positive outcomes. These church activities would probably be less effective without reinforcement from schools and social service organization programs.

Faith Temple began to serve as a bridging institution in the mid-1990s. The closed community of the church served as a center for activities in the aftermath of a racial incident in which a Kenosha resident ran down two young African American boys for no reason. The pastor began to work with some concerned whites, as well as his congregation members, to address racism in

Kenosha. This effort quickly led to the creation of a formal program, called "Kindness Week," meant to address intergroup relations. The program evolved into a series of forums on race related issues. Finally, an Alinsky coalition formed in 2000 continues these interfaith efforts to address inequities through the political process.[3]

As 5 percent of the Kenosha population, African Americans in this small city had always had contacts with whites. Many families already had strong closed social capital network connections to whites of the same class background through work, school, or neighborhood interaction. The aim of church bridging activities was to expand the contacts that African Americans had in homogeneous settings, to encourage bridging social and cultural capital that crossed both race and class. The goal of these activities was to right the imbalance in Kenosha citywide institutions that kept most African Americans out of leadership roles. Faith Temple sought both empowerment and change for its members and the African American community as a whole.

Bridging activities began slowly, with the middle-class church members who already had strong bridges with their white peers leading church efforts. However, the pastor quickly began to include the rest of the congregation through joint worship services with white congregations and other activities. At the same time, the pastor sought to include his congregants as volunteers in Sunrise, a citywide effort to feed the hungry and shelter the homeless in which previously only white churches had formally participated. This also brought congregants into contact with white volunteers from other organizations.

Faith Temple is an institution taking strong, clear measures to both build closed social capital and encourage bridging behavior. As in most bridging contexts, the church first built its internal community and strengthened social capital among its members. Next, it created programs aimed at individual empowerment, teaching bridging cultural capital, sustaining human capital development, and strengthening spirituality. Bridging activities soon followed. As it is for other strong bridging institutions, this church's expressed goal is to change the role of the African American community in Kenosha, not simply improve the lot of its members. Instituting social change is as important as building the faith community or improving outcomes for church members.

GRACE BAPTIST

Grace Baptist represents churches that serve as closed social capital networks for their members, providing both community and a range of instrumental supports for a small group of members and their friends. It is an offshoot of Faith Temple and in many ways illustrates the kind of church Faith Temple was before hiring its latest pastor. In addition to preaching values in line with mainstream U.S. expectations of work and family life, it upholds an alternative ethnic culture. The hallmark of this culture is avoidance of those considered in power and an expectation that mainstream institutions will try to hurt community members.

Grace Baptist was founded in 1961. The reasons for the split from Faith Temple are unclear, but the two congregations have remained on friendly terms. Relatives from some families belong to both congregations. The Grace Baptist preacher occasionally spoke at Faith Temple, and the two congregations held joint worship services during the holidays.

The majority of Grace Baptist members appeared to be stable-working-class or low-skilled workers with limited resources.

Comparing Faith Temple with Grace Baptist, the Faith Temple pastor commented, "You see, some African American churches do not believe in doing anything but waiting on God. And they believe that it is unethical to be involved in social situations." Our fieldwork supported this view. Most of the sermons focused on either salvation in the future or discontinuing destructive personal behavior. The church did not participate in any of the antiracism or social equity activities sponsored by other faith communities. The pastor did not attend interfaith meetings. Nor were any of the church members visible in government or social service jobs.

Grace Baptist's fear of mainstream Kenosha appeared well founded. When the congregation held a groundbreaking ceremony for a new, larger church building, the local news media did not cover it. However, when the congregation's treasurer was arrested for embezzling some of the building funds, several articles appeared on page one of the local section of the newspaper. This incident simply reinforced church members' suspicion of the outside world.

However, Grace Baptist maintained ongoing fellowship with churches whose members had the same class and race background. The congregation regularly had visits with similar churches in Milwaukee, north Chicago, and other places, thus maintaining a larger community but retaining racial and class boundaries.

Congregation members maintained a tight community with strong closed social capital networks. The organization maintained a ministry committee that kept careful track of the material concerns of the congregation. They also ran a "thrift house" offering clothing, but, although its hours were regularly posted in the service program, the house had no sign and was closed during its advertised hours. Our field-worker came upon an active church member there who was quietly organizing benevolence activities. The student who worked with this congregation, an African American whose roots were similar to those of many congregation members, knew this church member from her own social circles. Because of these prior connections, he agreed to talk with her about the church ministry activities but only "off the record." This conversation revealed a church that kept close contact among members and had a regular system to provide instrumental, social, and spiritual supports for members in need.

We saw in Grace Baptist a great deal of support for family and caring for congregation members. Social capital to support basic needs seemed to be a key component of this community, as in other African American congregations (Hall 1998).[4]

The family focus was part of the culture supported by this congregation. In many ways, strong family bonds are common in low-income African American communities (Stack 1974, 1996). Some of the behaviors we witnessed that seemed at odds with mainstream culture stemmed from this predominance of family needs over outsiders' concerns. For example, when a church member missed an appointment with the student field-worker because of a sudden death in the family, it did not occur to her to call to cancel the appointment or contact the student later to reschedule.

Outsiders to this closed social capital community were quietly ignored. Social service workers in the African American community reported that the pastor never returned phone calls. Families associated with the church received much support from the congregation, but the strong connections among several other African American churches and related community-based organizations appeared not to extend to Grace Baptist.

Behaviors tolerated at Grace Baptist, including not returning phone calls, missing appointments, being late, and not calling people outside the closed social capital network when plans or schedules needed to be changed, caused trouble in the larger world of work. For example, one nursing home manager reported that she had had to fire two African American nursing assistants because they missed work for two weeks without notifying the workplace, owing to a death in the family. These individuals otherwise exhibited good work habits but had so violated the rules of the workplace that they were laid off. Unlike Faith Temple, Grace Baptist did little to socialize members to the expectations of the mainstream world of work or school.

Clothing styles also reflected an alternative culture. Like Faith Temple, Grace Baptist insisted that congregation members dress up for church. However, the unspoken norms encompassed a wide array of appropriate attire. One Sunday, our field-worker observed:

> The mode of dress ranged from casual to too elegant, as one woman in the audience wore a gold lace dress with matching purse, hat, shoes, and nylons. Some of the teenage girls wore suits of various colors, ranging from bright red to velvet black with dressy pumps to match. Many of the women wore wigs, and many of the young girls and teens had a weave adorned in their hair. The young males wore white or multicolored shirts and permanent-pressed slacks. No T-shirts or tennis shoes were observed.

Dressing for church instills an important lesson: different clothes are appropriate in different settings. Grace Baptist conveyed this message, but it was less clear that it conveyed the differences between appropriate dress in the African American church community and that in the workplace. Other African American churches made a point of clarifying cultural differences regarding office work clothes. These cultural cues become particularly important for low-skilled workers attempting to move into white-collar employment. Grace Baptist paid less attention to these issues.

On the other hand, Grace Baptist consistently extolled members to steer away from vice. Every sermon focused on inappropriate behaviors: lying, infidelity, greed, gluttony, self-centeredness, "holding on to bad things." The cultural capital supported by the church reflected attempts to keep congregants from behaviors that could lead to poor family life, trouble at work, or jail. Church families should stay on the straight and narrow, like the "decent" families in low-income neighborhoods described by Anderson (2000). Sermons conveyed a dichotomy between people who stray and those who maintain God-fearing lives, and congregation members were to stay in the latter group.

The sermons, Bible lessons, and other messages of Grace Baptist worship constantly reminded members that they could rely on Jesus to meet their needs. The premise of its message was that focusing on God kept church members from straying into sin and led them toward a righteous life. Salvation was portrayed as succor in a world full of vice and pain. Devoting one's life to God provides a wellspring of support and relief from the ways of the world.

These messages were tied to the economic and cultural milieu that many congregation members faced in their outside lives. These low-income Kenosha residents were far more likely than Faith Temple's congregants to hold menial, dirty, and unfulfilling jobs. They were even more likely to face the temptations of the streets feared by families in poor neighborhoods. The church's focus on faith as an antidote to the difficulties of low-income life makes sense given these external conditions.

The messages of empowerment so evident at Faith Temple are missing at Grace Baptist. Instead, this church focuses on keeping members out of harm's way. Sermons convey a cultural message that members should lead an upright life but not move from their quiet, anonymous closed social capital community. The church does convey empowerment but in the form of Jesus's rewards for faith and a life lived well. Individuals are rewarded for avoiding the many sins of the world but are not encouraged to move beyond their community or situation in life.

In comparison towith the other two churches, Grace Baptist shows a community turned inward, a closed community bent on keeping its members away from the vices and oppression of the wider world through faith. The church serves as a spiritual well for its members, and it provides strong community and closed social capital to meet their needs. However, it discourages interaction with outsiders and does not build any bridging behaviors. The cultural capital encourages members to live a decent but unobtrusive life.

The social and cultural capital conveyed through this congregation is appropriate for a community engaged in low-skilled or stable-working-class work. Families receive the support they need. Messages are intended to sway younger members from the lure of the streets, but they also teach them not to stand out, potentially drawing the wrath of employers, customers, the police or government authorities. It is an appropriate strategy for faith communities that want to keep their members from harm. However, by reinforcing the closed community, Grace Baptist does little to encourage radical change within its members or the city as a whole.

ANNUNCIATION

Annunciation is a large Catholic church in Kenosha. The white congregation ranges from stable working class to middle class. The parish runs a large school and offers a number of services to its members, including a credit union and a food pantry and participates in St. Vincent de Paul and other service activities. It has an active membership and maintains a strong presence in this small city.

Annunciation also hosts the Spanish Mass in Kenosha. The Latino community maintains a separate congregation within this parish, complete with its own priest, church council, and social service mission project—the Ethnic Mission project profiled in chapter 4 and analyzed in more detail below. The white and Latino Masses are largely separate, with a distinct population attending each service. As such, Annunciation represents a closed community that exists as part of a larger institution. These separate Masses are common in Catholic dioceses with large immigrant populations, and the separation between congregations is similar to that found in other research (Goode and Schneider 1994). However, Annunciation is different because of the community control over the faith-based social service organization associated with the Spanish Mass.

Annunciation's Latino congregation also differs from Grace Baptist in that it includes several separate communities in one worship service. The Spanish-language Mass attendees at Annunciation nearly fill the large church, but most of the people are new Mexican and Central American immigrants. In contrast, many of the Sunday-school teachers and officers of the church council are more established Texas-Mexicans or Puerto Ricans. These are two very separate communities who share the same language.

In addition, Catholic worship and congregational practice is far less participatory than that of the African American Protestant churches profiled above. A few church members are active in the worship service and voluntary activities of the congregation. The others simply come to church once a week with few other expectations.

The Catholic Latino congregation started as a mission to migrant farm workers in the 1950s and 1960s. Until Latino migrants started settling in Kenosha in large numbers, priests came to the farms to celebrate Mass. As the population moved into the city of Kenosha and neighboring Racine, the Latino Mass moved into established community Catholic churches. In Kenosha, the Latino Mass was first hosted by a parish near where most newcomers lived. However, around 1995, the original host church requested that the congregation be moved elsewhere. No explanation was given for this request, and a variety of reasons have been put forth in the community for this change.

Annunciation's priest was friendly to a Latino mission and offered the congregation its new home. But the established white parishioneres still see the Latinos as simply using their space. There is little interaction between the two congregations, and the Latino congregation maintains a separate parish council and Sunday school in the guise of an advisory committee to a social welfare organization for new Latinos, also hosted by the parish.

This "advisory committee" is officially charged with administration of the social welfare activities of the Latino mission office. However, field observations of their board meetings reveal that two-thirds of the business conducted focuses on religious activities for the Spanish Mass. The current priest said, "You could cut the umbilical cord between the committee and the established congregation and have a fully functional parish council."

The Latino Mass consists of two closed communities centered on the church. The majority of both new émigrés and long-term Kenosha Texas-Mexican residents were Catholic, but many of the more established members were Protestant or "Catholic by tradition," that is, nonpracticing Catholics.

The original migrants formed a cohesive community in the camps that extended to their religious activities. For example, Anita said her parents' generation "did things like baptize each other's children. The godparents of my two younger siblings knew my parents in Texas, so the connection was that my parents maintained a friendship with the Hispanics that had come here just like they had."

Although these younger, English-speaking Kenosha Latinos often attended English Masses if they went to church at all, their parents became the mainstay of the Spanish congregation and its social service outreach activities. The social obligations of serving as godparents led to strong networks that carried forward into organizational activity. Social capital supports in this community were very strong, and the community maintained even tighter closed boundaries than the African American community in this small city.

The newcomer Latino population was equally strong as a closed community. Like other immigrants, they followed friends and family to the United

States and relied on the émigré community for jobs, housing, and other re-sources. The majority also attended this Spanish Mass.

Closed social capital in the Spanish Mass resembled the informal system of sharing information common in Grace Baptist and Faith Temple. Despite the existence of two separate communities relying largely on different social capi-tal networks outside of church, newcomer Latinos shared their needs with the more established parishioners. For example, in December, request forms for Christmas baskets began quietly appearing in the social mission project office.

Social welfare activities through the church reflect the nature of Latino pop-ular Catholicism (Espin 1994). Yolanda, a leader in the Latino congregation, noted, "The church is just a house, a building, the faith that carries some people. A place to go to ask for strength and support. . . . people go to church and ask God for things, healings, hopes." Notice that Yolanda sees church and faith-based social service as providing for the needy. In a traditional Catholic sense, church is seen as an institutional support. Yolanda added, "In the church you can ask for anything; ask the Father and if you don't get it you will understand why." Church is both provider and all-knowing authority. The faithful trust that God will provide, and they help God carry out this plan through their works.

Latino Catholic faith as practiced in Kenosha conceptualizes faith and works in the form of an omniscient family. The Father, in the form of the priest or God, either gives or withholds. The mother, in the form of Mary (or sometimes the Virgin of Guadalupe), gives and supports. This pattern stems from popular Catholicism that understands the Trinity as God the father who is feared and obeyed, "Mary the mother, Jesus as older brother, and many saints as members of the extended family and community networks" (Espin 1994:328–331). Latino Catholics turn to the church in the form of its mission activities for material and spiritual support, seldom questioning the bound-aries of this aid. The prevalence of women in key faith and social service roles in this community also derives from the strong role of women in the Latin American rural church (Diaz-Stevens 1994).

This Catholic church preaches service as an important aspect of faith in ways similar to the injunctions for service evident at St. Xavier's parish. In many ways, the established community seeks to aid the less fortunate without crossing social capital boundaries, as in the white Milwaukee parish. Service is part of the culture taught by both Catholic churches.

However, Annunciation differs from St. Xavier's in the sense that the estab-lished Latinos still see themselves as supporting the wider Latino community, despite the internal fissions between immigrants and ethnic Americans. Simi-lar to the African American services at Faith Temple, the activities of the social service organization that is part of Annunciation is meant to improve the lot of the entire Latino community. For example, the Spanish Mass publicized the U.S. census and encouraged parishioners to fill out their forms to ensure that

Latinos would receive the benefits they were entitled to. Undocumented aliens were reassured that the census had no connection to the Immigration and Naturalization Service.

The Latino congregation runs a large Sunday school predominantly in Spanish. The school serves to enculturate émigré children into U.S. Catholic culture. The church conveys mainstream Catholic cultural capital through this program. At the same time, Spanish Catholic songs and symbols in the Mass maintain the culture of the ethnic community. In this way, the Catholic service encourages bicultural behaviors in the next generation.

Comparing Annunciation with the other three churches shows that each church fosters community and social capital within the congregation. These faith communities also foster cultural capital among their members. The three churches for communities of color teach alternative cultures through the worship style, appropriate dress, and educational activities. Institutions with some bridging tendencies also offer bridging cultural capital through modeling or instruction.

While Annunciation's Latino congregation is largely a closed community with separate closed social capital networks, it uses its connections to the parish and the wider Kenosha Catholic institutions to create bridges for its community members. These bridges take the form of institutional efforts for change, not of promoting individual advancement as in the African American churches. Even while maintaining its separate structures, Annunciation reaches out to its white parish hosts and Kenosha as a whole.

Annunciation and St. Xavier's share a practice of service through formal ministries common in these Catholic churches. Because of its size, Annunciation's social welfare activities are more formalized than those of the smaller parish. Although the African American churches tend to be more informal and participatory in their social welfare provision, they are equally likely to institutionalize formal supports for the needy.

INSTRUMENTAL SUPPORTS

Most studies focus on the instrumental aspects of religious-based social service. Recent research by Cnaan (Cnaan et al. 1999; Cnaan and Boddie 2001; Cnaan 2002), Chang et al. (1998), Chaves (1999), and others describes faith communities as organizations that provide service. Chaves and Tsitsos (2000) demonstrate that churches often work with nonprofit organizations to help others. Other scholars (Costan et al. 1993) show government channeling aid to communities through churches.

All the faith communities studied here provided some form of instrumental assistance. Every church had informal mechanisms to provide material aid to families in need. These usually took two forms. First, pastors had funds ear-marked for families in need that they gave out at their discretion. Second, most churches had mission or material aid committees that visited the sick, and pro-vided food, transportation, and other forms of material assistance to people associated with the community. Often these committees were run by women active in the congregation and depended on congregation social capital. For ex-ample, Faith Temple identified the Women's Mission committee as the primary venue for instrumental supports. Either the pastor or committee members would bring a family to the attention of the committee.

The majority of churches also held special collections or developed a mech-anism to collect food, clothing, or money for local people in need; the dona-tions were frequently passed on to established social service organizations. For example, all collections from a joint Thanksgiving service involving two Kenosha churches were donated to the local Salvation Army chapter. These kinds of activities are examined in detail in the next chapter.

Church-based mission activities were linked to spiritual development. For example, the women's mission meetings at Faith Temple started and ended with Bible-interpretation lessons. Material support was linked to spiritual sup-port. Pastors clearly distinguished support through churches from aid through social service organizations. For example, one pastor commented:

> I was very reluctant to have a food pantry when I came to [this church] be-cause I didn't want another place where people run in, grab food, and run, because just to pass out food they can go to Neighborhood Settlement House to get that, maybe. So we're the church and we have a different set of responsibilities, so therefore we do give food for people but we also do try to connect people with what's really wrong with their life.

This pastor, like other people active in churches in the project, saw the in-gredient needed by poor families as an active spiritual life combined with the community created by church. Mission activities for the Protestant churches often attempted to draw the needy into the church family. The Catholic churches, particularly through their more formal activities such as the St. Vin-cent de Paul pantries, were less likely to stress interaction with aid recipients as a condition of service.

Social capital played a role in instrumental assistance through faith com-munities in two ways. Families receiving assistance from congregational com-mittees tended to be church members or known to members. In a few cases, the pastor would receive a call for assistance from outside the community. While these people would receive aid, often the pastor would first make sure that the family was contacted by someone in the church. For example, in one mission meeting, as described by a field-worker:

After some time of devotion, the ladies moved right in to discuss the sick and shut in. These are people who are sick in their homes or are in the hospital. They knew everyone, someone would mention a name and they would all throw it around until they all had figured out exactly who it was. They discussed who would go and see who and who would make phone calls to others. They seemed deeply concerned with them all.

Helping families in need draws on the social capital resources of the wider church community. Information about who needs help is passed to the committee through both informal conversations and referrals through the pastor or church secretary. The committee, in turn, develops an assistance plan that uses the resources of the church and its members. Most plans included distributing money, offering food or other material supports, and visits with the family.

The second use of church social capital to aid people in need was by drawing on church networks to collect goods or recruit volunteers. All the other faith communities also participated in such events to serve the community. In these cases, a need for assistance was usually announced in either the church service or the church bulletin. A formal committee usually used their social capital to organize the activity and receive and distribute goods. The same pattern applied to service opportunities. Institutional structures in the church served as a conduit to garner material resources or other forms of assistance. These formal structures then linked to the informal social capital developed through the church community.

All the churches reported an increase in need for instrumental supports after welfare reform had been implemented. In some cases, this extra demand impacted on the ability of churches to develop other ministries. For example, one pastor said:

> [My treasurer] tells me, "Reverend, don't join no more organizations where you have to pay." I said I need to. But when you go to your official board and they're saying, well, we can't afford this, because [it's] another thing that hit the black church as a result of W-2. This year we have given away over $12,000 from benevolence. We have given out over $6000 just to stop folks from being evicted.

Churches saw themselves as partners with government and social service organizations to provide for families in their communities. They felt that their major role was to develop the spiritual life of their members, build community, and help people lead an upright life. By cutting benefits and diversion tactics, churches saw firsthand how government supports were not fulfilling their part of the partnership. As described in chapter 13, some churches engaged in advocacy in order to change policy. Chapter 12 details how others worked more closely with social service agencies to address needs. Only a few developed formal social service missions to fulfill this role.

None of the individual faith communities studied here developed comprehensive social service programs in response to welfare reform. Instead, some churches increased their role as providers of instrumental supports and advice on obtaining services. Other churches, like Faith Temple and St. Xavier's, saw their role in welfare reform as increasing involvement in their traditional programs for children and youth. St. Xavier's felt that involvement in School Choice offered supports to former welfare mothers, despite the fact that few families that fit that description actually attended the school. Faith Temple planned to start a school and was in the process of developing a computer lab for community residents. These efforts were designed to better prepare community members for the world of work and facilitate their connections to employers or educational institutions. The limited tendency of congregations to develop formal social service activities and their focus on education are similar to findings by other researchers (Chaves and Tsitsos 2001; Chaves 1999; Grettenberger 2001).

I profile two formally organized mission activities here. Ethnic Mission is a long-standing program designed to aid newcomer Latinos in Kenosha currently under Annunciation's auspices. Share the Wealth was developed after W-2 to provide material assistance to families affected by welfare reform. Both organizations were profiled in chapter 4.

ETHNIC MISSION

Ethnic Mission was started by an activist priest who used his personal resources to help new émigrés find jobs, deal with material needs, and navigate the legal system in Kenosha. It currently offers translation services and assists with locating work, housing, and other needs. It also works closely with the formal social service organization for Latinos in this community.

As with mission activities through churches, this organization tries to look beyond the immediate need to address more comprehensive family needs. A staff member told us:

> This week, they called us for help for Christmas and I ask them about their situations. So there are people that ask me to help them find jobs . . . and make an appointment for them. And we look in the newspaper for them or in the computer and then we go to the place and make the applications.

Part of learning about individuals involves discovering the social capital resources that they have available through their own networks—the staff member could describe in detail specific family situations. She then used her own knowledge to assist families in need. This kind of social service involved one-on-one sharing of information through the agency-based social capital links.

Ethnic Mission formalized the same kind of one-on-one attention to family needs seen in the various congregation committees. As a separately constituted organization housed in Annunciation parish, the mission project was able to gather funds and enlist volunteer support from throughout the Kenosha Catholic and Latino community. Ethnic Mission also had formal oversight that provided it with a sense of direction missing from traditional congregation social welfare activities. However, the organization lacked the planning, accounting, and administrative structure of any of the formal 501c3 social service organizations. Although this project offered an important social service, it served as a supplement to the other organizations in the community-based and ancillary services sector of this small city.

Share the Wealth

We observed the same kind of personalized attention and limited administrative capacity at Share the Wealth, a thrift store for low-income families. The pastor also saw it as a way to train young people for jobs. The organization was not very successful in either role. Most of the volunteers who ran the store were older women involved in the church. The pastor also assigned community-service parolees work in the store. Given the limited supervision available from the pastor and volunteers, Share the Wealth could provide little training.

We saw very few people come into the store to shop, but a steady stream of people came in to ask the pastor for advice or favors. The social capital of the pastor was the major draw. His role was similar to that of the Ethnic Mission staff member—people wanted him to use his connections to help find jobs and deal with legal situations and other issues. The goods available through the organization were secondary.

The pastor saw Share the Wealth as intimately connected to the spiritual mission of the church. During the summer he held a free barbecue in front of the store in an effort to get people to come into the organization. His interactions with community members relied on spiritual messages and were aimed as much at getting people to come to church as to use the store.

Share the Wealth ostensibly was a separate organization; instead, it served as an extension of the pastor's other mission activities. His ministries to prisoners and addicts were an important resource in the community. Share the Wealth followed the same pattern as these other projects, offering material assistance, on-the-job training, and ways to fulfill community-service requirements mandated by the courts. However, these ministries did not have the staffing, funding, or ability to move beyond the closed networks of the pastor's community to make a long-term difference. Community members responded by treating the store as another venue in which to access church benevolence. The social welfare mission of the organization was never realized.

POLICY IMPLICATIONS

Analysis of congregational activities suggests that, although faith communities provide both instrumental and social supports for their members, most congregations have neither the administrative capacity nor the inclination to serve as social service agencies. Formal projects developed by the congregations studied in Philadelphia, Milwaukee, and Kenosha were an extension of congregation ministries, reflecting the level of expertise of church staff and volunteers. Although some faith communities can successfully develop welfare-to-work programs (Wineburg 2001), very few faith communities encountered in this study had the organizational capacity, expertise, and interest to become government contractors. Neither Ethnic Mission nor Share the Wealth had the sophistication to develop a welfare-to-work program; this was typical of the kinds of social service supports possible through faith communities. The prevalence of these kinds of activities suggests that a better strategy for welfare reform would be to build on faith communities' traditional role in supporting families rather than expect them to take over government or social service organization activities. As discussed in the next chapter, faith communities actively work with government and social service agencies. Expanding this support role may be a better strategy for welfare reform.

Faith communities do provide community, social, and cultural capital development for their active members. However, the choice to attend church is a personal decisions outside the mandate of any government social welfare program, in line with the Constitution's requirement for separation of church and state. As communities that sometimes serve as bridges for their members, nonprofit organizations and government can turn to faith communities for instrumental support, as a source of volunteers, and as a way to spread information to closed social capital communities. All these strategies are discussed in the next chapter.

SUMMARY

Religion loomed large in the lives of many families in these three cities. Faith communities became the major source of community, social and cultural capital, and empowerment. For both families and their surrounding communities, they were a source of spiritual support, community, and empowerment and change.

Faith communities build community, social and cultural capital, and empowerment through a combination of efforts designed to involve members in an array of activities and through messages conveyed through sermons and other formal events. Faith communities also created connections and socialized members through the informal interactions associated with worship and other activities.

The nature of available social capital and the cultural capital messages varied with class and race. Three of these churches also sought to build bridging social capital, but in different ways. Faith Temple encouraged empowerment and bridging behaviors for its members both as individuals and as a racial group. Annunciation attempted a milder form of group social change through its mission activities, but messages of individual empowerment and bridging were largely absent. St. Xavier's mission activities were intended to fulfill church injunctions to provide for the needy, relying on the social capital of the parish, but creating bridging social capital across boundaries was not among the church's goals.

Grace Baptist provides an example of a church with no intention to develop bridges outside its closed social capital networks. Instead, it serves as a haven from the dangers of the streets, rampant consumerism, and the oppression of the white world. Many of the behaviors and messages of this organization enforce closed social capital boundaries. These intense networks are essential to combat the difficulties that many members face. However, they do not build bridging behaviors or social capital.

Churches like Grace Baptist and Savior Independent Fellowship—the independent church founded by Pastor Rice, the minister who created Share the Wealth—are particularly important for welfare reform because many of the people targeted by these reforms belong to similar congregations. These institutions provide a safety net, spiritual supports, and social life for these families, but they are not likely to help them move out of low-skilled work. Like all faith communities, these institutions offer instrumental supports to their members and other community members in need. However, as examination of faith-based social service initiatives shows, the majority do not have the capacity or interest to develop successful welfare-to-work programs.

The previous chapter noted that social service agencies benefit from collaborations. Similarly, church supports are also most effective when combined with other institutional efforts. The major contribution by congregations to welfare reform is their ability to foster social capital and community for their members. One outgrowth of this primary role is working with other institutions. The next chapter looks closely at the ways in which faith communities, social service agencies, and government work together in communities.

CHAPTER 12

Faith, Works, and Community

Connections Among Nonprofits, Government, and Congregations

The previous chapter focused on activities within faith communities. In this chapter I look at the dynamic among congregations, nonprofits, and government. I explore the intertwining of the first two roles of congregations—as community and as spiritual well—as they work with other institutions to provide concrete social supports to neighbors in need. This chapter demonstrates that informal connections among churches, nonprofits, and government are as important as formal collaborations.

Ethnographic research in Milwaukee, Kenosha and Philadelphia indicates local church involvement in social welfare activities similar to patterns documented in quantitative studies (Cnaan 2002; Chaves 2001; Chaves and Tsitsos 2001; McCarthy and Castelli 1998; Grettenberger 2001; Saxon-Harrold et al. 2000). Faith communities are most likely to focus on short-term supports of such basic necessities as food, clothing, and housing and secondly on programs for children. Far fewer faith communities initiate complex programs (for example, job development or education) for low-income adults independent of their general support ministries for their congregations (Chaves 2001).

This chapter focuses on how and why congregations, nonprofits, and government connect to support families in need. I also examine the positive and negative effects of these collaborations. Their relative success depends on two factors. First, the nature of connections among these three types of entities is shaped by the ways active participants use bridging and closed social capital. People involved in particular congregations, nonprofits, and government may or may not come from the same closed social capital networks. When providers and receivers of social welfare activities come from different networks, they may choose to use their social capital either to build bridges among program participants and providers or to reinforce inequities through charity activities that maintain previous boundaries.

The second factor involves the theological concept of vocation. For religious people, calls to service arise from an obligation to practice faith through works. In Protestant traditions, people become coworkers and vessels for God in carrying out divine intentions on earth (Wingren 1957:207). Raines and Day-Lower (1986:104–105) outline four assumptions regarding vocation. First, each individual is called by God to a particular activity. For example, one person's vocation might be working as a caseworker in a social service agency, and another might be employed as a carpenter but also volunteer to organize mission activities to feed the poor. Second, each person's work contributes to the greater good. Third, everyone has a vocation; part of practicing faith is discovering how God intends the individual to contribute to the common good. Finally, all called activities should have meaning.

This last item is particularly important as it relates to congregation-sponsored social welfare activities. Many policy makers look to faith communities as a resource for volunteers, presuming that congregations supply ready labor for social welfare initiatives. Others suppose that faith-based employees will provide more sensitive and caring service because of the religious base of their work. People participate in congregation-sponsored activities for many reasons, among them to foster community within the congregation or to fulfill an obligation to it. People participating in social welfare activities for these reasons may limit their participation in the project. For example, one social service administrator described how he was volunteered by his pastor to participate in a faith-based initiative without having been called to do so:

> I think he said from the pulpit, and I'm positive of it now because it was a sore point . . . He says, "I have an announcement here and I'd like [Mr. Smith] to go to this one." And he got the congregation sitting there. It's Sunday and I'm mad, I don't come to church to be given an assignment unless I want an assignment. I'm a volunteer there for everything, even sitting there. That's why I was there for [the faith-based initiative]. . . . I did it until I felt the purpose was accomplished because they could become redundant.

Unlike some other people in the same initiative who continued with this effort for several years, this individual dropped out when he felt it was appropriate. As a forced volunteer activity, it became another required work duty rather than an act of faith.

In other cases, congregation-sponsored initiatives can lead to a lifetime of paid work as vocation. For example, several white elites who were key staff and board members of Latinos United were extremely committed to the organization. Asked how they became involved in the organization, they responded that they had started working with Kenosha's Latino community through church activities. That led to a call to service through employment, volunteer board commitments, or both. Motivations for continued service were intertwined with religious faith. As in other similar situations, these kinds of activities fostered bridging social capital. The same patterns were seen in all three cities.

Regardless of motivations, or whether or not social welfare activities foster closed or bridging social capital, collaborations among congregations, nonprofits, and government all contribute to fulfilling the needs of families. Delineating the different ways community institutions work together clarifies the range and potential of future initiatives drawing on private secular, sacred, and governmental institutions.

INFORMAL CONNECTIONS AMONG FAITH COMMUNITIES, NONPROFITS, AND GOVERNMENT

People employed in government and nonprofits come from communities in themselves (Milofsky and Hunter 1995) based in neighborhood, family, race/ ethnic group, class, and other institutions. As discussed in the previous chapter, faith communities may form the core community for people in a social network. Congregation-based closed social capital networks intersect with other networks based on race/ethnic group, school, or work as people develop strong and weak ties that they use to garner resources as adults (Granovetter 1973). People involved in social welfare activities often use these same resources to help families in need who may have no connection to the closed social capital networks of the congregation.

WITHIN-COMMUNITY CONNECTIONS

Informal social capital connections among congregations, nonprofits, and government take two forms. Some activities involve people of different class and racial backgrounds working together to support families. Activities that involve people of the same religious or racial/ethnic/national community working together appeared to be more common. These initiatives often crossed class lines and closed social capital networks but involved people from one community. One vignette from Kenosha illustrates such informal connections. I arrived at Pastor Rice's church to find waiting in his office two other African Americans active in social welfare in Kenosha. Sarah was a middle-class woman employed at a local public school as a parent liaison. Kenya was a former director of a social service agency currently employed as the officer of community outreach/multicultural affairs at a local college. Pastor Rice had invited them to the meeting to ensure that I met them. Neither belonged to his church; one was active in Zion and the other belonged to Faith Temple. However, all three people had connections through the wider African American community and a civil rights organization.

One of the women brought up a situation with a family in Pastor Rice's church. The children—who attended Sarah's school—had shown up to school dirty and hungry, prompting her to inquire about their home situation. Kenya also knew the family, through her community outreach work. Sarah, Kenya, and Pastor Rice compared information on the family and developed a short-

term plan to provide assistance that drew on resources of several of the churches, in addition to those available through the public schools. They also discussed involvement in the case of the citywide child welfare and W-2 system.

This incident shows three professionals active in social welfare in one small city working together informally to assist a family through the different arenas of church, government, and nonprofits . All three drew on institutional social capital resources, but the conversation originated from an informal meeting called for an entirely different reason. All three were members of the same race-based community, but each was an active member of different closed social capital networks. They developed bridging ties through participation in common nonprofit activities and through their paid employment.

These kinds of informal connections facilitated work among people involved in faith communities, government, and nonprofits in all three cities. As in this vignette, connections often developed most easily among people in one community or linked through either bridging or closed social capital networks. For example, student researchers working at Brotherhood Center, an African American nonprofit in Kenosha, reported children in their gang-prevention program going on outings with church youth groups from Faith Temple and Zion. These events were set up through informal connections by agency staff who attended these churches. The African American and Latino children in this program came from low-skilled-worker and limited-work-experience families. Some of the children attended Savior Independent Fellowship; others were sent on a bus to a white elite church with a mission to serve children from low-income neighborhoods. These joint activities enhanced Brotherhood Center's programming through collaboration with the two churches.

Families that belonged to the African American working- and middle-class churches reported volunteering for Brotherhood Center or participating on its board. For example, Roland Clark, the father of an African American stable-working-class family that belonged to Faith Temple, mentioned in an interview that his son was volunteering at Brotherhood Center as a tutor. The family was encouraged to help the center by their church.

These examples illustrate use of both bridging and closed social capital to facilitate social welfare activities that serve one racial community. The same ties are used to engender bridges to citywide resources. For example, Sarah and Kenya have connections in citywide government and nonprofit social service networks through their jobs that they use to help organizations such as Brotherhood Center. Latinos United relies on both whites and Latinos who belong to citywide elite networks developed through work or church. These individuals with bridging social capital ties bring additional citywide resources into institutions focused on communities in themselves.

However, bridging ties among faith communities, nonprofits, and government are more tenuous than closed social capital ties, particularly when cultural capital from different networks clashes. For example, Sarah, Kenya, and others with citywide social service connections, whose closed social capital ties were based in the stable-working-class and middle-class African American churches, gave limited support to Pastor Rice's Share the Wealth initiative.

Suspicion of outsiders among active supporters of Share the Wealth compounded the organization's problems. For example, I assigned Marcus—an African American college student who came from a low-income neighborhood in a nearby city and whose parents were storefront ministers—as an intern at Share the Wealth. I chose him because he had grown up in a culture similar to that of Pastor Rice's church members. However, irrespective of Marcus' abilities to fit into this environment, the volunteers who staffed the organization regarded him as an outsider because he was attending college. Marcus noted subtle actions that indicated that these people felt he was "acting white" or presumptions that he was "better than them." As a result, they were slow to include him in organization activities or share information.

Marcus was able to learn many things through his participation in Share the Wealth, but, unlike other students working on the project, he did not become a trusted organization volunteer.[1] As in other fieldwork projects in which students crossed class lines within the same racial community, people expected students to share their culture, but because Marcus had defied community expectations by attending college they refused to trust him.

These examples from Kenosha demonstrate that social capital can be used either to build bridges across cultural boundaries or to maintain existing inequities even within a single racial/ethnic community. On one hand, informal church/nonprofit activities brought together low-income children of color from the Brotherhood Center and Pastor Rice's church with their stable-working-class and middle-class peers at Faith Temple and Zion. These joint activities potentially build bridging social capital that can break down class-based boundaries. Children have the opportunity to learn to be bicultural through this shared experience.

On the other hand, by limiting support of Share the Wealth to material donations, middle-class African Americans maintain boundaries between themselves and Pastor Rice's lower-class constituency. The pastor's volunteers did the same through their lack of trust in Marcus, who was willing to help the organization in many ways. In each case, resources are provided across boundaries, but bridging social capital is not built. The same patterns were repeated in all three communities.[2]

As in all cases described here, closed and bridging social capital based on racial/ethnic, class, or geographic community combined with bridging social capital from other communities to help institutions work together.

ACROSS-COMMUNITY INFORMAL CONNECTIONS

Research in all three cities revealed an equal number of informal connections between nonprofits and faith communities across race/ethnicity/nationality, class, and neighborhood-based communities. Examples from Neighborhood Settlement House illustrate these patterns. The agency developed a relationship with a local Lutheran church serving predominantly stable-working-class and middle-class African American neighborhood residents. The church hosted a Neighborhood Settlement House–initiated home-ownership seminar, and both the church pastor and two key staff members of the settlement house spoke of future collaborations. Asked how the two organizations had decided to collaborate, all three people reported that they knew one another from citywide networks. The church pastor had worked in a faith-related social service organization before becoming an ordained minister. In this capacity, he had developed ties with key Neighborhood Settlement House staff. When he became a key actor in the neighborhood through his employment in a local church, the pastor and agency staff used these preexisting bridging social capital ties to foster cooperation.

Offers of informal support through faith communities may receive less attention when nonprofit staff members belong to different closed social capital networks. For example, one social service worker at Neighborhood Settlement House reported offering additional job-seeking resources through connections to a church program. As a paid employee, she sought to use her informal congregation social capital connections to assist Community Solutions, the government-funded W-2 agency, in carrying out its mission to help low-income women find family-supporting jobs. Whether for lack of time or lack of trust, the Community Solutions employee to whom she spoke failed to follow up on the good-faith offer. The Neighborhood Settlement House employee then took matters into her own hands and offered information on the congregation-based program to the women she served at the agency. Informal connections aimed at fostering bridging social capital across communities prevailed when efforts toward formal connections among faith-based and nonprofit programs failed.

Staff Capacity and Informal Social Capital   These examples highlight an additional factor that affects the ability of nonprofit organizations, government, and faith communities to develop joint initiatives. When such efforts fail, staff time and follow-through become key factors influencing the outcome of the potential collaboration, as exemplified by the Community Solutions employee who chose not to follow through on a program that could have benefited the population she served.

Another example from Kenosha illustrates a similar pattern. A white elite community activist with strong bridging social capital ties with the African American community offered to develop a public-school-based tutoring program that drew on volunteers from her church. A retired schoolteacher active in citywide social service networks, she chose a highly regarded citywide youth program serving African American and Latino children in area schools as the conduit for this new initiative. However, the overworked staff member at the nonprofit agency failed to develop the necessary connections with the schools. Church-based volunteers found that they were not assigned children to tutor or that the child was not available when the tutor arrived. Rather than risk straining trust among church members through more bad experiences, the community activist observed that the tutoring idea "still needed to be worked out."

The activist indicated that her trust in the nonprofit was weakened by this experience. She questioned whether it really had the capacity to live up to its reputation of offering quality programs, and she withdrew offers of informal support to the organization. Unless the agency is able to provide sufficient oversight of volunteer resources, it will no longer receive support from this church.

Policy Implications   These examples suggest that informal connections are enhanced by formal organizational support. Nonprofit organizations need the staff capacity to manage collaborations with congregations and must convey to their staff at all levels the importance of supporting such relationships. If the Community Solutions employee or the staff member at the Kenosha non-profit had received stronger messages to collaborate with congregations, they might have more eagerly facilitated church-initiated efforts. These informal activities could in turn lead to additional support for the organization through additional volunteers and donations.

Formal Connections Among Faith Communities, Nonprofits, and Government

The informal relationships among faith communities, nonprofits, and government suggest that individuals use their community connections as they carry out the work of their institutions. Each of the examples above involve individuals using social capital resources developed in one institution in order to aid another. In many cases, institutions like faith communities and social service networks serve as venues in which to develop community (Milofsky 1997: s140–s141).[3] Organization/community dynamics involve fluid interaction between community and organization (Milofsky 1997; Milofsky and Hunter 1995). As Selznick (1996) recognizes, understanding organizations entails examining behavior, not simply the cognitive, ritualized, and cultural aspects (Powell and DiMaggio 1991). Stinchcombe (1997:6) suggests that understanding organizations involves looking carefully at the work of the people involved in them.

As Chaves (2001:27) points out, churches are more likely to participate in a community-wide nonprofit-sponsored activity than to initiate an independent program. The ethnographic research here demonstrates the same pattern. Many more churches in Kenosha and Milwaukee support the food banks at Neighborhood Settlement House and Sunrise than have their own food pantries. In some cases, as in St. Xavier's and Annunciation's parishes discussed in the previous chapter, churches both maintain their own ministries for basic supports and contribute to nonprofit efforts. Like the Faith Community Welfare Support Project profiled in chapter 4, congregation-sponsored welfare-reform activities often develop as supplements to government programs rather than replacements for government aid.

In general, formal collaborations take two forms. First, faith communities provide supports for social service activities, for example, supporting a food bank, providing mentors or tutors to social service programs, offering space for nonprofit activities, or sponsoring refugee families. Second, agencies and faith communities collaborate on formal activities meant to support a particular population. Examples include Choice schools and staffed and funded social welfare activities involving congregations and either nonprofits or government such as Sunrise and Faith Community Welfare Support Project.

Congregations seek out social welfare collaborations to fulfill their missions as religious institutions. The joint programs help faith communities build community and foster social and cultural capital. For example, faith communities with many members needing educational programs may collaborate with educational institutions.

Collaborations can help faith communities build bridges and promote social equity. For example, the Kenosha community activist who developed the tutoring program drew on her vocation in order to promote equity across racial groups, which was in keeping with the social gospel mission of her church. She was also a church representative in several interracial and social justice collaborations among area faith communities, nonprofits, and government aimed at breaking down racial inequality and building bridging social capital in Kenosha.

On the other hand, church mission activities can fulfill a faith-based mandate to provide charity to the needy but maintain class and race boundaries. Many faith communities have different social welfare activities aimed at either their closed social capital community or the needy in the locality. For example, the pastor of a conservative, stable-working-class church near Neighborhood Settlement House responded to a question about social services offered through the church by saying, "Well, we offer all education, school, church. We don't offer a food pantry, we collect food here, but we don't distribute it here. We collect it and take it over to [Neighborhood Settlement House]." The educational programs served congregation members whereas the food collection provided assistance to predominantly African American needy families served by Neighborhood Settlement House.

SUPPORTING COLLABORATIONS

Supporting collaborations such as food pantries and mentoring recognize the strengths and weaknesses of many nonprofits and congregations. Congregations have the will to assist the wider community through calls to fulfill a vocation. Some members may possess expertise needed by nonprofits. As venues for community, faith communities offer natural places for nonprofits and government to educate the general public on a particular issue or request resources to meet a citywide need. Church communities also include people needing services offered by nonprofits and can help in identifying potential aid recipients. These assets supplement the limited resources and staffing of most small to midsized nonprofits. Large faith-related organizations often turn to congregations to locate sponsors for refugees, foster parents, and other community supports. Even large, professionalized faith-related institutions like Faith in Action, profiled in chapter 3, rely on donations from their founding religious body. Government sees congregations as a conduit to the communities they serve.

Most congregations lack the organizational capacity, professional staff, and funds to run independent social service programs and so turn to nonprofits to augment their activity. For example, the establishment of Neighborhood Settlement House's food pantry resulted from a request by churches. The key staff person for this program supplied the history:

> There was a sister, I'm not sure, in one of the churches. I think she called us wanting to know who would be willing to do a food pantry here. They had a pantry, but they had their pantry open once a month or every two months. We just felt kind of different, sometimes these people come here, they get food stamps, maybe they're working, but by the time you pay your rent, few other things, get the kids, you just don't have that much left sometimes. . . . people on the [agency] task force saying this is something that could benefit Uptown and the people in the service area.
>
> Getting back to the Food Pantry, we do thank God for the area schools, they do a food drive for us. We do have a church outfit, every two or three months they give us a lot of food. One church, religiously, almost every week, [another church], they bring food almost every week, and the Pantry's [open] on Thursday and I get anxious if I don't see their car pull up on Wednesday because we're just so used to it. They're just so great.
>
> *Interviewer:* How did all that start? How did these churches find out about you?
>
> The schools, [St. Xavier's], the area schools, 'course they know about it. The [children who attend those schools] going to programs, daycare, and other programs . . . schools make a little announcements.

This example shows how informal networks can lead to collaborations between churches and nonprofits. In this case, children from neighborhood schools learned about Neighborhood Settlement House through advertisements for the youth programs at school. They told their parents, who in turn shared the information with their church. When the churches found themselves receiving requests for assistance beyond their capacity, they used the information that their congregants had shared about Neighborhood Settlement House in formulating a solution.

With stable staff and the ability to raise funds through foundations, government, and community-based institutions such as churches and schools, Neighborhood Settlement House was the natural venue for food support in this locality. The pantry runs on a regular basis, also drawing donations from nonprofit organizations including Hunger Taskforce, the federal commodities programs, and corporations. Pastors at local churches sent parishioners and others in need to Neighborhood Settlement House when church food pantries were closed or running low on supplies. Area churches and schools knew that this resource was available. In this way, different types of community institutions supplemented the resources available through the other supporting institutions. Faith communities and nonprofits worked in partnership to meet community needs.

Nonprofits and government also sought out these kinds of supports from congregations. They sponsored informational forums about their services for congregations or simply sent them materials. In other cases, nonprofits and government openly asked congregation members or their leaders for donations of money, food, or clothing. Nonprofits also drew on congregations for families to serve as foster parents, mentors for low-income people, and tutors/mentors for children.

In many cases, social service organizations turned for assistance to citywide interfaith organizations. The smaller city of Kenosha attempted to include most area congregations in its interfaith coalition. However, smaller, minority-based churches and the more conservative white churches were less active than were mainline Protestant, liberal Catholic, Jewish, and denominational African American churches. During the three years that I attended meetings of the Kenosha Interfaith coalition, the type of social service organizations that approached the coalition and the nature of their message shifted as African American and liberal white activists were able to build bridging social capital into an organization that had previously been dominated by conservative elite whites. In 1997, Kenosha Interfaith did not welcome organizations seeking support for liberal causes or asking its member congregations to help social service organizations. By 2000, however, interfaith coalition meetings often featured presentations of this nature.

This shift involved changes in values as more established interfaith coalition members learned from the newly prominent African American members. Because the coalition brought together pastors from congregations with a wide array of political perspectives, trust between the more liberal and conservative churches was limited. In 1997, the conservative pastors dominated the coalition. Given the lack of consensus in the organization, the pastor in charge of programs did not want social service agencies asking faith communities for assistance.

Three years later, with a prominent liberal African American minister leading the coalition, that same pastor had changed his views on the role of congregations in supporting social welfare in Kenosha. By slowly developing bridging social capital with the more conservative members of the coalition, the more liberal members had succeeded in changing the values of some of the more conservative pastors. This man was one example. By 2000, he was an officer in the Alinsky-based advocacy coalition for social equity recently formed by the denominational churches of color and liberal white congregations. As the liberal faction gained sway in the interfaith coalition, they also took important leadership roles that determined coalition activities. The program committee's point person in 2000 was the pastor of a liberal Lutheran church that housed a social service mission activity funded by a number of Lutheran congregations and other citywide institutions. The African American minister leading the coalition also had significant input into presentations at the Interfaith meetings.

In 2000, coalition meetings regularly included presentations about government or nonprofit social welfare activities. Typically, the presenter would describe the community need and the organizational structure available to meet it and then suggest how churches could help. Questions from pastors focused both on the political or social ramifications of the program and on concrete ways that their congregations could assist.

POLICY IMPLICATIONS

These examples highlight the fact that social and cultural capital need to coincide for faith communities and organizations to work together. Notice that the churches that asked Neighborhood Settlement House to develop a food pantry already had feeding programs of their own. These organizations shared the same concern for supporting at-risk families in their neighborhood.

Case studies of supporting collaborations among congregations and nonprofits also reveal that each type of institution has a clear sense of its role and capacity. The churches that offer in-kind or financial support to social service agencies recognize that congregations have the structures to reach members with the means to offer assistance. They use the same mechanisms to recruit volunteers. However, most faith communities draw the line at creating formalized, professionalized programs that are open on a regular basis. They realize that their congregation does not have the capacity to mimic a formal social service agency. Instead, they turn to already established institutions with similar values to provide programs.

In turn, the nonprofits involved in these collaborations understand that they need the assistance of local community-based institutions to carry out their programs, and they know faith communities have the appropriate structures to garner donations and volunteers. At social service agencies that have effective collaborations with faith communities, is a clearly defined part of the job of the staff who run those programs. The social service agency sees its role as providing consistent service through regular hours, well-planned programs, and paid staff. Community supports through faith communities or other organizations become an important supplement to their mission. In many ways, the combined funding and in-kind support through government, other organizations, and the faith communities make nonprofits the locus for partnership between government and the private sector that has become the hallmark of nonprofit service.

Supporting activities sometimes led to formal programs involving both congregations and nonprofits. Sunrise is one example of such an endeavor. The Faith Based Welfare Support Project developed out of concerns raised by staff and church representatives during social welfare committee meetings. I next compare four types of collaborations through organized programs to explore additional dynamics involved in sacred and secular collaborations.

Seeking Government/Nonprofit Collaborations for Preexisting Church-Based Programs

Sometimes, as the size or age of a congregation changes, a church is no longer able to maintain an existing program. This is most often true of church schools in changing neighborhoods. In many cases, schools reach out to the surrounding community, creating different tuition structures for members and nonmembers. Faith communities may seek funding for their schools from local foundations or other organizations in order to allow low-income children to attend. In Milwaukee and other cities experimenting with School Choice programs, government becomes the funder for low-income children attending private schools.

Although programs like School Choice are generally considered outside the purview of adult-focused welfare programs such as TANF, schools are an important aspect of family needs for those using government-supported social welfare systems. The availability of safe and high-quality schools relieves some of the stress faced by low-income parents in public welfare programs. In Milwaukee and other cities where some public schools are inferior and unsafe, low-income families are often grateful for alternatives offered through Choice programs, magnet schools, and other educational enrichment programs. Good, community-minded public and parochial schools offer students an array of enrichment experiences that are likely to help them escape poverty. They can also be places where parents are able to develop helpful social capital bridges.

St. Xavier's parish school participated in School Choice. This program saved a school whose white, working-class population had largely moved away or aged to the point that families no longer had school-aged children. Keeping the school open also fulfilled St. Xavier's mission as an outreach church for Uptown residents and other low-income African Americans living in the neighborhood. Vouchers brought in needed tuition money and allowed the school to expand its programs. The major concession that the school made was not requiring non-Catholic students to attend religion classes. Parents from the surrounding community whose philosophy of education meshed with that of this Catholic school opted to send their children for a Catholic education. This kind of self-selection meant that most non-Catholic families shared many values with church staff and parishioners, as in other instances when African Americans sent their children to white-dominated Catholic schools (Irvine and Foster 1996).

The school principal interpreted the church mission to Uptown as creating a quality education for his students regardless of race or class background. The school had chapel and religion classes, but Catholicism was underplayed given the church–state issues related to the Choice program. The school recruited from throughout the neighborhood, and the resulting student body was very diverse in terms of race and, to a lesser extent, class. The parish priest reported that the school had never drawn many students from Uptown. Even with Choice, the African American and Asian parents who sent their children to St. Xavier's tended to be low-skilled or stable-working-class families living outside the housing project.

The church school–government collaboration built bridging social capital within the student population but maintained closed social capital boundaries among parents. Within the school, children from different backgrounds got along well, creating the kinds of multicultural communities common in similar schools or environments with shared purpose (Schneider 1997b; Goode et al. 1992; Conquergood 1992). Children who would not otherwise know one another became close friends through St. Xavier's. The friendships among the students we witnessed outside of school suggested that the school experience was creating bridging social capital between children of white parish members and the children of color from the surrounding community.

In contrast, in meetings of the Parent–Teacher Association, there was evident strain among the parish members, other long-term parents, and newcomer Choice parents. Throughout the PTA meetings we observed, active parents repeatedly asked the others to turn in forms and participate in the many fund-raising activities. Many of the newcomer parents may have had another view of their role in the school, given that they contributed through the public vouchers. However, as in other Catholic schools with newcomer and established parents (Goode et al. 1992:208–209), the complaints about participation mask the fact that there is little social interaction between the two groups. Neither the priest nor the principal spoke of active recruitment of school parents into the church, and announcements regarding the church at PTA meetings simply noted that all families were welcome to attend services. During PTA meeting breaks, the white parents who belonged to the parish gathered outside the meeting room to smoke and talk while the other parents remained in their chairs talking among themselves or simply waiting. Closed boundaries were maintained, with little effort to create bridging social capital.

The PTA mostly used preexisting social capital connections to the church to sustain the fund-raising activities for the school. This created another form of service for parish members. The principal tried to create links to the other parents by insisting that they attend PTA meetings, with little success. In large part, social capital connections in this school remained circumscribed to the small group of long-term active parents and those in their networks.

In its first year, St. Xavier's began to build bridges into the closed networks of Uptown by offering a positive educational experience to African American families who lived outside the housing project but had strong ties to Uptown residents. As the research project in this school ended, several Uptown parents spoke of sending their children to St. Xavier's. By building bridges with these parents who had access to Uptown's closed social capital networks, the school anticipated developing bridges with Uptown residents in the near future. As in all examples of bridging social capital, trust across closed networks developed slowly over time. However, the school did achieve its goal of offering outreach to its neighboring community.

COLLABORATIONS FOR CHARITY ACTIVITIES THAT BUILD THE CONGREGATION COMMUNITY

Research in all three communities found two very different motivations for congregations' involvement in formalized support activities such as homeless shelters and soup kitchens. Some projects were designed to break down barriers across class and race. In other cases, stable-working-class and middle-class faith communities saw these activities as charity responsibilities intended to build community within the congregation. The "needy" were viewed as very different "others" deserving of assistance but not people whom the congregation members would interact with on a regular basis. Charity work built closed social capital among the congregation by bringing people together in a shared activity that fostered closer relationships among congregation members beyond church walls.

The collaboration of St. Xavier's with Neighborhood Settlement House and the Uptown housing project tenants association to provide "luncheons" for Uptown residents is one example of this kind of activity. The church sought to build a stronger community of Catholics from among existing parish members and friends they might bring into the parish. In part, this meant making sure that the parish lost fewer members. The key volunteer responsible for evangelization through outreach to Uptown explained that the real goal of the Uptown mission activities for the parish was to build community internally. The parish youth groups served at the events and lay leaders strove to include less involved members as volunteers in these service activities as a way to practice vocation while helping build the church community.

The Uptown mission activities were understood as the church community helping the needy. Most key volunteers referred to the recipients of the services as *them*, those who do not have the good things that the working-class parish members enjoyed. Interviews about Uptown residents were replete with declarations that the parish was doing something nice for people who had nothing. The expectation that the parish should be helping Uptown went both ways. For example, Sally, the resident council contact person, reported approvingly that St. Xavier's "gave us a luncheon; they gave us an ice cream social."

These events for Uptown were the only occasions for Neighborhood Settlement House and the parish to work together. In this case, both church and community-based organization shared a vision of their role in the neighborhood; focused on the same community with the same goals, the two organizations were willing partners.

The line between parish hosts and Uptown guests was clearly drawn in these mission activities. For example, at the luncheon, parish members served the "guests," but the two groups had little interaction with each other. This was partly attributable to an understanding from a key parish volunteer that they should not be actively trying to convert non-Catholics. However, most of the noninteraction seemed to derive from assumptions about the roles of host and guest. Except in a few instances, the parish members spent the intervals between offering food and entertainment talking among themselves. The same was true of the people who came to the luncheon—they sat with their family and friends, accepted food and drink with little comment to the "hosts," and left after baskets of food were raffled off.

The bridge between the hosts and the guests was the small group of Uptown residents active in both the housing project and Neighborhood Settlement House. They became involved when the St. Xavier's lay leader contacted the agency to ask for help reaching Uptown residents. The settlement house sent the church organizers to their key participants/volunteers, using their organizational social capital networks to help the parish. The parish organizers spoke to the Uptown volunteers about logistical matters, but there was little social interaction. These joint activities simply reinforced preexisting closed social capital networks among organizations that served different communities.

These collaborations among St. Xavier's parish, Uptown Housing Project, and Neighborhood Settlement House succeeded as a social service activity providing resources to a community in need. It is one of many examples of outreach activities through congregations that supplement existing social welfare support activities through government (for example, food stamps) or nonprofits (for example, the food pantry). However, these activities are not meant to expand the boundaries of existing communities or build bridges across closed networks. They provide much needed social support to impoverished families but do not alter existing social inequities.

PROVIDING SUPPORTS TO COMMUNITY MEMBERS IN NEED THROUGH COLLABORATIONS

Sometimes participants in social welfare collaborations have mixed motives. The evolution of Sunrise is an example. As outlined in chapter 4, Sunrise began as a church mission project during a period when Kenosha lost many industrial jobs. The project was spearheaded by the wife of a college professor, an elite woman who belonged to one of the more liberal Lutheran churches, but her passion for this project quickly drew support from nonprofits and member benefit organizations serving the community of displaced workers: the unions, youth groups, other churches, and other community institutions. The project, envisioned as neighbors helping one another, developed into a large and efficient volunteer effort that ran a soup kitchen and food pantry without paid staff for more than ten years.

However, by the mid-1990s, many of the working-class families hurt by the earlier economic shifts had either found jobs or left town. This meant that fewer local working-class members felt a compelling need to contribute to the soup kitchen as a mechanism to support people in their closed social capital networks. People throughout the community still give generously of their time, material goods, and money, but the mandate for supporting Sunrise has largely shifted from helping one's own to helping others who are not benefiting from Kenosha's reinvigorated economy.

At the same time, the population using the organization began to shift toward people of color, particularly African Americans. Some white Kenoshans presumed that the African Americans served by the shelter were enmeshed in a culture of poverty (Lewis 1967) that kept them out of work. Others erroneously believed that the shelter served mostly people from Illinois who had come to Wisconsin for better welfare benefits.[4]

In either case, community residents increasingly saw Sunrise as an institution that served people who were different from the Kenosha mainstream. Helping in the soup kitchen or donating goods to the food pantry became a way to give to an unknown other in need, just as churches raised money for the poor in Africa or Latin America. College students volunteered at the soup kitchen in order to understand the values of disadvantaged people unlike themselves. These interactions often reinforced preexisting views of poor people as coming from alien cultures or practicing deviant lifestyles. In contrast to the sense that volunteering at Sunrise provided resources to "neighbors in need," this charity work now reinforced boundaries between the closed networks of givers and receivers. The givers came from the stable working class and middle class in Kenosha whereas the receivers increasingly consisted of people from the closed networks of low-income people of color in the surrounding area.

As the population using the shelter changed from temporarily needy displaced workers to more chronically needy low-income people, Sunrise sought government and private funding. However, the organization's budgets and operations indicate that local community supports through congregations and other member benefit organizations eclipse formal supports through government, nonprofits, and community foundations. Volunteer labor far outnumbers paid staff. Shelter for single adults and some families is provided in area churches.

All the churches providing supports to the organization are established white congregations. Several of the African American congregations provide teams of volunteers to serve at Sunrise but do not have the space to set up a shelter. Annunciation, the Kenosha parish hosting the Latino population, considered hosting the shelter, but found that its older building did not meet the code requirements. This more recent involvement in Sunrise of churches serving communities of color suggests a return to the ethos of helping neighbors in need in the community. However, given that the economic conditions of the community have changed, Sunrise volunteers will probably continue to have mixed motivations for their work even if stronger collaborations with churches serving people of color are established.

Sunrise represents a strong partnership among churches, nonprofits, and government to serve needy Kenosha residents. The social capital networks that support the organization developed when it was a community institution providing supports to then-unemployed auto workers, people from the dominant closed social capital community in this small city. These established relationships have continued even since the population using the organization has changed.

Reasons behind church collaborations to support Sunrise have changed as the population using the organization has shifted to more low-income people of color. The motivations of the volunteers participating in the organization vary. Some view their work with the organization as building community within the church and fulfilling charity obligations. Others see participation in Sunrise as helping more needy members of their own faith or racial/ethnic community. Regardless of motivation, the organization represents a partnership that involves a citywide effort to better the entire community The organization could not exist without both its volunteer supports from churches and other organizations and its formal programs through government contracts and community grants.

FAITH-BASED CONGREGATION–NONPROFIT COLLABORATIONS RELATED TO WELFARE REFORM

Faith-based efforts to provide more comprehensive programming to help the poor have been made since the beginning of social service in the United States (Cnaan et al. 1999). In recent years, African American churches are particularly known for involvement in community development and individual enrichment programs for people from their community (Lincoln and Mamiya 1990; Baer and Singer 1992; Chaves 1999), but congregations serving other race/ethnic/nationality groups also participate in formal social welfare activities (Cnaan 2002). Research in Milwaukee, Kenosha, and Philadelphia included some initiatives of this nature. For example, Milwaukee Interfaith developed connections to a Lutheran job-placement program that explained, "We do this as an outreach ministry, not as a job placement agency." Faith-based nonprofits related to congregations, but constituted as separate entities, were the norm for this type of activity. Mid-level adjudicatories such as the Catholic archdiocese and coalitions of churches were also more likely to develop these kinds of programs. For example, the Milwaukee archdiocese developed a mentoring program for welfare recipients.

A Milwaukee Interfaith workshop on welfare reform also included a presentation by a large African American church serving a mixed-class population that had developed a full range of educational, job development, and health services for community residents. The doctors, social workers, and other middle-class congregants volunteered time to help more needy people who either belonged to the congregation or were associated with their racial community. This program sought government contracts to help fund their work.

Although most congregations do not have the capacity to develop their own social welfare programs, others willingly participate in initiatives started by faith-based nonprofits. The Faith Based Welfare Support Project, profiled in chapter 4, was one such initiative. The program developed out of concerns about W-2 expressed by staff and volunteers in an interfaith coalition. Organizers were concerned that families transitioning from welfare to work would need supports in addition to those provided by government.

The program envisioned congregation-based volunteers providing friendship, guidance, and advocacy for low-income families involved with W-2. It clearly saw congregation activities as a supplement to government and professional social services. Mentors were expected to provide material resources such as food, clothing, and money only when they were not available through government, nonprofit, or congregation mission activities. Organizers also realized that few church volunteers could handle some of the more difficult cases, for example, adults dealing with substance-abuse problems or recovering from domestic violence. The role of the church mentor was seen as building social and cultural capital, fostering community, and, where appropriate, providing spiritual support. Finally, it was hoped that families served by the project would become mentors in the future. The model sought to build both closed and bridging social capital for chronically poor families attempting to move into the stable working class and rising middle class.

From the start, the program drew on significant social service and faith-based expertise. As a bridging institution, the parent interfaith organization knew most of the like-minded social service providers and faith communities interested in welfare reform in its locality. The coalition involved in the project included people from several faith-based and secular social service organizations providing welfare-related services, legal aid staff, representatives from a key church in the target neighborhood, and several other churches, the interfaith organization staff, and me.

The project envisioned a program in which selected low-income families would be matched with church-based mentors. The mentors would receive training and ongoing support provided on a voluntary basis by the professional social service organizations associated with the program. These professionals also developed a where-to-turn directory of formal services for both church mentors and families. Church mentors were also expected to accompany families to serve as advocates with government or professional social service agencies, in the expectation that the church member's presence would mitigate the power imbalances sometimes inherent in interactions between client and social service worker.

The project received a small grant from a local foundation that covered the cost of one staff person and some supplies. Staff salaries were set so low that the project had trouble locating appropriately qualified employees who would stay for its duration. Staffing was not helped by the fact that there was no guarantee that the grant-funded position would last beyond the initial seed grant.

The coalition of staff and volunteers successfully developed the training program, trained a small group of mentors, and helped some families. However, owing to staff changes and unanticipated difficulties among families involved in the project, it was not able to fully implement the model on a long-term basis. The project was shut down after funding ended, and the agency moved on to other welfare initiatives more in keeping with the expertise of the staff.

This coalition effort demonstrated some of the strengths and weaknesses of collaborations between faith-based and secular organizations. One of the hallmarks of the program was the fact that most people involved shared a language of faith that undergirded their actions. Most active participants and mentors shared a belief that the community and spiritual supports offered by faith communities constituted an important supplement to government and nonprofit social services. The project concentrated on working with families holistically, offering them the various supports available through the networks of a particular congregation. At the same time, the program drew on the resources of professional services and government, helping both the mentors and the families served by the program develop bridges into previously unknown social service systems.

The project also revealed the strains between secular and faith-based groups. The core program-development team included social service agency representatives uncomfortable with "God language" and the potential evangelizing aspects of faith-based initiatives. They provided an important check on team members who viewed congregation-building activities as central to a faith-based initiatives, but staff also had to resist attempts to remove the uniquely faith-based aspects of the program. Team members debated ways to convey availability of services to people from a range of religious and nonreligious backgrounds. These issues were not ultimately resolved.

Although the Faith Based Welfare Support Project was not a long-term success, it offers a model for similar initiatives. Social service agency representatives, advocates for the poor, professional faith-based service providers, pastors, and congregation volunteers all worked together to develop a program that included positive aspects of each type of institution. Professional social service organizations and advocates offered expertise on TANF and families served by welfare-reform initiatives. Faith-based providers, pastors, and congregation volunteers offered the spiritual, social and cultural capital, and community-building resources available through congregations. The interfaith organization, as a bridging institution, was able to bring together these various institutions to develop a unique program.

The limited funding and staff available for this initiative highlighted some of the problems facing similar faith-based initiatives. Funders of new social service projects often provide seed grants but are unwilling to offer long-term funding. The parent organization was leery of government funds because they wanted a program uncommitted to TANF goals, a concern expressed by many faith communities or faith-based nonprofits. Funders also assumed that the founding religious institutions could provide funding for such an initiative, but this kind of program stretched the capacity of a small interfaith organization and denominations that had many other areas of need to fund with their finite resources.

POLICY IMPLICATIONS

Analysis of congregation involvement in social welfare activities and collaborations among churches, nonprofits, and government suggests that faith-based

initiatives that focus exclusively on encouraging congregations to become social service providers will ultimately have little impact on service provision.
However, given the strong collaborations among faith communities, nonprofits, and government that already exist, government can build on current
strategies to strengthen support for families. The following specific recommendations arise from this research:

- Government faith-based initiatives should encourage collaborative programming involving nonprofits, faith communities, and government that
  recognize primary goals, strengths, and weaknesses of each type of institution. Government initiatives work best when they provide funding for
  safety-net services, guidelines for services, and such basic supports as cash
  assistance, food stamps, and medical insurance. Well-run, professional social service agencies offer effective case management and a diversity of
  program models to meet the needs of families using public assistance.
  Faith communities offer potential for community, social capital supports,
  and in-kind and human resources needed to round out government and
  social service agency programming.
- To effectively use supports available from congregations or other community-based voluntary institutions, nonprofits, and government need to
  have appropriate staffing and mechanisms to deal with volunteer efforts
  and manage relationships with community institutions. Policy initiatives
  and requests for funding for collaborations should include adequate
  funding and training in volunteer management, collaborative projects, or
  both.
- Given that faith communities offer entry into closed social capital communities of both people who need services and people who can offer resources to support programs for families in need, government and nonprofits should expand on initiatives to provide education, outreach, and
  access to services through congregations.
- Since informal connections among faith communities, government, and
  nonprofits provide as many resources as formal collaborations, policy
  initiatives should encourage expansion of these types of informal collaborations.

CONCLUSION

These examples show that collaborations among congregations, nonprofits,
and government can lead to programs that extend the social welfare abilities of
each type of institution. Each type of entity has different strengths to offer partnerships as well as varying capacity limits that can hinder collaboration. Non-

profit agencies and government have more stable staffing, greater resources, and ability to draw from additional resources to provide more consistent programming. However, nonprofits need the additional in-kind and financial resources provided through faith communities. The social and cultural capital and community-fostering aspects of congregations lend an additional element to government and nonprofit social service provision that is sometimes lacking. As the examples of disconnects between churches and nonprofits described here show, nonprofits and faith communities need to have the capacity to facilitate church efforts and manage volunteers for these kinds of partnerships to succeed.

Connections among faith communities, nonprofits, and government highlight the fluidity between organizations and their founding communities. The various formal and informal collaborations described here demonstrate an ability to draw on wider community resources through multiple organizational types to provide holistic, comprehensive supports to families in a locality. However, the examples illustrate two patterns of program: those that offer required necessities but maintain closed social capital boundaries and those that build bridges across closed networks. The second kind of initiative is more likely to break down social inequities and help persistently poor families find stable work. Both kinds of efforts are necessary, but they have different goals. Program designers and policy makers must recognize that collaborations among faith communities, nonprofits, and government do not necessarily foster citywide community or alter preexisting inequities.

The social service programs described in this chapter may empower and change individual families, but few of these efforts are focused on altering social welfare policy. The next chapter examines advocacy efforts.

CHAPTER 13

Advocacy and Social Capital

The three preceding chapters describe ways that institutions and individuals use their social capital to meet the needs of community residents. However, any social service or community-building activity is limited by the parameters of local economic conditions and policy rules. Efforts to move beyond individual improvement or institutional survival necessarily involves influencing public policy. This chapter discusses the role of social and cultural capital in changing welfare-reform policy to create a more equitable society that provides needed benefits to working families.

The previous chapter characterized social service efforts as fluid interactions among churches, nonprofits, and government. Public policy initiatives frequently entail interactions across the same three institutions. Such interactions can either involve conflict or cooperation. This chapter explores the effectiveness of different advocacy strategies in altering TANF policy to better serve community residents in each locality. I argue that social capital plays a key role in policy change. Advocates who succeed in changing public policy to better serve families build bridging social capital between policy makers and people using government services. Change requires fostering bicultural practices that enable community residents and policy makers from different closed social capital networks to communicate productively. Churches and nonprofits play a key role in organizing communities and facilitating social change. The chapter addresses the following questions:

- How do grass-roots advocates learn effective techniques for fostering social change?
- What kinds of welfare-reform advocacy existed in the late 1990s in these three cities?
- What kinds of advocacy activities succeed in changing public policy? Why are some strategies more effective than others?
- What role do social and cultural capital play in advocacy efforts?

Defining Advocacy

I define effective advocacy by the following criteria:

1. Advocacy leads to concrete policy changes to better the quality of life in communities and assist families in meeting their goals.
2. Although policy initiatives may focus on small changes to existing policy, the underlying objective is a society in which all citizens have access to the public goods needed to meet their goals.[1]
3. Advocacy efforts improve participation of community residents in the policy-making process, educating people about public policy and its impact on local citizens.

The last criterion envisions effective advocacy as increasing citizen participation across boundaries of class, race, and individual interest. I recognize that this criterion is at odds with the strategies used in many advocacy efforts, which rely on race and interest differences. Numerous policy scholars document the demise in U.S. politics of a commons where citizens assemble to participate in community governance (Boyte 1989; Putnam 2000; Warren 2001). Participatory democracy has been replaced by fragmented issues and identity politics based on the manipulation of an alienated and apathetic public by simplistic media campaigns. Citizens focus on bettering their communities through services, ceding politics to professionals. The examples used in this chapter show the effectiveness of advocacy that reengages grass-roots citizens.

The chapter focuses on advocacy efforts, defined as *policy initiatives that generally involve representatives speaking for either organizations or groups of people.* However, the third element of my definition of effective advocacy stresses the importance of community organizing, which starts by helping people define the problems they want to solve, decide on solutions, and fight for those changes. This chapter demonstrates that advocacy efforts that do not closely follow the wishes of the constituency are less successful than those that combine advocacy with organizing .

Participation in community institutions can build closed or bridging social capital, lead to self-improvement for families, or foster activities to alter community conditions. Although these activities may not lead to increased political participation, they are often a necessary first step in creating an involved citizenry. For this reason, I view self-empowerment activities through community institutions as linked to group-empowerment activities such as political participation.

However, like social service and self-help activities through nonprofits and congregations, community advocacy efforts can as easily lead to ineffective political strategies as to effective policy making. Examples below show that social change involves fostering bridging social and cultural capital among people in very different places in the power hierarchy of a community. Politics necessarily involves disagreement and conflict, but effective policy making is based on compromise. Advocates who succeed in policy change respect the views of those with different positions and know how to package their message in ways that can be heard. As outlined in chapter 1, the religious community served as the most effective advocates in the two larger cities of Philadelphia and Milwaukee. In Kenosha, the ability to foster individual social capital links with policy makers and effectively follow local cultural cues made the difference between effective and ineffective policy activities.

Developing Empowered Citizens

The first step in effective advocacy involves locating people with the skills and interest to participate in social change efforts. In most cases, advocates require training before they become effective spokespeople. Chapter 11 describes the links between individual and group empowerment. Some academic literature speaks against strategies that focus on the former, viewing these efforts as promoting the development of individual interest over group social change strategies. As Madine VanderPlaat (1999) recognizes, social service views of empowerment often envision those in power, such as government officials, giving disempowered individuals the skills to better their lives. From the leftist perspective, however, empowerment is *taking* power from those in control. As VanderPlaat (1999:4) observes, this perspective places the onus on "the dispossessed to 'claim' or choose an empowering experience. . . . If they do not avail themselves of the chance to become empowered, it is likely to be viewed as their own fault." I see empowerment as involving both individual development and group efforts for social change. Individual and group activities impact on each other. Effective advocacy entails groups of citizens who can effectively speak for themselves.[2]

The links between self-empowerment and group advocacy are best seen through an example. Delilah is a 63-year-old African American low-skilled worker currently active in the Kenosha Gamaliel project, on the board of a local community group, and in her church, Faith Temple. She grew up in the segregated South but moved to Kenosha in the 1940s when her husband heard about jobs at American Motors. She moved into an integrated low-income/ stable-working-class neighborhood, where she interacted with whites for the first time. She commented: "It was something to get used to. But I saw them as human beings. I saw the kids go to school together. . . . My neighbor was my neighbor, and we got along very well."

Delilah developed bridging social and cultural capital with whites in her neighborhood. These relationships created the comfort in biracial environ-

ments that led her to work on the PTA of her children's school, which eventually led to a job as an aide in the school system. She simultaneously developed closed networks in the neighborhood and in her all-black church. She had always been active in church, and she first began taking leadership positions in that safe community.

Delilah began advocacy work in her neighborhood when middle-class community organizers from outside the neighborhood talked to residents about forming an organization to work on housing issues. By that time, stable-working-class homeowners had started to leave and the neighborhood had begun to deteriorate. A concerned resident contacted a middle-class organizer about the situation. Delilah recalled:

> They came and talked to us about what we thought about it. [I became involved in the neighborhood advocacy organization] because I wanted to see our neighborhood improve. But before I became involved with [this organization], we had formed a committee from the neighborhood called Concerned Citizens for Better Housing because some of the housing was unlivable and the landlords, they weren't fixing them up, yet they were renting them to people.

As with most grass-roots advocates, Delilah's activism started through self-interest. Her first advocacy efforts focused on issues of concern to her closed social capital network. However, she needed to learn to bridge into Kenosha's mainstream power structure in order to work with funders and middle-class organizers associated with the nascent organization. The same was true of her earlier advocacy regarding landlords in her neighborhood. Participation at the neighborhood level led to expanding concerns about the needs of Kenosha as a whole. She was supportive of the Gamaliel organizing effort and became an active participant.

Delilah's movement from local concern to more broadbased advocacy is similar to the experience of other women involved in community advocacy and improvement efforts (Warren 2001; Wood 2002; Stack 1994; Susser 1982). Her work focuses on both direct service and advocacy. Her training as an advocate included informal lessons learned through working on local issues. She also possessed a natural willingness to participate in leadership roles in her community. This combination of training and natural talent is typical of advocates from communities that regularly use government social welfare programs. Local advocates like Delilah generally see their advocacy in citywide issues as connected to their personal concerns. Many community-based advocates remain focused on local issues; others translate these concerns into attention to state or national policy. However, moving from local to wider contexts often requires education about the connection between local issues and state and national policies.

The same connections between personal interests and advocacy are less common among concerned established middle-class citizens. Referring to the suburban middle class church members who participate in advocacy initiatives, one interfaith leader commented: "The other interesting thing is that a lot of our very strong policy advocate people aren't very much into direct service volunteering. They're so mad about the need, they'd rather be contacting legislators than going [to] work in a meal program because they're just mad it's needed at all."

Organizers like this interfaith leader build local advocacy capacity through educational initiatives because they want to ensure that, in his words, "people signing up for our Action Alerts are genuinely interested . . . [otherwise] who knows if they really care."

These events provide local advocates with information that they can use to effectively participate in advocacy initiatives. Individual development, in turn, leads to more effective group advocacy efforts. Letters produced by church members who have a real understanding of and empathy for policy issues are likely to be much more effective than mass campaigns.

The Gamaliel Foundation combines these kinds of education activities with training to teach local leaders to develop their own research on problems of concern. They start by teaching people to listen to one another through "one-on-ones," structured conversations meant to help organizers learn the interests of the people in their communities.[3] The same techniques are later used with policy makers, in an effort to understand their perspective. This technique, the first step in building bridging social capital, establishes initial empathy and rapport with others in the advocacy process. After the first phase within closed networks, one-on-ones are conducted with others from outside networks. In addition to helping local advocates develop issues and build consensus with others in their coalition, the technique enhances the ability of coalition members to work with policy makers and other stakeholders.

Gamaliel Foundation organizers also provide training in conducting research on issues. By teaching local leaders how to understand conditions in their community, they develop both individual and group empowerment. Rather than rely on the positions of outside organizers or national groups, these local grass-roots advocates provide the tools for people from these closed communities to connect local to global. They become more effective advocates as a result.

Progressive organization activities that include people using public assistance in the policy process take similar forms. For example, in 1995, the Alternative Work Experience Program (AWEP) education seminar prepared an op-ed piece on welfare reform,[4] beginning their research by asking participants to tell their own stories.[5]

The education seminar also provided information on welfare policy and welfare-reform proposals to give participants context for their personal experience. The op-ed piece was one product of participants' conversations about the policy initiatives. Participants were also offered opportunities to engage in Internet discussions of policy and to testify at local and statewide policy forums. To help them develop the cultural capital skills to speak in public forums, we practiced and modeled these activities.

As with welfare-rights groups training their participants to advocate for themselves with caseworkers (Kingfisher 1994), these activities focused on both individual and group empowerment. Our goal was to develop skills and confidence that would serve program participants well in many environments. We sought opportunities to build bicultural skills that would lead to bridging social capital.

Part of developing advocacy skills involved getting people to move beyond their frustrations with the system to present their stories in a way that could be heard by people in the power structure without provoking defensive reactions. This entailed helping people shift blame from a particular government worker to the system as a whole. The Gamaliel one-on-one technique achieves similar goals. Individuals who learn to see beyond their personal plight through education about the system as a whole are able to effectively advocate for changes beyond meeting their personal needs.

Without this kind of individual empowerment and training, grass-roots advocates were likely to reinforce the worst impressions of low-income people held by conservative community members and policy makers. Ineffective movements involving people using public assistance failed to provide this kind of individual development. These problems were compounded by other strategic errors by organizers, for example, ignoring the larger contexts of public policy and the economy in which advocacy efforts unfold.

THE ECONOMIC AND POLITICAL CONDITIONS
FACED BY ADVOCATES

Advocacy efforts in Philadelphia, Milwaukee, and Kenosha responded to labor-market conditions and federal and state TANF policy. As described in chapter 6, in patterns characteristic of globalization (Sassen 1998), all three cities faced a bifurcated labor market consisting of 1) high-paying jobs that required extensive education and 2) service-sector or small-industry jobs offering lower wages, fewer benefits, and more part-time schedules. Because many small businesses did not have the profit margin or resources to offer extensive benefits such as child care and expanded medical insurance, advocates had little success demanding higher wages and employer-sponsored benefits that larger, primary-sector employers could offer their workforce. Given the booming economy throughout most of the research period, advocates could not claim that no jobs were available in the community. Instead, advocates had to show how low-income populations were excluded from higher paying opportunities, could not support their families in the available jobs, or could not compete successfully for work owing to various "barriers to employment."

Advocacy efforts to obtain advanced education or expanded benefits for TANF recipients faced both national and local consensus in policy circles about the need for a work-focused welfare system.[6] Effective advocates in all three communities concentrated their efforts to reform local TANF programs on highlighting the difference between the two approaches of reducing caseloads and improving the quality of life of low-income people. Advocates also recognized that some families would need long-term assistance or additional supports. Policy-change initiatives were also directed toward developing unique programs for families escaping domestic violence, families with disabled family members, and grandparents caring for their welfare-eligible grandchildren.

Effective advocates recognized the goals of most families served by government aid programs. As I discovered when working with families on public assistance, users of the AFDC system were just as unhappy with "welfare as we know it" as policy makers were. Only a small percentage of families wanted a return to the old system. Their requests echoed concerns of other current and former welfare recipients.[7]

The changes sought by middle-class advocates were similar to those desired by welfare recipients. In all three cities, advocates also expressed concern about the behavior of government and nonprofit-agency workers in a system with time limits and sanctions. Government-contracted agency caseloads were a particular concern in Milwaukee. Disconnects between government caseworkers and local RESET providers caused similar problems in Philadelphia. Problems gaining access to supportive services such as child care, medical assistance, and food stamps also raised concerns in all three localities.

The local policy context differed somewhat in each city. Chapters 2 and 3 describe how both Wisconsin cities faced a state program that tried to rigidly enforce its policy through a steady stream of regulations. As explained in chapter 5, Kenosha's combined unitary and federative structure—which included for-profit, nonprofits, and government under one umbrella—blurred the lines between government and nonprofits in advocacy efforts. Agencies with government contracts seeking to advocate for change had to step out of their roles as participants in the government system to do so. In some cases, agencies found it awkward to play the dual role of policy implementer and advocate.

The limited ties between county and city government and agencies, churches, and communities that had limited participation in the government contract system also shaped local advocacy efforts. Organizations outside the government system received little attention and were sometimes considered simply "outside agitators" by government implementers, particularly for organizations associated with communities of color that had no bridging social capital with the Kenosha policy, social service, and business elite.

Advocates in Milwaukee addressed a system served by five social service agencies and the county government. These local actors responded independently to state government, as well as the local community. As outlined in chapter 1, the Milwaukee W-2 agencies developed their own advocacy strategy in response to government. Social service agencies and community advocates sought changes from a combination of the local W-2 and county government systems and the state wide system. Local advocates also expressed concerns about national policy.

The state government remained firm in its overall goals for the Wisconsin program, but each local contracted entity designed a unique program. This meant that advocates in Wisconsin could focus on local providers, the statewide W-2 program, federal TANF policy, or any combination of these policy-creating institutions. Advocacy in Wisconsin was much more diffuse and complicated for this reason.

The Philadelphia system changed over time in response to community concerns. In Pennsylvania, civil servants at both the commonwealth and local level provided a moderating influence on the governor's conservative agenda. The governor's appointed architect and implementer of Pennsylvania welfare policy was widely regarded as flexible and willing to listen to alternative strategies. This different tone shaped the relationship between advocates and government in Pennsylvania. Although many contractors were responsible for various pieces of Pennsylvania's TANF plan, all were responsible to the same government entity. Advocacy efforts, therefore, were directed more explicitly toward commonwealth or federal government policies than toward local providers. Despite these differences, advocacy efforts in all three communities included similar coalition activities with nearly identical tactics.

Advocacy Coalitions Working on TANF Policy

A number of constituencies were involved in welfare-reform policy in all three cities. These advocacy efforts, which in most cases consisted of broad-based coalition activities, fell into five general categories. First, agencies contracted to provide services had concerns about how policy affected both their organizations and the people they served. Second, formal advocates for low-income people—legal services, religious-based advocacy efforts, established welfare-rights groups, women's groups, progressive unions, and other nonprofit entities—monitored welfare reform to protect the interests of people they represented. Third, in the two larger cities, outside advocates sought to organize "the poor." Fourth, community-based advocacy groups and local churches organized forums in which low-income people voiced concerns. Fifth, liberal citizen groups, usually associated with colleges or faith communities, became involved in advocacy efforts for low-income families.

Some approaches to advocacy view political activity and social service provision as having very different agendas. In this perspective, activists seek to change society whereas direct service simply provides "charity" to ameliorate the needs of the poor.[8] However, as the following examples of advocacy coalitions demonstrate, the majority of effective advocates in these three cities are involved in both direct service and advocacy. Advocacy and direct service activities informed each other, leading to more effective activity in both arenas.

Middle-class members of faith-based coalitions and university-based advocates not already working in nonprofits or government were least likely to have direct experience with the subjects of their advocacy efforts. These people drew on their personal concern for "the poor," often using research materials, journalistic reports such as the books by Jonathan Kozol (1989, 1991, 2000) on impoverished children, or the positions developed by organizers claiming to represent "the poor." Outside organizers often used these concerned middle-class citizens as conduits to a wider audience, employees and volunteers.

Each of the five advocacy organization types had a different relationship with policy makers that shaped the nature of its messages, strategies for presenting positions, and the impact of policy initiatives. Service providers had strong ties to policy makers through contracting relationships. The relation-

ship between progressive advocacy agencies and policy makers varied enormously within each city, but larger coalitions developed links to policy makers
in local, and sometimes state, government, becoming bridging social capital
networks that were effective in changing policy. In other cases, policy makers
and advocates saw each other as familiar adversaries. Some pastors and group
organizers in low-income communities developed bridging social capital with
policy makers; others did not. Interested liberal church members, university
students and faculty, and outside organizers had the most attenuated relationship with policy makers.

Provider Associations

Advocacy efforts of provider coalitions grew out of already established trade
associations and vertical associations of agencies involved in similar activities.
For-profit organizations such as trade schools had formal lobbying arms with
paid staff. Nonprofit associations were less likely to have access to these kinds
of formal activities in the state capital, but most executive directors developed
relationships with key legislators, local government officials, and state-level
policy administrators.

In Kenosha, most advocacy involved one-on-one contacts between agency
administrators and policy makers. Strong relationships with policy makers
were key to effective advocacy. Representatives of agencies also sat on the W-2
committee that oversaw local TANF implementation, serving as advocates for
both providers and agency program participants.

In both Philadelphia and Milwaukee, coalitions of providers met regularly
to discuss their agency programs and develop advocacy positions related to
their contracts and their perceptions of the needs of agency participants. Citizens United, in Philadelphia, is an example of this type of coalition. The coalition drew on preexisting ties among progressive adult basic education and
training providers to work together to ensure that Family Support Act and
TANF policies best served the needs of the communities they served. Community Legal Services and several similar organizations also participated regularly.
Active coalition member agencies were all small to midsized citywide organizations run by progressive or liberal elites, and all had government contracts
through the PIC, the commonwealth, or the Mayor's Commission on Literacy.[9]
Each had an orientation toward local communities through direct service activities, strong ties to community-based organizations and constituencies, and
familiarity with left or liberal university- and policy-based research on the topics of concern. This emphasis came from understanding social problems as
caused by structural inequality.

Given these organizations' practices and progressive philosophy, organization representatives had bridging ties into both networks in communities

served by welfare programs and the citywide power structure. Participants were also knowledgeable about national legislation and research on their issues. The progressive orientation of coalition members meant that participants shared a culture oriented toward listening carefully to the needs of people they served and developing pragmatic policy positions targeting wide-ranging social change.

Advocacy groups compiled research on issues of concern through studies of Philadelphia agencies and their participants, participation in government-sponsored hearings, and informal advocacy with the PIC and commonwealth officials. Started in the early 1990s, the coalition first focused on combating PIC efforts to include more trade schools as contractors for JTPA and FSA. As TANF developed, coalition activities turned to influencing the shape and implementation of the commonwealth TANF.

The coalition had limited success until some members negotiated for an active member to be hired in a key position at the PIC. This strategy facilitated bridging social capital between the coalition and this local agency responsible for most government-contracted training. As TANF developed, the Pennsylvania Department of Welfare sought community participation in some of the TANF oversight committees. Some coalition members were asked to serve on these advisory commissions. Coalition research was shared with commonwealth and PIC officials.

Coalition members regularly submit testimony on commonwealth policy. Although the strength of ties between agency and government varied among coalition members, Pennsylvania officials view organization representatives as legitimate actors in the policy process, and commonwealth policy makers regularly accept and respond to policy initiatives from coalition member.

This coalition and its members most often speak for low-income communities, but some agencies actively attempt to include program participants in the policy process. Testimony is collected from program participants and sometimes they are asked to speak directly to government officials. Although few of these agencies are involved in community organizing themselves, several of them have ties to community-based groups that more actively engage community members in advocacy or community-improvement projects. This coalition thus involves some bridging social capital between low-income communities, provider networks, and local government.

Analysis of provider networks reveals the strengths and weaknesses of the social capital created by contracting. Providers had significant capacity to mold policy implementation through their interactions with government. This took several forms. First, best-practices models developed by providers were adopted in requests for proposals and implementation rules. Providers were sometimes able to alert policy makers to the implications of new programs for their participants. They were sometimes able to soften program rules to facilitate their management of government initiatives. Agencies developed trust with government that allowed access that organizations without contracts did not have.

On the other hand, the power relations of contracting meant that provider coalitions—in all three cities—had very little success in changing major policy goals or program rules. First, they represented a constituency with direct interest in policy outcomes, thus making them suspect as advocates. Second, as participants in the system, there were limits to their ability to argue against the government agencies that provided their funding. Finally, provider coalitions were considered just one voice in the policy process, not representatives of the community as a whole. Coalitions with fewer obvious direct ties had more success for these reasons.

PROFESSIONAL ADVOCACY ORGANIZATION COALITIONS

Professional advocacy organization coalitions were active in both large cities. These efforts brought together a number of organizations chartered to provide education about social welfare issues and to advocate for changes in policy. Advocacy organization coalitions developed citywide events to promote changes to TANF and related policies, brought media attention to problems with social welfare policy implementation, and participated in the policy process by developing testimony for legislative hearings or lobbying behind the scenes.

Many of the advocacy organization coalitions have interlocking membership with progressive agencies in the provider networks. They also overlap with formal organizations in the religious community, including interfaith groups and lobbying arms of large religious bodies such as the Catholic archdiocese and Jewish Federation. As such, they represent networks of city elites who share similar views on social welfare policy. Many of these coalitions also include local or nationally affiliated organizations (for example, 9 to 5) that represent program participants or low-income populations. Local advocacy efforts initiated by community organizers or outreach workers who worked with low-income residents on a daily basis also participated in these efforts. For example, in both Milwaukee and Philadelphia, nuns who ran outreach efforts for the most at-risk welfare families and the homeless participated in these coalitions.

Although the membership of these advocacy organizations included a significant number of providers, the lead organizers in all three cities were institutions focused specifically on advocacy. For example, in Philadelphia, one active coalition included a union-sponsored program for the unemployed, an advocacy organization for children's issues, and community legal services.

Coalition members had long-standing ties to one another. Most members participated together on a variety of boards and other coalitions. Although views on policies sometimes varied, coalition members, most of whom had similar progressive elite backgrounds, generally shared cultural capital attitudes toward social policy. As such, they were comfortable with each other. For example, one Milwaukee coalition includes a wide range of progressive organizations from the religious community, legal services, and groups working with the grass-roots community. Progressive researchers were also affiliated with this coalition. Its members purposely did not include the W-2 agencies because they want to remain separate from government-contracted entities.

The aim of coalition meetings was to share information and develop policy initiatives. This coalition has organized some activities together, but its members often maintain their own policy positions. For example, speaking about a colleague in another organization participating in the Milwaukee coalition, an agency executive said, "Our issues agendas aren't entirely the same, but if I've got six issues and she's got six, then three are usually the same. So we do a lot of work together . . . so there's a little overlap there and we all just know each other." Trust exists despite disagreements on some policy strategies.

Coalition activities are focused on state and federal policy, with some attention to the local W-2 agencies. Activities combine formal testimony on policy, research activities, and informal advocacy. Several participating organizations develop model projects or participate in the design of direct service initiatives. Some of the coalition members have developed ties with local legislators and state government, serving on advisory committees and regularly communicating with government. Most coalition participants know the cultural capital cues expected by policy makers and can present their message effectively.

Relationships with communities that use government social welfare programs resemble those of progressive provider coalitions. Coalition members speak for low-income people based on histories gathered by member agencies and affiliated researchers. In some cases, coalition members working directly with low-income people share insights from this experience. In this way, bridging individuals serve as conduits expressing the concerns of people in the closed networks of communities using government aid programs.

These professional advocacy coalitions were successful in bringing attention to the damaging effects of TANF and related legislation on low-income populations. They also had some success in changing policy. Success came from bridging ties among policy makers, progressive providers, and low-income communities, accurately representing a wide constituency of community institutions and residents. The broader the coalition, the greater its potential impact on the policy process.

However, these coalitions had boundaries based on shared culture and political views. Participants needed to have "three issues in common" to participate in a joint activity. More conservative and purist left organizations found little common ground with these coalitions. The ability to craft a broadbased, consistent message based on shared agendas and strategies led to the relative success of these efforts.

For example, some local advocates in the Milwaukee coalition expressed frustration with groups that supported positions out of step with the consensus on welfare reform or who identified themselves as uncompromising supporters of "poor people" in a capitalist society. One successful advocate reported the following experience with a purist left group initially involved in the coalition:

> We really debated some very basic questions for a long time. There was one group involved who said, "If you won't say every woman is entitled to stay home and receive support from the government until her youngest child is eighteen, then we're not part of this coalition." The rest of the coalition just looked at each other and nobody said anything. After weeks of arguing with these folks, they left.

Frustrations with purist left positions have increased over time. Like many pragmatic advocates, this agency leader considers some advocates—for example, Women Warriors and Energize, profiled later in this chapter—unproductive in the policy arena because of their refusal to compromise. He explained:

> We're the pure left. The people who think they're the pure left—we're having this debate about who [are] the progressive liberals. I think it's a bunch of crap. The progressives are so pure and holier-than-thou that they will refuse to get into anything that appears to be a compromise, and they watch things get worse while they stand on the sidelines being confident in themselves.

Instead, these policy advocates have a clear vision of a just society but work within the existing policy framework to move toward change. They are not afraid to disagree with policy makers or report abuses of the existing system. For example, Milwaukee advocates suggested that the U.S. Department of Agriculture look into food stamp diversion when it became clear that too many families eligible for this benefit were unaware of available supports. This led to an investigation that changed information and outreach strategies at W-2 agencies and contributed to national injunctions for all states to improve food stamp outreach.

Close ties to progressive providers, through either overlapping memberships or informal ties outside the coalition, enabled these advocacy efforts to focus on policy initiatives grounded in the current problems facing public assistance program users and the organizations that served them. By targeting pressing problems based on agency data, they were able to slowly move policy in both states toward more progressive agendas.

As one professional advocate's comment about arguments with the "progressives" indicates, these advocacy-organization initiatives are not the only active advocacy efforts on welfare reform in these two states. Advocacy efforts developed by groups active on the national policy stage evolved at the same time as these professional advocacy coalition initiatives. These outside organization activities differed from the strategies of the professional advocacy organization coalition in both their message and their methods.

OUTSIDE ADVOCACY GROUPS

Both large cities were sites for welfare-reform advocacy activities organized by newcomers to that city. In Philadelphia, Women Warriors was organized by a charismatic woman from outside the state who lived on welfare. Drawing on a small constituency of poor families in one neighborhood of Philadelphia, and a much broader constituency of middle-class college students, college professors, and other liberal, educated adults, she developed a series of creative actions designed to attract media attention to the plight of the poor and homeless. These activities had drawn national attention in liberal and radical policy forums, but, as illustrated in chapter 1, had little impact on local and statewide policy makers.

I profile the Milwaukee initiative here.[10] Energize, a national organization that develops grass-roots initiatives, had only a minor presence in Milwaukee before starting a campaign to "unionize" poor people to alter welfare reform. It brought in a professional organizer from the national office and hired established middle-class recent college graduates who were eager to act on empathy for the poor they had developed in college but who had little experience in the closed communities most likely to use public assistance. Energize's campaign began with a drive to encourage low-income people to sign pledge cards to join the poor people's union. They also staged a series of actions at W-2 agencies that included picketing to demand jobs and other resources. The group was involved in break-ins and vandalism at one facility. These actions failed to influence the local policy process or foster long-term organization in the local community.

The initial organizing campaign caused confusion in low-income neighborhoods. Energize's organizers told community residents that participating in the union could "help them get jobs." Unfortunately, many low-income people interpreted the message as "the organization would get me a job." When that didn't happen, disappointed residents complained that the organizers had let them down. Drawing on long-established mistrust of people of different class and race backgrounds within the closed networks that Energize sought to organize, these residents saw the organization's actions as yet another attempt to use poor people to promote the goals of the white elite.

Rather than create bridges into policy circles, Energize's actions sometimes served to reinforce preexisting barriers between members of these communities and others.

This disconnect with the grass roots resulted from a combination of limited social capital in the locality and the strategies used in developing the campaign. Key organizers and staff in the Energize initiative lacked ties in the low-income neighborhoods that they sought to organize. Of the people who signed pledge cards, very few actually participated in Energize's actions. The organization did not attempt to do the slow work of developing trust-based relationships in this community, focusing instead on recruiting people for mass demonstrations. Organizing campaigns relied on messages developed by the national office rather than reflect the concerns of community residents. Because campaign messages used the language of the educated advocacy community, they were frequently misunderstood by participants.

Energize had equally limited success working with existing advocacy organizations and faith communities. The problem came largely from the attitude of the lead organizers. One long-term citywide advocate reported:

> There's a little resentment in town among some organizing types: "Who's Energize; what are they doing here?" It's like Energize comes to town and says, "We'll organize because you all can't." Maybe they have a point. They didn't do it in a collaborative way. So fine, more power to them if they can organize this community and get some things changed. But they've not been friendly to some groups.

Energize's actions included picketing W-2 agencies and forcing one organization to cease operations during a key enrollment period crucial to maintaining cash-assistance benefits. The same citywide advocate described this action as follows:

> So they entered this private building with this megahorn and people singing and chanting. You're not going to be well received. So a couple of people were arrested for pushing and shoving, the pepper spray flew, they had to shut down. This happened during the peak enrollment time, in the last two weeks that people could enroll without losing their April grants and they had to shut down for five hours. Legal Action was furious: "we were there to do actions for people and we couldn't serve our clients because you forced this place to shut down." It was fascinating, how the rest of the advocacy community blamed Energize and didn't blame [the W-2 agency]. That was interesting.

The W-2 agencies also advocated strongly against this organizing effort. Ironically, two of the W-2 agencies had evolved from community organizing efforts and in other circumstances would have been supporters of Energize's positions. However, field-workers reported that the agency's staff feared Energize's actions, viewing them as disruptive to their attempts to serve low-income people. For example, at one Community Solutions training session, the project field-worker reported the following interaction:[11]

One woman asks about the protests. Richard [a W-2 agency caseworker] shows his annoyance at this request . . . going on a tirade against these groups, insinuating that these groups don't have their interests at heart and in fact are really trying to keep them down with their "advocacy." Speaking under the subtext of racial oppression, he equates traditional radical advocacy with disempowerment and another dependency—"they already got their degrees, they want to keep you trapped where you are"—at which several women comment out loud or nod in agreement.

Although this incident may represent attempts by a social service worker to maintain the power dynamics of his program in the same way that management disparages union organizing efforts, the format of Richard's message reveals a deeper distrust grounded in race- and locality-based social capital disconnects. In other contexts, Richard and other Community Solutions staff members demonstrated a commitment to advocacy tactics and working for the empowerment of the people they worked with. Although few in the advocacy community would state as strongly that they felt that Energize's actions were designed to "keep low-income people poor," many viewed the actions as counterproductive.

Outside advocacy organization activities drew much press and interest from left-liberal elites but were universally disliked by professional advocates, TANF providers, and policy makers. Despite claiming to represent the grass roots, this organization instead caused confusion and further alienation among the people using welfare. Lacking both appropriate social capital and cultural capital, these efforts were ineffective.

The behavior of outside organizers did nothing to build social capital with the preexisting advocacy community. Through tactics that alienated the people meant to benefit from organizing, the advocacy community, providers, and policy makers alike, these organizations created barriers to their positions rather than build bridging social capital that would foster a long-term place at the table for the communities they sought to represent.[12] Instead, the messages of structural inequality presented by Women Warriors and Energize raise awareness about welfare reform among people in the progressive advocacy community who had little personal contact with the "poor people" the organizations claimed to represent.

Outside activist strategies that ignored local social and cultural capital stemmed from the organizing strategies behind these organizations' campaigns. Both Women Warriors and Energize drew on advocacy strategy that entailed a charismatic organizer's seeking out disaffected populations as a base constituency. Advocacy tactics such as picketing W-2 agencies resembled injunctions from Saul Alinsky's later book, *Rules for Radicals* (1971), in which organizers conceive the world as divided between the haves and the have-nots. The purpose of such actions as closing down the W-2 agency honors Alinsky's (1971:116) rule that the "first step in community organization is community disorganization" through disruption of the current organization.

Organizing efforts like Energize and Women Warriors ignore the injunctions in Alinsky's (1946) earlier book that the organizer needs to listen to the local community and build advocacy positions from local concerns. Rather, these advocacy efforts draw primarily on established positions based on national policy initiatives, often using the complaints of the low-income people who join their organizations to support these views. Linking the self-interest of marginalized populations to national agendas, organizers use the grass roots to support their positions but ignore other ongoing strategies to resolve inequities in the locality. By disregarding local research and policy efforts, Energize simplified the welfare debate in ways that made themselves irrelevant in policy circles.

Theatrical tactics came out of media-oriented advocacy strategies popularized by groups like ACT UP, the AIDS advocacy group, similar to the way in which sound-bite messages and dramatic actions aimed at drawing media attention also appeal to the present-day media-driven political process. These campaigns are targeted to policy makers and the left or liberal middle class who vote and participate more actively in the policy process. It is no surprise that the Energize and Women Warriors campaigns appeal to progressive academics and college students, as they use cultural capital cues about welfare reform based on beliefs among this constituency.

The few low-income people who participate in these actions become the props for the organizers' events. Organizing was directed toward the national stage; local communities simply form the backdrop for a larger agenda. For this reason, organizers feel justified in ignoring the complexities of local policy implementation and preexisting activities in the local community.

In addition to their limited collaboration with local actors, these efforts failed to impress policy makers, who found them needlessly disruptive and inauthentic. One policy maker described a Women Warriors action as follows:

> From my experience, her timing was impeccable—welfare reform and people are making changes. And because it's hitting the news, she'd be out there,

instead of working with us, sitting at the table to discuss the issues. That never occurred; it would be more of "you're doing this." But she never had a dialogue with us—it was more of a shouting match, where with other organizations they would sit down, discuss, provide written comments. Public forums about the TANF plan, the advocates were there with written testimony, describing what they wanted to see, describing their concerns. What do they come in with? With a bunch of college kids and walk through with their placards and interrupt the speakers, who happened to be other advocates. Then they walked out and that's all they did. I said, "What's that all about?" You could scream and yell and it's not productive, while these other people are very productive.

Despite the lack of success that outside advocacy efforts had participating in the local policy arena, these campaigns showed a sophisticated understanding of politics from a particular point of view. They shared an understanding of professional social change tactics with both the provider coalitions and the professional advocacy coalitions. The middle-class people who served as leadership in all three types of coalitions shared a certain level of cultural comfort with policy makers in that they all had enough experience with educated-middle-class policy environments to be at ease communicating in policy forums. The final two types of advocacy efforts—low-income community advocacy efforts and liberal citizen advocacy groups—draw from closed networks of people in which the majority of community members generally do not interact with policy makers.

LOW-INCOME COMMUNITY ADVOCACY EFFORTS

Advocacy initiatives by organizations working with low-income communities often involved one-time events at which to voice emerging concerns. These events were usually precipitated by incidents in the community. Crisis focus events receive local media coverage and galvanize a neighborhood or closed community to demand action in response.[13] Relevant policy makers were invited to speak to the community by local leaders. These forums were often organized within a week of the incident and advertised via word of mouth, announcements at churches and other community organizations, and sometimes fliers posted in the community. Few people outside the closed networks of the concerned community heard about these events because advertising was concentrated locally. Media people were less likely to attend these forums than they were advocacy events organized by the more professional coalitions.

In some cases, these events led to longer-term policy initiatives such as antidrug efforts, town watches, and similar neighborhood-based activities. Issues forums that focused on problems with the power structure sometimes created longer-term relationships between policy makers and local community leaders but more often served as forums in which members of closed networks spoke to the elite power structure without either developing bridging social capital or changing policy. The focus of the events was primarily on city policy makers.

A student researcher with the Kenosha Social Capital Study reported on one forum to which she had been invited by a middle-class African American government employee. It was organized by Pastor Rice after racial profiling incidents both locally and in the national media:[14]

> Pastor Rice started out by saying that he receives many, many phone calls about the racial profiling that goes on by the police. He spoke of the time he himself was pulled over for no legitimate reason, [simply because of] the neighborhood he was in and the color of his skin. He asked the panel to discuss whether the police have the right to pull you over and search you and your car for no reason, without probable cause.
>
> The sheriff was the first to take the microphone over; he started by mentioning that he was recently appointed to the Governor's Commission on Racial Profiling. This commission was put together in order to develop a recommendation that accepts a specific level of racial profiling to the governor, and to figure out to what extent this is happening now. He then went on to discuss that profiling is a good thing; he wanted to clear up this misconception. And he also reminded everybody that he cannot control everyone that works for the department, nor their attitudes. But he will not tolerate racism on the force, so he stressed that any concerns anyone might have must be filed through a formal complaint or they cannot check into the problem.
>
> An African American woman asked if there was any type of policy set in place with regards to racial profiling. The sheriff replied that there was not, but that is what the commission is working on developing. Another man suggested having the officers partake in more cultural diversity classes. The sheriff confirmed that all officers go through an annual cultural diversity training program, and he assured that this would be expanding in the near future.
>
> Another African American man brought up the issue of there being such a prevalent double standard going on—blacks are treated one way, while white people are treated another way. The sheriff reminded us all that this is a national problem and asked that anyone who may have a suggestion as to how to eliminate this problem should speak up.

This event is a good example of people from a closed social capital network attempting unsuccessfully to talk with members of the city power structure. Community members and law-enforcement officials present their views, but the elite pay little attention to community concerns. Police view the complaints presented in this forum as illegitimate, noting that they are unable to act on incidents of racial profiling without a formal complaint. Government officials publicly support the concept of racial profiling but assert that they are against racism. Given the lack of trust between low-income people of color and the police, few community residents feel comfortable filing complaints. Because there is little trust between the communities of the people at this forum and the police, the event does not lead to social change.

The role of African American leaders in this event shows the intricacies of bridging social capital development. Pastor Rice is known among the power structure, but not trusted, because he has failed to develop bridging social or cultural capital with the Kenosha power structure. Policy makers comment that he only approaches them when he "wants something" and presents his case as demands for resources, a style that contradicts Kenosha's image of itself as an egalitarian, individualistic community. Policy makers interviewed about Pastor Rice commented that he never participates in the common social forums that facilitate governance in Kenosha like fund raisers for other organizations. He often sends a white community activist to represent him at events. All of these actions ran counter to practiced culture in Kenosha.

Despite lacking social capital to successfully advocate for social change, Pastor Rice understands local advocacy practice and taught many of the people in his community ways to effectively address government elite such as the law-enforcement officials who came to this forum. The field-worker reported that the low-income residents followed the cultural cues of Kenosha political forums, presenting their stories succinctly, politely, and clearly. The power elite had enough respect for this community leader to attend the meeting but did not have longer-term relationships that could lead to change. The adversarial nature of the forum also violated Kenosha's culture of polite, one-on-one interactions combined with written documentation. As a result, the town meeting failed to achieve its goal of getting the police to respond more appropriately to community complaints.

Lack of cultural capital was also reflected in inadequate research on the advocacy topic. Pastor Rice's constituents presented examples from their own experience, but he had not investigated local policy well enough to contest police assertions that they were "already working on" these issues. The forum offered no statistics on the prevalence of this problem in Kenosha or written complaints for police to address, and, rather than offer practical solutions, the forum simply implied that the police were racist. The lack of concrete information allowed police to retreat to their established position that no complaints would be addressed unless they were in writing.

The role of the African American middle-class government employee shows the limits of bridging social capital in this community. This administrator is active in interfaith antiracism initiatives and other social change efforts. She is widely trusted by the power structure. The sheriff invited her to the event, probably hoping that she would serve as a symbol of bridges between the low-income African American community and local government. She knows Pastor Rice, but she has not developed trusting relationships with him. For this reason, she had little to do with the forum other than announce it to the middle-class interfaith coalition members.[15]

This incident suggests that one-time, formal events that bring together people from different closed social capital networks in different parts of the power hierarchy have limited long-term value. However, as in Alinsky-style organizing efforts (Wood 2002; Warren 2001), if participants can develop either trust or political clout to influence the power hierarchy, these kinds of events can foster social change.

LIBERAL CITIZEN ADVOCACY GROUPS

Liberal citizen advocacy groups share several attributes with low-income advocacy efforts, most of which draw from faith-community members or community-organization members who do not usually interact with policy makers. Unlike the professional advocates and provider networks, the majority of people in these coalitions do not work with low-income families or in settings that would implement TANF policy on a regular basis. Although some members of these groups hold jobs in government or social service agencies, few have specific training in advocacy. Like the people involved in Pastor Rice's initiatives, participants in these coalitions need training to participate in the policy process.

Some participants in liberal citizen advocacy efforts have little familiarity with poor people or TANF programs from either their daily life or work. In general, however, these types of coalitions include a wide range of participants; the congregations and community groups profiled here included people active in policy circles as professional advocates, social service agency staff, and government employees. Some coalitions include families with personal experience with the welfare system. In some cases, social welfare professionals and advocates played leading roles in coalition activities. In other cases, these people remained in the background, allowing concerned citizens with less direct connection to welfare reform to lead community efforts. I profile two initiatives to show contrasts among different groups.

Kenosha Church Initiatives   The interfaith antiracism coalition in Kenosha mentioned above is one example of liberal citizen advocacy groups. Developed after an overt racial incident, the group brought together concerned members of the denominational African American churches and liberal white churches, along with several local university faculty members. The two African American church congregations represented a range of class backgrounds.

During that year, the coalition sponsored a number of forums on race-related issues that were widely attended by African Americans and whites. Bridging social capital relationships developed through this coalition led to the election to the school board of an African American pastor and a Latina with established social ties in Kenosha—the first people of color on the board. Because they had more progressive ideas than many of their predecessors, their election created the potential for social change in the schools. Many of the churches active in this coalition also formed the core for a Gamaliel chapter founded in Kenosha the following year.

As with other Alinsky-style church organizing activities (Warren 2001; Wood 2002; Warren and Wood 2001), the Kenosha Gamaliel chapter used a formalized organizing process to develop issues, train leaders, and advocate for social change. The Gamaliel Foundation provided paid organizers who worked with the local churches. Participating churches committed funding for Gamaliel activities and staff.

Churches that participated in the Kenosha movement came from already established social capital relationships developed through the local interfaith coalition and churches active in the antiracism coalition. The coalition included most of the liberal white Protestant churches in Kenosha, two of the more liberal Catholic parishes, and Faith Temple, the largest African American church. White churches were predominantly stable working class to established middle class. In the second year of the Gamaliel project, the Catholic church that hosted the Latino Mass also joined the coalition.

Gamaliel organizing techniques started with church members' interviewing one another to learn about community concerns. Each church then developed a set of issues for the organization to address and presented it to members of other churches at an issues event. At such events, participants vote on which issues to work on, smaller committees are formed, and committee members are trained in research and advocacy techniques. They lobby local and state officials at one-on-one meetings and formal events.

The style of the presentations made at the issues convention illustrates one of the goals of Alinsky-related citizen advocacy efforts. The presentations draw on the experience of community members. In addition, members have researched their topics using policy data and information from other advocacy campaigns. For example, Faith Temple's presentation consisted of five skits, and after each one the master of ceremonies presented hard data—research and statistics—on the pertinent issue.

This group's advocacy efforts included meetings of its leaders with government officials. They reported some positive response from county but not city officials. The advocacy efforts in the first year strengthened bridging social capital among member churches and the rest of the people who participated in the Gamaliel project. Outside observers commented that Gamaliel's adversarial approach, like that of Pastor Rice, clashed with the practice typical of Kenosha culture: calm, one-on-one conversations among people sharing closed or bridging social capital ties.

This example shows the evolution of advocacy efforts by the religious community from informal community-generated projects to a formalized advocacy process relying on training and expertise from a national organization. As with similar efforts, the churches became involved in local policy through a focus event—in this case, a hate crime that involved members of Faith Temple and drew wide media attention in Kenosha. Leaders in these efforts had already developed bridging social capital networks through common participation in Interfaith coalitions, work on similar issues, or connections made in other social settings. The initial leadership group included several social service agency administrators, pastors, and government officials who also had preexisting bridging ties to Kenosha's policy makers and power elite. These bridging connections facilitated the organization of local forums that engendered promises for social change from policy makers.

Recognizing that the forums had limited impact, organizers sought help from the Gamaliel Foundation. These national organizers changed the nature of the advocacy efforts in several ways. First, they provided training in advocacy strategies that had proved successful elsewhere. Second, their organizing techniques widened the circle of active participants, encouraging people like Delilah to take leadership roles. The pastors, government employees, and others who had run earlier coalition efforts were able to allow more grass-roots participation, freeing their time for behind-the-scenes advocacy efforts.

However, as noted above, the national strategies that the Gamaliel Foundation brought to Kenosha clashed with community culture, which hindered the development of social capital with the power elite. For example, one government administrator who was friendly toward the Gamaliel initiative and familiar with such efforts in other parts of country acknowledged that the Gamaliel leaders were "nice people, but . . ." and shook his head to indicate that they were not effective in Kenosha.

Since the Gamaliel effort was new when this research project ended, its long-term effects cannot be judged. Given the preexisting links that many participating churches had with policy makers prior to the Gamaliel project, it may be possible for local leaders to work with Gamaliel organizers to modify advocacy strategy to better fit local culture. The local Gamaliel leaders are just beginning to learn about the policies and government structures they hope to change. Only time will tell if this advocacy effort can develop the local social and cultural capital to effectively implement its national strategy in this community.

Congregations United   Congregations United, a Philadelphia interfaith coalition concerned with welfare, relied more on professional advocates to design initiatives and did not use a formal organizing strategy as the Gamaliel effort in Kenosha had. But the two groups have similar goals, and the members of both congregations were mostly liberal and middle class. The Philadelphia coalition included white and African American congregations, and some of these faith communities were involved in both advocacy and direct-service initiatives.

Congregations United included a number of denominations in a working-class to middle-class part of the city. Some of the active participants came from traditional religious circles: pastors, priests, rabbis, and concerned laypeople with little experience with welfare reform or government. This coalition also included most of the city's activists and social service providers: community legal services attorneys, city government employees, social service administrators, and union activists—many of the same actors as in the progressive provider association and the formal advocacy associations in Philadelphia profiled above. Most professional advocates in this religious-based coalition told me that they felt the coalition offered an opportunity to express the faith base for their paid work. Their presence added direction and authority to coalition activities.

One day the major government administrator for welfare reform in the city, Craig Jones, came to a coalition meeting. The professional activists were initially apprehensive about his presence and wondered why he had come. His pastor had sent him to represent the church social concerns committee. He participated in the coalition occasionally, organizing the relationship between his church and the coalition.

Mr. Jones's presence illustrated the parameters of social and cultural capital in this city for shaping welfare reform. He was a savvy political actor with Democratic roots implementing a Republican welfare-reform initiative. As such, he was usually at odds with the advocates and social service agencies that were concerned about the effects of welfare reform on the poor. While ably implementing the state program, he maintained a sense of moderation regarding some directions for reform. His participation in the religious coalition gave advocates an additional context in which to understand his behavior and created a sense of trust that might otherwise not have existed.

Representatives from one welfare-rights organization also attended these meetings. Women Warriors saw the coalition as a source for support for their activities. To a large extent, they were able to use the social capital of this coalition and similar networks to create visibility for their point of view on welfare reform. However, many coalition leaders questioned their motivations, and coalition members never unanimously supported them.

Given that the coalition included churches with a wide range of concerns and approaches, much of the activity during the year I observed this advocacy effort was focused on building bridging social capital within the coalition through joint prayer service and educational events. Leaders also developed educational materials for the churches. Although the coalition expressed concerns about welfare reform in Philadelphia, its activities were directed primarily toward state and federal policy.

These two initiatives share similar goals and orientation. Both draw on liberal, predominantly middle-class citizens concerned about local policy issues. They include professionals who work with welfare populations in their role as members of participating churches. Many of the coalition's activities entail educating congregation members so that they can effectively participate in the policy process. Coalitions also build bridging social capital among organizations with similar cultural capital values.

Although Kenosha's Gamaliel organizing effort included churches with impoverished members, the majority of the participants in both coalitions were rising educated middle class or multigenerational middle class. The members expressed concern for the people using government assistance, but few families that used public assistance actively participated in these coalitions. Members of a privileged closed social capital network were offering concern for people largely associated with different parts of the local and national social structure.

Members had had various interactions with government prior to development of the coalition. In both cases, coalitions included government officials and people involved in policy circles through other activities in their lives. The coalitions thus presented opportunities to develop bridging social and cultural capital between policy makers and concerned citizens.

However, the broad range of constituencies in these coalitions and their more attenuated connection to policy meant that they had less effect on TANF than the advocacy coalitions. For example, a policy official said of Congregations United that the group ultimately chose to focus on issues tangential to TANF implementation. At that point, the coalitions had limited ability to develop credibility in policy circles; they were too new to have created strong ties within the group that could lead to more effective interactions with policy makers. They offered the potential for widening the policy debate and involving a larger constituency in advocacy efforts but had not yet achieved their goals.

LESSONS ABOUT LOCAL ADVOCACY EFFORTS FROM THESE EXAMPLES

These examples show several patterns in the development of advocacy organization. First, most advocacy efforts draw on preexisting social capital among people working with populations in government programs, people who use government services, and other concerned citizens. Locally based advocacy coalitions tend to include many overlapping members. Contrary to presumptions that social service activities are equivalent to disempowering charity whereas progressive advocacy efforts enable social change, these advocacy activities show that many of the people who can accurately analyze TANF-related issues, present effective policy initiatives, and work with people from low-income communities are involved in both advocacy and direct service. Progressive service activities and advocacy efforts often inform each other.

Most of these advocacy coalitions involve elites who speak for low-income people served by government programs. Despite claims to the contrary, even the "poor people's movements," like Energize and Women Warriors, are staffed by middle-class, college-educated people schooled in advocacy. In the progressive provider coalitions and professional advocacy organization activities, elite activists worked with low-income people to present their stories and concerns. Some of these advocacy groups trained low-income people to speak for themselves in policy circles. The development of this kind of bridging cultural capital is evident in the progressive advocacy efforts, the faith-based concerned-citizen coalitions, and Pastor Rice's forums. The poor people's movements led by outside advocates were least successful in helping low-income people effectively communicate with policy makers.

Most of these coalitions also developed bridging links to policy circles. Their activities usually involved a combination of research, formal events to present information to policy makers, and informal meetings with government aimed at changing policy. The initiatives that included only short-term actions or formal events had the least success. This suggests that effective policy change involves developing bridging social capital with policy makers.

POLICY IMPLICATIONS: INGREDIENTS OF EFFECTIVE ADVOCACY

In both large cities, the faith-based coalitions were most effective in modifying welfare-reform strategies. Milwaukee's efforts to do away with the "job-ready" classification is the clearest example. As outlined in chapter 1, W-2 agencies could designate applicants for cash assistance as job-ready, requiring them to look for work without receiving any cash benefits for a period of time. This meant that poor families might have no income until they found work or were reclassified. Both nonsectarian welfare-rights activists and religious coalitions campaigned for changes in this policy for a number of months. The modifications proposed by various coalitions varied little, and the same actors participated in many of the efforts. Ultimately, the hearings and debates that had the most impact were those organized by religious-based coalitions. The authority attributed to church coalitions and the perceptions that churches were a moderating influence allowed policy makers to hear the message most clearly from them. Social capital resided in the recognized trust of religious coalitions based on cultural expectations of churches as community institutions, not in the relationships among individual actors participating in the debate. If relationships were all that mattered, the same advocates' nonsectarian initiatives would have been able to change this policy.

The fieldwork example in Philadelphia provided in chapter 1 shows similar patterns there. The differences among these religious-based efforts in the large cities, nonsectarian efforts, and the more adversarial approaches of welfare rights and Gamaliel advocacy efforts highlight aspects of effective advocacy:

- Effective advocacy draws on respected community symbols and uses moderating language to present positions.
- Effective advocacy draws on a large constituency that potentially participates in the policy process. The more effective religious coalitions represent a wide array of faith communities and work with an equally diverse group of advocates and direct-service providers who have bridging ties to policy makers. They are thought to represent a more established point of view than advocacy organizations representing a small group or one part of the population.
- Effective advocates use research and grass-roots examples in presenting positions. They are also well versed in policies they hope to change, offering concrete, feasible solutions. Effective strategies involved four components. First, coalition members developed detailed understanding of state, federal, and local policy before developing advocacy goals. Second, they used research conducted by national and local think tanks and/or academics. Third, they drew from data collected through the experience of agencies or program participants to support their positions. Fourth, they asked for changes that administrators could accomplish given the boundaries of existing policy.
- Effective policy advocates work with policy makers both through formal and informal mechanisms. The interfaith coalitions were most effective in influencing policy because they developed bridging social capital with key legislators, administrators, and service providers through participation in joint advocacy activities and oversight commissions on the county and state level.
- Effective advocates represent constituencies that can effectively participate in the policy process.

SUMMARY

Examination of advocacy efforts in Milwaukee, Kenosha, and Philadelphia reveals the importance of social and cultural capital in effective social change. The advocacy efforts that made a difference both in local communities and in state and national policy forums drew on coalitions of advocates with preestablished relationships. Interlocking coalitions from various types of organizations, congregations, and concerned citizens were able to expand bridging social capital within the local community and between advocates and policy makers. These advocates described problems caused by welfare-reform initiatives and sometimes gave voice to people served by these programs. These efforts also facilitated bringing low-income people to the table with policy makers. In Pennsylvania, welfare-rights and related groups sit on policy advisory committees. Owing to the bridging efforts of religious coalitions, similar groups now participate in advisory committees in Wisconsin as well.

Effective advocacy strategies contain several key ingredients. Campaigns draw from research on poverty issues, a clear understanding of policy, and a direct connection to the experience of people who use government social welfare programs. Advocates make use of public activities to promote their message as well as behind-the-scenes meetings with policy makers and key stakeholders. They develop enough trust with the various constituencies they work with to effectively communicate across closed social capital networks. In some instances, these activities build bridging social capital across the power hierarchy. In all cases, effective advocates present pragmatic initiatives using the cultural capital cues to which policy makers respond. Advocates educate their grass-roots constituency to practice the same skills. Most effective advocacy coalitions draw from people providing service and pay attention to the design of government or nonprofit programs to serve the disenfranchised.

The advocacy community is becoming increasingly bifurcated between the pragmatists who play a role in changing social welfare policy and the purists who refuse to compromise on a return to AFDC-style welfare or who look for global economic change. The same debates rage in the academic community.[16] Purist left academic analysis sees working with policy makers as supporting the current "neoliberal" policy regime or the "workist consensus." According to this view, only groups that claim to represent poor people and promote these idealistic strategies, like Energize or Women Warriors, are considered appropriate advocates on welfare policy.

Although I support the macro-level analysis of socioeconomic problems produced by these researchers and hope for universal benefits and social equity envisioned by the pure left campaigns, my research suggests that purist positions are counterproductive in changing welfare policy. For example, positions that focus on dismantling capitalism provide no concrete solutions whereas living-wage campaigns, which alter the compensation structure in local communities without demanding global change in the nature of work relationships, share the same philosophy but offer practical changes. I ask proponents of purist views to look to Marx's analysis of the transition from feudalism to capitalism. Our current economic system developed over several centuries in small steps, as a town-centered bourgeoisie slowly ascended to power, changing the legal and ideological assumptions about society in the process. The revolutions that brought capitalist landholders to power came after these gradual changes had taken place. Changing the current structure will happen in the same way, through gradually modifying policy and practice in a more progressive direction.

CHAPTER 14

Conclusion

Public Policy and Social Capital

Analysis of advocacy strategies in these three cities promotes gradual change aimed toward creating a just and equal society in which all families can meet their goals. Public policy that would make a difference in local communities contains several ingredients:

- Policy is based on research detailing the needs and resources of local families, the strategies of organizations providing service, and the realities of labor markets rather than on simplified theory about families' motivations or social structure.
- Policy solutions are flexible enough to provide a range of supports to families with different resources and needs.
- Social welfare policy should be based on an understanding that supporting working families involves much more than helping people find jobs and subsidizing child care, and that the organizational resources to meet those needs are currently provided through four interlocking but fragmented systems. Successful policy would work to integrate those systems and help families find the range of resources needed to meet their goals.
- Policy solutions address the unequal power relations among most of the persistently poor, their employers, and the agencies providing service. Rather than offer solutions crafted for the middle class or presume that everyone has equal opportunity, programs should provide the social and cultural capital skills, mentoring, counseling, and ombudsman support that families need to successfully navigate the labor market, educational system, and other resources.
- Policy makers recognize that government, social service agencies, and faith communities all make important contributions to the social welfare of local communities and their citizens. Rather than relegate policy implementation to one element of this system, successful policy would draw on the strengths of each type of organization, developing partnerships that take into account the different goals, resources, and strategies of each partner.
- Policy makers work with groups active in local communities to craft programs that address systemic problems across that locality.

This chapter draws on the analysis throughout this book to outline a social welfare system that meets these criteria. I offer suggestions for specific aspects of social welfare policy at the end of most chapters; here, I look at more general factors that impact on specific solutions. Most of the chapter details findings related to the first ingredient of successful policy: concrete research that informs policy development. I then return to the remaining five elements, outlining ways that policy creation and implementation could meet these goals.

Lessons from Research in Three Cities

In the first chapter, I identified five key factors that influence the implementation of social welfare policy at the local level:

1. The government policies that shape programs
2. The nature of the organizations providing service
3. The nature of the local implementation system
4. The socioeconomic system of the locality
5. The nature of the population receiving service

The social welfare systems in these three communities show local variation that impacts on public policy implementation. At the same time, commonalities across communities, service providers, and families stand out throughout this book.

Big City/Small City

Each city presented subtle differences regarding structure, labor market, and culture that influenced local-level outcomes, but the two large cities are very similar on most measures. Each large city includes an increasingly diverse racial, ethnic, national, and class mix. Although both cities have recovered somewhat from deindustrialization, they still lack the tax base, infrastructure, and jobs to provide a quality environment for all their citizens. The social and economic gaps between wealthy and poor residents continue to increase in both cities. Philadelphia and Milwaukee also remain centers for persistent poverty, containing the largest welfare caseloads in each state. These large cities are sites of significant racial segregation, but their power structures also include enough diversity that questions of both racial and class inequities can be addressed in policy and social service provision.

The large number of families needing service present policy-implementation problems very different from those in smaller communities like Kenosha. In the large cities, families can more easily fall through the cracks or disappear into neighborhoods with concentrated poverty. The existence of neighborhoods highly segregated by race and class means that socially isolated families are more likely to lack the connections and cultural capital to succeed in the current labor market.

These large cities also have the most complex and sophisticated systems to address social problems. Each has numerous organizations of varying quality that offer services to city residents. Some of these organizations have a long history of successful service provision, offering many strategies to address family needs. The wide range of service providers means that resources are available to address unique problems. At the same time, these service provision systems appear fragmented by kind of service and community.

Kenosha, on the other hand, reflects dynamics like those of small cities and towns across the country; I found many similarities to smaller towns where I have lived in recent years. The limited racial diversity and the focus on local-level knowledge in Kenosha were echoed elsewhere. In these communities, service strategies are individualized given smaller caseloads and cultural focus on particularistic solutions. The smaller number of persistently poor families in these communities promotes individual rather than systemic solutions.

In addition, in communities where most families can meet their needs through work, people on public assistance seem more at odds with local norms, particularly when an increasing percentage of welfare recipients have different racial/ethnic/national backgrounds than the majority of residents, as in Kenosha. Although people of color are more likely to interact with whites in these communities given common school systems, fewer places to shop, and fewer service providers, they also experience more overt racism and social segregation and their closed community networks and institutions often have fewer links to the city elite. The few people of color in power-dominant positions mean that these issues receive less attention in policy circles.

Kenosha differs from many smaller communities in the sophistication of its government welfare program. However, its program exhibits strengths and weaknesses similar to those of other small localities. The small caseload means that Kenosha's government can pay careful, individualized attention to each family it serves. At the same time, however, it lacks the economies of scale of the large cities. As funding decreases as a reflection of smaller caseloads, these localities increasingly run the risk of underfunding, which makes it difficult to offer the range of services needed.

The social service system in Kenosha has some of the same advantages and disadvantages as government. The small number of service providers know one another and their cases. They interact through a variety of formal and informal relationships that allow them to assist people in their community. However, these systems lack the range of unique services of the large cities. They are also significantly underfunded, affecting numbers and quality of

staff. This is a particular problem in community-based organizations, which face issues of staff turnover and a shortage of people with needed skills, making it necessary for staff to perform multiple functions. Kenosha residents contribute to their local organizations, but community resources are too limited to support these nonprofits. Other solutions to funding limitations are a critical need in cities like Kenosha.

These differences suggest that policy makers should tailor state and federal programs to address the different strengths and weaknesses of small versus large localities. In addition to the variation in numbers of residents and of people needing service, these two types of communities are qualitatively different. Quality of life, available work, social service systems, and local strategies to address problems are divergent characteristics of large cities versus small towns. Cities draw on the diversity and institutional complexity of large population centers, whereas smaller localities reflect tendencies toward homogeneity and individualized solutions. Neither type of community is better than the other; they simply use different strategies to organize social life. Successful policy can draw on the strengths of each type of locality while addressing its inherent weaknesses. Different funding formulas and strategies that make up for the narrower range of locally available social services would help small cities. In large cities, breaking up service provision into smaller units, as both Wisconsin and Pennsylvania have done, helps reduce the risks inherent in large caseloads. At the same time, state and local policy makers need to seek better ways to integrate service-delivery systems in the large cities.

LARGE ORGANIZATION/SMALL ORGANIZATION

Just as large cities differ from smaller localities, large and small organizations have different strengths and face different challenges. The economies of scale of large organizations give them greater capacity to provide government services. Given strong social capital relationships with government and long histories of offering government services, these organizations have become the winners in government devolution by garnering larger contracts. Smaller organizations represent much more institutional diversity and a greater range of social capital resources. These institutions, especially small to midsized organizations that link into community-based or faith-community social capital systems, may have stronger connections among communities of people receiving social welfare services, employers from particular racial/ethnic/national groups, and faith communities than some citywide organizations. While limited administrative capacity sometimes creates challenges for them, they also offer more possibilities to reach isolated populations and present a greater potential for innovative, community-specific programming. Government can address the differences between these two types of organizations by offering contracts to pool administrative functions for smaller organizations. Encouraging true partnerships between large and small organizations can also enhance service provision for both.

THE ROLE OF SOCIAL CAPITAL

Social capital makes a difference on all levels. Government that develops trust-based relationships with local service providers develops more sensitive strategies and is able to more quickly adjust programs to meet unanticipated situations. Organizations with strong social capital links to other organizations, government, and their participants are better equipped to obtain and manage contracts, provide a richer range of services for their program participants, and offer higher-quality service. Faith communities foster social capital and community, providing important resources to their members and the wider society. In some cases, congregations become centers to develop bridging social capital and social change initiatives. Families with divergent social networks have very different employment outcomes despite common efforts to improve human capital.

Despite this predominance of social capital as an element in social welfare systems, it receives the least attention in policy strategies. Policy makers would do well to build into policy factors that encourage social capital development. At an institutional level, including social capital as an aspect of policy implementation means fostering partnerships rather than market competition among providers. Acknowledging the existence of separate, siloed service-delivery systems for ancillary services, official welfare systems, and community-based systems and strategically building relationships across systems would also make a significant difference.

Policy makers can foster bridging social capital across constituencies by enhancing involvement of local-level actors from different parts of the community in policy creation and monitoring. Creating trust-based relationships implies doing more than expanding on already existing relationships between government and local constituencies. Government needs to be willing to share details of policy implementation with local-level actors and work with them on an ongoing basis to improve local systems. Government-sponsored monitoring committees for welfare reform in both states represent a first step in this process. However, to engage the resources available through local actors, government must use the data available through local-level constituencies and involve them in all aspects of developing policy. Pennsylvania shows more willingness to take this next step.

The same factors play a role in social capital development for individuals. If social and cultural capital involved only access to networks and learning the right behavior, social service agencies seeking to move welfare recipients into permanent work could simply enhance their placement mechanisms and focus on teaching communication and social skills. In fact, most contracts for these services require these two elements. However, offering "soft skills" training and hiring good job developers fall short for several reasons. Short-term classes cannot reverse the lack of trust in mainstream institutions of many program recipients, and appropriate cultural cues are seldom developed in a six-week program. The kind of cultural capital appropriate in one work environment may be counterproductive in another company. Finally, as the examples throughout this book demonstrate, success in the workplace depends on developing links to more established workers who will help new employees learn the rules of the workplace and support them as they develop in their careers. Without these social capital resources in the workplace, people moving out of the familiar employment patterns of their closed communities are likely to feel isolated and have a more difficult time succeeding in reaching their goals.

A number of proven service-provision strategies rely on creation of social capital. Mentoring, internships, On the Job Training, community-service positions, strategies to introduce program participants to different educational options through college classes at community-based organizations, workplace-based education, and public assistance outreach programs all draw on elements of bridging social capital. By introducing program participants to new people or institutions, all these programs create opportunities to develop long-term connections to a wider range of resources. Some of these strategies either offer new services in familiar settings or team people starting a new job or educational program with people from the same communities. Others—including internships and some mentoring programs—introduce people to new settings on a trial basis, giving them opportunities to learn over a set period of time. Internships, often combined with supportive mentoring, can provide a combination of social and cultural capital and work experience needed to move into new careers. Discussion throughout this book highlights the fact that social capital involves much more than connections; it depends on context-specific trust developed over time. Each of these strategies allows opportunities to develop these kinds of relationships.

However, each of these strategies can equally lead to busywork programs or placements that simply reinforce the inequities faced by many low-wage workers in the labor market. Several elements make the difference between effective and ineffective programs. First, in the assignment of mentoring or work, participants should be carefully matched with agencies or individuals that can best help them develop needed skills and experience. Second, these relationships should be carefully monitored to ensure that they continue to offer appropriate assets and that participants receive the supports they need to successfully meet mentor or placement expectations. Finally, participants should be viewed as potential employees in the same profession or workplace, fostering trust and long-term relationships between low-income participant and workplace or partner.

Carefully designed and executed programs such as these are much more successful than programs that offer connections without developing trust. Motivational lectures, placing people in jobs without providing case management or on-the-job mentoring, and merely providing information on available services or educational programs are much less effective than strategies in which either the program participant or the agency has long-term relationships that can ensure individual success.

Cultural capital proves equally important in putting social capital to use. People who understand the expected ways to dress, act, speak, and present information in a given setting are much more successful at finding work, assessing social service options, and presenting policy changes than people who lack appropriate cultural capital cues. Like social capital, cultural capital develops slowly through socialization and modeling rather than through job-readiness lectures or educational materials. Congregations and other community-based institutions often serve as sources of appropriate cultural capital as well as social capital. However, as a comparison of Grace Baptist and Faith Temple shows, not all churches and community institutions automatically offer struggling families the guidance they need to succeed in mainstream workplaces. In addition, advice from faith communities works only if the individual receiving guidance feels a part of the congregation and welcomes that advice.

As with mentoring and community-service programs, efforts to involve faith communities in social welfare service provision beyond their already existing programs must carefully match participants to congregations and ensure that these connections are voluntary and respect basic civil rights. Workplace or professional-association mentors offer similar opportunities. Developing partnerships between welfare-to-work providers and institutions offering appropriate cultural capital and supportive community could greatly enhance outcomes. Building bridging cultural capital through partnerships that bring together several organizations and faith communities offering different assets could do the most to foster both closed social capital supports and bridging relationships for participants.

BRIDGING AND CLOSED SOCIAL CAPITAL

Examples throughout this book highlight the need for both families and organizations to develop bridging social capital in order to succeed, particularly as communities and social service systems become more diverse. But closed social capital is equally important. Families rely on closed networks of similar people to find primary resources such as child care, social supports, and resources to fulfill instrumental means. Families help one another to meet their goals. Closed social capital networks are also instrumental in socialization and development of cultural capital. Most of the successful rising-educated-middle-class people relied on closed networks for support while bridging into new environments.

The same is true for organizations. Agencies with bridges across social service systems and into citywide and community-based networks had more capacity to address changes in the social welfare system and better serve their program participants. At the same time, organizations that could rely on resources from closed systems did better than isolated entities. Network associations of similar service providers offered best practices and advocacy clout that single organizations lacked. Agencies that could reach into local communities, draw resources from faith communities, or partner with organizations focused on the same population could supplement their own resources.

In general, though, successful partnerships generally depended on long-standing trust-based relationships. Partners shared similar service philosophies and respected the resource limitations of the other organizations. These partnerships often involve agencies with different strengths working together. For example, Neighborhood Settlement House and Empowerment Education partnered with Community Solutions in ways that benefited all parties. The two smaller organizations gained the contracting clout and administrative expertise that Community Solutions had as a large, citywide organization, and Community Solutions gained alternative service-provision models and additional community-service job-placement sites for their W-2 participants. All three agencies shared a general service ethos and an orientation toward low-income populations.

Partnerships created simply to meet government mandates for collaboration, in which partners have very different service philosophies or have unrealistic expectations of each other, are far less likely to succeed. For example, Citizens United's staff found that integration into FUTURE's employment program ran counter to the work philosophy and major goals long established by the nonprofit organization. These examples suggest that organizational partnerships need to be carefully constructed based on common social and cultural capital in the same way as for individuals.

Policy makers should place equal importance on developing closed and bridging social capital. This involves helping families and organizations identify resources in their own communities as well as partner across different systems. Enhancing resources at both the local and citywide levels would also help families meet their goals and enable agencies to better serve the community. Given that bridging social capital often depends on support from closed communities, fostering bridging programs with institutions such as bridging faith communities is one strategy to enhance social capital resources for families and communities.

One potential service-provision area for modeling these kinds of partnerships is day care. Many low-income families prefer home care or family providers over center-based care. However, these providers can prove unreliable, and the quality of care is uneven. Offering supports to family day-care providers through several mechanisms could make a difference and foster bridging social capital for both the provider and children in their care. First, developing backup supports for family providers through local faith communities could provide one form of additional support and stability. Next, involving both home care and faith-based support providers in enrichment and training programs could build additional human, social, and cultural capital. Offering opportunities for both children in care and their providers to attend on a regular basis larger centers with professionally educated staff or greater resources could also bridge some of the educational gaps between home care and high-quality center care.[1] These neighborhood-based or regional resource centers could also serve as bridges to wider enrichment experiences such as those offered by museums, theater, and music. Finally, enhancing resources through work with home care providers to develop both closed-culture-appropriate activities and bridging activities could expand the experience for both children and adults. As suggested in several chapters, this kind of program involves partnerships among local community members, faith communities, social service agencies, and government.

The Government Policies That Shape Programs

Wisconsin and Pennsylvania took different approaches to meet the same goal: moving people quickly into jobs. This book does not evaluate implementation of TANF policy, but responses from agencies and individuals yields examples of both successful and ineffective policy implementation at the local level. Both systems presumed that welfare recipients most needed work experience, and they used similar strategies to achieve their goals, including emphasizing rapid attachment to the workplace, community-service jobs for people who could not find work, and specific supports such as child care for working families. Pennsylvania placed much more emphasis on education and training, but adult education also was available in the Wisconsin system. Both policies succeeded in achieving these basic goals: welfare rolls declined and people found work. Although the most vulnerable limited-work-experience populations increasingly dominated caseloads, people in this category also found jobs.

Policies may have achieved their goals, but family responses show that rapid attachment may hurt the chances of the stable working class and rising educated middle class to return to jobs that offered pay and benefits similar to those for previous work. The emphasis on getting *any* job seldom allowed time to develop new social capital that could lead to more stable, family-supporting employment. Likewise, these programs placed low-skilled workers back into jobs that keep them poor. Retention and advancement become key issues for most program participants.

A focus on employment and separating cash assistance from food stamps, medical assistance, and other support programs exacerbated already existing fragmentation in the federal social support system. As a result, use of community resources such as food pantries and uncompensated medical care skyrocketed. Although government has taken measures to correct these problems, they highlight larger structural problems with the public support system rather than short-term issues caused by rapid policy change.

The experience in Pennsylvania and Wisconsin was echoed across the country. The uniformity of response suggests that common federal policy goals can impact on local programs. More important, other factors—for example, the labor market—play a much larger role in policy implementation than the form of particular state programs. Across the country, caseloads declined as the economy improved and began to rise again with economic decline.

Although policy plays a role in local outcomes, the uniformity of results in these three communities suggests that policy needs to focus much more on the labor market and local service-delivery systems than on ideology about the needs of program participants. This is supported by research that shows that the primary presumption about program participants—that they lack employment experience and a work ethic—proves false for most people using government assistance.

As outlined in earlier chapters, policy makers can help families escape poverty with a two-pronged approach. First, some families need additional training or social capital development to move into jobs that provide the wages and benefits to support their families. Initiatives focused on advancement should figure heavily in changes to TANF at both the state and federal levels.

The second critical need involves supplemental supports for families and communities. Ideas for changes to existing programs are suggested below under "The Socioeconomic System of the Locality." Child care and medical insurance are essential for all working families. People taking low-wage jobs also need income assistance as well as support with food, housing, and other basic needs. The TANF implementation experience in both states showed that these kinds of services need to be expanded and better integrated as part of TANF policy.

Analysis of welfare reform in these three communities also showed the importance of local-level differences. Kenosha drew on a cohesive culture of work for all citizens and a highly integrated social service system to craft a program that effectively served many city residents. The kind of federated system integration developed in Kenosha would not work in systems like those of Milwaukee or Philadelphia, which are characterized by more distrust among members of the service-provider community and more fragmentation within the system.

Milwaukee was particularly challenged to integrate the state's unitary service-delivery system into an adversarial union culture as the county offices teamed with W-2 agencies with very different agendas. Wisconsin recognized the racial/ethnic/national segregation in Milwaukee when it gave contracts to two agencies known for serving the Latino and African American communities. However, the state offered limited latitude for these organizations to develop programs geared toward the unique needs of their participants.

Pennsylvania officials acknowledge the very real differences between Philadelphia and other localities and tried hard to involve local service providers and other constituencies in program implementation, but the two-track contracting system exacerbates preexisting fragmentation of service provision in this large city. Although the various coalitions of service providers ameliorate this tendency, Pennsylvania would do well to take a regional approach to service provision. Developing ways to better integrate its many diverse programs would greatly enhance service provision overall.

THE NATURE OF THE ORGANIZATIONS PROVIDING SERVICE

All three cities used social welfare systems that relied heavily on nongovernmental entities to provide services. The same types of organizations—citywide, community-based, and faith-based organizations, both large and small—

offered programs in all three cities. Each type of organization relied on different social capital to carry out its work. These various providers struggled to maintain their missions as they provided government services. The unique programs offered by different types of providers highlighted the importance of this devolved system. It is potentially strongest when organizations with different characteristics partner with one another. Policies that make use of the unique role of various available service providers are more likely to succeed in the long run. Providing adequate funding so that organizations can maintain high-quality staff and reasonable caseloads also appears essential for service provision.

THE NATURE OF THE LOCAL IMPLEMENTATION SYSTEM

All three cities supported four interlocking systems: the official welfare services system, the ancillary services system, the community-based system, and faith communities. Organizations within each system developed relationships with other providers in that system as well as with local government. The ancillary services system had significant internal fragmentation because providers tended to connect with agencies like themselves rather than with those offering complementary services. Kenosha showed most integration across systems, but fewer providers meant limited options for service strategies.

Although both program participants and agencies needed services in all four systems, the connections among them were not well developed. This points to critical issues that need policy attention. First, government should adequately fund the full range of support services that families need to fulfill welfare-reform obligations. Second, funding should be provided for staff and materials to support outreach, education, and partnering across agencies in different systems. Finally, policy should foster better integration across these systems.

THE SOCIOECONOMIC SYSTEM OF THE LOCALITY

The local labor market is perhaps the most important issue affecting welfare policy. All three communities had bifurcated labor markets in which at least half the jobs offered low pay, limited benefits, and often only part-time schedules. Jobs that paid well often required advanced education and communications skills. The larger cities had more global enterprises, but smaller, more vulnerable secondary-sector employers predominated in all three communities.

These changed labor markets imply that social welfare policy needs to alter basic strategies on several levels. First, the better-paying jobs in these globalized labor markets stress communications and critical thinking skills as well as college-level human capital. Other jobs in the new economy call for similar skills. In all three cities, preparation for good jobs needed to start much earlier than adult-education programs—critical thinking, bicultural communications skills, and teamwork development have always come from childhood education. Changing the focus of local elementary and secondary schools is a critical component of preparing people for the new labor market. It is also the most difficult component, as local systems reflect local history, and parents, students, and teachers often resist change.

Adult education should focus on combining related training and work, along with development of social and cultural capital. Since many better-paying jobs have limited internal advancement structures, helping people develop on-the-job skills through internships becomes particularly important.

Given the suburbanization of jobs, both Philadelphia and Milwaukee also need to develop regional approaches to linking agencies and their participants to employers. Philadelphia has tried several mechanisms to achieve this goal in the past, with limited success. Kenosha does a much better job of working with employers, and some aspects of their employer recruitment strategies might work in the larger cities. However, given the large social, racial, and economic gaps between city and suburbs in both large cities, employer linkages in the two large cities also need to address these issues. As in development of any system, connecting employers to agencies or people needing work entails attention to all the social capital, cultural issues, skills, and supports needed to successfully link employers to a welfare-to-work system.

Support systems for all jobs in the new economy need improvement. Many jobs require flexible hours, and fewer provide benefits or income security. Some necessary supports call for policy changes at both the federal and state levels. Medical insurance continues to be a pressing issue that demands new solutions. Family-care systems, including child care, elder care, and related services, also need expansion and changes, but these systems are best designed at the local level to fit community culture and needs. Likewise, transportation is a problem in all three cities but requires local or regional solutions.

Finally, a growing number of jobs in the new economy are part-time, pay little, and expect limited skills. The number of these jobs is likely to increase as globalization continues. Because current trends suggest limited options to substantially improve wages and benefits, better mechanisms should be developed to supplement wages for people working in these kinds of jobs. Caregiving jobs, often provided by nonprofit organizations, are one rapidly growing employment category; offering government wage supplements to nonprofit agencies to raise wage levels for child- and elder-care aides could help raise wages across all organizations offering these services. Different types of wage supplements are needed for retail and clerical work and other low-wage jobs. The Earned Income Tax Credit makes a critical difference for many low-income families, and other strategies could complement this program.

THE NATURE OF THE POPULATION RECEIVING SERVICE

The populations using public assistance systems varied little in all three communities. Four policy-relevant factors stand out in assessing worker types and family strategies. The first is the high level of work experience among populations that use public assistance. Contrary to some policy makers' assumptions, most people start work as teenagers and continue to engage in productive labor throughout their lives. Welfare is most often a supplement to low wages or a form of unemployment insurance rather than a substitute for work. This fact suggests that welfare policy ought to address the limitations of jobs held by welfare recipients rather than focus on employment.

Second, the population using public assistance is diverse in consistent ways. The five family types discussed in this book have different social capital resources that lead them to different kinds of jobs. Education, training, and barriers to employment (for example, poor health, disability, and substance-abuse issues) impact on individual families in varying ways. This finding suggests that additional social capital development is a critical need for many families. Since most families have strong closed social capital networks, social capital development should focus on helping families bridge into systems that offer needed resources. Also, strategies to help individual families leave public assistance should be tailored for each worker type.

Caregiving responsibilities also loom large in family strategies. Many limited-work-experience people are designated caregivers in their family systems. Since both adults in two-parent households work more frequently now than in the past, caregiving responsibilities are a major issue even in multi-worker families and still more complicated for single parents. Adequately addressing timing, quality, and reliability of caregiving options for families, as well as costs, becomes a critical policy issue.

This research shows that caregiving is often accomplished through parents, other relatives, or closed social capital networks. This is true for the middle class as well as the poor. Given the community role in caregiving, government should foster caregiving strategies that draw on these already well-established systems. Improving the supports and quality of care among family providers, encouraging church-based caregiving programs for elders as well as children, and helping community health providers offer sick-child care or adult day care could promote stable caregiving systems needed by working families.

Finally, many individuals seek to enhance human capital skills, but people in some of the worker types may need assistance in assessing the appropriateness and quality of potential programs. Providing high-quality skills and aptitude assessment as well as building community and individual capacity to evaluate available educational opportunities could enhance the ability of individuals to successfully obtain and complete human capital development programs. Social and cultural capital are equally critical elements in advancement strategies: people lacking connections or appropriate cultural capital fail to get jobs despite enhanced skills. Building social and cultural capital development into educational programs is essential if these programs are to meet their goals.

ENVISIONING A BETTER SOCIAL WELFARE DELIVERY SYSTEM

The case studies throughout this book demonstrate successful strategies that families and agencies use to meet their goals. Examples also show instances in which systems break down, people fail to meet projected outcomes, or programs fail to provide needed benefits, and they highlight the importance of free will and agency individuality in program outcomes. Regardless of the structure and the incentives of policy makers or program designers, people respond to programs based on their own agendas, strengths, and weaknesses. Likewise, agencies bend policies to fit their missions, and individual staff members interpret program criteria differently. Rather than attempt unsuccessfully to impose a single model, successful policy would support creativity in programs and appreciate family choice to use programs in different ways.

Many of the ingredients of an integrated social welfare system exist today. Creating a program that successfully meets the divergent needs of community families primarily involves more flexible models, better system integration, ongoing training and social capital development measures for participating organizations, improved partnering with congregations and community-based institutions, enhanced funding, and establishing evaluation and ombudsman systems.

What would such a system look like? I outline one model for a service-delivery system, highlighting ways in which it fits the criteria established at the beginning of this chapter.

In keeping with the requirement of flexible solutions for families with different needs, the goals of the social welfare program would be to provide the family with assistance to meet income and benefit goals through an array of work-development strategies, supporting benefits, advancement opportunities, and measures to enhance social and cultural capital. Although this system would focus on work, as most people seek family-supporting jobs, strategies to find employment would take into careful account previous skills and work experience, short- and long-term goals, and family needs.

Entry to the system would start with a comprehensive assessment and development of a plan for each family. Current policy contains the seeds of such an assessment, but the goals are very different from those of the current employment plans in each state. This kind of assessment would require staff with smaller caseloads and adequate training to evaluate families' resources and needs. Assessment counselors would need ready access to specialists to address disabilities, substance abuse, and other highly specialized issues. Using a team approach, as in Kenosha, is a promising option. Enhancing training and hiring adequate staff may require additional funding or reassigning some staff members to focus on intake rather than case management. Assessment would recognize the differences among worker types and offer options in keeping with the skills, social capital resources, and expectations of individual families. Plans would also include the needs of various family members, so that individual goals take into account family responsibilities. Finally, plans would assess social capital resources available through local systems and determine how those supports shape options available to individual families. They would include strategies to develop new or bridging social and cultural capital in addition to guidance to find work, training, or social services.

Families could gain entry to services through a combination of government offices, social service agencies, and community-based agencies. Placing assessment workers in agencies in all three systems would provide benefits to the displaced-worker families and others leery of government offices. Providing ongoing training to staff at local agencies would enhance information about social welfare policy across the locality.

Once a plan was developed for a family, its members would be assigned a case-management team to help them achieve their goals. As with the integrated team in Kenosha, case management would be conducted by several people working together in order to balance strengths and weaknesses of individual workers. As in Philadelphia, case managers could be at different agencies—for example, the welfare department, a contracted employment-development agency, and an education program—but they would be required to coordinate with one another.

Families would be provided with a number of program options to meet their needs. As in the Vermont system and other social service programs that stress individuals' developing the skills to access services on their own, families would be encouraged to contact providers themselves. Individuals lacking the cultural capital cues to successfully access services on their own would receive modeling and support to learn these skills. Along with referrals to services, case management would also entail enhancing social capital through links to individuals or organizations related to goals. For example, someone seeking to develop stable family-supporting employment in a health-care field might be simultaneously referred to a training program, an employer in that field, and a mentor in that career found through a list of faith communities, professional organizations, and employers. Case management would provide variable supports and continue as long as needed to help the family firmly on the path toward long-term goals.

Payment for the range of services would be triggered through a locality-wide combined grant and fee-for-service funding system that included ancillary services system and community-based agencies. One disadvantage of voucher systems is that often local providers cannot depend on sufficient basic income; the combined system would yield more funding. Just as Kenosha provides grants to the homeless and domestic-violence shelters that serve their clients, the proposed system would provide grants to participating agencies to maintain basic staffing and anticipated services. Additional funds would be available for unforeseen need for a given agency's services. Organizations that function on fee-for-service contracts, such as training providers, would continue to receive payment in this way through case-management system triggers.

Families would also have access to ombudsman systems to address potential inequities in the system. Several models could work for this function. Offering "friendly advocates," as in the model faith-based welfare program in Milwaukee, is one strategy. Another might include training ombudsmen from community-based organizations, faith communities, advocacy organizations, or other agencies. Families would be introduced to these individuals at informal orientation events, where people could interact and identify for themselves the supporters who best matched them. Still another route would be offering connections to Community Legal Services and other watchdog agencies and expanding ombudsman capacity by providing ongoing training to social service and advocacy agency staff through legal services staff. These resource people would also be introduced to families through regular events at the case-management agency.

This family-support system depends on system integration across the official welfare-delivery system, the ancillary agency system, the community-based system, and faith communities. Integration of systems would start with contracts that promote partnerships across agencies offering complementary services and include faith communities and informal community voluntary organizations. These contracts would provide funding for interaction among agencies. Rather than expect congregations or voluntary organizations to become formal service providers, these partners would provide in-kind supports and one-on-one activities to build social capital and community. Contracts would locate administrative responsibilities in the agency with the best capacity to provide these services and foster development of simplified reporting procedures for other partners.

System-wide integration would begin with ongoing education, training, and information-sharing forums across the various systems. The events would encourage development of social capital across agencies. System integration would also involve creating communications mechanisms that allow agencies serving the same families to work together to meet holistic goals. The integration process would also include conversations focused on modifying policy based on observed outcomes.

Services in this expanded and integrated system would be available to a much wider range of families than currently qualify for needs-based support systems. Here, policy makers can take lessons from Kenosha, which eliminated separate systems for the poor and other citizens seeking help with employment, child care, and education. By expanding who qualifies for assistance, policy makers build wider social support for social welfare and help the entire community meet its needs. This is particularly effective with health care and family caregiving programs in which expanding benefits to working families lacking these benefits elsewhere enhances productivity, cuts down on costly emergency services, and impacts on crime prevention, remedial education, and future needs for emergency supports.

To improve links to employers and enhance social and cultural capital development, contracts for employment and training would include funding to foster internships, mentoring, on-the-job training, and increased connections to local employers. These initiatives could encompass a combination of direct connections to employers and support through professionals found through faith communities, business organizations, professional organizations, and associations of retired people.

POLICIES TO DEVELOP AN INTEGRATED SOCIAL SERVICES SYSTEM

This ideal program model depends on changes in social welfare policy at both the state and federal levels. Regardless of the details of local social welfare provision systems, policy changes would enhance social welfare provision in this country. First, social welfare policy needs to reduce the fragmentation of service provision in this country through federal policy that recognizes the interdependence of programs such as food stamps, medical assistance, family caregiving, and workforce development. The silo strategy of current policy makes it difficult for families to meet their needs given different program requirements and encourages fragmentation at the local level. Eliminating fragmentation would involve two simultaneous activities. First, federal policy should eradicate contradictory eligibility criteria across benefit programs and encourage states to develop integrated systems. Because many low-income working families quickly find that they earn too much to qualify for assistance, eligibility criteria should be linked to living-wage standards in local communities. Simultaneously, at the local level, state and local policies should promote social welfare approaches that address the needs of entire families by altering their contracting specifications and local service-delivery systems.

Second, policy should recognize the importance of developing links across agencies by stipulating that government funds can be used for enhanced community outreach through ancillary agencies and community-based agencies, allowing administrative costs for staff to develop social capital across agencies as well as for the families they serve. Policy should also promote diverse ways for faith communities, social service agencies, and government to work together, rather than foster initiatives to include congregations or other community-based entities in current contracting regimes.

Third, welfare in the United States has traditionally focused on providing income through either cash benefits or employment plans. The range of strategies and family needs documented throughout this book highlights the fact that welfare should be linked to workforce development and family care-giving programs in ways that provide flexibility for families and providers. The TANF block-grant system offers significant flexibility as well as local-level diversity. However, eligibility criteria, time limits, and the employment focus discourage more flexible plans. Acknowledging that public assistance is one strategy to meet family needs and developing policy that places benefits in this context would foster a system that supports long-term poverty reduction.

Finally, the United States offers much less in the way of comprehensive benefits than most countries. Wilson (1987, 1996), Skocpol (1995), and many others have long called for development of comprehensive benefits for health care, family care, and education in this country. This analysis adds one more voice calling for comprehensive benefit systems for all residents. Social capital implies access to basic resources by community residents. Increasingly, private systems offer uneven and insufficient supports. Government needs to step into a primary role as funder and facilitator for these basic needs so that families can productively contribute to society. Given current structures and political realities, the most promising proposal to date involves doing away with the current fragmented system of Medicare, Medicaid, and private insurance by giving everyone access to the health-insurance system offered to federal employees, funding health insurance through a combination of employer taxes, employee taxes, and general funds.

The structural and context-specific definition of social capital used throughout this book suggests that the United States will continue to have a much harder time developing universal benefits than other countries. Social polity is too fragmented into groups that mistrust one another. Political systems currently work to exacerbate existing divisions within society through identity politics and seeking simplified, generalized policies over the more community-defined solutions suggested here. Still, issues such as health care, wages, and other benefits touch all constituencies and remain crisis issues for all but the wealthy and those working for employers who offer comprehensive benefits. Using the strategies of developing linked coalitions across constituencies at the local level, as in successful welfare-reform modifications, and developing bridges to other constituencies concerned about the same issues could help advocates successfully bring about national changes. Advocates would do well to follow similar strategies used by early-twentieth-century reformers that created existing national benefits (Skocpol 1999).

Throughout the book I have consistently contrasted structural definitions of social capital with definitions that equate social capital with civic engagement. Social capital is one tool people use to address the existing fragmentation and inequities in U.S. society. Lack of civic engagement comes from limited generalized trust. Advocates of improved civic engagement, such as Putnam (2000), harken back to the golden age of the World War II generation when patriotism and civic engagement were high. Putting aside for a moment the very different pictures of society in the 1940s and 1950s painted by civil rights historians, let me end by examining several features of this time period that meant very different social capital resources for members of that generation. First, the war created opportunities for decent employment, for many different populations, that have rarely existed in this country. Women and people of color were offered jobs in primary-sector workplaces during the war that quickly disappeared as soldiers returned. The GI bill, which offered unprecedented class mobility to returning veterans, removed some of the potential employment pressure after the war. More people had opportunities to participate in generalized prosperity throughout their careers owing to a combination of the wage and benefit agreements established between government and employers during and after the war. The GI bill and the expanding economy created economic opportunities for that generation very different from those for more recent generations. Economic stability meant more leisure to participate in voluntary organizations and other civic activities. Finally, as Putnam rightly notes, the war created a unifying issue that drew many people into community activities.

Paying more attention to the structural issues that fostered community involvement would enhance bridging social capital and generalized civic engagement. Suggestions for integrated service-delivery systems and universal benefits are intended to boost employment prospects and economic stability across communities. Allowing more equitable distribution of social goods and building trust across parts of the service-delivery and employment systems, and changing advocacy efforts concentrate on truly empowering and including local communities, could begin a process of fostering the social conditions necessary for expanding civic engagement for various sectors of society.

In one good way, expectations of civic engagement in the twenty-first century are very different from those of the World War II generation. At that time, the different experience and needs of people of color and others in closed communities who generally were excluded from civic participation and social goods were largely ignored. Today, policy attempts to include these populations through a variety of initiatives. Paying attention to structural inequities and consciously building bridging social capital with these communities may eventually foster opportunities for a better quality of life for and more trust in the political process by currently disenfranchised communities.

Methods and Project Descriptions

RESEARCH STRATEGIES

This book's strategy of depicting systems in motion within a broader community is adapted from anthropology's approach to conceiving and researching social problems. Rather than begin research with a particular hypothesis to prove or disprove, anthropologists start with a set of theory-based general questions. Inquiry begins by exploring general patterns in the community as well as the macro-social factors that created it. The ethnographic method—as this research strategy is called—necessarily approaches problems historically and focuses on process as much as outcomes. More specific research goals come out of initial understandings of a community through months of less focused observation. Both research problems and solutions look broadly at a community and the way it works.

Anthropologists start research on poverty problems by asking general questions. Who uses government programs? How do they fulfill their needs? What do programs do to help or hinder their participants? What larger systems influence interaction in a particular setting? Researchers explore these questions by first observing people and programs. These initial observations lead to interviews with more direct questions, most of which address the generalized, process-oriented foci. Statistics are sometimes used in these analyses but as part of a larger whole rather than as ways to address specific hypotheses. Analysis brings together all the pieces of the research to describe a system and ways to make it work better.

The methodology in this book applies anthropology's holistic approach to comprehending poverty. Anthropologists traditionally rely on participant observation as a key research strategy: recording of events in a setting over time. As in much present-day anthropology, this study creates a comprehensive picture of social welfare in these communities by incorporating observation with several additional techniques. Research methodology combines quantitative statistical studies of various populations; qualitative questionnaires and structured life-history interviews; and ethnographic participant observation in the context of social service agencies, neighborhoods, and policy. The interaction among these factors is analyzed by comparing, contrasting, and aggregating findings from many research projects.

GOVERNMENT POLICIES THAT SHAPE PROGRAMS

Data on this issue came from secondary source documents, interviews with government officials, and observations of government forums. I collected and analyzed social welfare policy documents, requests for proposals, and an array of government statistics on labor markets, welfare, and related issues. Statistics were taken from the U.S. Census, the U.S. Department of Labor, the Pennsylvania Department of Public Welfare, and the Wisconsin Department of Workforce Development.

Interviews with government officials were conducted as part of the Kenosha Conversation Project, the Kenosha Social Capital Project, the Milwaukee Neighborhood Settlement House Evaluation Project, and interviews conducted specifically for this book. Formal interviews were conducted with local and state policy makers for each community. Both government administrators and politicians active in social welfare policy were interviewed. Among the topics discussed were policy details, the process of developing and implementing policy, the logic behind policy decisions, and the role of social networks in the policy process. The Kenosha Conversation Project also included focus groups on W-2 implementation with both the government officials and government welfare administrators.

Participant observation in Philadelphia primarily involved notes and materials from six years of meetings with policy makers as welfare reform and related policy evolved (1992–1997). The Institute for the Study of Civic Values (ISCV) also participated in a number of government hearings about welfare reform during this period. In addition, I participated in several advocacy coalitions as both an ISCV employee and a representative of the Central Philadelphia Monthly Meeting of the Religious Society of Friends. These observations form the core of my understanding of welfare policy in this locality. Participant observation related to policy in Milwaukee involved attendance of various advocacy meetings and discussions with local providers between 1997 and 2000. Students in an internship class focused on welfare in the spring of 1998, and student researchers working on the Kenosha Social Capital Study (1999–2000) and the Neighborhood Settlement House Evaluation Study (1998–1999) compiled observations of welfare-policy activities in Milwaukee and Kenosha that are used in this analysis.

THE NATURE OF THE LOCAL IMPLEMENTATION SYSTEM AND THE ORGANIZATIONS PROVIDING SERVICE

Research on these topics was conducted via interviews, participant observation, and one statistical study in Philadelphia. My experience as an administrator in Philadelphia from 1992 to 1997 included participant observation. Secondary source materials, including agency reports, advocacy coalition materials, and other information, were collected at the same time.

To better understand organization dynamics of agencies involved in education and training, a coalition of service providers in Philadelphia, with the support of the local Private Industry Council and the Mayor's Commission on Literacy, conducted a study of such agencies in the Philadelphia area, called the Survey of Training Providers. Participant observation in Kenosha included research that I and my students conducted during the Kenosha Conversation Project (1998) and the Kenosha Social Capital Study (1999–2000). The research in Milwaukee involved three projects. As part of the internship class, students were placed in several of the agencies with W-2 contracts to observe program development and interactions with program participants. The Neighborhood Settlement House Evaluation Project included one year of in-depth study of the major community-based nonprofit in a mixed class/race Milwaukee neighborhood. Finally, I participated in the advisory group for a faith-based initiative. Observations included the planning and implementation of this project. Students and I also participated in agency coalitions related to social welfare issues in both Milwaukee and Kenosha. Notes and other written materials from these efforts were added to information on individual agencies. Participant observation was combined with formal interviews with agency administrators, staff, board members, and participants in all projects. Both the Kenosha Conversation Project and the Neighborhood Settlement House Evaluation Project also included focus groups with key constituencies.

Research in all three cities also focused on churches. In Philadelphia, church activity consisted primarily of participation in church-related advocacy and direct service activities associated with one coalition involving numerous churches. This coalition was established in 1996. I continued to participate in its activities until I left Philadelphia in 1997 and kept track of its evolution through reports from other members through 1999.

Both the Kenosha and Milwaukee projects purposefully included observations of key churches and church coalitions. I observed interfaith meetings and activities in Kenosha from 1997 through 2000. Students and I observed church services and activities in key churches in the African American and Latino communities in Kenosha from 1999 to 2000 as part of the *Kenosha Social Capital Study*. Among my activities with Milwaukee Interfaith, I participated in several committees as well as the faith-based welfare-reform project. The Neighborhood Settlement House Evaluation Project in Milwaukee (1998–1999) included six months of observations in two churches central to social welfare activities in this neighborhood as well as limited observations in several other congregations.

By noting the different roles of formal organizations, churches, and government in social welfare provision, these various projects highlight the social welfare system in each locality as a whole. The scope of the research projects included both formal interorganizational dynamics and the flow of personnel and participants among organizations and churches. All the various data-collection techniques are used together, by comparing and contrasting data available through multiple sources, in order to understand the role of organizations and churches in social welfare provision and social capital formation.

The Socioeconomic System of the Locality

The socioeconomic data are primarily government statistics from the U.S. Department of Labor, the U.S. Census, and state welfare departments. Census maps of employment, poverty, and related issues were developed for all three localities. In addition, information on the socioeconomic system was gleaned from agency records and individual reports through life-history interviews. The Kenosha Social Capital Study also included a survey of 121 local employers regarding available jobs, benefits, and hiring practices.

The Nature of the Population Receiving Service

All participant observation projects included observations of people in programs and conversations with them about their experience. The observation data provide a rich understanding of individual experience and the ways people actually use formal programs and local institutions. These observations add background and contrasting information to data collected from individuals about their work, education, use of institutions, and social networks.

Most of the analysis of individual experience draws on two types of formal research: life-history interviews and quantitative statistical studies. Life-history, or depth, interviews collect information on a family or individual's experience over time. This book draws on three qualitative interview studies: Life Experience of Welfare Recipients in Philadelphia (twenty interviews conducted between 1993 and 1996), the Neighborhood Settlement House Evaluation Project (forty-eight families), and the Kenosha Social Capital Study (twenty-six family interviews).

The statistical studies were designed to examine education, work experience, and the role of social networks for families involved in education and training activities in Philadelphia. Each of the statistical studies (CWEP Study, Social Network Study, AWEP Evaluation, Rapid Attachment Study) independently revealed similar patterns for different low-income populations. The CWEP study (data from 1988 to 1992) included only women, the AWEP Evaluation studied two-parent families, and the Social Network Study (data collected in 1996–1997) looked at various groups in training programs. The different studies sought to both replicate findings in the other projects and build on the results of earlier research. The Rapid Attachment Study (data collected in 1996–1997) involved analysis of an administrative database from a mandatory welfare-to-work program in an agency that had participated in the formal research studies. The different samples added additional information on how patterns varied across populations.

In the initial analysis, each of the three statistical studies compared individual experience for different groups. Statistical analysis included cross-tabulations of demographic variables (race, gender, immigrant status, education, marital status) by work and training variables. Results reported here met tests of statistical significance. Since the significance levels varied across studies, this information appears with each project description.

After performing these initial tests, my analysis method departed from standard quantitative analysis. My goal was to comprehend complex patterns as opposed to discerning the variables that account for the most variance. Several multivariate statistical techniques allow researchers to identify complex patterns. I used cluster analysis to discern multivariate groupings of demographic, work history, and training data. Cluster analysis groups together cases with similar attributes, for example, individuals with similar work histories (see Schneider 1986).

I next used a time-line analysis to determine patterns over time for people in different demographic categories (Schneider 2000). The procedure is similar to path analysis but is designed for nominal data. It involves running a series of multilevel cross-tabulations across time-sequence data on clustered variables on jobs and training to identify patterns, which are then coded into nominal variables. These patterns are then compared with demographic cluster variables to clarify the relationship between demographic characteristics and work/training patterns.

As with data on organizations, analysis for individuals combined data collected through several studies using different techniques. Statistical studies outlined general patterns common in all three localities. Observations and interviews explain why and how people develop the strategies they use to meet their needs. Historical data show how some families or individuals develop over time. Taken together, these data suggest the role of social capital in shaping education and economic paths for families. Individual experience, in turn, is placed within the context of the local economic system and social welfare system to demonstrate ways that families use available resources.

DEVELOPING A HOLISTIC PICTURE IN THREE CITIES

In a final step, ethnographic research, interviews, and secondary source material were combined with statistical studies to develop a comprehensive picture of social welfare and social capital. Ethnography provided two kinds of data: 1) micro-level data on changing behavior patterns and ideology of program participants, agencies, and government through participant observation and life-history interviews of a smaller population and 2) macro-level data on government policy implementation, local labor-market conditions, and segregation. The ethnographic data explained patterns found through quantitative analysis of larger samples (macroanalysis). I further linked micro to macro by situating patterns of experience in sample populations within two contexts: 1) demographic data on segregation, gender, and poverty available through public-use data sets, included statistics from the U.S. Census, the U.S. Bureau of Labor Statistics, the Pennsylvania Department of Public Welfare, and the Wisconsin Department of Workforce Development and 2) local and national academic and policy literature on these topics.

RESEARCH PROJECTS

PENNSYLVANIA PROJECTS

1. Social Networks, Career and Training Paths for Participants in Education and Training Programs for the Disadvantaged (the Social Network Study) is a statistical study of 338 people enrolled in nine training programs or community college in Philadelphia, conducted from late 1995 through 1996. Study participants came from a stratified sample of people in training programs that served the range of low-income individuals in the Philadelphia area. The programs included training that drew both men and women and a combination of schools that offered adult basic education, job-specific skills, and college education. The project also included a mandatory community-service program for two-parent families on welfare and a mandatory job-development program.

Research questions for this study were: 1) What are the career trajectories of welfare recipients and other low-income individuals in Philadelphia? 2) What is the role of education and training in those career trajectories? 3) What is the role of gender, race, and immigration status in career trajectories? 4) What is the role of social networks in career trajectories? 5) Do different types of training programs lead to different employment outcomes? 6) Does the nature of the organization offering training (for-profit/nonprofit/government) make a difference in employment outcomes? 7) Do participants in mandatory programs have different outcomes than those who volunteer for training?

The questionnaire covered career and training histories of study participants, nature of public assistance use, and demographic information. Demographic information included age, gender, race/nationality, immigration information, number and age of children, highest level of education (and, if applicable, reason for not completing high school) and military information. The study gathered data on the type, length, and cost of training; the referral source for the training program; whether the program was completed; and employment placement for up to four programs. Data on student loans were also collected. The employment section requested data on benefits, length of employment, reasons for leaving, and social networks that led to the job. The final section solicited information on current source of income and use of government assistance.

Analysis consisted primarily of cross-tabulation comparisons for nominal data. Cluster analysis of participant, training school, and employment showed more complex patterns in these data. Finally time-line analysis illustrated patterns for different types of participants. Chi-square, measures of linear relationships for nominal data, correlations, and analysis of variance were used to determine statistical significance. Findings were considered statistically significant at the $p < .01$ level. Most patterns reported were significant at the $p < .000$ or $p < .001$ level.

Findings for this study are available in the Social Network Study Technical Report and Pathways to Opportunity: The Role of Race, Social Networks, Institutions and Neighborhood in Career and Education Paths for People on Welfare.

2.   Life Experience of Welfare Recipients, the qualitative companion project to the Social Network Study, includes life-history interviews of twenty individuals and participant observation of more than 100 public assistance recipients in education and training programs offered by the Institute for the Study of Civic Values. These data were supplemented with data from case files from the Alternative Work Experience Program from 1992 through 1997.

Research questions for this study were: 1) What are the career trajectories of welfare recipients and other low-income individuals in Philadelphia? 2) What is the role of education and training in these career trajectories? 3) What is the role of gender, race, and immigration status in career trajectories? 4) What is the role of social networks in career trajectories? 5) Do different types of training programs lead to different employment outcomes? 6) Does the nature of the organization offering training (for-profit/nonprofit/government) make a difference in employment outcomes? 7) Do participants in mandatory programs have different outcomes than those who volunteer for training? 8) What is the role of government assistance in the lives of low-income families?

Life history interviews were conducted by students from Bryn Mawr College and participants in the Alternative Work Experience Program from 1993 through 1997. The questionnaire contained open-ended questions regarding education, family experience, neighborhood where the respondent was raised, current neighborhood experience, work experience, education experience, public assistance use, and feelings about the public assistance system. Data on past and current social networks, patterns of support for network members, and regular communication patterns were also collected. Finally, data on activities during a typical day and week were gathered.

3.   The Community Women's Education Project (CWEP) Anonymous Survey Analysis is a statistical study of all 373 of the people enrolled in the CWEP Workstart program over five years. CWEP is an innovative adult basic education and career-preparation program for women. Questionnaires included work and training history, nature of welfare use, and demographic information. Demographic information included race, marital status, and extent of high school education. Information on training programs included type, completion, and cost of training and employment out of the program. Employment information included type of employment, wages, benefits, and reasons for leaving jobs. Subjects were also asked about welfare use and defaulted student loans.

Research questions for this study were: 1) What are the career trajectories of welfare recipients and other low-income individuals in Philadelphia? 2) What is the role of education and training in these career trajectories? 3) What is the role of race in career and training trajectories? 4) Are there differences in the career and training trajectories of people who have received welfare versus those who have never received public assistance? 5) Do different types of training programs lead to different employment outcomes? 6) What percentage of CWEP participants have defaulted student loans that prevent them from obtaining adequate low-cost training?

Analysis of these data consisted of frequencies, correlations, and cross-tabulations. Types of training programs as they related to employment were compared to show the frequency with which participants with certain kinds of training were able to find jobs using those skills.

4.   The Alternative Work Experience Program (AWEP) Evaluation is an evaluation of a model service–learning workfare program for two-parent families on welfare, based on program statistics for 154 individuals and ethnographic observations of that program from 1993 through 1995.

Research questions for this study were: 1) What are the career trajectories of welfare recipients and other low-income individuals in Philadelphia? 2) What is the role of education and training in these career trajectories? 3) What is the role of gender, race, and immigration status in career trajectories? 4) What is the role of social networks in career trajectories? 5) What factors influence successful completion of the AWEP program (placement in employment)? 6) What are the program's rates for participation, noncompletion due to lack of cooperation, and noncompletion for other reasons, and what factors influence those rates? 7) What are the strengths and weaknesses of the AWEP program model?

The AWEP fulfilled the community-service requirement for two-parent families on AFDC under the Family Support Act of 1988. The program combined work experience in nonprofit agencies with a service–learning seminar that covered a range of topics.

Data came from three sources. Intake forms collected demographic data and information on current income. The participant database contained data on work-experience internship placement, some demographic data, and program outcomes. Program outcomes included placement into employment, transfer to another education program, status changes due to illness or other factors, and failure to comply. Most of the analysis focused on factors that influenced placement outcomes.

Participant observation comprised both my notes from the program and case files. These data provided a rich understanding of participants' interactions with the welfare system, employers, and one another. Seminars on anger management, race relations, employment, training, small-business development, and other topics revealed participants' apprehension of the factors that played a role in their lives. Because the seminar relied on program participants' previous and current experience, it provided a wealth of stories about related topics. Participants shared work history, family issues, church involvement, and other information through seminar and caseworker interactions.

Findings from this study are available in the *Alternative Work Experience Program Two Year Evaluation Report*.

5.   The Economic, Racial, and Educational Census Mapping Project analyzes census maps of Philadelphia and the Philadelphia region. A series of maps for the city of Philadelphia and the SMSA that included data on race, Hispanic origin, income, poverty, education levels, employment, unemployment, types of employ-

ment, housing, welfare use, and travel to work. These maps were copied onto colored overheads and overlaid to determine patterns for various groups and neighborhoods. A transportation map for the city of Philadelphia showed transportation routes and costs for major neighborhoods with low-income residents. Research questions for this study included: 1) What are the sociogeographic patterns in Philadelphia for income, occupation, race, housing, education, and time traveled to work? 2) How do those patterns overlap?

6.　The Survey of Training Providers in Philadelphia is a questionnaire-based study of twenty-nine training programs in Philadelphia conducted in 1992–1993. Questionnaires were sent to most of the programs that provide education and training under contract to the Philadelphia PIC or with Commonwealth of Pennsylvania Adult Basic Education funds.

Research questions for this study were: 1) What are the organizational characteristics of the programs providing education and training to low-income populations in Philadelphia? 2) What role does government funding play in these organizations and their programs? 3) What are the characteristics of the staff of these programs? 4) What are the characteristics of the participants of these programs? 5) How does the organization define successful outcomes for their participants, and how successful are they in meeting their goals? 6) What does the organization think it needs in order to develop an ideal program?

The questionnaire gathered data on program funding, goals and ability to meet them, staff and participant demographics, and interaction with government contracting agencies. Analysis consisted of qualitative evaluation of responses and hand computation of information on different types of programs.

7.　The Education and Training System in Philadelphia is the companion qualitative study to the Survey of Training Providers, examining Philadelphia PIC, commonwealth, and federal documents on training and welfare reform, as well as drawing from my notes on working with training programs. Research was conducted between 1992 and 1997.

Research questions for this study were: 1) What are the organizational characteristics of the programs providing education and training to low-income populations in Philadelphia? 2) What role does government funding play in these organizations and their programs? 3) What are the characteristics of the staff of these programs? 4) What are the characteristics of the participants of these programs? 5) How does the organization define successful outcomes for their participants, and how successful are they in meeting their goals? 6) What does the organization think it needs in order to develop an ideal program? 7) How does the labor market, public assistance regime, and nature of the participants influence agency strategy and outcomes? 9) What role do coalitions and social networks among organizations play in development of programs and organization strategy?

8.　The Rapid Attachment Study is a statistical study of an administrative database for a short-term job-readiness and job-placement program in Philadelphia. The database includes demographic data; information on government program utilization; substance-abuse and criminal history; work and training history; interviewer assessments of presentation, attitude, dress, and interviewing techniques; TABE math and reading scores; and job-placement information for 718 people in this program from February 1996 to February 1997.

Research questions for this study were: 1) What are the career trajectories of welfare recipients in this mandatory program? 2) What is the role of education and training in these career trajectories? 3) What is the role of gender, race, and immigration status in career trajectories? 4) What role does previous substance abuse and criminal history play in career trajectories? 5) Are participants with different career trajectories perceived differently by program staff? 6) What role does career trajectory, education experience, gender, race, other barriers to employment (number of children, substance abuse, criminal record), and staff perceptions of attitude and deportment play in determining completion of the program? 7) How does social geography affect these factors?

The analysis focused on the relationship of previous work and training experience to placement and the relationship between where participants live and where they work. Statistical analysis included cross-tabulations on relevant variables; cluster analysis for types of participants, jobs, and training; and logistical regression on placement and program completion. Statistical results were considered significant at the $p < .000$ and $p < .001$ level.

WISCONSIN PROJECTS

1.   The Kenosha Conversation Project was a community-needs assessment project on welfare reform in Kenosha. Research consisted of focus groups with stakeholders involved in welfare reform (program participants; Kenosha County Job Center [KCJC] and Department of Human Services administrators, program managers, and line staff; social service agency staff; employers; government officials; church representatives; concerned advocacy organizations), along with interviews with key people involved in welfare reform and participant observation in KCJC and one advocacy organization.

Research questions for this study were: 1) How do different participants in the welfare system in Kenosha perceive W-2 and the needs of families using the KCJC? 2) What strengths and weaknesses do participants see in the social welfare system in Kenosha? 3) What features need to be added or changed to support families in Kenosha, particularly low-income families using the KCJC and its public assistance programs?

Results from this study, and description of the community planning model developed for the project, are available in the Kenosha Conversation Project education booklet.

2.   The Neighborhood Settlement House Evaluation Study was a study of the effects of changing welfare and child-welfare policy on a Milwaukee community-

based organization, its neighborhood, and its participants. This multimethod team study consisted of four components: 1) ethnography of the Neighborhood Settlement House and the agencies associated with the facility, 2) a depth-interview study of Neighborhood Settlement House participants (forty-eight families), 3) community-resource analysis through statistical mapping of the neighborhood, a windshield survey of community organizations, and interviews with selected organizations and churches, and 4) analysis of Neighborhood Settlement House administrative databases and correlation of those data with available demographic resources on the community.

Research questions for this study were: 1) Who are the participants in Neighborhood Settlement House programs, and how do they differ from others in the organization's catchment areas? 2) What are the other organizations and churches in the catchment area, and how do they relate to this organization and one another? 3) How have changes in welfare and child welfare affected Neighborhood Settlement House as an organization, its program participants, and its neighborhood? 4) How has hosting government programs changed the organization? 5) How can Neighborhood Settlement House better serve its community? 6) What are the roles of education, social networks, organization, and church involvement in the career trajectory and other life factors of people in the organization's catchment area? 7) How do people in the catchment area use organizations and churches to fulfill their needs? What is the role of processes within the organizations in the way people use them? 8) What is the role of social geography in the organization and its neighborhood?

The ethnographic component included nine months of in-depth work in the agency accompanied by interviews with key staff and board members. Ethnography included participant observation in welfare-serving programs, the after-school program, and agency events. The University of Wisconsin–Milwaukee produced an independent ethnographic evaluation of the alternative school. Between three and nine months of ethnography was also conducted in two key churches and one church school. Key parishioners and clergy at these institutions were interviewed. University of Wisconsin–Parkside students conducted shorter ethnographies and interviews at several other churches.

The depth-interview study included questions on demographics, work and education history, involvement in community organizations churches, feelings about the neighborhood, and experience with the Neighborhood Settlement House. Participants came from all the center's programs as well as community residents who had never participated in the center. To follow up on the interviews, three focus groups were conducted with interview participants at the end of the study.

3.   The Kenosha Social Capital Study was a study of the Latino and African American subcommunities of Kenosha focusing on the dynamic between Latino- and African American–focused community-based organizations and churches, community residents, employers, and the citywide community organization and church context. This multimethod team study consisted of four components:

1) ethnography in key organizations and churches serving these communities, 2) life-history interviews with twenty-six families (fifteen Latino, eleven African American) regarding social resources, work, education, and involvement in organizations and churches, 3) interviews with key actors in Kenosha and the African American and Latino communities, and 4) a survey of employment practices of Kenosha employers.

Research questions for this study were: 1) What is the life experience of families in the Latino and African American communities of Kenosha? 2) What is the role of institutions in those communities? 3) How does social capital influence the lives of people in these communities and their organizations? 4) What is the relationship between these two communities and the rest of Kenosha and its institutions? What role does social capital play in this relationship?

The ethnographic component included nine months of participant observation in four churches and five social service agencies. Observations included agencies' day-to-day activities, board meetings, and events. Participant observation was also conducted at the interfaith coalition and with community-wide efforts pertaining to race relations. Key actors in all these institutions plus key city stakeholders were interviewed.

The life-history interviews drew participants from all the organizations involved in the study, as well as some people who were not associated with organizations. The interviews focused particularly on social network information regarding the various topics as well as interactions with people from different groups.

The survey of employers was developed with Kenosha Women's Commission prior to the Kenosha Social Capital Study and conducted both before and during this study. The study consisted of a survey of a stratified sample of Kenosha County businesses, government agencies, and nonprofit organizations. Questionnaires were collected from 121 businesses, approximately 5 percent of Kenosha businesses that hired people outside of their families. The survey gathered information on business size, workforce breakdown by types of jobs and gender, wages and benefits, hiring practices, mentoring and retention practices, and familiarity with government-sponsored employment and welfare programs. Analysis consisted primarily of cross-tabulations and cluster analysis comparing business size and type with wages and working conditions. The use of government welfare programs was also analyzed.

In addition to data collected for this study, the project used census data, other local employment surveys, and government welfare-department statistics to develop a holistic picture of social capital for African Americans and Latinos in Kenosha. Results from this study are available in the Kenosha Social Capital Study.

4.   Research for the Milwaukee Interfaith Welfare Projects consisted of three activities. First, a student and I conducted participant observation of the agency and its advocacy programs for approximately a year and a half. In addition to participant observation notes, ethnographic research was based on written material from the agency and interviews with key staff members.

Research questions for this study were: 1) How does a faith-based organization develop a welfare project? 2) What are the outcomes of such a project? 3) How is the faith community involved in welfare reform and related issues?

I also observed meetings of the Urban/Suburban Task Force sponsored by Milwaukee Interfaith and participated for approximately six months in an Alinsky-style interfaith church program that involved a number of Milwaukee churches. Research from these activities include field notes from meetings and events as well as written materials from the agency.

Finally, for approximately two years I participated in the development of a mentoring project sponsored by Milwaukee Interfaith for former welfare recipients. Participation included attending planning meetings, writing grant applications for the program, and discussing the program with participants and staff.

Organizations

AGENCY TYPES AND EXAMPLES

Large citywide agencies. Established organizations that provide a significant share of services throughout the locality to address a given social problem. Their boards generally include city elites. Agencies usually have multiple sites, budgets of several million dollars, numerous funding sources, and large, diverse staffs.

Faith in Action: A Philadelphia agency offering vocational education, counseling, and rehabilitation. This institution has a faith-related affiliation but provides services to a wide range of city residents through a combination of grants, contracts, and fee-for-service programs.

Community Solutions: A Milwaukee agency providing education, training, and other employment-related services. This organization is an affiliate of a national organization, but its funding and planning are independent of the parent organization

Quaker Residence: A housing program started by Quaker House. The program has grown in recent years to include multiple sites across the city. As a faith-related institution, it maintains ties to the Religious Society of Friends as well as affiliations with other organizations working on similar issues. Staff and board also have strong political networks.

Small to midsized citywide agencies. Organizations founded by citywide elites that focus on a single social problem. These institutions may form network affiliations with large city wide organizations or participate in social capital affiliations with organizations tied to a specific approach to solving problems. They also tend to participate in associations affiliated with the social problem they address. In addition, most have ties to government and political circles. These organizations have budgets under $500,000 and fewer than twenty staff members.

Citizens United: A Philadelphia organization focusing on partnerships with community-based organizations. The agency offered welfare-to-work and adult basic education programs. Paid staff consisted of fewer than ten people and was supplemented with volunteers.

Empowerment Education: A. Milwaukee organization that was founded to provide GED and adult basic education but has expanded to offer W-2 services and day care. The agency had few paid staff members until subcontracting as a W-2 agency and now has a small, paid staff. Staff was supplemented with workers in the community-service job program.

Sunrise: A Kenosha homeless shelter offering various emergency services. The organization was all-volunteer for many years and now has a small paid staff. It is a faith-related institution founded by active church members and affiliated with several local churches. This agency is unique in structure because volunteers are still responsible for its soup-kitchen program. Individual shelter is offered through local churches.

For Profit Organizations. For-profits ranged widely in size and form.

Bakers: A for-profit proprietary school in Philadelphia offering several curricula. It functions within the network of vocational schools and maintains strong ties to the trade associations for employers that hire their graduates. It has a staff of twenty-five, most of whom are teachers, as well as a designated administrative staff and a job developer.

Midsized community-based organizations. These organizations usually have budgets of several million dollars and provide several types of service. In contrast to citywide institutions, they focus on one neighborhood or ethnic/racial community. Board and staff members often have connections to citywide institutions addressing the same community or type of service.

Neighborhood Settlement House: A Milwaukee settlement house that hosts a W-2 agency, alternative school, various youth programs, a health clinic, and related services. The organization partners with a large citywide social service agency, the school district, and a local university to offer its programs. It has a multimillion-dollar budget and a diverse front-line staff.

Small community-based organizations. These organizations range in size and form. The agencies in this study are formal 501c3 incorporated entities with budgets under $500,000 and paid staff of fewer than twenty. These organizations may or may not have affiliations with citywide institutions or others serving similar communities. Often they form associations with other small organizations serving the same closed social capital community.

Latinos United: A Kenosha organization providing multiple services for the Spanish-speaking population. It hosts Kenosha County Medicaid staff as outreach to the Spanish-speaking population and under contract to government provides city services to people from all races and nationalities. They work closely with other community-based organizations and citywide organizations serving the same populations.

Second Chance: A program for African Americans based in one of the poorest neighborhoods of Philadelphia. It claims a staff of twenty-two, but most of these people are part-time or volunteer workers. Ninety-five percent of staff and all participants are African Americans. It offers a combination of GED and skills training, working in partnership with a larger training program as well as their own programs.

Faith-based organizations. Institutions whose program staff, mission, and funding are closely tied to a religious community. They take a variety of organizational forms. Their programs may not directly refer to religion, but program design and staff activities represent a particular faith in action. Most of the faith-based organizations in this project had staffs of under thirty and budgets of under $500,000.

Share the Wealth: The mission project of a well-known clergyman serving low-income African American residents in Kenosha. The program consisted of a thrift store for low income residents. Funding and donations came from throughout the African American community, and the store was staffed with volunteers from the pastor's church and community-service workers from his other ministries.

Faith Community Welfare Support Project : A model welfare initiative of a Milwaukee interfaith organization. The parent organization is an umbrella institution for parts of Milwaukee's religious community. Funding comes from the member religious bodies, as well as some small foundation grants. Most programs were run by volunteer committees of people from the constituent denominations with staff support from one of the interfaith organization's paid staff. Before starting Faith Community Welfare Support, the parent institution had initiated another social service activity that had spun off into a separate organization.

Ethnic Mission: A Catholic church-based mission project in Kenosha designed to provide social service supports and outreach to a marginalized segment of the Kenosha community. It was developed by a priest serving that community and is funded by all the Catholic churches in the Kenosha diocese. It has a staff of one part-time person. A church committee acts as the board.

CHURCHES

Annunciation: Catholic church that hosts the Spanish-language Mass in Kenosha. The Latinos operate a separate congregation within the predominantly white parish, complete with its own social service organization. The church also hosts Ethnic Mission, the archdiocese outreach for the local Latino community.

Faith Temple: A large African American denominational church in Kenosha. This church has moved from being a small, isolated church to one of the major bridging institutions in the city. It has greatly expanded its membership and widened the class range of its congregants to include rising-educated-middle-class families.

Grace Baptist: A small church serving stable-working-class and low-skilled-worker African Americans in Kenosha. The church is a spinoff from Faith Temple that maintains closed social capital networks.

Savior Independent Fellowship: An independent African American church serving the limited-work-experience and low-income community in Kenosha. Its pastor fostered a number of ministries to help the most at-risk families in this small community. This book focuses on Share the Wealth, one mission project.

St. Xavier's: A predominantly white Catholic parish in Milwaukee. The parish has struggled as the neighborhood has changed from largely Catholic to a mix of religions and its original population has aged. It has sought to redefine its relationship to its neighborhood and the Uptown housing project on its borders.

Zion: An African American denominational church in Kenosha that serves rising-educated-middle-class and stable-working-class families. The church worked closely with Faith Temple on several initiatives.

Family Types and People Profiled in the Book

Limited or no work experience. This group included long-term welfare recipients with limited work histories.

Christine: An African American woman in her early twenties from an impoverished, segregated neighborhood in Philadelphia. She had completed high school and an associate's degree focusing on clerical skills at community college. She had limited work experience as an adult.

Jaysa: An African American single mother with four children from Milwaukee. She is a high-school graduate and certified as a day-care aide. She went on welfare when her first child was born and stayed on public assistance until the late 1990s. She found her first job as a day-care aide through volunteer work at Neighborhood Settlement House.

Linda: An African American single mother from Milwaukee in her mid-twenties with a three-year-old son. Her parents were both on SSI owing to various health problems, and Linda herself is on SSI because of poor health. Linda quit school at fifteen after spending most of her school years in special education. She is currently enrolled in a GED program as well as other intensive services because reports of child neglect have put her at risk of losing her son.

Margaret: An African American woman from a segregated neighborhood in Philadelphia. She was married to a disabled man and had school-aged children with learning disabilities. She had finished high school but read and wrote at a second-grade level. The family had relied on welfare for several years. She had no paid work experience.

Mary: A single parent of six children from Chicago who had moved to Kenosha to be near her mother. She had no high-school diploma and limited work experience. She began volunteering in a day-care program associated with her mother's church.

Low-skilled workers. This group includes people who go from one low-skilled job to another. Between jobs, these families rely on welfare to survive.

Anna: An African American single mother from Philadelphia with a high-school diploma and an associate's degree in business (secretarial work). Work experience included numerous sales jobs. She used welfare between jobs to support her family.

Chrystal: An African American single mother, aged thirty-five, from Philadelphia with three school-aged children. She had completed a GED and was attending community college when interviewed. She held numerous jobs as a nursing assistant and in housekeeping, and other service-sector jobs, using welfare between jobs.

Delilah: A sixty-three-year-old African American woman from Kenosha who had worked as a domestic and a teacher's aide. Her husband worked in low-skilled positions in factories. She has one grown son.

Megan: An African American single mother in her late twenties from Milwaukee with one school-aged son. She began work at sixteen and has since held multiple jobs in retail. She has used medical assistance since she became pregnant in her senior year in high school and has gone on and off welfare between jobs. She did not graduate from high school because one teacher gave her an incomplete grade but was enrolled in a GED program when interviewed.

Rachel: An African American low skilled worker from Kenosha with two adult children. She worked as a nursing assistant for several years. Her husband had a stable, working-class job, but Rachel separated from him after her children were grown and has survived on her own income and welfare. She stopped working as a nursing assistant because of the hours and an injury. When interviewed, she was on welfare and babysitting her grandchildren for income.

Sally: An African American single parent from Milwaukee with two children and three foster children. Sally completed two years of college. She worked as a printer for six and a half years before stopping work to care for a disabled child. She has been on government assistance for more than twenty years. She is a community leader for Uptown Housing Project and an active volunteer/board member for Neighborhood Settlement House. She works part time for the housing project and supplements these wages with SSI and other government benefits.

Sam and Tanya: An African American family in an impoverished, mixed-race neighborhood in Philadelphia. They had three school-aged children; the oldest daughter, Lydia, wanted to be a doctor. Sam had finished high school and one year of college in the military—he served for more than five years. He moved between welfare and various jobs. He wanted to found a nonprofit organization to help neighborhood children but took a job as a maintenance man. Tanya also had significant employment experience but chose to stop working to raise her children.

Stable-working-class/displaced workers. In these families, men worked in factory or other blue-collar jobs that paid family-supporting wages with benefits but lost their jobs when factories were closed. Women usually had high-school diplomas and sometimes high-quality training. Working-class women worked in factories or held clerical, or entry-level social welfare positions. Unless they stopped working to care for children, the women in these families, like working-class men, remained in the same job for long periods of time

Christina: An African American woman in her mid-thirties. She is married and has two teenaged daughters. Her husband works in a blue collar job. She finished her GED through a Neighborhood Settlement House program and is employed part time as a bus driver. She intends to return to school soon to obtain a college degree and move into more professional employment.

Jeff: A white man in his early thirties from Philadelphia, married with several small children. His wife stayed home to care for the children. His education included high school and one year of technical college training in the military. Before his military service, he worked at a casino and in construction, among other jobs. After four years in the Air Force, he held several skilled blue-collar positions. When he lost his last job during the economic downturn of the early 1990s, he ran through his unemployment compensation and turned to welfare.

John: A white man in his mid-forties from Philadelphia without a high-school diploma. John was illiterate, and his work experience included factory work and driving a truck. He lost his job when his company downsized in the early 1990s. When his unemployment benefits ended, he went on welfare.

Sandy and Jake: An African American family from Philadelphia with school-aged children. Sandy had graduated from a high-quality technical high school with clerical skills. Jake worked in maintenance and caretaking positions. Alicia, the oldest child, planned to manage a hotel. She enrolled in a technical high school focusing on food service and later attended community college.

Xavier and Maria: Texas-Mexicans in their fifties from Kenosha. Both have completed high school. Xavier completed one year of college, and Maria has a secretarial certificate from a technical college. Xavier has spent his entire career working in factories, mostly in large, unionized workplaces. However, during an economic downturn, he worked in a small factory employing Mexican migrants. Maria worked first at a nonprofit agency and then switched to the local electric company, where she has worked for many years. Their children are high-school-aged and young adults.

Rising educated middle class. Families in this group had at least one adult member who had completed some college and worked in a professional, technical, or white-collar managerial position. These families focused strongly on college education for their children. In many cases, these families were the first generation to have attended college, and they had limited social and economic resources in hard times.

Javier: Formerly a supervisor in a factory in Philadelphia, he was placed in a community-service organization doing work with youth and maintenance.

He became involved in community-improvement activities in his neighbor-hood as well as citywide politics. He was hired as a front-line worker for a so-cial service agency.

Karen: A single African American professional woman from Kenosha. Karen came from a stable-working-class background and has completed a master's degree. She is a management-level government employee and active in Faith Temple church.

Lydia and Juan: Middle-aged American-born Latinos from Kenosha with three young adult children. Lydia is the first generation of her family to attend col-lege. She has a bachelor's degree in education and has spent her career as a teacher. Juan has a welding certificate from the local technical college but works as a low-skilled worker in a meatpacking plant that hires many Latinos. Their oldest daughter is currently in college, and the two youngest are finish-ing high school.

Mark: African American man in his late thirties from Philadelphia. His wife was also a college-educated professional but worked part time to care for their six young children. The family relied on public assistance for health insurance, food stamps, and some cash support for several years while he transitioned to another career after being downsized by a high-technology company. He was a few courses away from a bachelor's degree in engineering and had worked at a primary-sector high-technology firm since he was recruited through an af-firmative action program out of an associate's degree program.

Martha: An African American woman from Philadelphia, married with several school-aged children. Prior to the study period, she had completed high school, high-quality clerical training, and a legal secretarial certificate at the community college. She intended to return to school to obtain a bachelor's de-gree in social work. She had a history of clerical work before stopping to raise her family. When her husband lost his job as a result of downsizing, the family turned to welfare to survive. She entered a welfare-to-work community-service program to fulfill Family Support Act requirements. Initially hired as a secretary, she moved into a casework position at the nonprofit agency that hired her.

Migrants and refugees. Newcomers to the United States in these studies included mostly Puerto Rican citizens, Mexican migrants, and refugees. They fell into two subgroups: highly educated and skilled people who needed to learn English and gain U.S. mainland experience and people with few skills and limited education.

Assan: Nigerian legal immigrant living in Milwaukee. He came to the United States in the late 1980s. Fifty years old when interviewed, he had recently brought his wife and youngest daughter, age ten, to the United States. Assan finished high school in Nigeria and completed computer-repair courses in the United States. His wife has a college degree and a health-care certificate from

Nigeria. Assan has worked in a variety of temporary service-sector jobs since coming to this country. His wife is just beginning to look for work. His daughter attends a local Catholic school and attends after-school programs at Neighborhood Settlement House.

Jaime: A Puerto Rican man in his early twenties from Philadelphia, married with two preschool children. In Puerto Rico he had finished high school and worked in a factory. After coming to the United States, he relied on welfare while attending community college. He was hired as a bilingual housing counselor through a welfare-to-work program.

Li-Tran: A refugee from Vietnam trained as an accountant in his homeland. He had resettled in Philadelphia and attended the local community college to improve his English skills and learn U.S. accounting practices. He was married, with several children in the United States and members of his extended family living nearby. The family lived on welfare while adjusting to their new country.

Yolanda and Angel: Undocumented Mexican migrants in Kenosha. In their early thirties, they have two school-aged children and a new baby. Their household includes Angel's four brothers, who recently arrived from Mexico. Yolanda completed the ninth grade in Mexico, and Angel has completed high school. She speaks only Spanish; he negotiates English-speaking systems for the family. Angel works in a meatpacking plant that employs many Latinos and Yolanda earns extra money by babysitting another brother's children. The children attend Kenosha's Spanish bilingual school, and Yolanda and Angel are active in its parent–teacher association.

NOTES

1. Introduction

1. All names of individuals and organizations have been changed to protect privacy.

2. This landmark legislation follows the strategy for turning domestic programs into block grants to the states that was used for housing in the Community Development Block Grant program in 1974 and some social service programs in the Community Services Block Grants in 1981.

3. Drawing on Weberian and neo-Kantian traditions, he sees the golden age of social capital in the United States built by the "social habits and values" influenced by World War II, concluding that civic renewal requires finding "the moral equivalent of war" (Putnam 2000:275–276).

4. Although Putnam's (2000) discussion of social capital refers to social networks on many levels, his argument assumes that engagement with others will most often lead to participation in society as a whole, thus increasing civic engagement. The exception to this rule is bonding social capital, defined as participation in a closed group, for example, a white supremacist organization. For this reason, social capital is often linked to civic engagement in his formulation of the concept. Less sophisticated thinkers than Putnam who subscribe to his general understanding of social capital often use the term to signify civic engagement.

5. Bourdieu (1986:243–244) does not use the term *human capital*, instead subsuming the attainment of skills and education under cultural capital. While I agree that human capital is a subset of culture in the anthropological sense of culture as a people's whole way of life, I use *human capital* to refer to skill sets in the U.S. sense because, in a fluid democracy like the United States, people can acquire skills that are recognizable outside a given cultural context.

6. Fernandez-Kelly (1995) describes how alternative cultural styles are an essential part of fitting in in oppressed neighborhoods. The cultural capital that defeats people like Christine in mainstream labor markets is important to access social capital in her home community.

7. Fifteen employers accounted for 121 jobs, or 31 percent of the placements. Nine percent of the placements overall and 31 percent of the large block placements were within the agency.

Part I. Factors Influencing Implementation of Welfare Reform

2. The Federal and State Policy Context for Welfare Reform

1. See also Skocpol (1992).

2. The COS, founded in 1877 in Buffalo, New York, sought to "organize the charitable impulses and resources of the community" (Trattner 1994:90–95). Although COS's efforts fo-

cused on the moral uplift of the poor through "friendly visitors"—the precursors to social workers—the society's careful documentation of poverty later provided data for social welfare legislation.

The more progressive settlement-house movement brought middle-class and elite reformers in direct contact with low-income families through neighborhood-based organizations aimed at improving conditions for the new industrial working class. The settlement-house movement included a combination of church-based missions, nonsectarian organizations, and race-based settlements.

3. The large number of widows and orphans created by the Civil War also contributed to the spread of mothers' pensions. Civil War pensions, which were also available to widows and orphans, were the first large-scale public assistance program in the United States and provided one model for later veterans' benefits and government-sponsored social insurance programs. See Skocpol (1992) and Trattner (1994).

4. This pattern contrasted with two-parent working-class households, in which men and older daughters left the home for wage work. Working-class mothers in multiple-adult households sometimes supplemented household earnings with home work or by keeping boarders, but were more available to watch children. See Lamphere (1987), Haraven (1982), Schneider (1990), Skocpol (1992:424–479), and Trattner (1994:134, 224–225).

5. For example, Spatler-Roth et al. (1994) report that only 11 percent of the women in their study of people who combine work and welfare received unemployment insurance benefits, even though most worked approximately half time, the same number of hours as for most working mothers. The average total earnings for unemployment insurance recipients ($7,945) was less than $600 more than for those who did not receive assistance ($7,296). The major significant difference between those who did and did not qualify for unemployment insurance was the type of job. Those who did not receive unemployment insurance were more likely to be employed in service occupations (nearly 42 percent) whereas the unemployment insurance recipients more often worked in administrative support and clerical jobs. Housekeepers were least likely to qualify for unemployment insurance.

6. SSI benefits are based on wage contributions by the deceased worker.

7. This policy was an artifact of the initial conception of AFDC as income support so that widows could stay home to care for their dependent children (Gordon 1994). The 1967 Work Incentive Program (WIN) refocused AFDC toward employment for public assistance recipients, requiring states to operate employment and training programs. WIN was dramatically underfunded, resulting in limited programs that seldom reached beyond registration for work or job search.

8. To develop the workforce and help workers improve their skills, the U.S. government has either directly funded or contributed to education and training programs for several populations. For example, the GI Bill training programs started after World War II provided opportunities for veterans through education grants. The government's first nonmilitary job-training initiatives since the New Deal programs of the 1930s were the 1961 Area Redevelopment Act and the 1962 Manpower and Development and Training Act.

9. The FSA maintained AFDC cash assistance but required that an increasing percentage of the caseload participate in twenty hours of mandatory activities designed to move them toward economic self-sufficiency. States were required to enroll 7 percent of their AFDC caseload in FSA activities in 1990, with an incremental increase to 20 percent by 1995.

10. Domestic-violence survivors were specifically named as one category of potentially exempt recipients, at a state's discretion. Both Pennsylvania and Wisconsin chose to exempt

certain classes of pregnant participants and participants with very young children. Pennsylvania gives domestic-violence survivors a "time-out" until they can stabilize their domestic situation and deal with the immediate emotional issues related to escaping a violent home.

11. Participants were required to be involved in twenty hours of activity in 1997 and 1998, twenty-five hours per week in 1999, and thirty hours per week in subsequent years. Participation rates were different for single-parent and two-parent families. The single-parent participation rate started at 20 percent in 1997 and was incrementally raised 5 percent per year until it reached 50 percent in 2002. Seventy-five percent of two-parent families were required to participate in work-related activities in 1997 through 1998, rising to 90 percent in 1999 and later. Activities for recipients under age eighteen were much more restrictive. Minors were required to complete a high-school diploma or GED.

12. http://www.dwd.state.wi.us/desw2/w2overview.htm. Accessed October 28, 1997.

13. The description of Wisconsin legislative initiatives on welfare comes primarily from interviews and informal conversations with J. Jean Rogers, David Riemer, and others familiar with the legislative process at the time. See also Kaplan (2000) for a discussion of Wisconsin welfare-reform development. Many of the Democratic ideas for welfare reform were piloted through the New Hope project. An evaluation of New Hope was conducted by the Manpower Demonstration Research Corporation. See Bos et al. (1999), *New Hope for People with Low Incomes: Two-Year Results of a Program to Reduce Poverty and Reform Welfare,* New York: MDRC.

14. Prior to 24 months on TANF, sanctions applied only to the adult recipient, reducing the level of cash assistance in the household. Sanctions for post-24-month clients applied to the entire assistance group.

15. Data provided by the Pennsylvania Department of Public Welfare.

16. Programs were accredited through regional bodies that ranged from the respected higher-education associations to state accreditation programs for proprietary schools that community legal services advocates describe as consisting primarily of trade-school executives (Ackelsberg n.d.:2).

17. These standards were based on a Department of Labor regression model that took into account local labor-market conditions and characteristics of the client base. In 1986, the national standards were overall adult entered-employment rates of 62 percent (51 percent for welfare recipients), wages of $4.64 an hour, and cost per entered-employment of $4,373 (Dickinson et al., 1988:20). States and localities could amend these standards.

18. Comparisons of WIA with previous legislation come from http://usworkforce.org/archive/sideby810.htm.

19. Pennsylvania programs should meet the state goals of an entered-employment rate of 50 percent, average cost per employment placement of $9,000, an average cost per participant of $4,500, and average hourly wages of $6, and half the jobs should provide medical insurance. As with JTPA, standards were modified to take into account local conditions. According to a commonwealth official, the Philadelphia entered-employment performance standards for 1993 were 34 percent entered-employment at a wage rate of $180 per week. Statewide performance standards were 43 percent with wage rates of $193 per week (Yorkievitz, personal communication, 1993).

20. TANF stipulates that families with children under the age of six cannot be sanctioned for failure to participate in work-related activities if suitable child care is not available.

21. In Pennsylvania during the 1990s, child-care payments were notoriously slow, and the system of providing vouchers to welfare parents had numerous problems. To resolve this

problem, the state makes direct payments to child-care providers for TANF recipients. It has also instituted a "fast pay" invoicing system in which enrolled providers are reimbursed within fifteen days of submitting bills.

22. See Skocpol (1997) for an analysis of the failure of the Clinton health-insurance initiative.

23. Betsy Vieth, *Primer on the Health Care Safety Net.* Produced for the National Governors Association. Available on the NGA Web site, http://www.nga.org.

24. See http://www.covertheuninsuredweek.org.

25. Nearly 70 percent of recipients are enrolled in a Badgercare HMO, which covers basic health care, prescription drugs, and hospital stays. Families earning above 150 percent of the federal poverty level pay a premium equal to 3 percent of their income.

26. Pennsylvania also instituted a Medicaid managed-care system in 1997. Philadelphia residents currently have a choice of three managed-care corporations.

3. LOCAL GOVERNMENT SYSTEMS

1. From PIC Request for Proposals. Feeders were required to submit contracts for programs consisting of 60–70 percent basic skills, 10–15 percent each of life skills and job readiness, and including case management for everyone; job-specific skills programs must include 60 percent occupational skills, 10–15 percent basic skills and job readiness, 10–20 percent life skills, and case management and job development for all participants.

2. The PIC offered "fixed unit cost" contracts to nonprofit and for-profit programs that had commonwealth-approved tuition rates (primarily for proprietary schools). For example, if a school had a tuition rate of $7,000, the contract amount would be $7,000 times the number of students to be served regardless of actual staffing or operations costs. Nonprofits, on the other hand, had to specify all costs related to the program and were reimbursed only for expenses that they could account for and were allowable within government regulations. See PIC response to public comment, 1994:8–9.

4. SOCIAL SERVICE ORGANIZATIONS

1. For example, most refugee resettlement organizations are tied to religious bodies.

2. For example, Smith and Lipsky (1993:22) describe nonprofits as "tangible, significant manifestations of community."

3. See Schneider (2001:15–29) for discussion of Kenosha's history and culture.

4. Community Legal Services of Philadelphia collected numerous case studies of problems with trade schools. Students were promised quality training but discovered that they had not been taught the basic skills required for the target jobs (for example, nursing assistant or in a skilled trade). These programs cost the maximum allowed for student loans but ran for less than three months. Several schools closed down before students could complete their programs and did not refund tuition. People in the education and training programs involved in the Institute for the Study of Civic Values' Campaign for Self Sufficiency reported similar stories. The Social Network Study (Schneider 1997a) documented that students in some tuition-based programs did not find jobs, but others used their training as the basis for a stable career. The Social Network Study did not have information on the profit status of tuition-based programs, but its findings suggest that the quality of trade schools varies widely.

5. Although all for-profit trade schools used a variety of media to advertise their programs, the low-quality trade schools were more likely to advertise on daytime or late-night

television or on public transportation. Their participant base often included people lacking social capital through either social service organizations or informal networks that would help them make choices about quality schools. This lack of access to people knowledgeable about training programs allowed these schools to continue luring unsuspecting people into their programs.

6. These included four youth-serving nonprofit organizations; ten local, regional, or national nonprofits; four local community organizations; eight governmental and quasi-governmental organizations; and three higher-education schools.

7. For a more in-depth discussion of the role of locality culture in social welfare systems, see Schneider (2001).

5. Social Service Systems

1. For additional discussion of Kenosha's culture and its influence on social service organizations, see Schneider (2001).

2. Data provided by the Wisconsin Department of Workforce Development.

3. Data provided by the Pennsylvania Department of Public Welfare.

4. Data provided by the Pennsylvania Department of Public Welfare. Analysis of prior contracting relationships through refugee resettlement and programs for people of color comes from research conducted for my dissertation (Schneider 1988) and as part of the Changing Relations: Newcomers and Established Residents in Philadelphia Project (Goode and Schneider 1994).

6. Labor Markets and Individual Career Paths

1. Wisconsin technical colleges train people for specific working-class or paraprofessional vocations such as welding, secretarial work, and nursing assistance. They have recently begun to offer some liberal arts courses; in the past they did not provide the basic liberal arts curriculum offered by the community-college system throughout most of the United States.

2. Data provided by the Pennsylvania Department of Labor from annual economic surveys.

3. Data provided by the Wisconsin Department of Labor from annual economic surveys.

4. Seventy-one percent of the employers had fewer than 10 employees (KABA 1999:58).

5. These tables use statistics from the Pennsylvania portion of the Philadelphia SMSA (Standard Metropolitan Statistical Area), Milwaukee County, and Kenosha County. These geographical areas reflect the wider set of opportunities in nearby suburbs but restrict the labor market to areas that most low-income city residents can reach relatively easily via public transportation. I did not use Philadelphia County because the county and the city have the same boundaries. In both Wisconsin cities, the county includes some nearby suburbs.

6. Source: Pennsylvania and Wisconsin Department of Labor figures for employment by industry.

7. These data come from U.S. Department of Labor annual wage surveys in each community. The figures are a subset of the total employment picture and do not add up to the employment figures in table 6.1.

8. Data come from annual wage surveys conducted by the Pennsylvania and Wisconsin departments of labor.

9. My categories differ significantly from general categories used by the Department of Labor because those groupings place dissimilar jobs in the same category, for example, teaching assistants, nurses, and engineers. A full list of job titles in each category is available from the author.

10. The Family and Medical Leave Act requires employers with 50 or more workers to offer unpaid leave for childbirth or to care for an ailing relative. The Americans with Disabilities Act requires employers to make reasonable accommodation for workers with disabilities.

11. Data provided by the Pennsylvania and Wisconsin departments of labor.

7. FAMILY SURVIVAL STRATEGIES AND SOCIAL CAPITAL

1. Each study examined a slightly different population. The Rapid Attachment Study reached the most vulnerable welfare population with the highest percentage of people who had worked in the informal sector as housekeepers or in child care, and 46 percent who had not obtained a high-school diploma or GED. However, this study also included a significant population of people who had taken college courses (9 percent) and worked as professionals (11 percent). The AWEP study, which focused on two-parent families on welfare, contained the highest percentage of displaced workers and refugees. The social network and CWEP studies included a range of low-wage people. The Wisconsin studies, which focused on everyone in a particular neighborhood or ethnic community, included a higher percentage of people with limited experience with the public assistance system. These studies included more participants from the stable working class and rising middle class.

2. Following historical Marxist scholars (Williams 1976, 1980), class identity comes from the position in the labor market of the working family members. As outlined in an earlier article (Schneider 1986), class position comes from a combination of an individual's function in the work process and his or her relationship to others at work. For example, a factory line worker performs repetitive tasks and has very little say in the production process. A low-level service worker in a store or restaurant may be in a very similar position. A mid-level manager or professional has much more control over the work process and interacts with others in a more equal fashion.

A family's class status is determined by the employment position of all adults responsible for a share of family income, including those working for wages, business owners, the self-employed, and others. Except in families whose economic position had recently changed, most parents had similar class backgrounds, and others in their key social networks shared the same values and lifestyle strategies.

3. Any family whose adult members had settled on the U.S. mainland for the first time within the past 15 years was classified as migrant/refugee.

4. During the late 1990s, when many types of workers easily found jobs, limited-work-experience individuals began to dominate the welfare rolls in some localities. However, the numbers on welfare of families of other worker types began to rise again during the economic downturn starting in 2001.

5. Young people working at a hamburger chain she calls Flips find that their family members and friends all hold similar jobs. Low-skilled workers are unable to develop networks of people with different wok experiences who can help them find jobs. Their alternative is to send out résumés or call on potential employers in person.

6. African Americans' northward migration from the rural South began in significant numbers after World War I, but the majority did not come until after World War II (Wilson

1978:62–87). Many African Americans maintain ties with the South, with relatives moving back and forth in search of work, family support, and safe environments in which to raise children (Stack 1996).

7. Pre-TANF welfare-to-work programs tended to exclude people older than fifty-five from Rapid Attachment and community-service requirements.

8. Particularly in the two large cities, the majority go to schools with people like themselves, work as equals with people from similar backgrounds, and often choose to live far from people from other class or racial backgrounds. Given the social divisions of most workplaces, established middle-class people are likely to have few equal relationships with people from different class and racial/ethnic backgrounds.

9. For example, an established middle-class man from Kenosha commented that he has developed long-term relationships with the white middle-class children he grew up with but does not have similar relationships with people of color from any class background. For this reason he tends to judge others based on his own values. In this research, established middle-class people who cherish class and racial diversity actively chose to live or work among people from different backgrounds.

10. In the early 1970s, the migrant social service organization began a program to move farm workers into primary-sector factory work as mechanization of agriculture increased and the larger factories began to open to people of color because they received government contracts that required them to hire minority workers. Most of Kenosha's Mexican American farm laborers were able to move into the stable working class through these programs and the social capital established by relatives and friends hired by these factories.

11. As Carol Stack (1974) demonstrates, African American low-income subculture emphasizes mutual sharing among closed social capital networks. Katherine Newman's research (1999, 2001) also shows more affluent African Americans developing strategies to maintain some ties with lower-income family, but they avoid spending all their resources on less fortunate family members.

12. For example, in an earlier study (Goode and Schneider 1994), we found that Korean merchants in inner-city neighborhoods used extensive security measures in response to news reports in Korea and among the émigré community describing crime in the United States. Cultural expectations combined with social capital networks to circumscribe interaction with the local community.

13. Scholars of emergent ethnicity (Yancey et al. 1976) show that U.S ethnic cultures are unique forms created through the interaction of émigrés with U.S. structures. The émigré generation is also likely to maintain transnational identity, with a foothold in both countries (Basch et al. 1994). Faith communities and community-based organizations serve as centers for both types of activities.

CHAPTER 8. COMPARISONS AMONG WORKER TYPES

1. The Rapid Attachment Study data included information on significant barriers to employment such as addictions, disabilities, and criminal history. People with these barriers were spread equally among worker types. Seven percent of the participants reported having a history of drug abuse, but only 1 percent had been in a drug rehabilitation program. Nine percent reported that they were disabled. Most of the disabled people were older: 22 percent of those aged 45 and older had disabilities, many due to work injuries. However, these two barriers had no impact on whether an individual was placed by the

program. In addition, 4 percent reported that they had criminal records and 2 percent were on parole.

2. The U.S. federal poverty level is based on a formula that calculates the costs of a fixed set of consumer goods and is indexed based on family size. Many scholars and policy makers are critical of the U.S. federal poverty measure. McFate et al. (1995:31), in a book chapter entitled "Markets and States: Poverty Trends and Transfer System Effectiveness in the 1980s," note that the U.S. poverty measure is usually 40 percent of the median wage whereas most European countries consider 50 percent of the median wage the cutoff for poverty.

3. Margaret's case is profiled in Schneider (2000:76, 79).

4. The database includes 718 people who participated in the program.

5. Men were more likely to be married: 34 percent of the men in the sample were currently married, compared with 4 percent of the women.

6. Worker type was determined through cluster analysis based on the variables in table 8.2.

7. Three percent said that they had a language barrier, and only two participants were Asian refugees.

8. I used logistical regression based on placement status and multiple regression based on wage levels to determine the importance of demographic, education, work experience, and other variables in program success.

9. Together, these two variables accounted for less than 25 percent of the variance.

PART II. SOCIAL CAPITAL AND COMMUNITY CONTEXT

9. SOCIAL SERVICE AGENCY USE AND SOCIAL CAPITAL

1. Fees are currently $2 for a child, $6 for a teen, $8 per adult, and $10 for a family The membership fees are not collected from people in some of the categorical programs or from anyone who cannot afford them. They do not generate more than a few thousand dollars in income per year.

2. For example, Kingfisher (1996) observes that "good" clients often have the potential to gain education and enter the helping professions.

10. AGENCIES AND SOCIAL CAPITAL

1. Discussion of the Kenosha audit is based on conversations with J. Jean Rogers and several officials in Kenosha. I also analyzed newspaper accounts of the audit and its results.

2. The community-reinvestment clause in W-2 contracts gave nonprofit and government agencies access to funds remaining in their W-2 contracts after they had fulfilled their program goals. Agencies that quickly placed participants in jobs spent less of the cash-assistance portions of their contracts, leading to large surpluses. For-profit contractors were able to keep some of this surplus as profit.

3. For example, the Child Welfare League of America recommends a supervisor-to-caseworker standard of one to five. For child-welfare caseworkers, caseload recommendations ranged from ten to twenty active cases per worker (Child Welfare League of America's Standards for Organization and Administration, part 3). Caseloads for case managers working with adults tend to be higher; generally accepted standards among agencies in Philadelphia ranged from twenty-five to forty, with thirty as a preferred maximum.

11. Faith Communities and Social Capital

1. According to the parish priest, the archdiocese considers 700 families the minimum number for an active parish.

2. It did not purchase a building until 1957 and broke ground for its present location in 1962. The congregation remains in a midsized building with an educational wing. In recent years, Faith Temple has tripled the size of the sanctuary and plans to completely rebuild shortly.

3. Saul Alinsky sought to organize local community groups through an organizing and leadership training method that has inspired several generations of social activists. Alinksy saw churches as a key resource from which to draw constituency for advocacy efforts. After Alinsky's death, IAF, the organizing institute he founded, developed a coalition advocacy model based in church congregations that now has chapters in communities across the country. Several other organizations based on the same model have been spun off from IAF. Philadelphia had an IAF chapter, and both Milwaukee and Kenosha had Gamaliel Foundation coalitions under the aegis of the same organizing team. I had limited involvement with the Milwaukee coalition but observed the development of the Kenosha initiative as part of the Kenosha Social Capital Project. See Warren (2001), Warren and Wood (2001), and Wood (1997) for discussion of church-based, Alinsky-based organizing efforts in other parts of the United States.

4. Cnaan (2002) notes that congregations tend to draw like -minded people, becoming homogeneous communities based on a number of factors, including world view and belief.

12. Faith, Works, and Community

1. Marcus's experience contrasted with that of other students of very different race and class backgrounds from the people involved in the organizations and churches where they studied; many such students were able to develop trust with the participants in the organizations.

2. In Philadelphia, Quaker House relied on social capital connections with members of the Religious Society of Friends, the citywide social service community, and the African American neighborhood-based community to find resources for the organization. Quaker resources were given less freely when social and cultural ties between the nonprofit and the founding religious body became strained. Quaker organizations with closer ties to Friends Meetings had better access to funds and volunteers (Schneider 1999c).

3. This study contrasts with research that views institutions as bounded units influenced by outside stakeholders (DiMaggio and Powell 1988) or sees interorganizational dynamics as stemming from the networks among key staff in an institution (Chang et al. 1998).

4. This idea was particularly ironic because W-2's rules for access to public assistance were much more restrictive than those in neighboring states.

13. Advocacy and Social Capital

1. For example, effective advocacy on health care may concentrate on providing coverage to the uninsured as a step toward universal health-care coverage.

2. For example, legislative aides can easily recognize letter-writing campaigns that are based on a form message. These letters carry much less weight than those that speak from

the personal experience of program participants and that advocate practical change This observation comes from my year as an American Anthropological Association Congressional Fellow as well as current observations of the policy process.

3. Gamaliel training document, *Workshop on Doing One-on-Ones*, provided by the Gamaliel Foundation.

4. Welfare Recipients Want to Work, *The Philadelphia Inquirer*, September 25, 1995. The op-ed piece was prepared with input from participants of AWEP, a mandatory welfare-to-work program under the FSA that offered participants the opportunity to combine mandatory community-service requirements with education using a service-learning model. The seminar was a weekly event that incorporated conversation about community-service experience and either practical training (for example, anger management) or discussion of such topics as the economy and public policy. The evaluation of this program is available through the Institute for the Study of Civic Values (Schneider 1996).

5. When Paul, a rising-middle-class program recipient with research skills entered AWEP, I asked him to take over this initiative to meet his community-service obligation for the program. This represented a shift from established middle-class facilitators working with people using government assistance to welfare recipients working with one another.

6. Early TANF evaluation efforts showed that welfare reform was "working," as demonstrated by a rapid reduction of cash-assistance caseloads across all states (Wiseman 2000). However, poverty did not decrease dramatically with caseload decline, and many families were not getting supplemental supports, such as food stamps, needed to survive on low-wage jobs (Zedlewski and Gruber 2001).

7. Additional discussion of welfare attitudes using this research is available in Schneider (1999b). Quint et al. (1999), Rank (1994), and Kingfisher (1994) provide other examples of attitudes of many welfare recipients toward work and assistance. Generally, recipients assert that some recipients abuse the system, stressing, however, that they and the people in their social networks legitimately use it but want to find stable work if they have appropriate supports.

8. Much of this bifurcation of advocacy from direct service stems from the writings of Saul Alinsky (1946, 1971), who saw the development of direct-service organizations as drawing energy away from local advocacy efforts. Present-day organizations based in Alinsky advocacy models have somewhat softened the enjoinder against direct service but still see advocacy and direct service as distinct, often competing, activities (Warren 2001).

9. The director of the Mayor's Commission on Literacy during the period that this coalition was most active was a progressive community organizer active in the Women's International League for Peace and Freedom and several neighborhood-based organizing efforts. Unlike the PIC, which was under the control of administrators with no ties to elite progressive circles, this agency was sympathetic to coalition activities. It provided social capital support in the form of mailing lists and support letters for coalition research activities.

10. Discussion of the Energize initiative is drawn from conversations with its staff, advocates for low-income people involved in various coalitions, policy makers, and students' field notes from W-2 agencies during this period.

11. Field notes collected by Jamie Harris.

12. Boyte (1989:59) criticizes similar organizing efforts as ineffective precisely because they avoid preexisting community organizations, instead focusing on disaffected community members.

13. See Goode and Schneider (1994:188–206) for a discussion of crisis-based focus events.

14. Data collected by Theresa Embury.

15. The antiracism coalition also sponsored a forum on the police in which similar incidents were reported. The white police power structure responded in similar ways, but in the forum sponsored by liberal elites who belong to citywide networks conceded that they were "working on" the issue and open to community complaints.

16. See, for example, Maskowsky (2001).

14. CONCLUSION

1. I envision these centers as having a small professional staff and the kinds of educational resources available at high-quality centers. Developing partnerships in which home providers brought the children in their care once or twice a week on a rotating basis could offer the advantages of both home and center care at a lower cost.

REFERENCES

Cited References

Abramovitz, Mimi. 2001. *In Jeopardy: The Impact of Welfare Reform on Nonprofit Human Service Agencies in New York City.* New York: National Association of Social Workers.

Adams, Carolyn, David Bartelt, David Elesh, Ira Goldstein, Nancy Klenuewski, and William Yancey. 1991. *Philadelphia: Neighborhoods, Divisions and Conflict in a Postindustrial City.* Philadelphia: Temple University Press.

Adelman, Robert, and Charles Jaret. 1999. Poverty, Race and U.S. Metropolitan Social and Economic Structure. *Journal of Urban Affairs* 21 (1): 35–56.

Alinsky, Saul. 1946; Vintage edition, 1989. *Reveille for Radicals.* New York: Vintage Books.

———. 1971; Vintage edition, 1989. *Rules for Radicals.* New York: Vintage Books.

Ammerman, Nancy. 1997. *Congregation and Community.* New Brunswick, NJ: Rutgers University Press.

Anderson, Benedict. 1983. *Imagined Communities: Reflections on the Origins and Spread of Nationalism.* London: Verso.

Anderson, Elijah. 1990. *Streetwise: Race, Class and Change in an Urban Community.* Chicago: University of Chicago Press.

———. 2000. *Code of the Street: Decency, Violence, and the Moral Life of the Inner City.* New York: W. W. Norton.

Baer, Hans, and Merrill Singer. 1992. *African American Religion in the Twentieth Century: Varieties of Protest and Accommodation.* Knoxville: University of Tennessee Press.

Bane, Mary Jo, and David Ellwood. 1994. *Welfare Realities: From Rhetoric to Reform.* Cambridge, MA: Harvard University Press.

Bell, Colin, and Howard Newby. 1972. *Community Studies: An Introduction to the Sociology of Local Community.* New York: Praeger.

Berg, Linnea, Lynn Olson and Aimee Conrad. 1991. *Causes and Implications of Rapid Job Loss Among Participants in a Welfare-to-Work Program.* Working Paper. Evanston, IL: Center for Urban Affairs and Policy Research.

Berger, Peter, and Richard Neuhaus. 1977. *To Empower People: The Role of Mediating Structures in Public Policy.* Washington, DC: American Enterprise Institute for Public Policy Research.

Bischoff, Ursula, and Michael Reisch. 2000. Welfare Reform and Community Based Organizations: Implications for Policy, Practice and Education. *Journal of Community Practice* 8 (4): 69–91

Bodnar, John, Roger Simon, and Michael Weber. 1983. *Lives of Their Own: Blacks, Italians and Poles in Pittsburgh, 1900–1960.* Chicago: University of Illinois Press.

Boger, John Charles and Judith Welch Wegner. 1996. *Race, Poverty and American Cities.* Chapel Hill: University of North Carolina Press.

Bos, Johannes, Aletha Huston, Robert Zgranger, Greg Duncan, Thomas Brock, Vonnie McLoyd. 1999. *New Hope for People with Low Incomes: Two Year Results of a Program to Reduce Poverty and Reform Welfare.* New York: Manpower Demonstration Research Corporation.

Bourdieu, Pierre. 1984. *Distinction.* Richard Nice, trans. Cambridge, MA: Harvard University Press.

———. 1986. The Forms of Capital. In *Handbook of Theory and Research for the Sociology of Education.* John G. Richardson, ed. Richard Nice, trans. New York: Greenwood Press.

Bourdieu, Pierre, and Loic J. D. Wacquant. 1992. *An Invitation to Reflexive Sociology.* Chicago: University of Chicago Press.

Bourgois, Philippe. 1995a. *In Search of Respect: Selling Crack in El Barrio.* Cambridge, U.K.: Cambridge University Press.

———. 1995b. The Political Economy of Resistance and Self-Destruction in the Crack Economy: An Ethnographic Perspective. In *The Anthropology of Lower Income Enclaves: The Case of East Harlem.* Judith Freidenberg, ed. *Annals of the New York Academy of Sciences* 749: 97–118.

Boyte, Harry. 1989. *Commonwealth: A Return to Citizen Politics.* New York: Free Press.

Browne, Irene. 2000. Opportunities Lost? Race, Industrial Restructuring and Employment Among Young Women Heading Households. *Social Forces* 78 (3): 907–929.

Buenker, John. 1976. Immigration and Ethnic Groups. In *Kenosha County in the Twentieth Century: A Topical History.* John Neuenschwander, ed. Kenosha: Kenosha County Bicentennial Commission: 1–50.

Carlson-Thies, Stanley W., and James W. Skillen. 1996. *Welfare in America: Christian Perspectives on a Policy in Crisis.* Grand Rapids, MI: William B. Eerdmans.

Chambre, Susan Maizel. 1977. Welfare, Work, and Family Structure. *Social Work* 22 (1): 103–108.

———. 1982. Welfare Use as Status Attainment: Similarities Between Factors Influencing Socio-Economic Status and Welfare Use. *Journal of Social Service Research* 5 (3–4): 17–32.

———. 1985. Role Orientations and Intergenerational Welfare Use. *Social Casework: The Journal of Contemporary Social Work* 13–20.

Chang, Patricia, David Williams, Ezra Griffith, and John L. Young. 1998. Church–Agency Relationships and Social Service Networks in the Black Community in New Haven. In *Sacred Companies: Organizational Aspects of Religion and Religious Aspects of Organizations.* N. J. Demerath, Peter Dobkin Hall, Terry Schmitt, and Rhys Williams, eds. New York: Oxford University Press, 340–348.

Chaves, Mark. 1999. Religious Congregations and Welfare Reform: Who Will Take Advantage of Charitable Choice? *American Sociological Review* 64 (6): 836–846.

———. 2001. Religious Congregations and Welfare Reform. *Society* (January–February): 21–27.

Chaves, Mark, and William Tsitsos. 2000. *Congregations and Social Services: What They Do, How They Do It, and with Whom.* Unpublished paper presented at the ARNOVA meetings.

Cnaan, Ram A. 2002. *The Invisible Hand: American Congregations and the Provision of Welfare.* New York: New York University Press.

Cnaan, Ram, and Stephanie Boddie. 2001. Philadelphia Census of Congregations and Their Involvement in Social Service Delivery. *Social Services Review.* 559–580.

Cnaan, Ram, Bob Wineberg, and Stephanie Boddie. 1999. *The Newer Deal: Social Work and Religion in Partnership.* New York: Columbia University Press.

Cohn, Samuel, and Mark Fossett. 1996. What Spatial Mismatch? The Proximity of Black Employment in Boston and Houston. *Social Forces* 75 (2): 557–574.

Coleman, James. 1988. Social Capital in the Creation of Human Capital. *American Journal of Sociology* 94 (suppl): S95–S120.

Coleman, John. 1998. *The Nature and Location of Religious Social Capital.* Unpublished paper presented at the Religion, Social Capital and Democratic Life Conference, Calvin College, Grand Rapids, MI, October.

Conquergood, Dwight. 1992. Life in Big Red: Struggles and Accommodations in a Chicago Polyethnic Tenement. In *Structuring Diversity: Ethnographic Perspectives on the New Immigration.* Louis Lamphere, ed. Chicago: University of Chicago Press, 95–144.

Costan, Jennifer, Terry L. Cooper, and Richard Sundeen. 1993. Responses of Community Organizations to the Civil Unrest in Los Angeles. *Nonprofit and Voluntary Sector Quarterly* 22 (4): 357–373

Couto, Richard. 1999. *Making Democracy Work Better: Mediating Structures, Social Capital and the Democratic Prospect.* Chapel Hill: University of North Carolina Press.

Crane, Jonathan. 1991. The Epidemic Theory of Ghettos and Neighborhood Effects on Dropping Out and Teenage Childbearing. *American Journal of Sociology* 96 (5): 1226–1259.

Cruikshank, Barbara. 1994. Revolutions Within: Self-Government and Self Esteem. In *Foucault and Political Reason: Liberalism, Neo-liberalism and Rationalities.* A. Barry and N. Rose, eds. Chicago: University of Chicago Press, 231–251.

Diaz-Stevens, Ana Maria. 1994. Latinas and the Church. In *Hispanic Catholic Culture in the U.S.: Issues and Concerns.* Jay Dolan and Allan Figueroa Deck, eds. Notre Dame, IN: University of Notre Dame Press, 278–307.

DiMagio, Paul, and Walter Powell. 1988. The Iron Cage Revisited: Institutional Isomorphism and Collective Rationality in Organizational Fields. In *Community Organizations: Studies in Resource Mobilization and Exchange.* Carl Milofsky, ed. New York: Oxford University Press, 77–99.

Dodson, Lisa, Tiffany Manuel, and Ellen Bravo. 2002. *Keeping Jobs and Raising Families in Low Income America: It Just Doesn't Work.* Boston: Radcliffe Public Policy Center and 9 to 5 National Association of Working Women.

Dudley, Katherine Marie. 1994. *The End of the Line: Lost Jobs, New Lives in Postindustrial America.* Chicago: University of Chicago Press.

Edin, Kathryn, and Laura Lein. 1997. *Making Ends Meet: How Single Mothers Survive Welfare and Low Wage Work.* New York: Russell Sage Foundation.

Edwards, Bob, Michael Foley, and Mario Diani. 2001. *Beyond Tocqueville: Civil Society and the Social Capital Debate in Comparative Perspective.* Hanover, NH: Tufts University Press.

Elliot, James. 1999. Social Isolation and Labor Market Insulation: Network and Neighborhood Effects on Less Educated Urban Workers. *Sociological Quarterly* 40 (2): 199–217.

Ellis, Eileen, Vernon Smith, and David Rousseau. 2000. *Medicaid Enrollment in 50 States.* Washington, DC: The Kaiser Commission on Medicaid and the Uninsured.

Espin, Orlando. 1994. Popular Catholicism Among Latinos. In *Hispanic Catholic Culture in the U.S.: Issues and Concerns.* Jay Dolan and Allan Figueroa Deck, eds. Notre Dame, IN: University of Notre Dame Press, 308–359.

Fendt, Pamela, Kathleen Mulligan-Hansel, and Marcus White. 2001. *Passing the Buck: W-2 and Emergency Services in Milwaukee County.* Milwaukee: Institute for Wisconsin's Future, Interfaith Conference of Greater Milwaukee, and University of Wisconsin–Milwaukee.

Fernandez Kelly, Patricia. 1995. Social and Cultural Capital in the Urban Ghetto: Implications for the Economic Sociology of Immigration. In *The Economic Sociology of Immigration: Essays on Networks, Ethnicity and Entrepreneurship.* Alejandro Portes, ed. New York: Russell Sage Foundation, 213–247.

Foley, Michael, and Edwards, Bob. 1997. Escape from Politics? Social Theory and the Social Capital Debate. *American Behavioral Scientist* 40 (5): 550–561.

———. 1999. Is it Time to Disinvest in Social Capital? *Journal of Public Policy* 19 (2): 199–231.

Foley, Michael, John D. McCarthy, and Mark Chaves. 2001. Social Capital, Religious Institutions and Poor Communities. In *Social Capital and Poor Communities.* Susan Saegert, J. Phillip Thompson, and Mark Warren, eds. New York: Russell Sage Foundation.

Fordham, Signithia, and John Ogbu. 1986. Black Student's School Success: Coping with the Burden of "Acting White." *Urban Review* 18 (3): 176–206.

Freedman, Stephen, and Daniel Friedlander. 1995. *The JOBS Evaluation: Early Findings on Program Impacts in Three Sites.* Prepared with U.S. Department of Health and Human Services and the U.S. Department of Education. New York: Manpower Demonstration Research Corporation.

Frumkin, Peter, and Alice Andre Clark. 1999. The Rise of the Corporate Social Worker. *Society* 36 (6): 46–53.

Fukuyama, Francis. 1995. Social Capital and the Global Economy. *Foreign Affairs* 74 (5): 89–103.

Furstenberg, Frank, Thomas Cook, Jacquelynne Eccles, Glen Elder, and Arnold Sameroff. 1999. *Managing to Make It: Urban Families and Adolescent Success.* Chicago: University of Chicago Press.

Galster, George. 1996. Polarization, Place and Race. In *Race, Poverty and American Cities.* John Charles Boger and Judith Welch Wegner, eds. Chapel Hill: University of North Carolina Press, 186–227.

Gans, Herbert. 1982. Symbolic Ethnicity: The Future of Ethnic Groups and Subcultures in America. In *Majority and Minority: The Dynamics of Race and Ethnicity in American Life.* Norman Yetman and C. Hay Steele, eds. Newton, MA: Allyn and Bacon, 495–508.

General Accounting Office (GAO). 1991. *Job Training Partnership: Inadequate Oversight Leaves Program Vulnerable to Waste, Abuse and Mismanagement.* Washington, DC.

———. 1993. *Unemployment Insurance: Program's Ability to Meet Objectives Jeopardized.* Washington, DC.

Goode, Judith, and Jo Anne Schneider. 1994. *Reshaping Ethnic and Racial Relations in Philadelphia: Immigrants in a Divided City.* Philadelphia: Temple University Press.

Goode, Judith, Jo Anne Schneider, and Suzanne Blanc. 1992. Transcending Boundaries and Closing Ranks: How Schools Shape Interrelations. In *Structuring Diversity: Ethnographic Perspectives on the New Immigration.* Louis Lamphere, ed. Chicago: University of Chicago Press, 173–214.

Gordon, Linda. 1990. The New Feminist Scholarship on the Welfare State. In *Women, the State, and Welfare*. Linda L. Gordon, ed. Madison: University of Wisconsin Press.

———. 1994. *Pitied But Not Entitled: Single Mothers and the History of Welfare*. Cambridge, MA: Harvard University Press.

Gordon, David M., Richard Edwards, and Michael Reich. 1982. *Segmented Work, Divided Workers: The Historical Transformation of Labor in the United States*. Cambridge, U.K: Cambridge University Press.

Goto, Stanford. 1997. Nerds, Normal People and Homeboys: Accommodation and Resistance among Chinese American Students. *Anthropology and Education Quarterly* 28 (1): 70–84.

Gramsci, Antonio. 1971. *Selections from the Prison Notebooks*. Q. Hoare and G. N. Smith, trans. New York: International Publishers.

Granovetter, Mark. 1973. The Strength of Weak Ties. *American Journal of Sociology* 78 (6): 1360–1380.

———. 1985. Economic Action and Social Structure: The Problem of Embeddedness. *American Journal of Sociology* 91 (3): 481–510.

Grettenberger, Susan. 2001. *Churches as a Community Resource and Source of Funding for Human Services*. Non-profit Sector Research Fund Working Paper 01–020. Washington, DC: Aspen Institute.

Grubb, W. Norton. 1992. Postsecondary Vocational Education and the Sub-Baccalaureate Labor Market: New Evidence on Economic Returns. *Economics of Education Review* 11 (3): 225–248.

———. 1995. *The Returns to Education and Training in the Sub-Baccalaureate Labor Market: Evidence from the Survey of Income and Program Participation, 1984–1990*. Berkeley, CA: National Center for Research in Vocational Education.

Gulati, Ranjay, and Martin Gargiulo. 1999. Where Do Interorganizational Networks Come From? *American Journal of Sociology* 104 (5): 1439–1493.

Hagen, Jan L., and Irene Lurie. 1992. *Implementing Jobs: Initial State Choices*. Albany, NY: Nelson A. Rockefeller Institute of Government, State University of New York.

Hall, Peter Dobkin. 1990. The History of Religious Philanthropy in America. In *Faith and Philanthropy in America*. Robert Wuthnow, Virginia Hodgkinson, and associates, eds. San Francisco: Jossey-Bass, 38–62.

———. 1996. *Founded on the Rock, Built Upon Shifting Sands: Churches, Voluntary Associations and Nonprofit Organizations in Public Life: 1850–1900*. New Haven, CT: Yale University Program on Nonprofit Organizations (PONPO).

———. 1998. *Two Models of Interorganizational Fields: African American Voluntary Associations, Congregations, and Nonprofit Organizations in New Haven, Connecticut, 1900–1996*. Unpublished paper presented at the Association for Nonprofits and Voluntary Action Meetings.

Handler, J. 1995. *The Poverty of Welfare Reform*. New Haven: Yale University Press.

Handler, Joel F., and Yeheskel Hasenfeld. 1991. *The Moral Construction of Poverty: Welfare Reform in America*. Newbury Park, CA: Sage Publications.

———. 1997. *We the Poor People: Work, Poverty and Welfare*. New Haven, CT: Yale University Press.

Haraven, Tamara. 1982. *Family Time, Industrial Time: The Relationship Between Family and Work in a New England Industrial Community*. Cambridge, UK: Cambridge University Press.

Harlan, Sharon L., and Ronnie J. Steinberg, eds. 1989. *Job Training for Women: The Promise and Limits of Public Policies*. Philadelphia: Temple University Press.

Hershberg, Theodore, ed. 1981. *Philadelphia: Work, Space, Family and Group Experience in the Nineteenth Century*. New York: Oxford University Press.

Hershberg, Theodore, Alan Burnstein, Eugene Erickson, Stephanie Greenburg, and William Yancey. 1979. A Tale of Three Cities: Blacks and Immigrants in Philadelphia: 1850–1880, 1930, and 1970. *Annals, AAPSS* 441: 55–81.

Higginbotham, Evelyn Brooks. 1997. The Black Church: A Gender Perspective. In *African American Religion: Interpretive Essays in History and Culture*. Timothy Fulop and Albert Raboteau, eds. New York: Routledge, 201–226.

Holzer, Harry. 1991. The Spatial Mismatch Hypothesis: What Has the Evidence Shown? *Urban Studies* 28 (1): 105–122.

———. 1996. *What Employers Want: Job Prospects for Less Educated Workers*. New York: Russell Sage Foundation.

———. 1998. Employer Skill Demand and Labor Market Outcomes of Blacks and Women. *Industrial and Labor Relations Review* 52 (1): 82–99.

Horten, Sarah, Joanne McCloskey, Caroline Todd, and Marta Henrickson. 2001. Transforming the Safety Net: Responses to Medicaid Managed Care in Rural and Urban New Mexico. *American Anthropologist* 103 (3): 733–736.

Hull, Glynda. 1992. *"Their Chances? Slim and None": An Ethnographic Account of the Experiences of Low-Income People of Color in a Vocational Program and at Work*. Berkeley, CA: National Center for Research in Vocational Education.

Hunter, Albert. 1974. *Symbolic Communities: The Persistence and Change of Chicago's Local Communities*. Chicago: University of Chicago Press.

Ihlanfeldt, Keith, and Madeline Young. 1996. The Spatial Distribution of Black Employment Between the Central Cities and the Suburbs. *Economic Inquiry* 34 (4): 693–708.

Institute for Wisconsin's Future. 1998. *Transitions to W-2: The First Six Months of Welfare Replacement*. Working Paper. Milwaukee: Institute for Wisconsin's Future.

Irvine, Jacqueline Jordan, and Michele Foster. 1996. *Growing Up African American in Catholic Schools*. New York: Teachers College Press.

Jargowsky, Paul. 1997. *Poverty and Place: Ghettos, Barrios and the American City*. New York: Russell Sage Foundation.

Kain, John. 1968. Housing Segregation, Negro Employment, and Metropolitan Decentralization. *Quarterly Journal of Economics* 82 (2): 175–197.

Kaplan, Thomas. 2000. Wisconsin Works. In *Managing Welfare Reform in Five States: The Challenge of Devolution*. Sarah Liebschutz, ed. Albany, NY: Rockefeller Institute Press.

Kasarda, John. 1989. Urban Industrial Transition and the Underclass. *Annals, AAPS* 501: 26–47.

Katz, Michael B. 1989. *The Undeserving Poor: From the War on Poverty to the War on Welfare*. New York: Pantheon.

Keehn, Richard. 1976. Industry and Business. In *Kenosha County in the Twentieth Century: A Topical History*. John Neuenschwander, ed. Kenosha, WI: Kenosha County Bicentennial Commission, 175–222.

Kenosha Area Business Alliance (KABA). 1999. *Kenosha County Overall Economic Development Program Plan, Annual Report*. Kenosha, WI.

Kingfisher, Catherine. 1996. *Women in the American Welfare Trap*. Philadelphia: University of Pennsylvania Press.

Kozol, Jonathan. 1989. *Rachel and Her Children: Homeless Families in America*. New York: Fawcett Columbine.

———. 1991. *Savage Inequalities: Children in America's Schools*. New York: Crown.

———. 2000. *Ordinary Resurrections: Children in the Years of Hope*. New York: Crown.

Lamphere, Louis. 1987. *From Working Daughters to Working Mothers: Immigrant Women in a New England Industrial Community*. Ithaca, NY: Cornell University Press.

Le Roy, Barbara. 2000. *The Effects of Welfare Reform and Children's Health Insurance on Families Whose Children Have Disabilities*. Detroit: Developmental Disabilities Institute, Wayne State University.

Lieberson, Stanley. 1980. *A Piece of the Pie: Blacks and White Immigrants Since 1980*. Berkeley: University of California Press.

Liebschutz, Sarah. 2000. Public Opinion, Political Leadership and Welfare Reform. In *Managing Welfare Reform in Five States: The Challenge of Devolution*. Sarah Liebschutz, ed. Albany, NY: Rockefeller Institute Press.

Lincoln, Eric, and Lawrence Mamiya. 1990. *The Black Church in the African American Experience*. Durham, NC: Duke University Press.

Lipsky, Michael. 1980. *Street Level Bureaucracy: Dilemmas of the Individual in Public Service*. New York: Russell Sage Foundation.

Lopez, Lisette, and Carol Stack. 2001. Social Capital and the Culture of Power: Lessons from the Field. In *Social Capital and Poor Communities*. Susan Saegert, J. Phillip Thompson, and Mark Warren, eds. New York: Russell Sage Foundation.

Lurie, Irene. 2001. *Changing Welfare Offices*. Washington, DC: Brookings Institute Policy Brief Number 9.

Lynd, Robert, and Helen Lynd. 1929. *Middletown: A Study in American Culture*. New York: Harcourt, Brace.

Maskowsky, Jeff. 2001. Afterword: Beyond the Privatist Consensus. In Goode, Judith and Jeff Maskovsky, eds. *The New Poverty Studies*. New York: New York University Press.

Massey, Douglas S., and Nancy A. Denton. 1993. *American Apartheid: Segregation and the Making of the Underclass*. Cambridge, MA: Harvard University Press.

Mauss, Michel. 1954. *The Gift*. I. Cunnison, trans. Glencoe, IL: Free Press.

McCarthy, John, and Jim Castelli. 1998. *Religion Sponsored Social Service Providers: The Not-So-Independent Sector*. Queenstown, MD: Aspen Institute Working Paper Series.

McFate, Katherine, Roger Lawson, and William Julius Wilson. 1995. *Poverty, Inequality, and the Future of Social Policy: Western States and the New World Order*. New York: Russell Sage Foundation.

McFate, Katherine, Timothy Smeeding, and Lee Rainwater. 1995. Markets and States: Poverty Trends and Transfer System Effectiveness in the 1980's. In *Poverty, Inequality, and the Future of Social Policy: Western States in the New World Order*. Katherine McFate, Roger Lawson, and William Julius Wilson, eds. New York: Russell Sage Publications, 29–66.

Mead, Lawrence M. 1992. *The New Politics of Poverty: The Nonworking Poor in America*. New York: HarperCollins.

———. 1997. *The New Paternalism: Supervisory Approaches to Poverty*. Washington, DC: Brookings Institute Press.

Merry, Sally Engle. 1981. *Urban Danger: Life in a Neighborhood of Strangers*. Philadelphia: Temple University Press.

Milofsky, Carl. 1988. Structure and Process in Community Self-Help Organizations. In

Community Organizations: Studies in Resource Mobilization and Exchange. Carl Milofsky, ed. New York: Oxford University Press, 183–216.

———. 1997. Organization from Community: A Case Study of Congregational Renewal. *Nonprofit and Voluntary Sector Quarterly* 26 (suppl): S139–S160.

Milofsky, Carl, and Al Hunter. 1995. *Where Nonprofits Come From: A Theory of Organizational Emergence.* Unpublished paper presented at the Southern Sociological Society Meetings, Atlanta.

Morgen, Sandra. 2001. The Agency of Welfare Workers: Negotiating Devolution, Privatization and the Meaning of Self-Sufficiency. *American Anthropologist* 103 (3): 747–761.

Moss, Philip, and Chris Tilly. 2001. *Stories Employers Tell.* New York: Russell Sage Foundation.

Newman, Katherine. 1999. *No Shame in My Game: The Working Poor in the Inner City.* New York: Alfred A. Knopf and the Russell Sage Foundation.

Orum, Anthony. 1995. *City Building in America.* Boulder, CO: Westview Press.

Pawasarat, John. 1997. Employment and Earnings of Milwaukee County Single Parent AFDC Families: Establishing Benchmarks for Measuring Employment Outcomes Under W-2. University of Wisconsin–Milwaukee: Employment and Training Institute.

Pawasarat, John, Lois M. Quinn, and Ann Hendrix. 1998. *Employment Patterns of Larger Milwaukee Area Companies: Occupational Shifts, Job Expansion and Progress Toward Diversity.* Employment and Training Institute, University Outreach, University of Wisconsin–Milwaukee.

Perlmutter, Felice. 1997. *From Welfare to Work: Corporate Initiatives and Welfare Reform.* New York: Oxford University Press.

Piven, Francis Fox, and Richard A. Cloward. 1977. *Poor People's Movements: Why They Succeed, Why They Fail?* New York: Pantheon.

Portes, Alejandro. 1995. *The Economic Sociology of Immigration: Essays on Networks, Ethnicity and Entrepreneurship.* New York: Russell Sage Foundation.

———. 1998. Social Capital: Its Origins and Applications in Modern Sociology. *Annual Review of Sociology.* 1–24.

Portes, Alejandro, and Patricia Landolt. 1996. The Downside of Social Capital. *The American Prospect* 26: 18–21.

Portes, Alejandro, and Julia Sensenbrenner. 1993. Embeddedness and Immigration: Notes on the Social Determinants of Economic Action. *American Journal of Sociology* 98 (6): 1320–1350.

Portes, Alejandro, and Alex Stepick. 1993. *City on the Edge: The Transformation of Miami.* Berkeley: University of California Press.

Podolny, Joel, and Barron, James. 1997. Resources and Relationships: Social Networks and Mobility in the Workplace. *American Sociological Review* 62: 673–693.

Portney, Kent, and Jeffrey Berry. 1997. Mobilizing Minority Communities: Social Capital and Participation in Urban Neighborhoods. *American Behavioral Scientist* 40 (5): 632–644.

Powell, Walter. 1988. Institutional Effects on Organizational Structure and Performance. In *Institutional Patterns and Organizations: Culture and Environment.* Lynne Zucker, ed. Cambridge, MA: Ballinger Publishing, 115–138.

———. 1990. Neither Market nor Hierarchy: Network Forms of Organization. *Research in Organizational Behavior.* Vol. 12. Barry Straw and L. L. Cummings, eds. London: JIA Press, 295–336.

————. 1996. Trust Based Forms of Governance. In *Trust in Organizations: Frontiers of Theory and Research*. R. Kramer and T. Tyler, eds. Thousand Oaks, CA: Sage.

Powell, Walter, and Paul DiMaggio. 1991. *The New Institutionalism in Organizational Analysis*. Chicago: University of Chicago Press.

Putnam, Robert. 1993. *Making Democracy Work: Civic Traditions in Modern Italy*. Princeton, NJ: Princeton University Press.

————. 1995. Bowling Alone: America's Declining Social Capital. *Journal of Democracy* 6 (1): 65–78.

————. 2000. *Bowling Alone: The Collapse and Revival of American Community*. New York: Simon and Schuster.

Putnam, Robert, and Lewis Feldstein. 2003. *Better Together: Restoring the American Community*. New York: Simon and Schuster.

Quadagno, Jill S. 1994. *The Color of Welfare: How Racism Undermined the War on Poverty*. New York: Oxford University Press.

Queen, Edward, ed. 2000. *Serving Those in Need: A Handbook for Managing Faith-Based Human Services Organizations*. San Francisco: Jossey-Bass.

Quint, Janet, Kathryn Edin, Maria Buck, Barbara Fink, Yolanda Padilla, Olis Simmons-Hewitt, and Mary Eustace Valmont. 1999. *Big Cities and Welfare Reform: Early Implementation and Ethnographic Findings from the Project on Devolution and Urban Change*. New York: Manpower Demonstration Research Corporation.

Raines, John, and Donna Day-Lower. 1986. *Modern Work and Human Meaning*. Philadelphia: Westminster Press.

Rank, Mark. 1994. *Living on the Edge: The Realities of Welfare in America*. New York: Columbia University Press.

Rankin, Bruce, and James Quane. 2000. Neighborhood Poverty and the Social Isolation of Inner City African American Families. *Social Forces* 79 (1): 139–165.

Riccio, James, and Stephen Freedman with Kristen S. Harknett. 1995. *Can They All Work?: A Study of the Employment Potential of Welfare Recipients in a Welfare-to-Work Program*. New York: Manpower Demonstration Research Corporation.

Rich, Paul. 1999. American Voluntarism, Social Capital, and Political Culture. *Annals of the American Academy of Political and Social Science* 565: 15–35.

Riemer, Frances. 1997 From Welfare to Working Poor: Prioritizing Practice in Research on Employment-Training Programs for the Poor. *Anthropology and Education Quarterly* 28 (1): 85–110.

Rodriguez, Cheryl. 1996. African American Anthropology and the Pedagogy of Activist Community Research. *Anthropology and Education Quarterly* 27 (3): 414–431

Rose, Nancy E. 1995. *Welfare or Fair Work: Women, Welfare, and Government Work Programs*. New Brunswick, NJ: Rutgers University Press.

Rose, Damaris, and Paul Villeneuve. 1998. Engendering Class in the Metropolitan City: Occupational Pairings and Income Disparities Among Two-earner Couples. *Urban Geography* 19 (2): 123–159.

Salamon, Lester. 1987. Partners in Public Service: The Scope and Theory of Government–Nonprofit Relations. In *The Nonprofit Sector: A Research Handbook*. W. Powell, ed. New Haven, CT: Yale University Press, 99–117.

————. 1995. *Partners in Public Service: Government, Non-profit Relations in the Modern Welfare State*. Baltimore: Johns Hopkins University Press.

Sassen, Saskia. 1998. *Globalization and Its Discontents*. New York: The New Press.

Saxon-Harrold, Susan, Susan J. Weiner, Michael T. McCormack, and Michelle A. Weber. 2000. *America's Religious Congregations: Measuring Their Contribution to Society*. Washington, DC: Independent Sector.

Schneider, Jo Anne. 1986. Rewriting the SES: Demographic Patterns in Divorcing Families. *Social Science and Medicine* 23 (2): 211–222.

———. 1988. *In the Big Village: Economic Adjustment and Identity Formation for Eastern European Refugees in Philadelphia, PA*. Ph.D. dissertation, Department of Anthropology, Temple University.

———. 1990. Patterns for Getting By: Polish Women's Employment Patterns in Delaware County, PA, 1900–1930. *The Pennsylvania Magazine of History and Biography* 114 (4): 517–541.

———. 1996. *Making Workfare a Success: Alternative Work Experience Program Two Year Report*. Philadelphia: Institute for the Study of Civic Values.

———. 1997a. *The Social Network Study Technical Report*. Philadelphia: Institute for the Study of Civic Values.

———. 1997b. Dialectics of Race and Nationality: Contradictions and Philadelphia Working Class Youth. *Anthropology and Education Quarterly* 28 (4): 493-523.

———. 1998a. Linking Welfare Recipients to Jobs: Connections Between Client Abilities, Previous Work and Education History, Social Isolation and Placement in a Rapid Attachment Program. Unpublished paper presented at the 28th Annual Urban Affairs Association Meetings, Fort Worth, TX, April.

———. 1998b. Kenosha Conversation Project Education Booklet. Kenosha: University of Wisconsin–Parkside.

———. 1999a. *We're Not Just Making Widgets: Non-profit Training Providers and Welfare Reform in Philadelphia*. Unpublished paper presented at the 29th Annual Urban Affairs Association Meetings, Louisville, KY, April.

———. 1999b. And How Are We Supposed to Pay for Health Care? Views of the Poor and the Near Poor on Welfare Reform. *American Anthropologist* 101 (4).

———. 1999c. Trusting that of God in Everyone: Three Examples of Quaker Based Social Service in Disadvantaged Communities. *Nonprofit and Voluntary Sector Quarterly* 28 (3): 269–295.

———. 2000. Pathways to Opportunity: The Role of Race, Social Networks, Institutions and Neighborhood in Career and Educational Paths for People on Welfare. *Human Organization* 59 (1): 72–85.

———. 2001. *Kenosha Social Capital Study*. Online: http://www.nonprofitresearch.org/newsletter1531/newsletter_show.htm?doc_id=17368.

Seder, Jean. 1990. *Voices of Kensington: Vanishing Mills, Vanishing Neighborh*oods. McLean, VA: EPM Publications.

Selznick, Philip. 1996. Institutionalism "Old" and "New." *Administrative Sciences Quarterly* 41: 270–277.

Sherman, Amy L. 1997. *Restorers of Hope: Reaching the Poor in Your Community with Church Based Ministries that Work*. Wheaton, IL: Crossways Books.

Sider, Ronald. 1999. *Just Generosity: A New Vision for Overcoming Poverty in America*. Grand Rapids, MI: Baker Books.

Skocpol, Theda. 1992. *Protecting Soldiers and Mothers: The Political Origins of Social Policy in the United States*. Cambridge, MA: Harvard University Press.

————. 1995. *Social Policy in the United States: Future Possibilities in Historical Perspective.* Princeton, NJ: Princeton University Press.

————. 1997. *Boomerang: Health Care Reform and the Turn Against Government.* New York: W. W. Norton.

————. 1999. How Americans Became Civic. In *Civic Engagement in American Democracy.* Theda Skocpol and Morris Fiorina, eds. Washington, DC, and New York: Brookings Institution Press and Russell Sage Foundation, 27–80.

Smith, Sandra. 2000. Mobilizing Social Resources: Race, Ethnic and Gender Differences in Social Capital and Persisting Wage Inequalities. *Sociological Quarterly* 41 (4): 509–538.

Smith, Stephen, and Michael Lipsky. 1993. *Nonprofits for Hire: The Welfare State in the Age of Contracting.* Cambridge, MA: Harvard University Press.

Smith, Stephen, and Michael Sosin. 2001. The Varieties of Faith Related Agencies. *Public Administration Review* 61 (6): 651–670.

Spalter-Roth, Robert, Heidi Hartmann, and Beverly Burr. 1994. *Income Insecurity: The Failure of Unemployment Insurance to Reach Out to Working AFDC Mothers.* Presented at the Second Annual Employment Task Force Conference.

Spar, Karen. 1983. *Job Training Partnership Act: Background and Description.* Congressional Research Service Report 83–76 EWP. Washington, DC: Library of Congress.

Squires, Gregory. 1994. *Capital and Communities in Black and White: The Intersections of Race, Class and Uneven Development.* Albany, NY: SUNY Press.

Stack, Carol. 1974. *All Our Kin: Strategies for Survival in a Black Community.* New York: Harper and Row.

————. 1996. *Call to Home: African Americans Reclaim the Rural South.* New York: Basic Books.

————. 2001. Coming of Age in Oakland in *The New Poverty Studies.* Judith Goode and Jeff Maskofsky, eds. New York: New York University Press.

Stepick, Alex, Guillermo Grenier, Steve Morris, and Debbie Draznin. 1997. Brothers in Wood. In *Challenging Fronteras: Structuring Latina and Latino Lives in the U.S.* Mary Romero, Pierrette Hondagneu-Sotelo, and Vilma Ortiz, eds. New York: Routledge, 265–278.

Stinchcombe, Arthur. 1997. On the Virtues of the Old Institutionalism. *American Review of Sociology* 23: 1–18.

Stoesz, David. 2000. *A Poverty of Imagination: Bootstrap Capitalism, Sequel to Welfare Reform.* Madison: University of Wisconsin Press.

Summers, Anita, and Thomas F. Luce. 1988. *Economic Report on the Philadelphia Metropolitan Area, 1988.* Philadelphia: University of Pennsylvania Press.

Susser, Ida. 1982. *Norman Street: Poverty and Politics in an Urban Neighborhood.* New York: Atheneum.

Susser, Ida, and John Kreniske. 1987. The Welfare Trap: A Public Policy of Deprivation. In *Cities in the United States: Studies in Urban Anthropology.* Leith Mullings, ed. New York: Columbia University Press, 51–70.

Takagi, Dana. 1994. Post-Civil Rights Politics and Asian-American Identity: Admissions and Higher Education. In *Race.* S. Gregory and R Sanjek, eds. New Brunswick, NJ: Rutgers University Press, 229–242.

Teachman, Jay, Kathleen Paasch, and Karen Carver. 1997. Social Capital and the Generation of Human Capital. *Social Forces* 75 (4): 1343–1359.

Thomas, William, and Florian Znaniecki. 1927. *The Polish Peasant in Europe and America.* New York: Alfred A Knopf.

Tienda, Marta, and Haya Stier. 1996. Generating Labor Market Inequality: Employment Opportunities and the Accumulation of Disadvantage. *Social Problems* 43 (2): 147–165.

Tigges, Leann, and Irene Browne. 1998. Social Isolation of the Urban Poor: Race, Class and Neighborhood Effects on Social Resources. *Sociological Quarterly* 39 (1): 53–78.

Trattner, Walter. 1994. *From Poor Law to Welfare State.* New York: The Free Press.

Turner, Susan. 1997. Barriers to a Better Break: Employer Discrimination and Spatial Mismatch in Metropolitan Detroit. *Journal of Urban Affairs* 19 (2): 123–142.

Vanderplatt, Madine. 1999. Locating the Feminist Scholar: Relational Empowerment and Social Activism. *Qualitative Health Research* 9 (6): 773–785.

Vieth, Betsy, *Primer on the Health Care Safety Net.* Produced for the National Governors Association. Online: http://www.nga.org.

Wacquant, Loic. 1998. Negative Social Capital: State Breakdown and Social Destitution in America's Urban Core. *Housing and the Built Environment* 13 (1): 25–40.

Wacquant, Loic, and William Julius Wilson. 1989. Poverty, Joblessness and the Social Transformation of the Inner-City. In *Reforming Welfare Policy.* D. Ellwood and P Cottingham, eds. Cambridge, MA: Harvard University Press, 70–102.

Wagner, Regine, Paul van Reyk, and Nigel Spence. 2001. Improving the Working Environment for Workers in Children's Welfare Agencies. *Child and Family Social Work* (6): 161–178.

Waldinger, Roger. 1995. The 'Other Side' of Embeddedness: A Case-Study of the Interplay of Economy and Ethnicity. *Ethnic and Racial Studies* 18 (3): 555–580.

Warren, Roland. 1967. The Interorganizational Field as a Focus for Investigation. *Administrative Science Quarterly* 12 (3): 396–419.

Warren, Mark. 2001. *Dry Bones Rattling: Community Building to Revitalize Democracy.* Princeton, NJ: Princeton University Press.

Warren, Mark, and Richard Wood. 2001. *Faith Based Community Organizing: The State of the Field.* A report on the findings of a national survey conducted by Interfaith Funders, Jericho, NY. Online: http://www.comm-org.utoledo.edu/papers2001/faith/fait.htm.

Waters, Mary. 1990. *Ethnic Options: Choosing Identity in America.* Berkeley: University of California Press.

Weber, Max. 1948. *From Max Weber: Essays in Sociology.* H. H. Gerth and C. Wright Mills, eds. and trans. London: Routledge and Kegan Paul.

Williams, Raymond. 1980. *Problems in Materialism and Culture.* London: Verso.

Wilson, William Julius. 1978. *The Declining Significance of Race: Blacks and Changing American Institutions.* Chicago: University of Chicago Press.

———. 1987. *The Truly Disadvantaged: The Inner City, the Underclass, and Public Policy.* Chicago: University of Chicago Press.

———. 1996. *When Work Disappears.* New York: Alfred A. Knopf.

———. 2000. Rising Inequality and the Case for Coalition Politics. *Annals, AAPSS* 568: 78–99.

Wineburg, Bob. 2001. *A Limited Partnership: The Politics of Religion, Welfare, and Social Service.* New York: Columbia University Press.

Wingren, Gustaf. 1957. *Luther on Vocation.* Philadelphia: Muhlenberg Press.

Wiseman, Michael. 1999. *In the Midst of Reform: Wisconsin in 1997.* Assessing the New Federalism Project. Discussion paper 99–03. Washington, DC: The Urban Institute.

Wittman, Laura. 1998. *In Our Own Words: Mothers' Needs for Successful Welfare Reform.* Report produced by the Women and Poverty Public Education Initiative. Kenosha, WI: University of Wisconsin–Parkside.

Wood, Richard. 2002. *Faith in Action: Religion, Race, and Democratic Organizing in America.* Chicago: University of Chicago Press.

Wyly, Elvin. 1999. Local Labor Markets and Occupational Sex Segregation in an American Metropolis. *Journal of Urban Affairs* 21 (1): 1–34.

Yancey, William, Eugene Erickson, and Richard Julaini. 1976. Emergent Ethnicity, Review and Reformulation. *American Sociological Review* 41: 391–402.

Zedlewski, Shiela. 2002. Family Incomes: Rising, Falling or Holding Steady. In *Welfare Reform: The Next Act.* Alan Weil and Kenneth Finegold, eds. Washington, DC: Urban Institute Press.

Zedlewski, Shiela, and Amelia Gruber. 2001. *Former Welfare Families Continue to Leave the Food Stamp Program: Assessing the New Federalism Project.* Discussion paper 01–05. Washington, DC: The Urban Institute.

Zhang Zhongcai. 1998. Indirect Tests of the Spatial Mismatch Hypothesis in the Cleveland PMSA: A Labor Market Perspective. *Urban Affairs Review* 33 (5): 712–724.

Zhang Zhongcai and Richard Bingham. 2000. Metropolitan Employment Growth and Neighborhood Access in Spatial and Skills Perspectives. *Urban Affairs Review* 35 (3): 390–422.

Zippay, Alison. 1995. Tracing Behavioral Changes Among Discouraged Workers: What Happens to the Work Ethic? *Psychological Reports* 76: 531–543.

Zophy, Jonathan. 1976. Invisible People: Blacks and Mexican-Americans. In *Kenosha County in the Twentieth Century: A Topical History.* John Neuenschwander, ed. Kenosha, WI: Kenosha County Bicentennial Commission, 51–82.

PRIMARY SOURCES

Ackelsburg, Irv. Testimony on hearing on trade school legislation. Philadelphia Community Legal Services.

De Parle, Jason. Shrinking Welfare Rolls Leave Record High Share of Minorities. *New York Times,* July 27, 1998: A1, A12.

Dresang, Joel. Welfare Caseload Expected to Stabilize: February Drop Just 0.5% as W-2 Changeover Nears Completion. *Milwaukee Journal Sentinel,* March 27, 1998: B1, B2.

Foodstamp Use Plunges 32% in State, Federal Report Finds. *Milwaukee Journal Sentinel,* August 4, 1999: 1A, 9A.

Gamaliel training document *Workshop on Doing One on Ones.* Provided by the Gamaliel Foundation, Chicago.

Philadelphia in Straits During the Recession. *Philadelphia Inquirer,* April 2, 1997: B1, B3.

Schneider, Jo Anne. Welfare Recipients Want to Work. *Philadelphia Inquirer,* September 25, 1995.

Suburbs Gain Jobs; City Avoids Loss. *Philadelphia Inquirer,* March 19, 1997: A1, A12.